The Kivas of Heaven

Ancient Hopi Starlore

Gary A. David

Adventures Unlimited Press

Adventures Unlimited Press
P.O. Box 74
Kempton, Illinois 60946 USA
www.adventuresunlimitedpress.com

ISBN: 978-1-935487-09-8

Cover art and design: by the author.
Photographs and illustrations: by Gary A. David
or non-copyrighted Internet sources unless otherwise noted.

Acknowledgments

Earlier versions of some the information in this book appeared in *World Explorer* magazine and *Sagenhafte Zeiten* (German language magazine) as well as on antiguosastronautas.com (Spanish language website) and on Gary Vey's website viewzone.com.

I want to express my appreciation to Mark Borcherding for his help with matters regarding the Maya. Thanks as well to Dorothy Prior and Roberta Ruth Hill for writing about my work, to Gisela Ermel and César Reyes for translating some of my articles into German and Spanish respectively, and to Kymberlee Ruff for attempting to bridge Hopi-Tibetan cultures. I would especially like to thank my friend and colleague Rob Milne for introducing me to the magnificent landscape and skyscape of South Africa in September of 2009, and to his wife Slava Milne for her hospitality and delicious food during my stay. They provided both photos and invaluable information, especially for Chapters 15 and 16.

Finally, as always, I wish to thank my wife Anita Descault. Her continued encouragement and support have sustained me over our nearly thirty years together.

Contents

Right half of 1903 stereopticon photo looking southwest
toward Walpi village on First Mesa, Arizona.
The highest building in the background is the Bear Clan house.

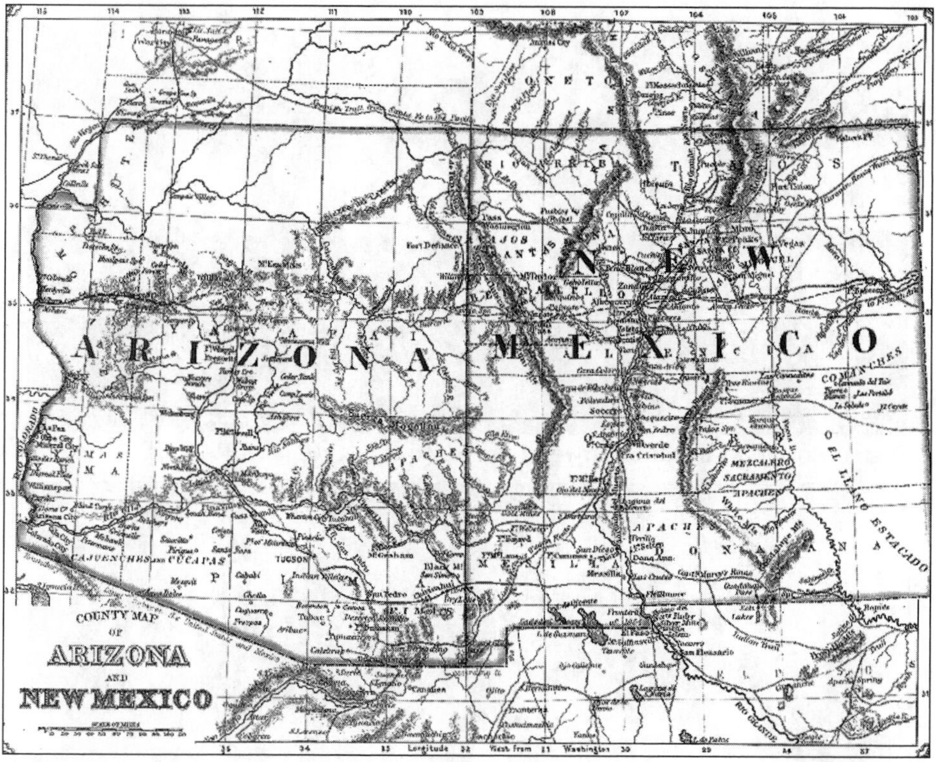
COUNTY MAP
OF
ARIZONA
AND
NEW MEXICO
ARIZONA
NEW MEXICO
TUCSON
COMANCHES
EL LLANO ESTACADO
APACHES
MEZCALERO
SACRAMENTO
Longitude West from Washington

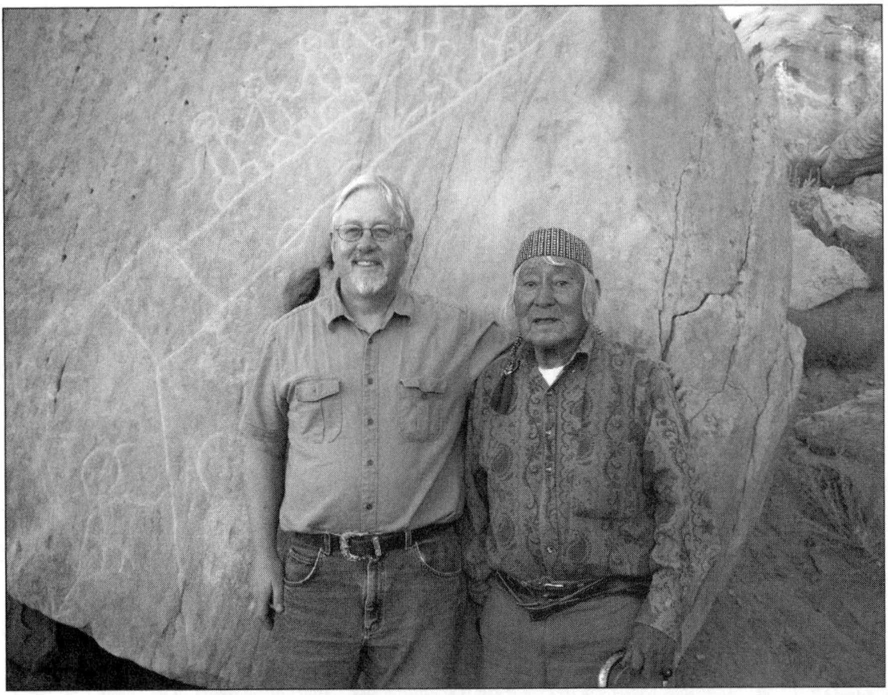

The author and Martin Gashweseoma in front of Prophecy Rock, August 2010.

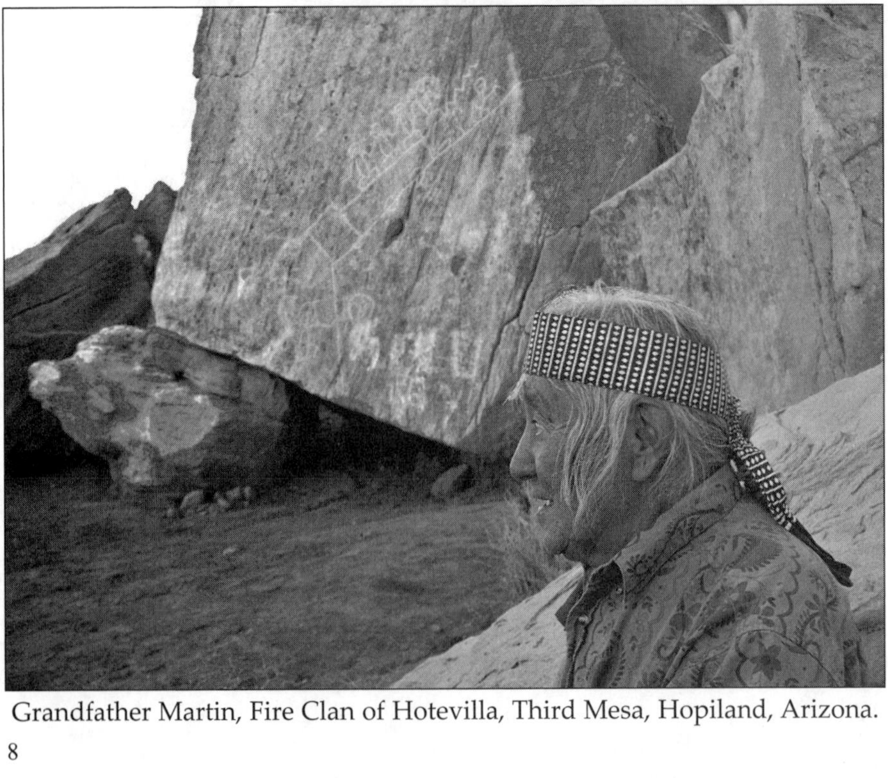

Grandfather Martin, Fire Clan of Hotevilla, Third Mesa, Hopiland, Arizona.

Preface
Bio-Brief and Disclaimer

I am a *wasichu*. But I am not a "fat-taker," the literal meaning of the Lakota (Sioux) word for white person. I am also a *pahana*, the Hopi term for a person of Caucasian descent. But I am not a member of the Wannábe tribe (white folks who want to be Indians). I am *not* in any way, shape, or fashion a spokesperson for the Hopi or any other tribe, nor am I qualified to be such. The observations and opinions expressed in this book are strictly my own; they do not reflect the policies (either official or non-official), attitudes, cultural orientations, philosophies, cosmologies, or religious beliefs of any particular native group.

During the fifteen years I have lived with my family in rural Arizona, I have learned to cherish the land of the indigenous Hopi and other Ancestral Pueblo People. When I finally settled here, it was as if I were coming home. In one sense, however, non-Indians can never truly be home on the North American continent. On the other hand, I believe that, with a little luck and a lot of discipline, some are able to touch the unique spirit of this land. The British fiction writer D. H. Lawrence, who lived for a time in the Southwest and attended a number of religious dances, including a Hopi Snake-Antelope Ceremony, remarked in regard to the spirit of place. "Different places on the face of the earth have different vital effluence, different vibration, different chemical exhalation, different polarity with different stars: call it what you like. But the spirit of place is a great reality."[1]

Before moving to the Four Corners region in the American Southwest, I resided for nearly fifteen years in South Dakota, where for part of that time I was an instructor of English composition at Oglala Lakota College on Pine Ridge Reservation. I also taught creative writing for the State arts council on the Rosebud Reservation, among other places. I additionally served as a proud member of the CIA (Cowboy and Indian Alliance), which I helped to found in 1987. This ad hoc organization was instrumental in halting the Honeywell Corporation's plans to build a testing site for radioactive munitions in the sacred He Sapa (Black Hills). It also garnered the support of notable Lakotas such as Charlotte Black Elk (great granddaughter of the *Black Elk Speaks* narrator) and AIM (American Indian Movement) member Dennis Banks, as well as many on the tribal council. I have participated in genuine Lakota *inipis* (not New Age sweat lodges) led by elders such as Reginald Bird Horse of the Standing Rock Reservation, and I prayerfully supported the dancers at a *wiwanyag wacipi* (sun dance) on the Rosebud.

Born and raised near Cleveland, Ohio (where the only Indians I really knew were the baseball team), I earned a bachelor's degree in English from Kent State University (1974) and a master's degree in creative writing and literature of the American West from the University of Colorado, Boulder (1992).

In my two previous books titled *The Orion Zone* and *Eye of the Phoenix*,[2] I revealed no sacred lore or secrets of Hopi spirituality. The occasional ceremonial details described are already part of common knowledge, most of which is available in any substantial college library (in my case, primarily Northern Arizona University). For better or worse, early ethnography has already let the genie out of the bottle. This is simply a case of freedom of religion (to remain concealed) clashing with freedom of speech (to be revealed).

In writing this book, for the most part I consulted no Hopi elders, medicine people, or spiritual leaders. For better or worse, I relied instead on my own idiosyncratic perceptions, fleeting intuitions, and assiduous research to describe the star pattern of the constellation Orion projected upon the high desert of the

Colorado Plateau. During frequent trips to the Hopi Mesas at my own expense, I witnessed numerous kachina (also spelled *katsina*) dances and encountered certain elements about which I choose not to write. I have tried to respect the wishes of the Hopi for their utmost privacy in spiritual matters. If I have inadvertently discussed something that otherwise should have remained hidden, I am deeply sorry.

My goal in doing this research is not financial gain. Although a few of my articles have appeared in national publications and my two books on Hopi archaeoastronomy, mythology, and religion are generally available, I can honestly say that the remuneration has been minimal—certainly not enough to survive on. To date, I have given a few radio interviews, for which I was paid nothing, and a few lectures, for which I received mere honoraria.

As a regionalist, I choose to live in the place that I primarily write about—northern Arizona, where economic opportunities are limited. I live in a single-wide trailer house, drive a 20-year-old Ford Aerostar van, eat from a free food pantry, and have health insurance only intermittently. Nevertheless, I don't want to "cash in" on the Hopi. I merely wish to see if the fifteen-years-worth of my observations on their venerable culture have some merit.

Although I was formerly a college instructor, I am not currently employed by or associated with any school, institution, foundation, corporation, or agency. The fabrication of Hopi rituals or the facile mimicry of the Hopi way of life by non-Hopis is utterly distasteful to me, especially if a profit motive is involved. Sooner or later, the charlatans and exploiters will be recognized and discredited.

Let me repeat: *I do not wish to speak for the Hopi*—only for myself. I do, however, wish to speak *to* the Hopi, establishing a dialogue as a bridge between cultures. My goal is not to obtain any restricted religious or ceremonial information, but instead to see if my findings are verified in Hopi cosmology.

Perhaps the Arizona Orion correlation that I discussed in my first book as well as the other star correlations I describe in the current one are just gigantic coincidences, or, more precisely, one small coincidence piled upon another upon another upon another, etc. Personally I do not think so, or I would not have worked almost full time for more than a dozen years to elucidate this mystery.

The elegant complexity of these celestial templates both intrigues and bewilders me. If nothing else, one must admire the vision and tenacity of the *Hisatsinom* (ancestral Hopi) who conceived and implemented them over the course of three centuries. Time will tell whether this mirroring of sky and earth is merely the fanciful yearnings of a misguided *pahana* or the true cultural heritage of the Hopi.

For the sake of convenience, my use of the term "Hopi" is sometimes representative of both their ancestors and those of other Pueblo People of the Southwest, such as the Zuni, Acoma, Laguna, Jemez, Zia, and the various native groups living in the pueblo villages along the Rio Grande. Although linguistic variation and some cultural differences among these pueblos are apparent, the basic cultural structure is remarkably similar. The term "Anasazi" has fallen into disfavor, partly due to the fact that this is actually a Diné (Navajo) word that literally means "ancient enemy." Archaeologists now commonly identify these ancient people by the general phrase "Ancestral Puebloans."

In this book I do not directly deal with the Mayan Long Count calendar and its end date of December 21st, 2012, except in Chapter 17. This is not my expertise, and plenty of authors are more qualified to speak about it—John Major Jenkins and the late Linda Schele, to name a couple. I do, however, discuss what I call the Hopi "legacy of prophecy" in the context of what many Hopi spiritual elders consider to be the current conclusion of the Fourth World and the traumatic transition to the Fifth World.

The Hopi and other Pueblo People of the ancient Southwest undoubtedly had contact with the Maya, Toltec, and Aztec of Mesoamerica. The discovery of macaw feathers and whole bird bodies in burial sites throughout the Southwest is proof of an extensive cultural interaction. Macaws, of course, are indigenous to the humid jungles of southern Mexico and were transported north to the arid Four Corners region.

Did the Hopi know about the Mayan calendar and the latter's obsession with temporal cycles? Probably so. A sharing of ideas most likely accompanied the trading of goods. It has been said that the Hopi are the masters of space, whereas the Maya are masters of time. Each native group was assigned specific duties by the Creator. The Hopi assumed the daunting task of keeping the whole world in balance via the performance of sacred rituals in the seasons' ceremonial cycle, whereas the Maya kept track of the calendrical and astronomical aspects of that cycle.

In Hopi cosmology the whole notion of a particular, arbitrary date –namely, December 21, 2012– is itself rather pointless. As linguist Benjamin Lee Whorf discovered in the mid-20th century, the Hopi conceptualize space-time in a manner radically different from the culture of the *pahanas*.

> "According to the conceptions of modern physics, the contrast of particle and field of vibrations is more fundamental in the world of nature than such contrasts as space and time, or past, present, and future, which are the sort of contrasts that our own language imposes upon us. And the Hopi actually have a language better equipped to deal with it than our latest scientific terminology.... Hopi may be called a timeless language. It recognizes psychological time, which is much like "Bergson's 'duration,' but this 'time' is quite unlike mathematical time, T, used by our physicists. Among the pecular properties of Hopi time are that it varies with each observer, does not permit of simultaneity, and has zero dimensions, i.e., it cannot be given a number greater than one."[3]

Given the Uncertainty Principle of any verbal communication, we start, here and now, with one—the only one there is.

Chapter 1
What *Is* a Kiva?

Kiva Culture

At the very time Gothic cathedrals were raising their spires in Europe to pierce the firmament, ceremonial prayer chambers called kivas were sinking deep into the earth of the American Southwest to reach for a spiritual underworld. It was simply a matter of opposing cosmologies. The former system located God in the heavens, while the latter believed that the Afterlife lay in the subterranean realms.

For the Ancestral Puebloans (the ancient Hopi, for example), to go downward was to return to the sacred source of being. Because fertility rose from the soil in the physical form of the corn plant seeking sunlight, they assumed that a divine matrix that nurtured all life on Earth was naturally located at the nadir, not the zenith. Archaeoastronomer Dr. E. C. Krupp comments on the kiva's agricultural link.

> "The kiva's connection with the Underworld associate it with the idea of creation and birth. ...the earth, through these same parallels, is part of the metaphor of the creation of life. Sprouting plants emerge from the ground. As an architectural space, the kiva parallels the idea of the womb, the place from which we are born or emerge into the world. Religious initiation of the young Hopi men is itself a kind of 'birth' and so

occurs at the Wúwuchim ceremony [in November], when the emergence myth is ritually reenacted."[1]

In his essay "When Is a Kiva?", archaeologist Watson Smith provides a definitive description of the structure:

"The kiva, defined as a specialized ceremonial room, with few or no functions of a domestic nature, is apparently limited to the Anasazi area, and seems always to have been one of the basic criteria of Anasazi culture. It has certainly not been recognized in the Hohokam [of the Phoenix Basin in central Arizona] or on the Plains and the determination of its presence or absence in intermediate areas occupied by people of such clouded legitimacy as the Sinagua [of northern Arizona] or the Mogollon [of southeastern Arizona and southwestern New Mexico] becomes obviously a matter of great importance to the establishment of their proper social status. If they had kivas, perhaps they were culturally affiliated with people on the right side of the tracks; if they lacked them, perhaps with those on the other, since presumably a feature so intimately integrated into the usually conservative religious and ceremonial pattern of a culture would likely be both consistent and persistent throughout the extent of that culture in both areal and temporal dimensions."[2]

Smith enumerates a few essential criteria of the kiva: (1) It was located close to a surface dwelling that supported a large enough population to require or at least desire it. The kiva was sometimes located to the southeast of the pueblo, which is the direction of the winter solstice sunrise—to be discussed shortly. (2) It was never lived in. It contained few or no domestic artifacts such as pots, grinding stones, mealing bins, or evidence of food consumption such as bones. (3) It incorporated ceremonial features into its architecture.[3]

Kivas were constructed of masonry—usually flat stone slabs with little or no mortar. Historically, earlier kivas tended to be circular, while later ones were rectangular. Apparently there was an "unbelievable explosion" in the construction of round kivas in about AD 1100.[4]

Kiva in Ceremonial Cave, Frijoles Canyon,
Bandelier National Monument, New Mexico.

The difference in kiva morphology might also be viewed geographically. Circular kivas belong to the Eastern Pueblo tradition (for instance, Chaco Canyon and Mesa Verde in northwestern New Mexico and southwestern Colorado respectively), whereas rectangular kivas belong to the Western Pueblo Tradition (Homol'ovi and the Hopi villages in northern Arizona).

The circular version usually incorporated either four or six pilasters around the interior circumference, which supported a cribbed roof made of small timbers. A masonry banquette, or bench, also lined the round inner wall. A fire pit was located in or near the center of the structure. On one side of the circle a recess provided altar space, under which was a ventilator shaft. In front of the shaft a flat rock deflector was sunk into the kiva floor, so the flames of the sacramental hearth would not be extinguished by wind gusts.

On the side opposite the fire pit was a small hole in the floor called a *sipapu*. This was both the icon and the embodiment of a direct connection to the underworld, which in Hopi terms was called the previous Third World (or Era). A legend describes the migration of righteous Hopis from the corrupted Third World to the pristine Fourth World. They ascended a ladder –or in some versions they climbed through a giant reed– which is inserted through a hole in the Third World's celestial dome. By entering the hole (or in modern terms, a stargate), they passed into, to quote the Book of Revelation, "a new heaven and a new earth," from which they could start civilization afresh. The *sipapu* in the kiva represents this cosmic tunnel to a previous existence.

BUREAU OF AMERICAN ETHNOLOGY

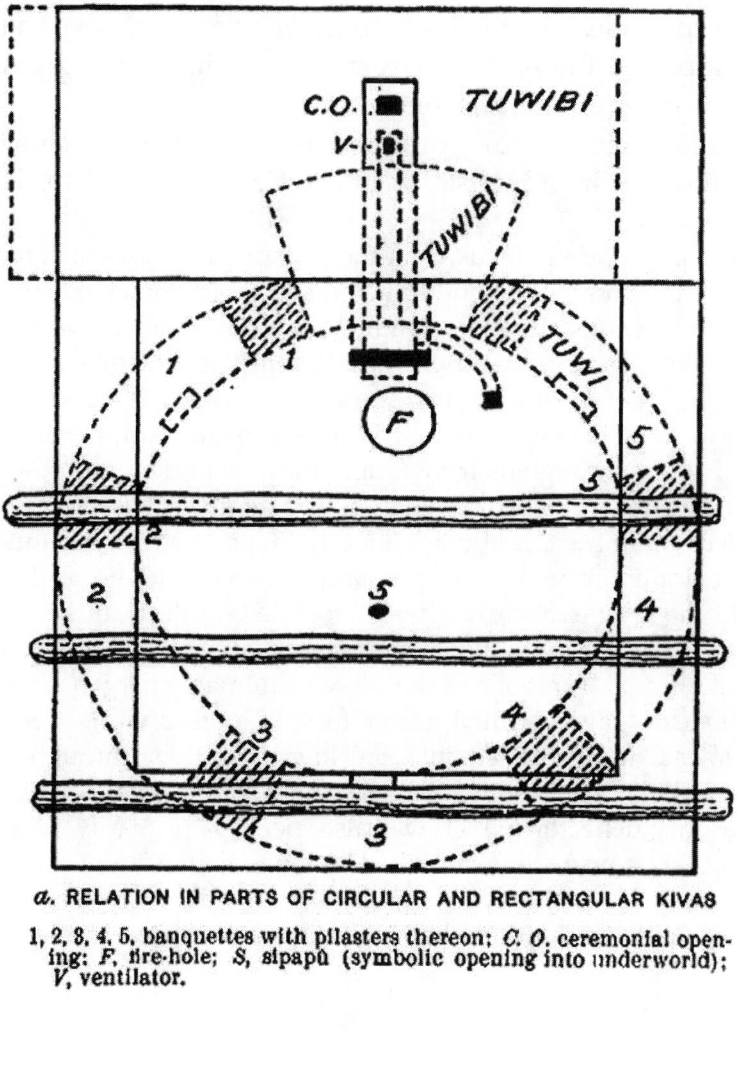

a. RELATION IN PARTS OF CIRCULAR AND RECTANGULAR KIVAS

1, 2, 3, 4, 5, banquettes with pilasters thereon; *C. O.* ceremonial opening; *F*, fire-hole; *S*, sipapû (symbolic opening into underworld); *V*, ventilator.

Through an overhead hatchway in the center of the kiva's roof protrudes the top of the wooden ladder bathed in sunlight, moonlight or starlight. This is used to climb down into the ritualized space of myth, chant, and dance. After the ceremony one could ascend the ladder and return to the world of quotidian normality. The ladder remains as a reminder of the ancestors' journey into a new world, which the Hopis still inhabit—though many elders believe we are actually at the end of the Fourth World (or Era).

The structural variations of the round kiva include either a lack of pilasters in smaller ones (i.e., the clan kiva, which may have been roofless) or their replacement by four massive columns that supported the roofs of larger ones designed for communal use. This latter type is referred to as a great kiva.

Scholar Vincent Scully describes the kivas that were incorporated into the Great Houses of Chaco Canyon, New Mexico.

> "Ritual was surely focused on the cylindrical kivas which penetrate the body of the building and spatter its contained courtyard like enormous drops of rain. The kivas intensify the effect of an obsessive geometric order. When placed above ground among the dwelling and storage cubicles they are built upwards to whatever height is necessary to permit entrance and egress through their roofs, and they are packed round with earth to retain their original and, apparently, *ritually necessary subterranean character* [italics added]. Stepped altars, mountain and cloud at once, would probably have been found in them, and the *te'wi* circled their walls, rock ledges deep in this ultimate cave. Yet in the floor the round, shallow navel-like notch of the *sipapu,* symbolic of the place of human emergence from the earth, gave spiritual access to still another world deeper below. One descended into the kiva by ladder through the smokehole in the ceiling over the fire, which was shielded by a masonry deflector (which was also, perhaps primarily, part of the altar) from an air vent, called by the Indians a 'spirit tunnel,' in the wall behind it. In some areas that wall often flared out into a keyhole shape, perhaps to facilitate the spirits' passage."[5]

The rectangular kiva contained all the ritual elements of the circular kiva. Generally aligned on a north-south axis, the four-sided structure also added a slightly raised platform at the south end for spectators. Note that the performers were not placed on a raised stage but were spatially lower than the audience, and thus closer to the primal source of life.

Writer Jon Manchip White colorfully imagines a ceremonial kiva scene.

> "Here, in this sophisticated edifice with its subtle warm brown hues, the ancient inhabitants of the Southwest felt themselves close to those chthonic deities whose existence was so intimately bound up with their own. Here the shamans and rain-makers danced round the sacred fire in their horned head-dresses. The flames sent forth their scented fumes, while the men on one side and the women on the other sang, chanted, and shook their gourds and rattles, their bodies oiled and glistening in the crimson glow."[6]

The circumference of the circular kiva reflected the round desert horizon, where earth meets sky. The four corners of the rectangular kiva, on the other hand, reflected the four summer and winter solstice sunrise and sunset points on the horizon—not cardinal directions but the inter-cardinal points of northeast, southeast, northwest, and southwest.

Archaeologist E. Charles Adams attributes the shift from round to rectangular kivas as a result in the evolution of what he calls the "katsina cult." About the time of the Great Drought beginning in 1275 AD, the size of pueblos generally increased. In addition, open plazas –rectangular or square– surrounded by domiciliary or storage rooms replaced circular great kivas as ceremonial spaces. At the same time, kivas also became rectangular. One explanation is that the flat wall surface of the kiva provided space for painted murals depicting the *katsinam* (plural of *katsina* or kachina). These spirit messengers were increasingly called upon to usher in rainfall during this period of greater aridity. Plaza and kiva thus demonstrate both the public and the semi-private aspects respectively of *katsina* ritual.

"The enclosed plaza allowed the public portrayal of the cult. This facilitated the integration of those initiated to the symbolism of the cult and emphasized the difference between those initiated and those not initiated. The rectangular kiva completed the plaza as the focus for the private aspect of katsina ritual."[7] It was as if they were squaring the circle in order to bring rain.

Imago Cosmo

Whether kivas were circular or quadrilateral, their primary function was to create an *imago mundi*, or "image of the earth." This architectural form basically linked both the underworld and the heavens to the terrestrial plane. Like most archaic cultures, the Ancestral Puebloans believed that the terrestrial mirrored the celestial. The ancient hermetic maxim "as above, so below" was certainly an essential component in their cosmology. Thus, the kiva could also be considered as an *imago caeli*, or "image of the sky." But as we have seen, the kiva was a representation of both cosmology and cosmogony—not only how the world now is but also how the world came to be in the beginning.[8] Writer Evan Hadingham explains how kiva mirrors cosmos.

> "Why was this careful ordering of space within the underground sanctuary important? According to modern Pueblo beliefs, the *kiva* symbolizes the place where the first humans emerged from the lower world. The traditions of the Acoma Pueblo, New Mexico, assert that the first *kivas* were circular, even though the present-day examples are all rectangular. One Acoma informant interviewed in 1928 explained how supernatural ancestors had decreed the layout of the *kiva* so that it would be a sacred model of the world. The four central pillars supporting the roof were to represent the trees planted in the underworld for the first humans to climb. Each pillar was associated with a different sacred direction and a special color. 'The walls represent the sky, the beams of the roof (made of wood of the first four trees) represent the Milky Way, *wakaiyanistiaw'tsa* (way-above-earth-beam). The sky looks like a circle, hence the round shape of the kiva.'"[9]

Was the kiva a structure used solely for religious purposes? It is likely that it also served secular or social events, just as churches today are sometimes used for non-religious meetings or even theatrical occasions. The kiva may have even been something of a social club, functioning like contemporary fraternal lodges, which sometimes provide a refuge for single men, widowers, or husbands beleaguered by domestic troubles. (Examples of such charitable organizations today include the Shriners, the Kiwanis, and the Odd Fellows, or totemic organizations like the Elks, the Moose, the Lions, and the Eagles, which may also be philanthropic in nature.) Finally, the kiva may have provided a workshop, a specified place where men crafted ceremonial objects, such as *katsina* masks and ritual paraphernalia, or where they wove cotton blankets and *katsina* sashes.[10]

As I mentioned, the kiva probably served a dual function-both religious and secular. This dichotomy is more apparent today than it was to ancient people, who artfully wove their spiritual demands and everyday exigencies together in order to create a holistic tapestry of life.

High Desert Archaeoastronomers

An essential feature of the kiva was its use as an astronomical observatory. The hatchway in the ceiling provided a window to the stars. Because specific constellations appeared at certain times of night during certain times of the year, the sky-window could also be used as a clock to synchronize various rituals.

One of the most important constellations for the Hopi is Orion. The Hopi term *Hotòmqam* means "strung together" or "beads on a string"—perhaps a reference to the belt, although the triad may instead be Betelgeuse (Orion's right shoulder), Alnilam (middle star of the belt), and Rigel (Orion's left leg). (My book *The Orion Zone* profusely details the mythical and ceremonial importance of this constellation, especially to the Hopi.)

Contemporary archaeoastronomer Ray A. Williamson stresses the importance of the constellation to the Ancestral Puebloans.

"The belt of the Western constellation Orion was only about a degree from the [celestial] equator in A.D. 1250. A very important winter constellation for the historic Pueblo, Orion was very likely important for the Anasazi as well. Because it is an easily recognizable winter constellation, it today serves as a timing device for winter kiva ceremonies. When it appears above the eastern horizon, when it is overhead, and when it sets are all important milestones in the course of Hopi kiva celebrations."[11]

Writer Frank Waters, who lived for a time with the Hopi, describes the appearance of Orion vis-à-vis the kiva entrance during the crucial winter solstice ceremony.

"On the twelfth night [of the Soyal, or Hopi winter solstice ceremony] the altars are consecrated. All must be ready when the group of seven stars in Pleiades (Chööchökam—the Harmonious Ones, the Stars That Cling Together) is halfway between the eastern horizon and directly above, and the first star in Orion's belt below it is just rising into view through the ladder opening, about ten o'clock.... All songs must be finished when the Pleiades stand halfway between the midnight sky and the western horizon, and the three stars in Orion's belt lie across the roof entrance of the kiva.... All these dances, songs, and spinning of the sun are timed by the changing position of the three stars, Hotomkam, overhead."[12]

Thomas O. Mills, who along with his mother opened and operated the Hopi Cultural Center on Second Mesa in the early 1970s, remarks on the necessity of realigning the kivas due to effects of precession.[13] "I watched the Hopi construct a new kiva and it took them three years to determine where the doorway would be located. Orion has to enter the doorway precisely on time. That is why many kivas are retired and new ones have to be built. Orion appears to be moving, just like the [other] constellations, as the earth travels through space."[14]

If, for instance, a kiva had been built in AD 1100 , by the year 2000 the shift in astronomical orientation would total 12.5°. (The rate of precession: 1° = 72 years.) The width of a full moon (and coincidentally, the sun's disk) is .5°. This gives us an idea just how far off the hatchway would be to the original alignment of a constellation such as Orion after a period of 900 years—the width of 25 full moons!

Orion was in fact a Hopi timing device for both the December Soyal ceremony and the November Wúwuchim (or *Wuwtsim*) ceremony, previously mentioned. In this context it is interesting to note that the Hebrew word *Kislev*, the name of the tempestuous ninth month (which includes both November and December), may be etymologically related to the Hebrew name for Orion, or *Kesil*, which literally means "impious." This adjective refers to a characteristic of the legendary race of giants, of which Orion, striding across the sky, is a sidereal version. In fact, Orion is sometimes also referred to as Nimrod, eternally bound to the heavens for his rebellion against Jehovah.[15]

> "Canst thou bind the sweet influences of Pleiades, or loose the bands of Orion?
> Canst thou bring forth Mazzaroth in his season? or canst thou guide Arcturus with his sons?
> Knowest thou the ordinances of heaven? canst thou set the dominion thereof in the earth?" (Job 38: 31-33)

Ethnographer Richard Maitland Bradfield comments on the association of Orion and the final two months of our calendar.

> "...the constellation first becomes visible a few days after the summer solstice, when it appears shortly before dawn above the eastern horizon; during the next four months, as it rises earlier and earlier (four minutes earlier each night), the constellation becomes more and more prominent in the night sky, until, during the months of November and December, it is visible virtually all night long. Now these six months are precisely the period over which the Hopi evince a keen interest in the approach of cold weather; and it is surely not far-fetched to suppose a conceptual link between the waxing of Orion and the Pleiades, and the return of cold weather? Nor to suppose a more specific link between the cold, glittering stars of the night sky in November and December, and the glittering frost and

ice with which those stars co-incide?"[16]

But, as mentioned in the quote, Orion is not only important in winter. The constellation is also used to synchronize the summer Flute Ceremony. This ritual is performed in mid-August of every other year, alternating with the Snake-Antelope Ceremony, sometimes known as the Snake Dance. These August ceremonies assist to mature the crops and bring the final rainfall of the monsoon season.

"After an interesting interchange of ceremonies, the Flute priests return to their kiva to prepare for the public dance on the morrow. When at 3:00 a.m. the belt of Orion is at a certain place in the heavens, the priests file into the plaza, where a cottonwood bower has been erected over the shrine called the entrance to the underworld. Here the priests sing, accompanied with flutes, the shrine is ceremonially opened and prayersticks placed within, and they return to the kiva."[17]

The Hopi share with other modern pueblos in the Southwest a common ancestry. Although some geographical variations exist, this proto-culture had related worldviews, customs, and ceremonies. These sacred rites in sync with celestial mechanics were performed in accordance with an agricultural calendar system. The stars were thus rooted in the earth. Archaeoastronomer J. McKim Malville sums up the system.

"The Rio Grande Pueblos watched the paths of the Great Bear, Orion, and the Pleiades, relying on the regularity of their movements for ordering nocturnal rituals. In some cases, these rituals were timed by the passage of these constellations over the kiva hatchways. Tewa religious officials anxiously watched for the rising of Orion's belt near both solstices, believing that an early May appearance would mean a long growing season. Seen as a bridge between this world and the celestial realm, the Milky Way remains important to all the Pueblo peoples and may once have been viewed as a god in its own right. Possibly it, too, was once a metaphor for the omnipresent Sky God."[18]

Snakes and Ladders

When people descend the ladder, every kiva ritualistically becomes the center of the world. There the children of the Earth Mother find shelter in this iconic womb. The world-axis rises from her navel, the burning heart of the fire pit. Incense of juniper and piñon rises through the smoke hole and mingles with the Milky Way overhead. The *sipapu* is the snakelike, umbilical passageway to the underworld, where live the ancestors in a parallel universe that mirrors the terrestrial plane. Like the corn plant, the ladder represents the vertical pole where the four inter-cardinal directions meet.

Historian of religion Mircea Eliade, who has also written the definitive text on shamanism, outlines the architectonics of sacred space. This archaic concept exists in contradistinction to our modern concept of profane space –rootless, centerless, and chaotic– where, as W. B. Yeats has said, "Things fall apart; the centre cannot hold…"

> "Where the break-through from plane to plane has been effected by hierophany, there too an opening has been made, either upward (the divine world) or downward (the world of the dead). The three cosmic levels –earth, heaven, underworld– have been put in communication. As we just saw, this communication is sometimes expressed through the image of a universal pillar, *axis mundi,* which at once connects and supports heaven and earth and whose base is fixed in the world below (the infernal regions). Such a cosmic pillar can be only at the very center of the universe, for the whole of the habitable world extends around it. Here, then, we have a sequence of religious conceptions and cosmological images that are inseparably connected and form a system that may be called the 'system of the world' prevalent in traditional societies: *(a)* a sacred place constitutes a break in the homogeneity of space; *(b)* this break is symbolized by an opening by which passage from one cosmic region to another is made possible (from heaven to earth and vice versa; from earth to the underworld); *(c)* communication with heaven is expressed by one or another of certain images, all of which refer to the *axis mundi*: pillar (cf.

> the *universalis columna*), ladder (cf. Jacob's ladder), mountain, tree, vine, etc.; *(d)* around this cosmic axis lies the world (= our world), hence the axis is located 'in the middle,' at the 'navel of the earth'; it is the Center of the World."[19]

The word "hierophany" is used to designate the appearance of a higher power or divine presence. The Hopi and other pueblo people are historically heir to the deep native tradition of shamans-cum-hierophants. The "break-though" from one level to another is achieved in the kiva by the ladder.

Jacob's ladder, which Eliade cites as an example of the *axis mundi*, is significant because the biblical figure's staff or rod was traditionally known as Orion's belt.[20] The phallic connotations here are even more obvious when we consider that Orion's "sword" hanging from his belt contains the star-seed of the Orion Nebula (M42 and M43).

We also recall that Jacob erected (no pun intended) and anointed a pillar made from the stone pillows whereon he had slept and dreamed of a colossal ladder. "And he dreamed, and behold a ladder set up on the earth, and the top of it reached to heaven: and behold the angels of God ascending and descending on it. And, behold, the LORD stood above it, and said, I am the LORD God of Abraham thy father, and the God of Isaac: the land whereon thou liest, to thee will I give it, and to thy seed;"(Genesis 28:12-13) On a macrocosmic level, this vertical shaft variously corresponds to the Tree of Life in the Jewish Kabbalah, the World Tree in the Nordic Eddas, the green Ceiba Tree in the Mayan *Popol Vuh*, and the Flowering Tree, or sacred cottonwood, which the medicine man Black Elk saw in a vision on the highest mountain in South Dakota's Black Hills—the heart of the Lakota (Sioux) territory.

But on a microcosmic level, the vertical axis is associated with the *kundalini* channel that runs parallel to the spine. Through this psycho-spiritual conduit the serpent power of enlightenment flows.

Jacob called the place where his dream occurred Bethel ("house of God"), but it was originally named Luz, which incidentally means "light" in Spanish. Rather than uplifted, Jacob seemed quite disturbed by this dream. "And Jacob awaked out of his sleep, and he said, Surely the LORD is in this place; and I knew it not. And he was afraid, and said, How dreadful is this place! this is none other but the house of God, and this is the gate of heaven." (Genesis 28: 16-17) (This "stargate" is a reference to the Gate of Capricorn, discussed in Chapter 2.)

In addition to the Jacob's staff/Orion's belt connection, other sources identify Jacob's ladder as the Milky Way. "It appears from Eusebius, that tradition, at least, represented Israel [Jacob] as an astrologer, who believed himself under the influence of the planet Saturn. Even at this day, the three great stars in Orion are called *Jacob's staff*, and the milky way [sic] is familiarly termed *Jacob's ladder*. This Patriarch had twelve sons, and tradition has allotted to each a sign of the zodiac."[21] Traditionally there existed a direct correlation between Saturn and Orion. (See Chapter 9.) We should also note here that infused in the Milky Way are Orion's upper torso and upraised right arm. The Milky Way is also located in close proximity to the constellation Gemini, so perhaps it is no accident that Jacob had a fraternal twin named Esau.

Kiva Coda

The recently published, comprehensive Hopi dictionary predictably defines kiva as "an underground or partially underground ceremonial chamber." However, a secondary definition of the same word is a verb: "bring many things."[22] Thus, the kiva also denotes abundance or bounty. Contained in this architectural structure unique to the Ancestral Puebloans, a plethora of iconography is undeniably found: the fire pit with its heart-source of heat and primal energy, the wormhole *sipapu* tunneling to the nether realms of departed spirits, and the ladder of stars extending from frigid earth to Orion's fiery loins.

But is the kiva really unique to the American Southwest? One of the premier archaeologists of this region, Jesse Walter Fewkes, discovered an interesting correlation between the main area he studied and the Maghreb (northern Africa). In a Smithsonian report he describes the southern Tunisian Berber town of Matmata as follows:

> "As the visitor approaches it, we are told, he sees no sign of a village but only a number of cisternlike depressions in the earth, each measuring about 30 feet in diameter. But standing on the edge of one of these depressions and looking over the side into it what a strange sight meets his eyes. Deep in these sunken areas he sees the inhabitants, dogs, camels, and human beings. This depression is a breathing place or sunken plaza into which rooms open through lateral passageways, which are excavations in the walls of the depression. Some of these chambers are adorned with rugs and furniture. The sunken plaza is apparently the living place, entrance to it being by means of a subterranean tunnel, slanting upward, large enough for passage or man or beast. The troglodytic people which inhabit these subterranean chambers now number 1,200, and there is historical evidence that they have lived in these sunken pits for centuries. The court or sunken area into which the different rooms open is a common gathering place for the inhabitants, in which most of the household work is performed, the excavated chambers being often arranged one above another, serving as the sleeping rooms."[23]

Incidentally, Hotel Sidi Driss in Matmata was the filming location for Luke Skywalker's moisture farm on his home planet Tatooine in the *Star Wars* saga.

The common area of the Berber structure is called a *qaba,* or "hub," and is analogous to the circular great kiva.[24] The people excavated sleeping rooms radiating off this central portion, which correspond to the observation rooms lining the circumference of the great kiva, such as the one at Aztec, New Mexico.

The Hopi word for the fire pit at the center of the kiva is *qöpqö*. Both this word and the Berber one sound somewhat similar to the Arabic word *Ka'ba,* which refers to the black cube located at Mecca—the center and holiest locus of the Muslim world. In addition, the Sumerian phrase INA QABAL means "in the middle of."[25]

Old photograph showing circular depressions of the kiva-like Berber structures.

This may be related to the Hebrew *qabbalah*, literally "receiving, accepting," as a tradition. "Kabbala" is the word from which the English "cabal" is derived.[26] Furthermore, the Egyptian words *ka* and *ba* mean "spirit-double" and "soul" respectively. Finally, the Mayan word *qaba* denotes "name." (Read about the incredibly rich legacy of the simple, single syllable *ka* in my book *Eye of the Phoenix*.)

The Berbers were known historically as Meshwesh (*mšwš.w*) by the ancient Egyptians, Libyans by the ancient Greeks, and Numidians or Mauri by the Romans.

Fewkes goes on to mention the "deep-seated similarities" in the cultures of "Tunisian pueblos" and those of the Southwest, citing parallels in "...house ownership, matriarchal rights, and clan descent..." Fewkes also admits to common ground between Berbers and the Hopi or other ancient Pueblo people in terms of "...their customs, arts, and institutions..."[27]

This seems to be the case in, for instance, textile arts, to which scholar Sophia Gates attests.

> "A few matriarchies still survive, among them the Berber and Tuareg of North Africa and the Hopi of North America. The Dineh –the Navajo [of Arizona and New Mexico], are matrilineal if not outright matriarchal– land stays with the woman's family and the husband moves in with the wife's family. These groups, interestingly, are still active and highly productive in the ancient arts of weaving and pot-making and jewelry manufacture; and although they are under extreme stress from modern times, Christianity, Islam, and Arabism, their art flourishes still."[28]

The Berbers call themselves the *Imazighen* (singular, *Amazigh*), or "free people." Coincidentally (?), the Hopi word *ímangyam* specifically means "members of these particular clans or this particular clan (already referred to)."[29] Even today in Muslim North Africa, the women go unveiled and tattoo their chins, whereas the men wear blue-indigo veils over their lower faces and turbans on their heads.

A number of symbols from the Berber and Hopi cultures show a strong congruence in both image and message. (See facing page.) In the case of the Berbers, they are manifested in woven carpets, ceramics, and tattoos; in the case of the Hopis, they find expression in blankets and pottery.

The cultural diffusionist Barry Fell even found a correlation between one Libyan word and the design on a ceremonial kilt worn by the Hopi priest leading the Snake Dance in 1891.

> "This kilt is now preserved at Harvard, and shows alternating symbols which may be read as the Libyan letters W-t repeated as a decorative motif. Is it merely an accident that W-t is the spelling adopted by the Egyptians (and presumably by Libyans) for the name of the sacred serpent known to the Greeks as the uraeus, and worn by the Pharaohs as a forehead ornament symbolic of divinity? It is facts such as these that force us to recognize that Libyan writing as well as Libyan language must once have been current in some southwestern regions of North America."[30]

The two letters were painted upon the undulating body of a snake, which was also painted on the cotton kilt. The "W" is represented by what looks like an equal sign (= , sometimes rotated 90°); the "t" is represented by a modern peace symbol turned upside down but sans circle, which in Hopi iconography is called a "crows foot" and relates to war.

Coincidentally (here we go again), this exact same glyph is also the Nordic rune *Algiz*, which signifies protection. "*Algiz* serves as a mirror for the Spiritual Warrior, the one whose battle is always with the self."[31]

[continued on p. 32]

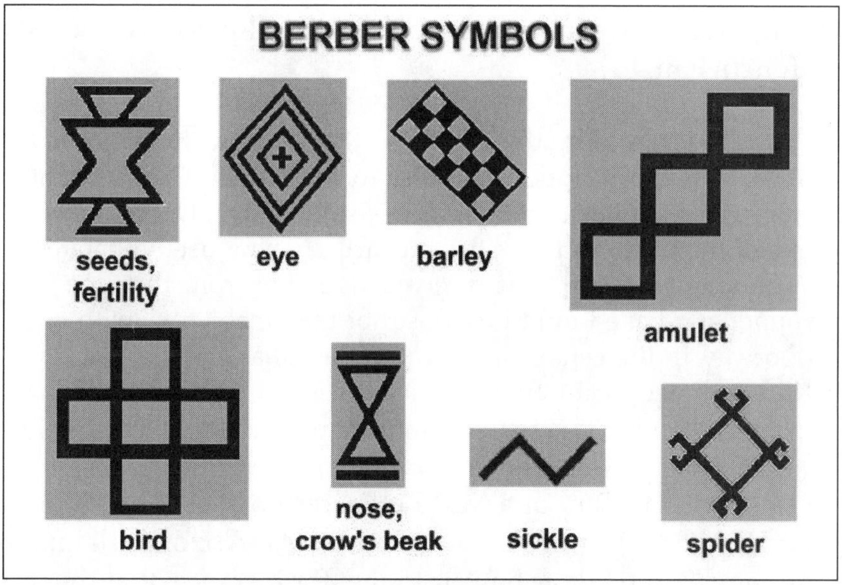

The geometric iconography of these two cultures from opposite sides of the globe is remarkably similar. The lozenge refers to a celestial portal. The Egyptians considered Orion as the Barley God, so the checkerboard night sky is appropriate. In the Hopi world, equilateral crosses are emblematic of stars; thus, the war shield of the sky deity Sótuknang also makes sense. In addition, the crow is symbolic of war. The breath is a positive spirit, and the Berber metallic sickle warded off evil ones, or *jinns*.

Scholar Gene D. Matlock speculates that long ago the Hopi may have been part of a snake cult in, of all places, Uzbekistan or Afghanistan.

> "The Hopi origin myth mentioned their nuclear home, called **Kiva**. This word appears similar to the name of the ancient city-state of Khiva in today's Uzbekistan. **Khiva**, Uzbekistan is one of the most ancient cities on earth, having been inhabited since about 8,000 B.C. It received its name from the type of round, sun-baked mud pit-houses of the inhabitants, with the doorway in the center of the roof. The inhabitants of ancient Khiva entered their homes by a ladder. Khiva's name is derived from two Sanskrit words: **Ki** (ant hill) plus **Va** (dwelling)."[32]

Other sources hint at a Middle Eastern or East Indian origin of the Hopi. Mr. Jasper Poola of First Mesa, Arizona, claims the following: "Some Hopis have told me, for instance, that the original *sipapuni* (earth navel) was in Egypt, India, or Jerusalem—that is, somewhere in the Old World."[33] I might add here that the Hopi were the least affected of all the Pueblo people by Christian evangelism.

In the Hopi culture, men are the weavers and women are the potters. Southwestern archaeologists still find "loom holes" in the floors of excavated kivas. Although Hopi society is matriarchal, one tradition that modern Puebloans inherited from their ancestors –perhaps even those of the Old World– is still vibrant. The male-dominated kiva culture remains a key factor in religious life of the American Southwest.

Chapter 2
Stargates In Antiquity

Gate of Cancer, Gate of Capricorn

In the current development of Western civilization, the popular imagination has seized with a peculiar ferocity upon the notion of the stargate as a sort of cosmic corridor leading to a whole new world or a dimension radically different from ours. The cult classics *Stargate* and *Contact* as well as astrophysists' theories about wormholes –a household word in the wake of *Star Trek* and its ilk– invest such ideas with an almost mythical potency.

This phenomenon is not new but may instead have accompanied human beings' first realization of their own individual mortality. Even if Near Death Experiences may not have been common in our evolutionary history, they were certainly not unknown either. NDEs could have correlated the long tunnel that takes us to brilliant white light of the afterlife and the birth canal that brings us into this life. Both may be considered as forms of stargates—the soul's passageway to and from the celestial realm.

In essence, there exist two separate stargates at opposite ends of the Milky Way. First I need to discuss two astronomical terms: celestial equator and ecliptic. The celestial equator is a great circle formed by the projection of the Earth's equator onto the sky. At 0° celestial latitude, it is 90° from each of the celestial poles. The ecliptic is another great circle that forms the apparent path of the Sun, Moon, and planets. It is also the track along which the twelve constellations of the zodiac appear to travel in the night sky. The ecliptic forms a 23°27′ angle with the plane of the celestial equator.

In their scholarly tome *Hamlet's Mill,* Giorgio de Santillana and Hertha von Dechend discuss these sidereal terms in the context of the Platonic cosmology found in *Timaeus,* written about 360 BC. "When the Timaean Demiurge had constructed the 'frame', *skambha* [Sanskrit word for *axis mundi*], ruled by equator and ecliptic –called by Plato 'the Same' and 'the Different'– which represent an X (spell it Khi, write it X) and when he had regulated the orbits of the planets according to harmonic proportions, he made 'souls.'"[1]

In other words, "the frame" is the point where the celestial equator crosses the ecliptic. Called by astronomers the First Point of Aries, this juncture where the Sun crosses the equator in its northward journey marks zero point in the measurement of right ascension, which can be conceptualized as celestial longitude.

The celestial equator now passes very near Mintaka (one of three stars in the *Zona,* or Orion's belt—see my book *The Orion Zone* for more on this). Conversely, the ecliptic always passes through Gemini, just above the right hand of Orion and between the horns of Taurus. The point at which the celestial equator presently crosses the ecliptic is located between Pisces and Aquarius—hence we are entering the celebrated "Age of Aquarius."

About 6,150 years ago, however, the fiducial point of the vernal equinox occurred on April 25th. It was located equidistant between Gemini and Taurus above Orion's upraised weapon with the axis of the Milky Way passing directly through it near the galactic anticenter. The early 5th century AD Latin grammarian and philosopher Macrobius states that during that age, souls ascended through what in his time he called the "Gate of Capricorn" and descended to be reborn through the "Gate of Cancer."

Because of the precession of the equinoxes caused by the slight wobble of the Earth's axis, the Cancer Gate is currently located between Pisces and Aquarius. This is called the northern stargate.

[continued on p. 36]

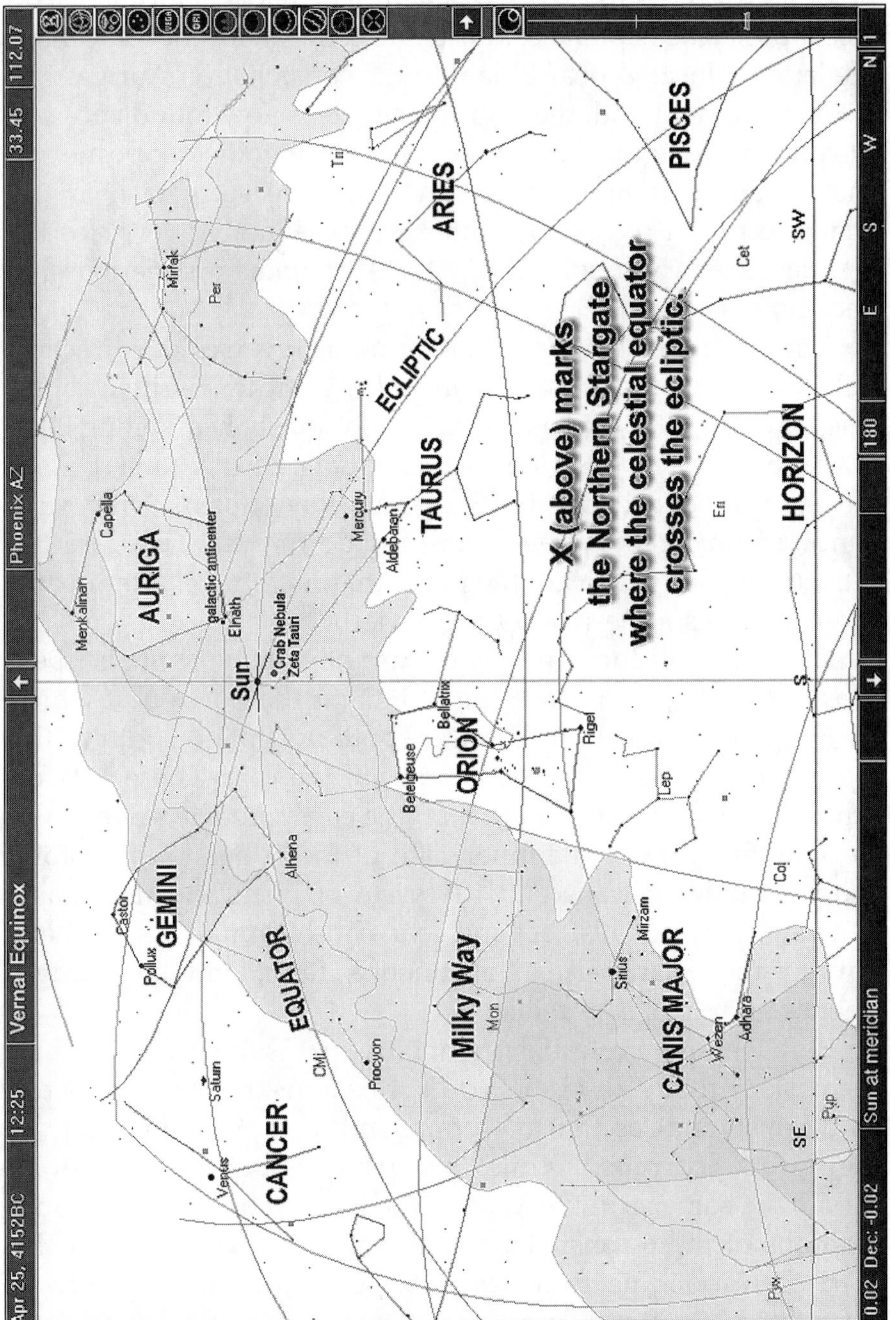
Fri Apr 25, 4152BC
12:25
Vernal Equinox
Phoenix AZ
33.45
112.07
X (above) marks
the Northern Stargate
where the celestial equator
crosses the ecliptic.
CANCER
GEMINI
AURIGA
TAURUS
ARIES
PISCES
ORION
CANIS MAJOR
Milky Way
EQUATOR
ECLIPTIC
HORIZON
Sun
Sun at meridian
RA: 0.02 Dec: -0.02

The theoretical point in the heavens that lies directly opposite the center of the Milky Way is called the galactic anticenter. The axis of the galactic plane connects the center with the anticenter. The latter is located near Elnath in the constellation Auriga.

On the other hand, the Capricorn Gate is now found between Scorpius and Sagittarius on the end of the zodiac opposite the Gate of Cancer. This is called the southern stargate near the galactic center. The galactic center, which is located very close to Sagittarius A* (pronounced "A-star"), contains a supermassive black hole.

A source much earlier than Macrobius reverses the direction of the two stargates. *Prasna Upanishad,* a Vedic text written sometime between 900 BC and 600 BC but obviously hearkening back to a far earlier age, describes two celestial paths: "Prana [primal energy, symbolized by the Sun] and Rayi [form-giving substance, symbolized by the Moon] divide the year. Two are the paths of the Sun—two are the paths that men travel after death. These are the southern and the northern."[2]

The solar and lunar references are obviously symbolic, perhaps alchemically so, since the points on the horizon at which the Sun and Moon rise and set are both north and south of the equinox points during various times of the year. Those seeking either progeny or reincarnation on the earth piously travel Rayi, the southern way, or the lunar path of the fathers or ancestors. Those seeking to transcend the cycle of birth and death and achieve a place of rest beyond fear chose Prana, the northern way, or the solar path of abstinence, faith, and knowledge, whence no return is possible.

Here we find a celestial orientation that is the exact opposite of the skies today. In other words, this Sanskrit text deems the southern stargate as Taurus-Gemini and the northern stargate as Sagittarius-Scorpius. While the psycho-spiritual functions remain the same as in the Macrobius description, the directional positions of these constellations along the Milky Way fit a sky chart corresponding to at least 10,500 BC or earlier—halfway around the 26,000 year precessional cycle.

In his book *Signs in the Sky,* Adrian Gilbert cites Matthew

16:19, where Christ gives the "keys of the kingdom of heaven" to Simon Peter and appoints him its gatekeeper. "Using a different but related metaphor, Peter also was to become the door-keeper of heaven, as he was to be given the keys to the gates of Hades. In church art and statues of St. Peter he is usually shown holding the keys: one gold and the other silver, suggesting two different gates."[3]

The reference to the two most precious metals corroborates the solar/lunar symbology found in the Hindu version. These portals to the afterlife were obviously important components in the cosmologies of many diverse cultures around the globe.

The Dual Stargates of Egyptian Cosmology

The *Book of the Dead,* an ancient Egyptian manual of resurrection technology, identifies both the falcon and the heron/phoenix as key icons, each of which is apparently associated with a specific directional portal or doorway in the sky.

In Spell 13, the *Spell for going in and out of the West* (symbolic of the underworld), the afterlife journeyer states: "I have gone in as a falcon, I have come out as a phoenix..."[4] The former bird corresponds to the southern stargate of what may be termed "post-carnation," ("gone in" to the underworld), providing a conduit for the soul to leave the body after death. The latter bird corresponds to the northern stargate of incarnation ("come out" of the underworld and back to the Earth), allowing the soul to return to a new body, being reborn from the ashes of a previous existence like the mythical phoenix.

In the *Spell for being transformed into a divine falcon,* the Messenger addresses Osiris: "O Lord of the Soul, greatly majestic, see, I have come, the Netherworld has been opened for me, the roads in the sky and on earth have been opened for me, and there was none who thwarted me."[5] In the same manner the *Spell for being transformed into a heron* states: "I am vindicated on earth, and the terror of me is in the sky – and vice versa; it is my strength which makes me victorious to the height of the sky, I am held in respect to the breadth of the sky, my strides are towards the towns of the Silent Land [the realm of the dead]."[6] Spell 17 proclaims: "I am that great phoenix which is in Heliopolis, the supervisor of what exists... I go on the road which I know in front of the Island of the Just. What is it? It is Rosetjau. The southern gate is in Naref, the northern gate is in the Mound of Osiris; as for the Island of the Just, it is Abydos."[7]

Heliopolis is in Lower Egypt to the north. Rosetjau (or *Rostau*) refers to the netherworld. Naref is the necropolis at Herakleopolis, near the Faiyum, or the lake and marshy area west of the Nile in Middle Egypt. The mythical Mound of Osiris (or the primeval Mound of Creation) was located at Heliopolis. Abydos is in Upper Egypt, far to the south.

The oasis of the Faiyum was probably the naturalistic origin of the concept of the Field of Rushes, or Field of Reeds, a sort of Egyptian Elysian Fields. Some of the vignettes for this region in The *Book of the Dead* depict the Heron of Plenty perched upon a small pyramid. It is interesting to note that the hieroglyphic of a heron upon a pyramid corresponds to the word *bah,* meaning "to flood, to inundate."[8] Also shown is a celestial bark containing a staircase, which connotes transcendence. It is rather like half of a stepped pyramid cut vertically. (See drawing on p. 60.)

Commenting on Egyptian funerary literature, the renowned but controversial scholar Zecharia Sitchin writes:

> "The pictorial depictions which accompanied the hieroglyphic texts surprisingly showed the Stream of Osiris as meandering its way from an agricultural area, though a chain of mountains, to where the stream divides into tributaries. There, watched over by the legendary Phoenix birds, the *Stairway to Heaven* was situated; there, the Celestial Boat of Ra was depicted as sitting atop a mountain, or rising heavenward upon streams of fire."[9]

In papyrus illustrations of The Field of Rushes, either the falcon or a small, human-headed bird representing the *ba,* or soul (homonym of *bah*), perches atop a pylon, which is a massive rectangular gateway to a temple or hypostyle hall.[10] Thus, the pylon is a perfect symbol for the stargate. In addition, the walls of the Field of Rushes are made of iron, presumably meteoric iron, which further stresses its supernal connotation.[11]

Egypt is known as the Two Lands: Lower Egypt and Upper Egypt. This division corresponds to the northern and southern stargates respectively, located along the celestial Nile River, or the Milky Way. "The Milky Way will not reject me, the rebels will not have power over me, I shall not be turned away from your *portals*, the *doors* [italics added] shall not be closed against me..."[12]

In addition, Spell 109 asserts: "I know the northern gate of the sky; its south is in the Lake of Waterfowl, its north in is the Waters of Geese..."[13] In other words, the northern gate's *southern* limit is where the heron's domain begins, which is probably a reference to the Faiyum. On the other hand, the northern gate's *northern* limit is symbolically inhabited by geese.

The goose is frequently equated with Geb (sometimes written Seb or Keb), the god of earth and husband of Nut, who is the personification of the sky. Geb's chief seat is in Heliopolis to the north where with his wife he produced the great Egg, whence sprang the sun god in the form of the phoenix.[14]

> "The doors of the sky are opened for me, the doors of the earth are opened for me, the door-bolts of Geb are opened for me, the shutters of the sky windows are thrown open for me. It is he who guarded me who releases me, who binds his hand on me and thrusts his hand on to me on earth, the mouth of the Pelican is thrown open for me, the mouth of the Pelican is given to me, and I go out into the day to the place where I desire to be."[15]

The pelican is significantly related to the phoenix in alchemical literature, and both are associated with the color red. Perhaps it is not coincidence, then, that the Red Crown (Deshret) comes from Lower Egypt, whereas the White Crown (Hedjet) is from Upper Egypt. The two lands (or Crowns) were united when King Menes of Hierakonpolis (about forty-five miles south of Karnak, or Thebes) conquered the Delta circa 3100 BC.[16]

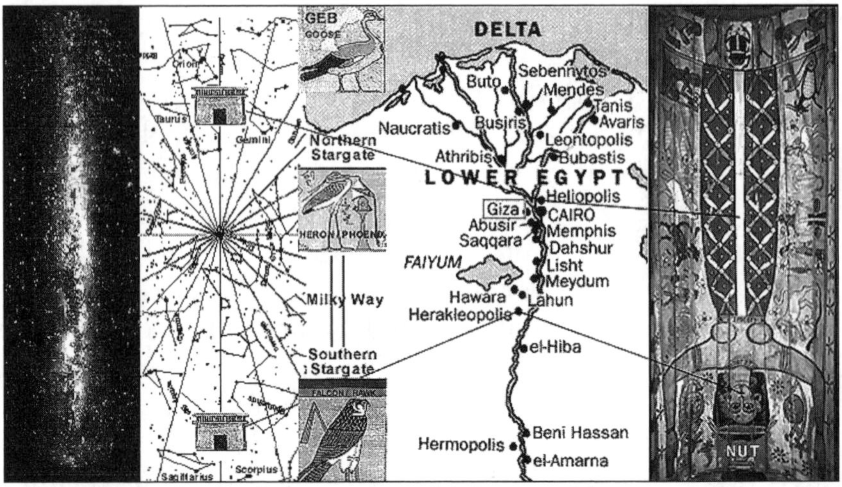

Left to right: galactic plane, stargates, birds, map, Nut on sarcophagus lid.

As an anthropomorphism of the sky, Geb's wife Nut is conceptualized as arching face down over her supine husband, who is sometimes portrayed in an ithyphallic manner. (See p. 262.) Her fingers and toes form the horizon, while stars scintillate like semen on her dusky belly. Both figures are positioned in the same direction, though some confusion exists about exactly which direction they are oriented. Although the couple is sometimes seen with their heads pointing toward the west, it makes more sense that the torso of Nut would represent the north-south orientation of the Milky Way/Nile as seen during the pre-dawn and post-dusk periods of the vernal and autumnal equinoxes. If we accept this positioning, her four outstretched limbs could represent the sunrise and sunset solstice points on the horizon, while her vagina could signify the northern stargate and her mouth the southern stargate. (Her *mons veneris* may in fact be the same as the Mound of Creation at Heliopolis.) In this case, her head would be pointed south. Egyptian lore recounts that when the Milky Way hugs the northern horizon, arching from east to west during the pre-dawn winter solstice, Nut comes down to Earth to lie with her husband Geb.

I have previously discussed the biblical Jacob's Ladder and its association with the Milky Way. Indeed, the Egyptian "bible" contains similar passages. Psychologist C. G. Jung observes:

"In one of the Pyramid Texts he [namely, Set, brother of Osiris] and Heru-ur (the 'older Horus') help Osiris [Orion] to climb up to heaven. The floor of heaven consists of an iron plate, which in places is so close to the tops of the mountains that one can climb up to heaven with the help of a ladder. The four corners of the iron plate rest upon four pillars, corresponding to the four cardinal points. In the Pyramid Texts of Pepi I, a song of praise is addressed to the 'ladder of the twin gods,' and the Unas text says: 'Unas cometh forth upon the Ladder which his father Ra hath made for him, and Horus and Set take the hand of Unas, and they lead him into the Tuat [or *Duat*, the underworld].'"[17]

This narrative occurred before the two brothers became fierce enemies. Set's abode was traditionally in the north[18], so in the context of these "twin gods" (akin to the Mayan Hero Twins and the Hopi warrior twins) we may assume that Horus belongs to the opposite direction.

Continuing the ladder imagery, the *Spell for fetching a ferry-boat in the sky* reads in part:

"Hail to you, you plateau which is in the sky north of the Great Waterway [the Milky Way], for whoever sees it will not die. I stand upon you, I appear as a god, I have seen you and I will not die. I stand upon you, I appear as a god, I cackle as a goose [of the north], I fly up as a falcon [of the south] upon the branches.

"O Dew of the Great One, I cross the earth towards the sky, I stand up as Shu [god of air, one of the Heliopolitan Ennead], I make sunshine to flourish on the sides of the ladder which is made to mount up to the Unwearying Stars, far from decapitation."[19]

The heart-rending tone of this pilgrim's words echoing through the realms of the dead is readily evident as he/she expresses an ultimate desire for eternal wholeness in bodily form and life everlasting in spirit. Moreover, many passages from the *Book of the Dead* emphasize the paramount role of Orion and his northern stargate in achieving this spiritual goal.

In the *Spell for opening the mouth*, a ceremony in which the falcon god Horus uses an adze of meteoric iron to pry open the deceased mouth, thereby allowing the latter to regain his/her faculties in the netherworld, we find the following proclamation: "...I am Orion the Great who dwells with the Souls of Heliopolis."[20] Another spell avers: "I am Orion who treads the land, who precedes the stars of the sky which are on the body of my mother Nut, who conceived me at her desire and bore me at her will."[21]

Still another spell speaks in the voice of the guardian of the northern stargate: "I am the guardian, I am his [Osiris'] heir on earth. Prepare a path for me, O you who are at peace; see, I enter into the Netherworld, I open up the beautiful West, I make firm the staff of Orion..."[22] In the reproductive sense this staff is the phallus of Orion, whose star-seed is packed with nebulae such as M42 and M43. In a more war-like aspect Orion holds this staff in his right hand and points to locus where the ecliptic crosses the galactic plane of the Milky Way, the location of the northern stargate.

Orion's warrior image (facing page) is artfully conveyed on the reverse side of a shield-shaped palette depicting King Narmer (or Menes, as previously mentioned) of the south vanquishing his northern foes. Wearing the White Crown and holding upraised staff in his right hand ready to strike, he holds his kneeling enemy with his left hand. Behind him is what has been deemed the "sandal-bearer," with a seven-pointed star blazing above her in the exact relationship that Sirius (Isis) is to Orion (Osiris).

In front of Narmer is a falcon perched on a fan of six papyrus stalks symbolic of Lower Egypt, which perhaps corresponds to the V-shaped Hyades. This image indicates that the bird of the southern stargate has conquered the quintessential plant of the north. The bird also holds a rope in his claws that apparently binds the head of another bearded captive seen in profile (perhaps Phoenician). At the bottom of the palette is a pair of figures that on the celestial plane may represent Gemini, although the constellation in the sky is seen above rather than below Orion.[23]

[continued on p. 44]

Narmer Palette, early First Dynasty (3100–3050 BC), carved schist. It was deposited at Hierakonpolis (or Nekhen, "City of Hawks," the southern city where a Horus cult was located). King Narmer was probably the son of King Scorpion, who may be associated with the constellation Scorpius.

The Spell of the northern gate's guardian continues: "...I am the mysterious phoenix, I am one who goes in that I may rest in the Netherworld, and who ascends peacefully to the sky. I am the Lord of Celestial Expanses, I travel through the lower sky [that is, over Lower Egypt] in the train of Re[24]; my offerings in the sky are in the Field of Re; my gifts on earth are in the Field of Rushes."[25] In this incantatory longing for peace in the afterlife, the earth-sky duality is obviously a sine qua non of Egyptian spiritual cosmology.

As sundry passages from ancient Egyptian texts have shown, the heron/phoenix complex and its associated deities Osiris and Set are associated with the northern stargate of incarnation, whereas the falcon and Horus are connected with the southern stargate of post-carnation. Two contrasting terms clearly illustrate this dichotomy: chronology and horology.

Chronos is the lord of time in its linear procession—of time tables and stone tablets; in essence, the Masonic square. More than one source has identified Chronos (the Greek Kronos or the Roman Saturnus) with the constellation Orion.[26] On the other hand, horology is the measuring of time in its cyclical sense—the passing of the "hours," from which both the word "horology" and the name Horus derive; in essence, the Masonic compass. A "horo-scope" allows one to view the wheel of the zodiac, the group of twelve archetypal constellations spinning through the solar year, as it affects the individual. On a much larger scale it permits us to see the influence of the precessional year (equaling 25,920 solar years) as it impacts the rise and fall of civilizations. (for instance, the Age of Taurus, the Age of Aries, of the Age of Pisces, the Age of Aquarius, etc.)

Horology has a deeper meaning, however. According to Jung, "Horos (boundary) is a 'power' or numen identical with Christ, or at least proceeding from him." Its synonyms are "he who leads across," "emancipator," and "redeemer."[27]

The Egyptians conceptualized the phoenix –a.k.a. the *bennu* bird of the northern stargate– as "the patron of reckoning time" and "the soul of Osiris."[28] He was basically an agent of purification by fire in the netherworld, allowing souls to be reborn on the earth plane. Conversely, Horus was perceived as the falcon god who ushered them through the southern stargate, out of this temporal world and into eternity. Hence, the dual stargates of immanence and transcendence served as ports along the great sidereal river whereon all souls sail.

Ninja Turtles Versus Turtledoves

If we return from the Egyptian celestial realm to the terra firma of the American Southwest (actually Tierra Zia), we see the dual stargates concept manifested in the structure of the pueblo societies, some of which live along the Rio Grande in New Mexico. The underlying principle of these people is the concept of duality: dark/light; winter/summer; north/south; yang/yin; male/female; active/passive; and, in Jungian terms, animus/anima. Frank Waters eloquently sums up this primary cultural structure.

> "All Indian life is permeated with an exaggerated sense of duality. One of its two great polarities is Encircled Mountain which extends invisibly upward toward the Sun Father. The other is the canyon, the *sipapu* which leads back down into the depths of our Mother Earth. Day and night, winter and summer, sun and moon, male and female, mountains, rivers and rains, the colors and the fictions, the kachinas, the sand-painting figures with their stylized round or square heads, the dual Hero Brothers—everywhere in nature, ritual, and legend is manifested this duality."[29]

This dichotomy is more clearly exemplified in the Tewa, for instance, than in the Hopi of Arizona (excluding the Tewa village of Hano on First Mesa of Arizona). The Tewa have adopted what is called a moiety system. Basically, this indigenous society exhibits a duality that consists of Winter People and Summer People, each with their own kiva and ritual duties. Each moiety is headed by a caciaque, or spiritual leader, who directs the ceremonies during the half of the year for which he is responsible.

Once selected, he retains his authority for life.

During spring and summer, the Corn Dances prevail, performed in the village plaza in order to assist in the annual agricultural cycle. In fall and winter, also held in the plaza, the Animal Dances take precedence, invoking, for instance, the buffalo, antelope, deer, mountain sheep, eagle, and turtle. The Winter People dancers paint their bodies a dull blue, whereas the Summer People dancers paint their bodies a dull red. These colors respectively correspond to the directions north and south. (In addition, East corresponds to white, and west corresponds to yellow.)

Winter People, regardless of gender, are symbolically identified by male qualities and turquoise stone. Summer People are, conversely, identified by female qualities and squash blossoms. (An interesting aside: the Tewa consider men to have both male and female traits, while women have only female traits. How did they know about XY and XX chromosomes?) Winter People are associated with hunting and warfare, whereas Summer People are connected with the gathering of wild plants and agriculture.

At the Keresan-speaking Cochiti Pueblo (native name *Kotyete*) we find a Turquoise Kiva on the eastern side of the village and a Pumpkin (Squash) Kiva on the western side.[30] This directional orientation may be the result of the initial proto-Puebloan migration from *Sipofene,* or Sandy Place Lake, located to the north in south-central Colorado. (This is analogous to the primordial Place of Emergence that the Hopi call the *Sipapuni,* found at the bottom of Grand Canyon.) The Winter Chief proceeded from their original homeland southward along the eastern side of the Rio Grande; the Summer Chief, on the other hand, traveled in the same direction along the western side of the river.[31]

Common sense tells us that winter is associated with the north, while summer is related to the south. Equally obvious is the universal relationship between the east with its burgeoning life at birth (dawn) and the west with its declining life that leads finally to death (sunset). Respecting the moiety system, the ancestral Winter People followed a path on the eastern bank of the Rio Grande. It may at first seem counter-intuitive that the class of people who kill animals (hunters), and this same class of people who also may kill humans (warriors), are connected with the direction associated with life. However, if we remember that the northern stargate, to which the Winter People are linked, allows for the birth of souls on the material plane, then we can see the underlying rationale of this relationship. On the other hand, the Summer People on the western bank of the river must rely on the germinating power that resides in the underworld. The southern stargate is the main portal to that underworld, which of course includes the watery stellar plane found in the Milky Way.

The directional placement of kivas within the plaza varies from pueblo to pueblo. I previously commented on the east-west orientation of the kivas at Cochiti Pueblo. Frank Waters has noted that the Tiwa-speaking Taos Pueblo (native name *Tua*) is divided by a stream in the middle of a central plaza. Located at one end is the "north pyramid," or housing block, which is called *Hlau-oma,* literally "cold-elevated." At the other end is the "south pyramid," which is called *Hlau-gima* ("cold-diminished").[32]

The Tewa-speaking San Ildefonso Pueblo (native name *Pokwoge*) is also aligned to a north-south axis, with the rectangular kiva of the Winter People located in the northernmost housing block. The rectangular kiva of the Summer People is detached and positioned in the southwestern part of the village. A large, circular kiva with a stairway on the side is also located aboveground on the southern side of the village—the direction of the winter solstice sunrise. This kiva belongs to both moieties.[33] (See a photo of the San Ildefonso round kiva on p. 115 of my book *Eye of the Phoenix*.)

The sacred Turtle Dance is performed at the winter solstice or shortly thereafter. Like the Hopi Soyal ceremony (see p. 22), this Puebloan dance is probably synchronized by the appearance of Orion in the overhead hatchway of the Winter People's kiva. Edward S. Curtis, the famous early photographer of Native Americans, describes the scene at the Tewa-speaking San Juan Pueblo (native name *O'ke*):

> "One of the most prominent of these public ceremonies is Okuhyare ('turtle dance'), which takes place annually on Christmas day. ...the dancers file out of the kiva and dance in a row, first on the east, then on the south, last on the north side of the plaza. They are painted black from neck to ankles, and wear white and black loin-cloths terminating in a tail, moccasins with skunk-skin anklets, and turtle-shell rattles on the right ankle. Below the left knee is a yarn band with bells or rattles suspended from it, around each bicep is a green band with spruce sprigs thrust fanwise under it, and on the head are upright eagle-feathers and transverse parrot-feathers. In the right hand is a gourd rattle, in the left a bunch of Douglas spruce."[34]

Note that when the dancers exit the kiva, they first go to the east (the Winter People's side of the river), then they walk to the south to acknowledge the Summer People, and finally they end up on the north side. This latter direction is laden with symbolic and mythological resonance. North is the original homeland, the eternal residence of the ancestors, an Edenic place that knew no death, which began to occur only after the migrations southward were undertaken. Thereafter dying became a fact of life due to sorcery. The lake in the north was essentially a paradise lost.

This Turtle Dance song from Santa Clara Pueblo (native name *Ka'po*) captures the primal power of the boreal spirit:

> "Long ago in the north
> Lies the road of emergence!
> Yonder our ancestors live,
> Yonder we take our being.
> Yet now we come southward
> For cloud flowers blossom here
> Here the lightning flashes,
> Rain water here is falling!"[35]

The two moieties basically traded in their subterranean water world for one where water came from "cloud flowers" in the sky.

And the Turtle Dance is all about water and entreaties for it, as the aquatic reptile symbolizes. But it is also about a renewal of the annual cycle.

> "The Turtle Dance is easily the most important public religious ceremony of the San Juan calendar, defining as it does the end of one year and the beginning of a new one. The dance is named for the turtle, believed, to be the first hibernating being that moves about after the year has turned; thus, the turtle is seen as symbolizing the beginning of each new annual cycle."[36]

Among the clan names belonging to the winter moiety include some expected ones, such as the sky-stone Turquoise and water in its crystalline form: Snow, Ice, and Hoarfrost. Also included, however, are clan names designating the glittering celestial bodies of Orion's Belt, Pleiades, and Evening Star ("Yellow Dim Old-woman") as well as animal clans, such as Coyote, Snake, and, of course, Turtle.[37]

As I mentioned, *O'ke* is the Tewa word for San Juan Pueblo, located at the confluence of the Rio Chama and the Rio Grande. Its full native name, *Okhay Owinge,* possibly means "place of the strong people."[38] *Oku share* is the name for the Turtle Dance. *'Oku* means "turtle" but it also means "hill," the latter perhaps suggesting the shape of the turtle's shell. The turtle may in fact be a precise anagogue or hieratic analogue for the Quiché Maya concept of "sky-earth." (See p. 62.) The upper shell, or carapace, would correspond to the dome of the sky, while the lower shell, or plastron, would correspond to what appears to be relatively flat ground—the plain of the earth plane.

I will be dealing in greater depth with the Maya concept of the Cosmic Turtle in Chapter 8 and Chapter 9. Suffice to say here that the Mayan word for turtle is *ak,* very similar to the Tewa prefix *Ok-,* suggesting this creature whose dorsal shell mirrors the sky. The Mayan word for star is the near homonym *ek.*

In fact, a Mayan mural on the north wall of Room 1 at Bonampak in Chiapas near the Guatemalan border depicts Orion's belt on a turtle's back. (See top of p. 357.)

[continued on p. 51]

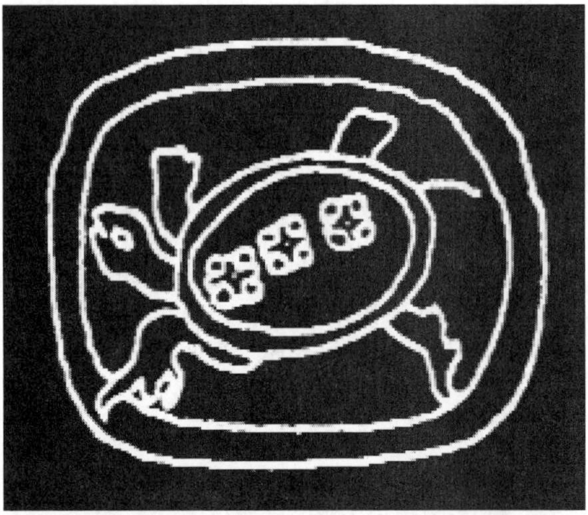

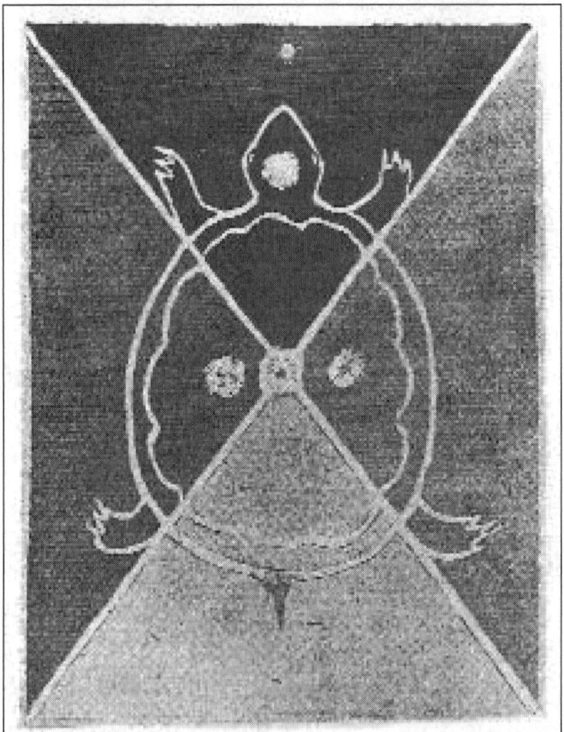

Drawing (above) shows a detail of a multicolored Mayan mural at Bonampak, star glyphs on its shell. The sand painting (below) is an offering for a child-naming ceremony at Acoma Pueblo, New Mexico. Orion's belt is clearly shown in both depictions. The lower rendition shows four directional colors plus opposing triangles that suggest Orion's shape. 12 scallops on shell represent the 12 zodiac constellations. Pyramid-shaped head is also like Orion's.

A similar motif is found in the American Southwest: an Acoma painting of a turtle shows three dots in a row on its shell. The native name of this pueblo is *Ako*. The words *O'ke, Oku, ak, ek, Ako*... Can all these similar syllables connected with the turtle and Orion's belt be merely a coincidence?

At this point we might ask what the archetypal significance of the turtle or tortoise is for cultures around the globe. Slow and steady wins the race, as we were taught as children by one of Aesop's fables. The turtle may represent gradual evolution as opposed to lightning-fast revolution. Linear time (Chronos) rather than cyclic time (Horos) is suggested by the stolid creature. Longevity, strength, and endurance are its hallmarks. (By the way, the Japanese word *ninja* literally means "person who endures.") Astrologically, the turtle invokes turgid Saturn instead of rebellious Uranus.

The Sumerian figure of Enki (Ea), Lord of the Earth and god of waters, had a few dealings with the turtle. In one fable the quarrelsome and malevolent turtle harasses the "gift-bringing" heron in her nest among the reeds. He turns her nest upside down, dumps her chicks into the water, and scratches her forehead until she is bloody.

Although the text is fragmentary, Enki seems to be assisting the heron by building some sort of sluice or gate (stargate?) to protect the heron's nest. Mention is made of Enki filtering "holy water" and making "a copper box." The badly damaged story cryptically ends: "...of Enki. ...did not catch; ...the hunting net. The turtle ...Enki ...something from his fingernail. Its inside is five ...; its exterior is ten... A crevice..." Or a stargate portal?

At any rate, Enki in his domain of lagoons and reeds helps the heron, which is a naturalistic model of the Egyptian phoenix or *bennu* bird. Whenever the universal symbol of the reed is used, it signifies civilization, high culture, and writing. On the other hand, the turtle curiously has "snake's eyes" and a "snake's tongue." The dichotomy of this story is clear: female/male; peaceful/martial; fertile/destructive.[39]

Although the turtle is a destabilizing element, it is still associated with water in whatever context it is found. The chief of the

Hopi Patki (Water) Clan, for instance, performs a ritual for new turtle shells.[40] By the way, the sun chief (*tawa mongwi*) is selected from the Patki Clan. He also tracks the position of the Sun on the horizon around the time of the solstices.

For the ancient Egyptians the turtle represented darkness, evil, and the night.[41] Their Turtle-god was associated with the fourth sign of the Egyptian zodiac known as *shetau*, which probably corresponded to Cancer, where the northern stargate was once located.[42]

Some tribes claim that the North American continent was called Turtle Island. The *Walam Olum*, purportedly a series of translations of pictographs made by the Lenni Lenape (or Delaware Indians), states the following: "In that ancient country, in that *northern country* [italics added], in that turtle country, the best of the Lenape were the Turtle men."[43]

The Akimel O'odham (Pima) of southern Arizona have a song that in part goes: "The Black Turtle approaches us, / Wearing and shaking his belt of night."[44] This may refer to the Milky Way, the ecliptic, or perhaps even Orion's belt. The turtle reputedly causes sores, and the singing of this song with a turtle shell rattle is a remedy.

The Zuni (native name *A'shiwi*) of New Mexico gather turtles from the sacred lake named *Kothluwalawa* around the time of the summer solstice. It is here that the departed souls are thought to reside. The turtles are brought back to the village, where they are tenderly and reverently treated as if they were relatives. Then they are ritually killed, their flesh and bones placed in a nearby stream and their shells carefully saved for use as dance rattles. The apparent purpose of this ceremony is to send the souls of the ancestors that inhabit the turtles' bodies back to the spirit land.[45] Like the Tewa, the Zuni also have a Turtle Clan.

The Australian Ngarinyin and Worora tribes (also mentioned on p. 62) believe that their Creator god Wandjina favors the long-necked, sweetwater turtle above all creatures. The waterholes where they live contain healing earth energies. The souls of humans also live there and enter either one of the parents before or during pregnancy. These tribes also believe that Wandjina put his own image into the turtle in the form of its jaw and neck bones, which, they say, resemble miniature human skeletons.[46]

The /Xam Bushmen of southern Africa believed that Orion's belt was "Three Male Tortoises (hung on a stick)."[47] The Fali tribe of northern Cameroon are divided into two clans: the Tortoise and the Toad. The world originally came into being from two eggs, one from each creature, and the insides of this pair of eggs revolved in opposite directions. The Tortoise was thought to represent "human earth," whereas the Toad was of "wild earth."[48]

In addition to the aforementioned connection of the turtle with Orion's belt, the Maya knew this aquatic reptile as the patroness of childbirth named Mayauel (Maya-uel). She was also the goddess of pulque, the intoxicating milky drink made from the agave, a large cactus that was considered by the Nahua people to be the Tree of Life.[49] This corresponds in Mayan cosmology to the celestial Maize Tree, or the *Wakah-Kan* ("Raised-up sky"), that sprouts from the Turtle's carapace at the point where the Milky Way crosses the ecliptic at nearly a right angle.[50]

In the plaza at the Classic Mayan site of Copán in western Honduras, a king named 18-Rabbit erected a number of stelae in the early 8th century to commemorate the first Katun (7,200 days) of his rule. Stele C is a square stone column about fourteen feet high and three feet wide with elaborate carvings on all surfaces. The east-facing side depicts the youthful monarch, while the western side shows him with a false beard and mustache. The late art historian Linda Schele refers to him by his native name: "Waxaklahun-Ubah-K'wil's features appear to be relatively young, but he wears a long beard, a rare feature among Mayan men. We suspect the beard was false, but its meaning is not entirely clear."[51] Perhaps he faces the west and wears facial hair to honor the members of some Chinese expedition that sailed eastward and landed on the coast of Central America. We can only speculate.

I bring up this particular monument because of the large turtle altar located at 18-Rabbit's feet. Looking at the western side of the stele, it appears as if he is rising like the Maize God from the portal of the turtle's cracked carapace, just like the momentous event described in the *Popol Vuh*. Thus, this 13th sovereign of

Copán was attempting to synchronize his reign with the cosmic cycles of Creation. (More on his resurrection in Chapter 8.)

Certain Mayan texts note a dichotomy of two creatures that possess shells: the tortoise and the snail. To the former they assigned the summer solstice, to the latter the winter solstice.[52] This is exactly opposite of what I have been discussing in terms of the Tewa with their winter solstice Turtle Dance. Three possible explanations exist for this discrepancy.

(1) If the Mayan underworld is anything like that of the Ancestral Puebloans, then there is a direct reciprocity of the two realms; in other words, the upper world mirrors the underworld. When the people above are doing the winter solstice ceremony, the spirits below are performing the summer solstice ceremony, and vice versa.

(2) Another explanation is similar to the reversal that I mentioned on p. 36 in regard to the Vedic texts. With this turtle-summer/snail-winter schema, the Maya may well have been referring to a time halfway around the precessional cycle—nearly 13,000 years ago. As masters of time, the Maya certainly had the ability to make such calculations.

(3) During the solstices the Sun achieves its maximum swing to the north and south along the horizon at sunrise and sunset. In the northern hemisphere at summer solstice, the Sun rises and sets as far north as it will get during the year; at the winter solstice it rises and sets as far south. In this way the tortoise-summer makes sense because the solar directions are northeast and northwest, while the snail-winter indicates the solar directions of southeast and southwest.

What is important, though, are the two disparate morphologies of these creatures. The tortoise or turtle represents the cup or bowl shape, while the snail takes on a spiral or vortex shape. (Read about the spiral's significance in my book *Eye of the Phoenix*.) As you will see shortly, these morphologies are precisely the way the dual stargates are described.

Similar to the north/upper and south/lower division of the ceremonial city of Cuzco in Peru, the Inca society at large also had two moieties: *banan* and *burin*. The former represented worldly authority, prestige, and, empire; on the other hand, the latter suggested spiritual authority, intrinsic self-worth, and the individual soul.

> "The upper moiety was more secular, military, and administratively oriented, while the lower moiety was more traditional, agricultural, and religiously oriented—shades of Wari and Tiahuanaco. Thus the conflicting reports on Wiraqocha Inca and Pachakuti Inca may be understood as the conflicting viewpoints of the warrior and peasant classes in pre-imperial Cuzco."[53]

A wooden engraving from an erotic Renaissance romance called *Hypnerotomachia Poliphili (Poliphilo's Strife of Love In a Dream),* published in 1499, precisely exemplifies the dichotomy I have laid out here. On one page a young woman is shown sitting on what appears to be a three-legged stool with her own legs spread apart in a very uncharacteristic fashion for the time. In her left palm she holds a turtle, while her right arm grabs a pair of extended wings as she gazes toward the latter. She is resting upon a rectangular dais with a pediment above her, thus suggesting the quadrilateral symbol of the earth. If she is facing east, as is likely for illumination by the dawn's light, then the turtle is positioned to the north and the wings to the south.[54]

SOL Travel

For our purposes here, SOL refers to the "speed-of-light" (*not* feces sans fortuity). However, it also resonates with the homonyms "Sol" (or Sun) and "soul." I am essentially talking about souls crossing immeasurably great distances at unimaginably great velocities.

I have also used the term "stargate" to describe those two celestial portals at opposite ends of the great loop of the zodiac—one to the north, the other to the south. In addition, the Milky Way (or Jacob's Ladder) crosses these two points on the ecliptic.

Macrobius actually uses a specific word to identify these. The following passage specifically describes the northern stargate, the place where souls enter the physical world: "...[the] Starry Cup (Crater) of Father Bacchus placed in the space between Cancer and Leo..."[55] A round "cup" or "crater," one at each end of the zodiac, is essentially an inter-dimensional bowl that allows ingress or egress of souls either to mix with matter or to be separated out from it. (The Greek word *krater* literally means "mixing bowl.") The fact that Bacchus creates this sky portal is perhaps an analogy to his wine cup, which when drunk sometimes produces mystical ecstasy and an upwelling of the unconscious.

In addition to being circular, these cups are shaped like a vortex or whirlpool—a spiral leading from one realm to another. "Plato, as we have seen, in his psychogony, speaks openly of this Cup or Crater (Mixing Space, or Vortex) in two aspects, in it the Deity mixes the All-Soul of universal nature from the purest Cosmic elements, and from it He also 'ladles out' the souls of men, composed of a less pure mixture of these Elements."[56] The term "psychogony" refers to the creation of the psyche, or the soul. Souls are "ladled out" like a spiritual fluid emptied into the cup of the northern stargate, eventually to be reborn. The Milky Way itself is a liquid metaphor, and we recall that many ancient cultures conceived of the underworld as a riparian realm flowing into the sea of stars.

As we have seen, the dual stargates were a primary component of many cosmologies in antiquity. Near the galactic anticenter, the northern stargate between the Bull and the Twins was ruled by Orion, the Hunter. At the other end of the zodiac near the galactic center, the southern stargate between the Scorpion and the Centaur was ruled by Ophiuchus, the Serpent Handler. Orion, especially his belt, was associated with the turtle in many cultures. Ophiuchus was also known as Asclepius, the Greek god of healing. We remember that the medical profession uses the icon of a pair of wings, much like that seen in the *Hypnerotomachia* engraving shown on p. 55. To these wings a staff with two entwined serpents that resemble the DNA double helix is sometimes attached, forming a caduceus.

In this chapter we have encountered many diametrically opposed concepts: north/south; up/down; incarnation/post-carnation; human/immortal; earth/sky; upper world/underworld; lower Egypt/upper Egypt; Red Crown/White Crown; Geb/Nut; goose/falcon; Chronos/Horus; Winter People/Summer People; hunting/agriculture; turtle/heron; turtle/snail; tortoise/toad; warrior/peasant.

The dynamic duo of stargates comprises a celestial dialectic. A cup... a crater... a whirlpool... a vortex... These in duplicate light the way into the matrix of matter, and the way out of it. These are the wormholes of Eden's apple. These are the cosmic tunnels of love. These are the liquid ladders of song. These are the spiral's Arc of the Covenant. These are the round portals to the worldwide dream-web. These cause the spectral Maya of time to collide with the large hadron of space. These provide the means of SOL travel. These justify the End. These ring in the Alpha that comes after the Omega. These ditto-stargates echo the deuces of the plumed ouroboros.

These are *the kivas of heaven*.

Aztec god Quetzalcoatl as ouroboros.

Chapter 3
The Hopi Cosmos

A Way Up and a Way Down: Ladders, Pyramids, and Helixes

In the first chapter I mentioned the biblical patriarch Jacob and his dream of a great ladder. With some trepidation he raises a pillar from the stones he had used as a pillow, calling the place Bethel, or the "house of God," and "the gate of heaven."[1]

Adrian Gilbert comments: "If we equate Jacob with Orion and his ladder with the Milky Way, then it would appear that this 'gate of heaven' is the same star-gate that Macrobius describes as being at the crossroads of the latter with the ecliptic. We have, therefore, the image of Jacob seeing the angels passing through the star-gate that lies at the top of the ladder of the Milky Way."[2] This association is reinforced by the notion that Orion's belt, as I previously mentioned, has been traditionally known as Jacob's staff or Jacob's rod—in other words, his phallus.

The Hopi word for 'stepladder' is *saaqa*. Perhaps it is more than a coincidence that the one of the world's most famous Step Pyramids is located at Saqqara, Egypt. In addition, the Hopi word *atsva* means "above."[3] The similar Egyptian word *Aatt* refers to either "pyramid region" or "Other World," while *aaut* means "pillars."[4] All across the globe, the pyramid is the primary symbol of ascension, whether it is the pointed-capstone pyramids of Egypt or the flat-topped pyramids of Mesoamerica. The ancestral Hopi of the American Southwest also carved petroglyphs resembling Step Pyramids, which represented stylized, stepped clouds.

[continued on p. 60]

Step Pyramid at Saqqara, Egypt. Photo © by Max Gattringer.

Petroglyphs of four-pointed star and stepped figures. The Hopi term for the latter is *tutuvengveni.* Coincidentally, petroglyphs are called *tutuveni.* Note the sharp, pyramidal shapes carved horizontally along the top of the rock. Petroglyph National Monument, New Mexico.

Stepped icons of the *Tuat* (or *Duat*) in *The Egyptian Book of the Dead*. The Hopi word *tu'at* (also spelled *tuu'awta*), which means "hallucination" or "mystical vision," sounds very close to the Egyptian *Tuat*. E. A. Wallis Budge, former director of antiquities at the British Museum, used this orthography rather than the more commonly spelled *Duat*. Whatever way it's spelled, this refers to the illusory realm of the afterlife.

In a painting called "Jacob's Ladder" (see facing page) by mystico-occult poet and artist William Blake, the ladder is actually a golden spiral staircase leading to the Sun, with angels (a few with wings but mostly wingless) going up and down, while a dreaming Jacob is sprawled at its base. The angel at the bottom is holding above her head some sort of curved platter –curiously resembling an Egyptian boat– with what looks like a sheep's head on it. Behind and to her right appears to be the Pleiades cluster.

If we conceptualize the three-dimensional spiral, or helix, as a unification of the eternal and the temporal, we may also see this geometric shape linking sky and earth. Historian of religions Mircea Eliade provides evidence of this from an initiation ceremony performed by the Wiradjuri tribe of New South Wales, Australia.

> "... the men cut a spiral piece of bark which symbolizes the path between sky and earth. In my opinion this represents the reactivation of the connections between the human world and the divine world of the sky. According to the myths the first man, created by Baiame [highest of the Gods], ascended to the sky by a path and conversed with his Creator. The role of the bark spiral in the initiation festival is thus clear—as symbol of ascension it reinforces the connection of the sky world of Baiame."[5]

[continued on p. 62]

William Blake, "Jacob's Ladder," 1800-03.

Wandjina pictographs (rock paintings), northern Kimberley, Australia. These ancient eerie figures resemble modern representations of ETs with their large eyes and heads but usually no mouths or ears.

Reciprocity of terrestrial and celestial is also a key cosmological concept for Aboriginal elder David Mowaljarlai of northern Kimberley, Australia. "Everything under Creation is represented in the soil and in the stars. Everything has two witnesses, one on earth and one in the sky.... Everything is represented in the ground and in the sky. You can't get away from it, because all is one, and we're in it. As you see, the Milky Way, it ties up the land like a belt, right across."[6] For instance, the Ngarinyin and Worora tribes consider the Milky Way (*Lejmorro*) as the spirit center, and the corresponding locus on earth is where the most powerful Wandjina (Raingod or Creator) paintings are located.

The Quiché Maya of the Guatemalan highlands use the term *cahuleu* to describe the dual nature of what we call the world. It literally means "sky-earth."[7] Scholar John Major Jenkins sums up the cosmology of the Maya in regard to the celestial realm.

> "Astro-mythology, astro-theology, archaeo-astronomy, mytho-astronomical ideation—however you phrase it, the connection between celestial cycles and cultural ideas on earth defines the highest insight of Mesoamerican religion, which can best be described with the Hermetic principle "as above, so below." Sky and earth, subjective and objective realities, are interrelated, two sides of the same coin. We see this tangibly in astronomically timed rites of Maya kingship. We also see it in city names and city planning, in which cities were oriented to astronomically significant horizons and reflected the structure of the cosmos."[8]

Most archaic societies, it appears, maintained a complex interrelationship between the terrestrial and the celestial, which not only determined where and how their temples and cities were to be placed but also regulated the rhythms of their daily lives, both in their mundane and spiritual aspects.

The Hopi also have a dual spiral figure similar to the Wiradjuri incorporated into their cosmology: a spiral situated at each of the Earth's polar regions.

> "It has been said that there are two water serpents coiling the earth, from North to South pole. On each of the poles sits a warrior god on the serpents' head and tail, now and then communicating messages of our conduct and behavior toward each other; now and then releasing light pressure which causes the great serpents to move, resetting earth movements—a message also commanding nature to warn us by her actions that time is getting short and so we must correct ourselves. If we refuse to heed the warning, the warrior gods will let go of the serpents and we will all perish. They will say: we do not deserve the land given to us because we are careless."[9]

Archetypally resonating with the Hero Twins found in the Mayan book of Creation called the *Popol Vuh,* the Hopi warrior twins are called Pöqanghoya, god of solidity, and Palöngawhoya, god of sound vibrations. The former sits on the North Pole, while the latter sits on the South Pole. Although the suffix *hoya* refers to "youth," Pöqanghoya (literally "son of the

Sun") is known as the elder, and Palöngawhoya (literally "water-dripping Sun") is known as the younger deity. Never functioning independently of each other, these two legendary characters frequently assume a mischievous character.

On the other hand, the dyad also plays the role of culture heroes, sometimes performing such Herculean tasks as the slaying of monsters.[10] Not only were these twins responsible for the creation of mountains and canyons, but they also monitored the vibratory centers of the earth, such as various vortex points on the globe.

Their primary duty, however, was to assure proper rotation of the planet. The dual spiral is represented by the pair of water serpents, each assigned to its polar station. The following quotation further describes the two spirals revolving from each pole outward into space, thereby providing the sort of divine connection to which Eliade refers.

> "The Spiral Force of Pöqanghoya, which turns the Arctic ice, is so powerful that it extends into Space. In other words, the Spiral Force coming from Pöqanghoya is Spiraling into Space over the North Pole and making a giant invisible Tornado going up into Space. The same is happening in the South Pole; with His Spiral Force Palöngawhoya is making a giant invisible Tornado going up into Space. These giant invisible Tornadoes are different from other Tornadoes in two ways: First, they stay in one position, always over the Poles, never moving from Place to Place, and second, they are turning more slowly than other Tornadoes, but always in a Spiral Motion like a giant funnel."[11]

In another version of the myth, the duo lives in the Grand Canyon, location of riparian whirlpools known as the Gate of Masau's House.[12] Masau (also spelled Masau'u or Masaaw—see picture on p. 247) is the Hopi god of the underworld, fire, death, and transformation—similar to the Greek god Hades or the Roman god Pluto. It is significant in this context that the Hopi climbed up from the previous Third World located underground and emerged into the current Fourth World on the Earth's surface via a giant reed—a wormhole-like passageway at the bottom of Grand Canyon. The underworld is conceived of as a great subterranean lake that paradoxically merges with the ocean of stars. In other words, the nether realm and the celestial realm are seen as one great circle of water surrounding the earth plane.

The northern Arizona rock carving seen below shows the spiral on the left (north) touching the three-pronged instrument (facing east), its power continuing across the line to the spiral on the right (south).

In the symbolism of rock art, the spiral represents a whirlpool or whirlwind but it also signifies a portal, vortex, or inter-dimensional space of numinous influence. Starting from the center, a clockwise spiral signifies ascension. Perhaps the spiral on the left energizes the instrument whose origin is the underworld. On the right-hand side the line of force dips –energy pauses?– before rising to the Earth's surface (the carved circle touching the arc at about a two o'clock position) and continuing onward into the sky. The spiral on the left is somewhat smaller than the one on the right. So, if the petroglyph is indeed depicting a 3-D perspective, the former could be seen as lower than the latter. (For a full discussion of spirals, see my book *Eye of the Phoenix*.)

As I mentioned, however, the underworld of Hopi cosmology also contains the realm of the stars. This rock carving may, then, represent the dual stargates—north and south. (See Chapter 2.)

Double spiral petroglyph: clockwise on left, counterclockwise on right, trident in middle. Homolovi Ruins State Park, Arizona.

What the tripartite emblem signified for the ancestral Hopi is unclear, but it may have represented the stylized bud of a squash plant, which is generally used in rock art and pottery design to embody fertility, germination, and the female principle. If this is the case, then the northern stargate/spiral juxtaposed to the trident was a visual schematic for the soul's process of incarnation on the earth plane.

Although the figures of both Shiva (the Hindu destroyer god) and Poseidon (the Greek sea god) traditionally used a trident, the statue of Pluto (the Roman underworld god) at the Nymphenburg Palace in Bavaria holds a three-pronged weapon as well.

The type of Roman gladiator known as *retiarius* also employed this instrument. "The fact that the trident was the weapon of the Roman *retiarius* is highly significant, for the net which he also used relates him to the Uranian deity, whereas the sword wielded by the *mirmillo* gladiator suggests the heroic, solar son. Hence, the trident, in the hand of the *retiarius*, would seem to be an attribute of archaic, paternal power, as opposed to the unique heroism of the solar son."[13]

Urania was the Greek god of astrology, so the distinction is made here between the stellar and the solar as well as between the father and the son. Thus, for the Hopi the trident was seemingly a female symbol; for the Roman a male one.

Shiva with trident, statue
on Delhi-Gurgaon Highway, India.

Pluto with trident, statue
in Munich, Germany.

The Hollywood blockbuster movie called "The Mummy Returns" shows two scantily clad female combatants of ancient Egypt using trident-like truncheons, but this weapon is actually of Japanese origin. Called a *sai,* the blunt, martial arts weapon was used to deflect swords but may have originally developed from a farming implement employed to make furrows.

Now You See It, Now You Don't

During the latter part of April, all of May and June, and about half of July, Orion's influence is significant by virtue of either its departure or its total absence from the sky. At present Rigel (the left leg of Orion) is approximately 15 degrees above the western horizon on April 20 at 8:00 p.m., an hour after sunset, and by 9:15 in the evening it is just touching the horizon. Orion is last seen on the western horizon in early May, and by mid-May it is blotted out altogether in the Sun's glare. This astronomical phenomenon is called heliacal setting. After that the constellation does not reappear until about July 21st—its heliacal rising in the east.

However, some nine centuries earlier when the first villages on the Hopi Mesas of Arizona were being settled, Rigel touched the western horizon on April 20 at 8:00 p.m., again an hour after sunset, and by early May achieved its heliacal setting. At the same time (about 1100 AD) it was not seen again until about the second week of July. Its heliacal rising coincided with the annual arrival of the monsoons. Much like the flooding of the Nile in Egypt, monsoon rain fulfills the agricultural and ceremonial cycle.

But what is the meaning of all these star positions? If the Ancestral Puebloan and modern Hopi planting schedules coincide, then sweet corn (*tawaktsi*), whose symbolic direction is designated as Below, was planted in late April when Orion was departing for his two-month sojourn in the underworld. The importance of sweet corn is reflected primarily in its customary harvest at the Niman Ceremony in July. It is used as a gift from the

Hemis kachinas (masked intercessory spirits) to the children. The remainder of the corn was planted from late May until the summer solstice, when Orion was inhabiting his subterranean abode.

The constellation's influence may in fact cause the spirits of the corn to rise from the underworld and enter into the sown seeds, acting as a catalyst for germination. Orion is planted in the nether realm at the same time as all the various types of corn, thereby assuring their germination and quickening growth during the lengthening days of the year.

During this part of the seasonal cycle a minor agricultural rite of planting is performed in the fields. This is actually a sort of native Passion play involving Masau'u, who, as I previously mentioned, is the Hopi god of the underworld. (He is also the counterpart of the Egyptian god Osiris.) "...Masau'u strikes down his challengers and strips them of their clothes, until in the end he also falls down as if dead. Then he rises to accept prayers and gifts. On one level this is a mime depicting the life cycle of the corn plant; the ear is stripped from the plant, the cob is stripped of its seeds, and some of these are buried... but he, as a corn symbol, rises again and accepts the thanks of the people."[14]

Thus, Masau'u/Orion functions as not only as symbol of resurrection imitated by farmers assisting the forces of nature but also as a manifestation of the corn itself, which is planted in the spring and returns after a few months to provide the people with its bounty.

Domesticated in Mesoamerica about 5000 BC, corn is undoubtedly the most sacred and ritualized of all Hopi foodstuffs. The symbolic color directions for each type of corn are as follows: yellow for northwest, blue for southwest, red for southeast, and white for northeast. This encompasses the terrestrial (horizontal) plane of Masau'u's domain. In addition, black (or purple) corn, known as *kokoma,* or Masau'u's corn, symbolically representing the direction of Above, is planted in May for the fall harvest. When Masau'u's dark corn of the zenith is brought down and placed in the dark earth together with Orion, then no major ceremonies can be held. The resumption of the ceremonial cycle will have to wait until Orion once again rises in the east just before dawn in July, when the ripening sweet corn reaches its full maturity and the life-giving monsoon rains begin.

We have seen here a direct relationship between the perceived absence of Orion and the vernal sowing of corn. The placement of seeds in the soil at the very time Orion in the chthonic realm is urging the life force forward and upward into the light must have seemed to the ancient Hopi as a cosmically ordained synergy. Fettered by the paradigms of science, we moderns rarely have the opportunity to witness a synchronistic magic of such magnitude.

The (Hopi) World According to Whorf

The linguistic work of Benjamin Lee Whorf demonstrates that the Hopi language has three tenses: present-past, future, and generalized. This makes it much better equipped to describe the vibratory and transformative phenomena of modern physics than English. The latter language imposes the two Newtonian universal forms on existence: static, three-dimensional space and perpetually flowing, one-dimensional time. On the other hand, the Hopi language structures the world and the perception of it via their language in a completely different manner.

> "It imposes upon the universe two grand cosmic forms, which as a first approximation in terminology we may call MANIFESTED and MANIFESTING (or, UNMANIFEST) or, again, OBJECTIVE and SUBJECTIVE. The objective or manifested comprises all that is or has been accessible to the senses, the historical physical universe, in fact, with no attempt to distinguish between present and past, but excludes everything we call future. The subjective or manifesting comprises all that we call future, BUT NOT MERELY THIS; it includes equally and indistinguishably all that we call mental—everything that appears or exists in the mind, or, as the Hopi would prefer to say, in the HEART, not only the heart of man, but the heart of animals, plants, and things, and behind and within all the forms and appearances of nature in the heart of nature, and by

> an implication and extension which has been felt by more than one anthropologist, yet would hardly ever be spoken of by a Hopi himself, so charged is the idea with religious and magical awesomeness, in the very heart of the Cosmos, itself."[15]

Hence the subjective world of emotions, thoughts, hopes, and desires as well as the inner life of everything in the natural world are engaged in a perpetual dynamic process of becoming objectively manifested in the world of the senses. Unlike Western cultural perception, the Hopi view makes no distinction between the manifest physical world (the present) and the world as heretofore manifested (the past). Thus, the former world of the ancestors is always close at hand.

But as the past becomes sufficiently vague and distant enough to encroach upon the insubstantiality of the mythical dimension, it again takes on the characteristics of the subjective. Hopi language uses primarily verbs rather than nouns (as European languages do) to describe metaphysical concepts in general and this mythical realm in particular, which in its own way is as mercurial as small particle physics. However, the word meta-physical is not quite appropriate to denote this subjective state, since it is not truly "beyond." In lieu of this, I must coin the word "intra-physical" to better describe its potentiality.

Whorf further designates the subjective, or unmanifested, realm as "a vertical and vitally INNER axis" symbolically connected to the pole of the physical zenith and subterranean nadir. This mirrors the verticality of the growing corn plant, a dietary mainstay that has substantial spiritual connotations for the Hopi. The cosmological axis is "the wellspring of the future" that flows from the inside outward to manifestation on the horizontal plane of the desert landscape.

All Hopi ceremonies, both exoteric and esoteric, are an attempt by one means or another to urge forward this process of germination and development. This resembles the alchemist whose opus includes both chemical and psychological transmutations in order to assist and hasten the natural "growth" or evolution of baser metals into spiritual gold, of which physical gold is merely the tangible result. The Hopi perform their elaborate and time-consuming ceremonies primarily to promote the flux of life. As a by-product, their physical needs are fulfilled. In other words, they are keeping the world in balance, thereby meeting their basic requirements, epitomized by corn (maize).

The life force constantly streams from the inner heart of the Hopi world outward across mesas and plateaus of the physical realm toward distant vistas of mythical consciousness (the intra-physical), where its energy is again transformed into the subjective realm and brought via chthonic pathways back to the sacred center. This circuit is the proprietary function of Masau'u, god of metamorphosis, whose domain includes both the horizontal plane of the inter-cardinal directions and the vertical *axis mundi* ranging from the underworld to the stars.

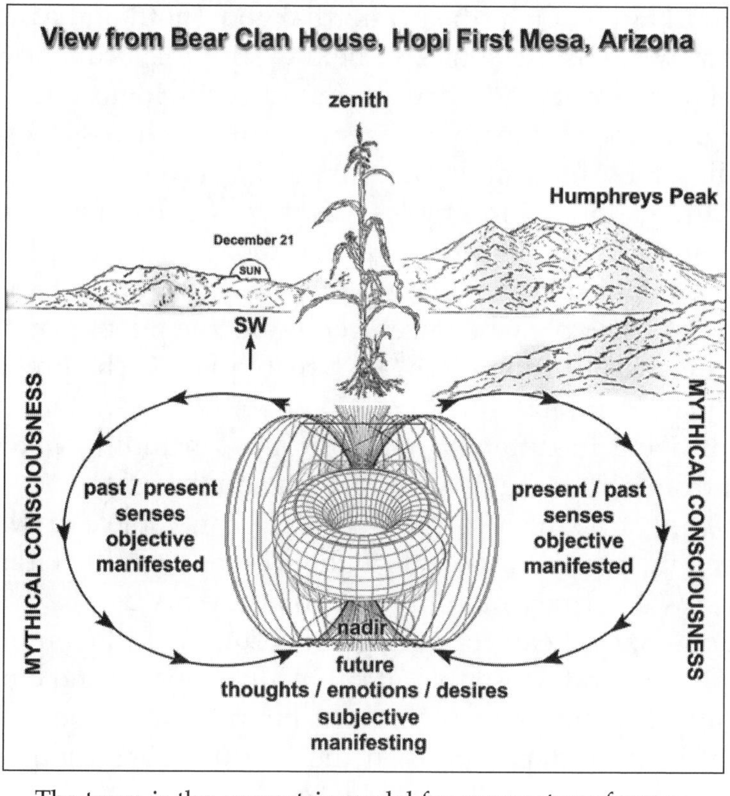

The torus is the geometric model for energy transference from the "inner axis" to the manifested physical world.

Chapter 4
New Mexico's Orion Kivas

Some readers may be familiar with the "Orion Correlation Theory" proposed by Robert Bauval in his 1994 bestseller *The Orion Mystery*. This theory basically states that the belt stars of Orion correspond to the three major pyramids on the Giza Plateau in Egypt. Or as the primordial god Thoth of that ancient land has written: "As above, so below." But this brilliant winter constellation apparently had profound cosmological and spiritual significance for many indigenous cultures across the globe, including the American Indians of northern New Mexico.

Secluded in idyllic Frijoles Canyon is a circular masonry building with an almost unpronounceable name: Tyuonyi (Chew-OHN-yee, or something like that). In the Keresan language of the people who once lived there, the pueblo's name literally means "meeting place" or "treaty place." The prehistoric "apartment complex" on the canyon floor may have thus been a hub, drawing in different native groups, including Keres and Tewa, from across the Pajarito Plateau and beyond.

Pajarito is Spanish for "little bird." This tableland wedged between the Jemez Mountains to the west and the Rio Grande to the east was formed more than a million years ago by volcanic eruption. The plateau consists of soft, crumbly tuff (compressed volcanic ash) and denser basalt cut by deep gorges and crowned with forested mesas of piñon and juniper. In fact, one of the largest volcanic depressions in the world, Valles Caldera, lies about a dozen miles to the northwest.

[continued on p. 74]

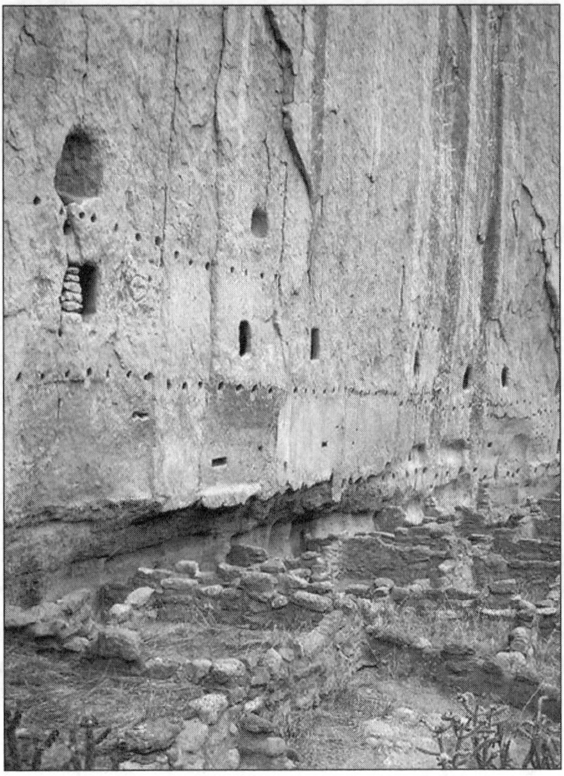

Above: Tyuonyi Ruin in Frijoles Canyon, Bandelier National Monument. Only one kiva out of the three has been reconstructed. Seen on the left, it is about 21 feet in diameter. The southern side of the canyon is in the background. Note snow in the shadows of northward-facing slope.
Photo © by Mohammad Faisal Hadi.

Right: Roof beam holes and interior wall niches at Long House Ruin.
Photo © by Jacob Rus.

The two-to-three story pueblo had 300 ground-floor rooms –about 400 total– arranged around a central plaza in tiers extending from three to eight deep. The back rooms would have been used for storage more than for living quarters. An easily defensible entrance on the east side allowed the only access to the D-shaped plaza, which contained three kivas at the north end arranged in a row like Orion's belt. But more on these subterranean communal prayer chambers shortly.

Although the canyon had sporadically provided indigenous peoples a refuge for thousands of years, the main habitation period ranged from 1300 AD until 1540—about the time Spanish conquistadors arrived in the region.

People also constructed so-called "talus houses," or cliff dwellings, built along the north side of the canyon for more than a mile. They took the natural caves formed from tuff and in some cases shaped or enlarged them, then put porch-like structures made of stone slabs in front of the cave entrances. The most extensive talus ruin is called Long House, containing over 350 rooms in five clusters. In order to construct this pueblo rising from three to four stories tall, large roof beams called *vigas* made from straight ponderosa pine were put into round sockets gouged in the cliff face.

About a half mile up the canyon from Long House is Alcove House, formerly called Ceremonial Cave. Located about 150 feet above the permanently flowing El Rito de los Frijoles (Bean Creek), this cave with a view is accessed by stone stairs and a series of wooden ladders. Over 20 masonry-walled rooms are connected to the alcove. The main feature of the site, however, is the reconstructed kiva. (See photo on p. 16.)

The kiva was the focal point of the spiritual life of these "delight makers." This phrase comes from a novel of the same name written by Adolph F. A. Bandelier, a preeminent Swiss-American archaeologist and ethnologist who did extensive research in the region between 1880 and 1886. He used the phrase specifically to refer to the sacred clowns known as the *Koshare*. Named in his honor, Bandelier National Monument was established in 1916 and encompasses nearly 50 square miles with numerous ruins as well as the unique Shrine of the Stone Lions and an alcove thick with ancient pictographs called Painted Cave.

Bandelier was the mentor of another archaeologist who worked in this area, Edgar Lee Hewett, who explains the deep significance that the kiva held for the Ancestral Puebloans (formerly called Anasazi):

> "The structural germ of every community house was the kiva, the circular subterranean room that is found in conjunction with all community houses, small and great, of the Rio Grande and San Juan Valleys. This was the clan sanctuary, the place set aside for prayer and religious ceremony.... In it centered all that was vital to the life and happiness of the people. It was the place of silence, the sanctuary to which those charged with sacerdotal functions retired for thought, for prayer, for offering, for sacrifice. It was the place of secret religious rites and preparation for public ceremonials. In gathering about the sipapu, men approached the Earth Mother; they sought the sources of ancient wisdom; they were at the portal whence life emerged."[1]

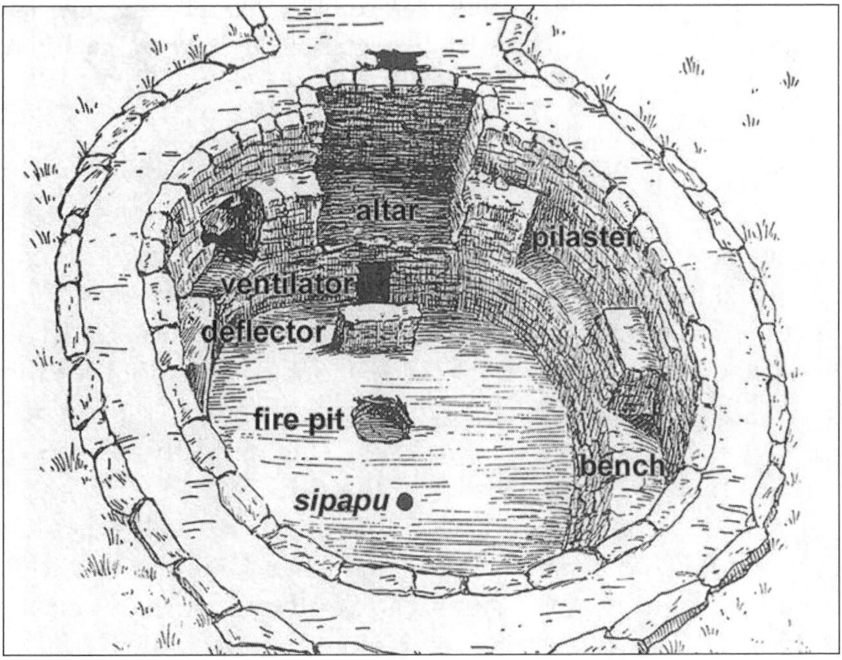

Round kiva with major components labeled.

As stated in Chapter 1, the *sipapu* was a small hole located on floor of each kiva. It formed part of a cosmic subway system, so to speak, by which spirits traveled to and from the underworld. The round kiva would have been covered with a wooden and earthen roof supported by six wooden pillars set atop stone pilasters. A ladder extended from the center of the roof to allow entrance and exist. Also part of the standard architecture were an altar, a ventilation shaft, a deflector, a fire pit, and a round bench on the inner wall. (See sketch on preceding page.)

Bandelier's journal for 1885 describes a dance he witnessed at Cochiti Pueblo some 12 miles south of Frijoles Canyon, where the ancestors of this pueblo once lived. This striking dance called the "Ah-ta Tany" was traditionally performed by the Warriors Society (*Umpa*) on December 21st, the winter solstice.

> "The 'Matadores' or (Matalotes) or *Umpa* are painted black, the front hair combed down on the forehead and painted with almagre. There is a crown of white down [eagle's] over the head and down the side locks, and there is a feather of the painted eagle hanging from the topknot. They are dressed in buckskin and white shirt, the buckskin hanging down almost to the ankles. Bead-strings around the neck and an iridescent shell suspended from them. In the left hand a bow painted red, with eagle feathers at each end, and some red-painted arrows. In the right hand, a wooden or iron hatchet, also red."[2]

The Spanish word *matadore* literally means "killers." Almagre is red ocher, or iron oxide. For the Keresan of Cochiti, the color red symbolizes war, starvation, epidemics, and hail.[3] The artifacts that members of the Warrior Society hold for their winter solstice dance are particularly significant. In the left hand is a bow, in the right hand a hatchet. This perfectly mirrors the weapons that Orion brandishes in the sky.

The winter constellation is alternately conceptualized as having a nodule club in his upraised right hand, similar to various ceremonial figures of the American Southwest such as *katsinam* (kachinas). In the corner of a room where a person dies, relatives place an ear of blue corn (symbolizing the soul) and a small club.

They surround these two items with a protective circle of crosses scratched on the floor to represent roadrunner tracks.[4] Sometimes also referred to as "crows-feet," these tracks are emblematic of warfare.

The Tewa have an emergence myth that involves the "first Made person," who was called the Hunt chief. This primeval figure ascended from the *Sipofene,* or the underworld tunnel beneath Sandy Place Lake in the north. (The Hopi conceptualize a similar cosmic conduit, the *Sipapuni,* located at the bottom in Grand Canyon. The *sipapu* orifice in the floor of every kiva microcosmically represents the subterranean passageways of both cultures.)

The Hunt chief came to an open space and saw many predatory mammals including wolves, coyotes, mountain lions, and foxes as well as carrion-consuming vultures and crows.

> "On seeing the man these animals rushed him, knocked him down, and scratched him badly. Then they spoke, telling him: 'Get up! We are your friends.' His wounds vanished immediately. The animals gave him a bow and arrows, and a quiver, dressed him in buckskins, painted his face black, and tied the feathers of the carrion-eaters on his hair. Finally they told him: 'You have been accepted. These things we have given you are what you shall henceforth use. Now you are ready to go.'"[5]

With friends like these, who needs enemies? At any rate, this Tewa hunter paradoxically received his weapons from his quarry. Moreover, he resembles in great detail the members of Keresan Warrior Society as they perform their winter solstice dance. As noted in Chapter 2, among the obsessively dichotomous Tewa, the Winter moiety (half the social group) is associated with hunting, whereas the Summer moiety relates to farming. Needless to say, Orion is the primary constellation dominating the winter sky.

Also relevant is the architectural form of Tyuonyi. Many people comment on its circular shape, but upon looking closer we see that the inner courtyard is actually bow-shaped, with the straight northern wall forming the bowstring. This may be another link to Orion the Hunter as an archer.

Archaeologists face a challenging task to reconstruct a kiva once it has fallen into ruin after seven centuries or more of neglect, erosion, and deposition. But it's an even greater feat to reconstruct the spiritual life of the people who lived for two-and-a-half centuries at Tyuonyi and then –suddenly and mysteriously– departed, leaving their artfully crafted masonry to the ravages of the harsh elements.

Satellite photo of Tyunonyi Ruin in Frijoles Canyon. The three kivas aligned on a northwest-southeast axis correspond to Orion's belt. Aldebaran corresponds to the area in front of Long House, with the rest of the constellation Taurus extending northward. Sirius (the brightest star in the heavens in Canis Major) corresponds to the Great Kiva, measuring 42 feet in diameter, seen at the lower right-hand corner. The binary Rigel (the brightest star in Orion) corresponds to the area north of Tyuonyi where are located Sun House (named after a sun symbol petroglyphs behind it) and Snake House (named for the plumed serpent painted on a plastered wall of its kiva). © 2008 Google Earth.

Ethnological research done primarily in the late 19th and early 20th centuries allows some insight, even if the inherent biases of that period distort the overall picture. The sacred rituals of modern pueblos along the Rio Grande as well as a few others to the southwest (namely, Laguna, Acoma, and Zuni) or even farther west (Hopi) provide anthropologists with additional clues to the ceremonies of the Ancient Ones, though the links through time are increasingly tenuous. And then there are the legends.

The Tewa, we recall, was a native group, some of which either lived at Tyuonyi or interacted with its inhabitants. In about 1300 AD the Tewa began to live primarily at the "mother pueblo" of San Juan, less than 25 miles to the north near the confluence of the Rio Grande and the Rio Chama. Other Tewa speakers also settled at Santa Clara and the four smaller pueblos of San Ildefonso, Nambe, Pojoaque, and Tesuque.

One Tewa story, in particular, involves Orion. The wise warrior Long Sash desired to take his people to a land of peace, for enemies were constantly attacking their village. He led them along the Endless Path (the Milky Way), but the road was long and arduous, and they soon began to quarrel. Long Sash stopped at the Place of Decision, where he built two campfires (Castor and Pollux, the Gemini twins) by which the people could sort out their differences.

Eventually even Long Sash himself wearied of the journey and began to question his ability to lead, so he set down his headdress at the Place of Doubt (the Pleiades). After resting a while, he finally found the fortitude to bring the Tewa to their new home called the Middle Place (Orion's belt). (Long Sash's name may itself refer to the Great Nebula of Orion's "sword," which hangs down from the belt.)

Is this Middle Place actually the three kivas in a row inside the village plaza at Tyuonyi? The sacred center of the Tewa universe, the *sanctum sanctorum,* is the southern end of the plaza-called *Nan echu kwi nan sipu pingeh,* or literally "Earth mother earth navel middle place."[6] *Sipu* means 'navel', which of course is located above the belt. In terms of Tyunonyi, this umbilicus rests either in the middle or on the southern side of the plaza.

So, is Orion both a warrior/hunter and an earth mother? Both a male in the sky and a female on the ground?

One very curious fact involves the way the Tewa traditionally view gender. As mentioned previously, they see a man as possessing both male and female qualities, whereas a woman has merely the female quality. This highly dualistic culture is structured in a ritual sense by the annual twofold division: masculine winter and feminine summer. Thus, it holistically conceives a man's role as incorporating both, namely, hermaphroditic.

Author and ethnographer Frank Waters evokes the quintessence of the kiva in his classic novel *The Man Who Killed the Deer*: "The circular, soft adobe wall sinking like a womb into the dark resistless earth, with a ladder sticking out for men to enter by. The female symbol of fertility imbedded in Our Mother Earth. The Kiva. This was the Indian church."

The man enters the feminine chamber to become one with the Earth and his past—both personal and communal. He climbs down the ladder to humbly worship, but by descending into darkness, he paradoxically rises in triumph to the brilliant sky portal of Orion's belt. Once the quotidian realities of existence are transcended, the underworld and the stars become one—united in song and mythic time.

Waters continues:

> "The kiva, each kiva, was now itself a vibrating drum. A single star visible through the aperture at the top quivered as if painted on the vibrous, skin-tight membrane of the sky stretched overhead. In the middle of the round floor, like a dot within a circle was another symbol—a little round hole, the opening to the center of the world, the place of emergence. The circular walls quivered."[7]

A single point within a circle, the golden dream of wholeness, the soul's longing for oneness, the Sun's heart, the spark of divine consciousness seeking its star birth… these at last are achieved. And we, too, quiver with delight.

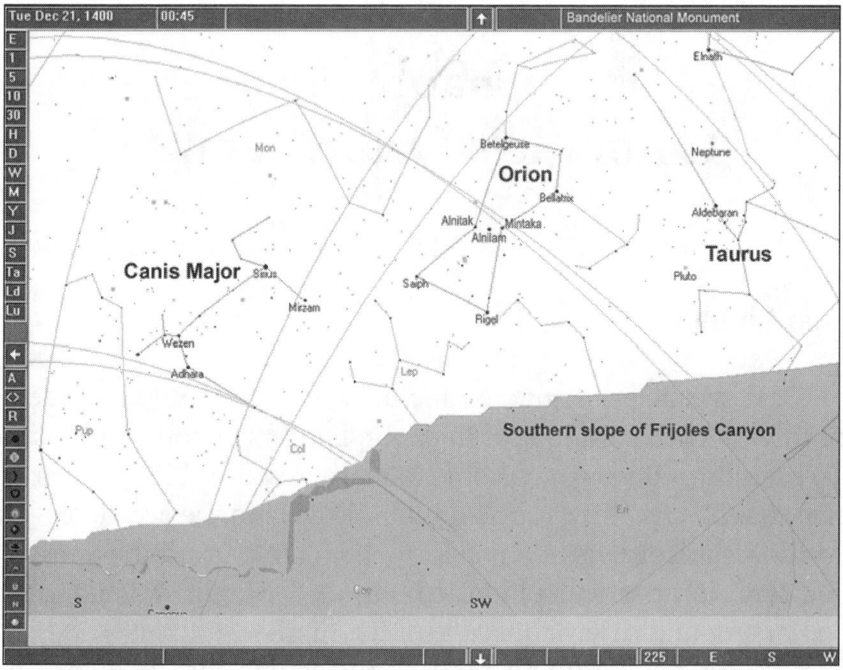

If someone stood either on the ladder protruding from the overhead hatchway of the middle kiva at Tyuonyi or at the base of the northern slope of the canyon at about 12:45 a.m. on December 21st in 1400 AD or so and looked southwest (225° azimuth), he/she would roughly see this vista: Canis Major (Sirius) on the left, Orion (the belt stars of Alnitak, Alnilam, and Mintaka) in the middle, and Taurus (Aldebaran) on the right. Hopi ethnographic evidence from the late 19th century shows that the winter solstice ceremony had been performed at approximately 1:00 a.m., when the Orion's belt begins to hang down in the sky. In addition, the mid-winter sunset is roughly in this direction—about 241° azimuth. (Azimuth is the clockwise measurement in degrees from true north, or 0°. 90° is east, 180° is south, and 270° is west.)

Chapter 5
Colorado's Orion Temple

—dedicated to Gwynne Carol Spencer (1946 – 2009)

Solar Line-up

Mesa Verde is a green sanctuary for the soul. Located in southwestern Colorado near the Four Corners region, this massive geological uplift was once home to many Ancestral Puebloans, the term that has recently supplanted "Anasazi" in the archaeological world. Mesa Verde is Spanish for "green table," and the area covered with juniper and piñon trees indeed provided refuge from the harsher and drier landscape of the high desert below.

Some of the continent's most spectacular cliff dwellings are found here, including Spruce Tree House and Cliff Palace. Occupied between 600 and 1300 AD, the mesa is cut by numerous canyons running generally north and south. These canyons are pocked with giant rock alcoves under which the ancient people built large villages of sandstone.

Cliff Palace, for instance, was inhabited between about 1190 and 1300. It contained some 220 rooms and 23 circular kivas (subterranean, ceremonial prayer-chambers)—the largest cliff dwelling in the American Southwest. This pueblo, a sort of ancient apartment complex, also included a round tower and a four-story square tower from which the sacred "sun watchers" made their celestial observations. (For round tower, see middle of the top of p. 92; for square one, see right side of same photo.)

Unlike the cliff dwellings, the so-called Sun Temple was used exclusively for watching the skies. It is located on top of the mesa rather along cliff sides within the canyons. Perched at the southern edge of the mesa near the juncture of Fewkes Canyon and Cliff Canyon, this D-shaped structure lies a bit more than 300 yards southwest of Cliff Palace, which is located on the far side of the latter canyon. As we shall see, the two complexes had a reciprocal relationship. These two canyons, by the way, contained a total of 33 habitation sites. (See satellite photo on p. 85.)

Most pueblo villages grew by accretion, as rooms were gradually added on to each other. On the other hand, the form of the Sun Temple was preconceived and executed with a single, coherent symmetry in mind. The structure, built probably about 1250 AD, consists of two concentric bows. Its southern wall (the metaphoric bowstring) is 122 feet long, while the curved north wall provides the temple's 64-feet width. The inner "bow" is bisected exactly to the inch by a recess a few feet wide in the outer southern wall. Although the reconstructed walls are now an average of six feet high, they once rose to an estimated 11 to 14 feet. They were generally about four feet thick and composed of a central core of rubble and adobe dressed with finely placed sandstone blocks. The floor of the consisted of the mesa's bedrock, with no additional adobe flooring added.

No external doorways or windows are found, except for one walled-up entryway near the southwestern corner of the structure. However, a number of inner windows and covered doorways connect to some of the rooms, which total 24. The lack of wooden beams shows that the structure was unroofed and open to sunlight and starlight. No household goods of any kind (i.e., bowls, baskets, grinding stones, etc.) were found in or near the building, which indicates the building's purpose was ceremonial rather than domiciliary. In other words, this edifice truly deserves the name "temple." Whether or not this was strictly a sun temple will be dealt with shortly.

The archaeologist Jesse Walter Fewkes, who worked initially to unearth and reconstruct it in 1915, observed the following: "...the building excavated shows the best masonry and is the most mysterious structure yet discovered in a region rich in so many pre-historic ruins."[1]

Almost every masonry block was assiduously pecked and shaped in order to fit perfectly into the walls. Some of the blocks were even sculpted or incised with geometric designs similar to those commonly found on the indigenous pottery of the region. Other designs in the blocks include the so-called crows-foot, flowing water, and what looks like a ladder leaning against a wall. A few blocks are cut with the T-shape that resembles many of the doors and windows of other pueblos (though not in this structure). The designs in these blocks suggest that the walls were not plastered. This style of sculpted stones is very rare in the American Southwest and indicates an influence from Mexico and Central America.

There are three circular kivas incorporated into the architecture. These are not typical kivas, however, because they lack the normal features, such as a fire pit, an air deflector, a banquette (bench along the wall), and a *sipapu* (a tiny hole in the floor that conceptually leads to the underworld). In addition, they are above-ground, not subterranean. The two eastern "kivas" (marked **B** and **C** on the diagram) each have a narrow subterranean trench that leads from the plaza through an inclined shaft to a spot just south of the center of each circular room. The western "kiva" (marked **A**) has a similar access from one of the small rooms to the south.

On the eastern two-thirds of the structure, fourteen mostly rectangular rooms enclose the plaza that contains two kivas, which are equal in diameter. On the western third, we find ten rooms: six nearly square rooms, one circular room, and three quadrilateral rooms that surround the single kiva and conform to its shape. This kiva is slightly smaller than the other two kivas. One small triangular enclosed space also lies just northeast of the circular room.

As the diagram on the facing page shows, the north-south axis of the structure is shifted five degrees west of due north. A line drawn from the southwestern corner eastward past the building is tangent with the inner wall of another kiva (marked **D**). This separate kiva lies just over twenty feet from the southeastern corner of the main structure.

[continued on p. 86]

Birds-eye view of the "Sun Temple," looking northeast.

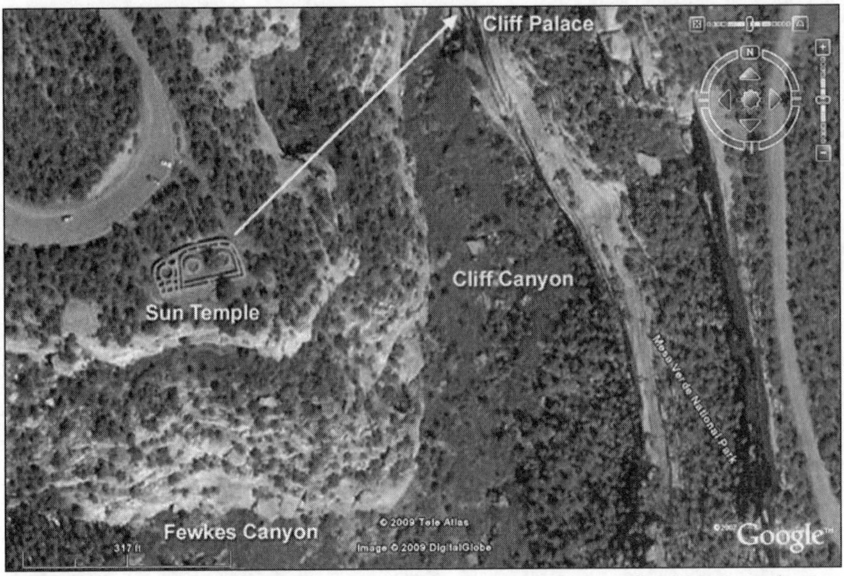

Satellite view of "Sun Temple," Cliff Palace to northeast. © 2009 Google Earth.

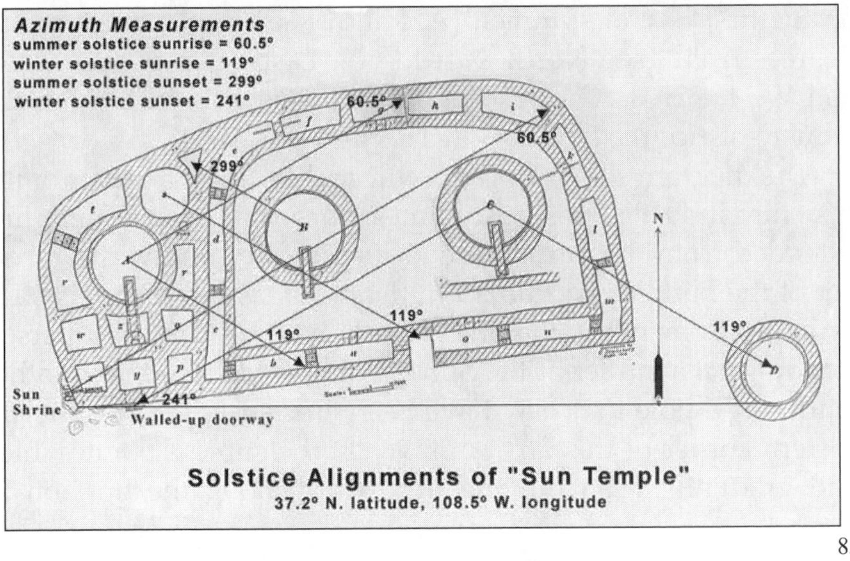

One of the most usual features connected to the Sun Temple, however, is the so-called Sun Shrine. Located at the southwestern corner of the building, this curious stone slab extends as part of the bedrock a few feet from the building. A masonry enclosure was constructed on two sides perpendicular to the outer wall in order protect it. The stone seems artificially worked, with sharp grooves radiating from a central basin. It has been suggested that these grooves represent solar rays. At the center of this depression are three indentations, one of which is offset. If a person sat on this stone, the masonry addition would be something like the arms of a chair. Gazing westward, an observer could watch the equinoctial sunset. Some researchers believe that this stone functioned as a kind of sundial.

But does the Sun Temple live up to its name? Apparently so. A number of what are termed solstice alignments are incorporated into the building as line-of-sight connections between two points. In the world of the Ancestral Puebloan, the four solstice points on the horizons are more important that the cardinal directions. That is, the exact spots on the horizon where the Sun rises and sets in either summer or winter are crucial to maintaining an agricultural calendar. The "sun watcher" performed the task of determining when to plant or harvest certain crops and when to perform various ritual activities.

At the latitude of Mesa Verde, the Sun rises at 60.5° azimuth on the first day of summer. (Azimuth is an angle measured in degrees from True North. North = 0°, East = 90°, South = 180°, and West = 270°.) On this same day it sets at 299°. During the winter solstice the Sun rises at 119° and sets at 241°.

The diagram shows how specific architectural features of the structure indicate the solstice times. For instance, a straight line extended from the Sun Shrine located in the southwestern corner of the building to ***Room i*** in the northeastern corner is 60.5° azimuth. Remember, the Sun Temple had no roof, so a person standing on a ladder at the Sun Shrine could see either another ladder or a pole that may have been erected in the very northeastern corner of this far room. When the sunrise point, which had gradually been moving northward along the horizon as spring progressed, finally reached this upright marker, the person would know it was the summer solstice. In other words, the Sun had reached its "summer house." Another summer solstice sunrise alignment can be found between the center of ***Kiva A*** and the northeastern corner of ***Room g***. (See diagram on p. 85.)

Three winter solstice sunrise alignments can be found in the building: (1) between ***Kiva A*** and the southeastern corner of **Room b**, (2) between the circular ***Room s*** and the center of the recess in the southern wall, and (3) between ***Kiva C*** and ***Kiva D***. This was probably the most important time of year for the ancient people. Solstice ceremonies were performed in part to usher the Sun northward from its "winter house." If these rituals were done poorly or not conducted at all, there was concern that the Sun might not return with its life-giving warmth.

A summer solstice sunset alignment can be found between ***Kiva B*** and the small triangular room. In addition, a winter solstice sunset alignment runs from ***Kiva C*** to the center of the walled-up door along the southern wall of the structure. The redundancy of alignments might have resulted from different ceremonial clans, each using either one of the three enclosed kivas or the single separate kiva.

Stellar Line-up

Was the Sun Temple used solely as a solar indicator? On the contrary, compelling evidence points to the possibility that it may have been a stellar temple as well, especially during the winter months.

The positioning of the three kivas within the structure perfectly reflects the belt stars of Orion. ***Kiva A*** corresponds to Mintaka, ***Kiva B*** to Alnilam, and ***Kiva C*** to Alnitak. It is significant that ***Kiva A*** is somewhat smaller than the other two and slightly offset—similar to Mintaka in the triadic row that forms the constellation's belt. The relationship of the measurements between the kivas is proportional to the apparent visual distances between the stars (as opposed to the light year distances).

Orion Temple at Mesa Verde, Colorado (overview)

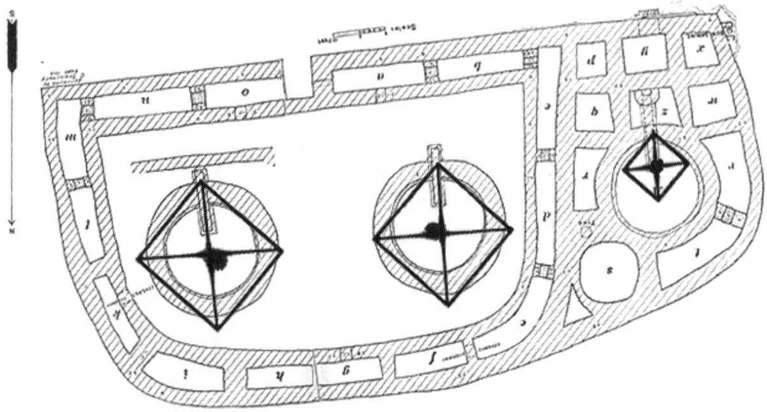

Alnitak, Alnilam, and Mintaka with corresponding Giza pyramids (Khufu, Khafre, and Menkaure) superimposed on the three kivas.

In the previous chapter, I mentioned the Orion Correlation theory developed by Robert Bauval in his book *The Orion Mystery*, co-authored by Adrian Gilbert.[2] The book posits that the arrangement of three major pyramids on the Giza plateau directly corresponds to the belt stars. As seen in the diagram above, the pyramids, the trio of stars, and in this case the three kivas all coincide.

Orion dominates the celestial landscape during December, rising in the east, arcing across the southern sky, and setting in the west. It achieves its highest point (meridian) around midnight. On December 21st, winter solstice in the Northern Hemisphere, the Sun rises and sets at the farthest point south on the horizon. During the night of the same date, the spot between Alnitak and Alnilam (the left side and the middle of the belt respectively) reaches 175° azimuth at exactly twenty minutes past midnight.

As the diagram on p. 89 shows, the nearly vertical line runs from a point halfway between the two kivas of the main part of the structure, past the recess in the southern wall and continues along an imaginary line to the stars just mentioned. Why 175° and not 180° (due south)? Was this the signal to begin the winter solstice ceremony—when the line-of-sight from a point equidistant between the two main kivas ran through the southern doorway and reached toward the corresponding position in the heavens?

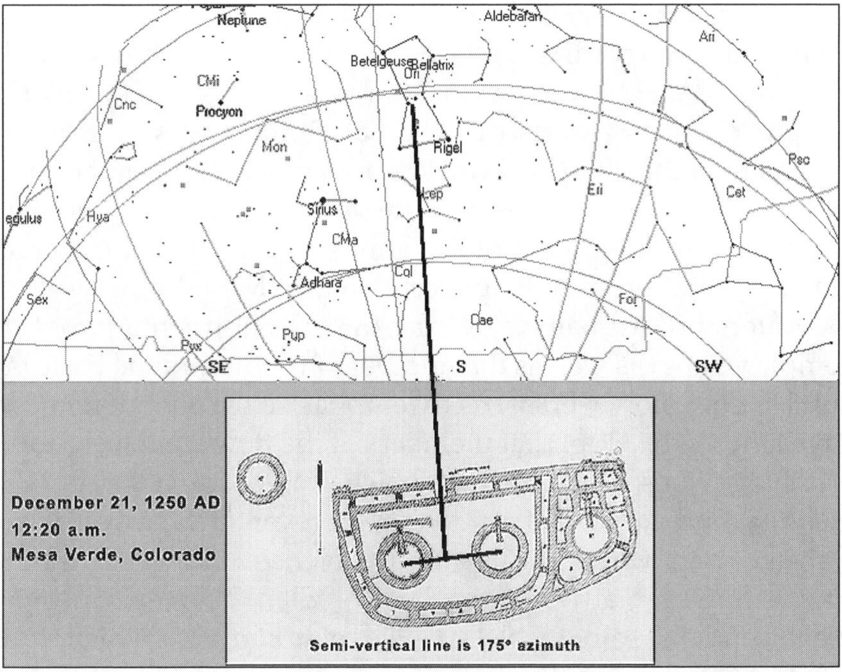

Another piece of architectural evidence in favor of a dual function –both solar and stellar– is the previously mentioned Sun Shrine in the southwestern corner. Although the basin has radiating from it like the Sun, its center also has three indentations, one of which is offset. These may have been artificially worked in order to resemble Orion's belt.

One tribe that claims to be direct descendants of the Ancestral Puebloans (formerly known as the Anasazi) is the Hopi.[3] For this highly ritualistic native group the most important part of the winter solstice ceremony, or Soyal, occurs after midnight. In fact, the ethnographer A. M. Stephen witnessed this ceremony in the village of Walpi in 1891. He claims that the "Star Priest" signaled the most crucial phase of the ceremony just after 1:00 a.m., when Orion's belt begins its descent toward the west.[4] Or as Frank Waters puts it, "...when Hotomkam [Orion's belt] begins to hang down in the sky."[5]

In regard to what I now may call with impunity the Orion Temple, the exact moment when the belt stars were just five degrees prior to reaching their highest point in the sky was the signal for the ceremony to begin. Thus, the "Sun Temple" may have been oriented according to the position Orion assumes when the most important ceremony of the year was supposed to commence.

Frank Waters asserts that the Sun Temple was built by the Bow Clan of the Hopi. This makes perfect sense, given the shape of the structure. "There seems little doubt that the Sun Temple is the one great monument of the almost extinct Bow Clan, offering additional proof of Hopi occupancy at Mesa Verde."[6]

Waters unfortunately gets the directional orientation of the Temple wrong, as well as the number of rooms and the basic layout. He does, however, correctly emphasize the common knowledge among the Hopi that members of the Bow Clan were rulers of the previous Third World, which was destroyed due to its inequity and moral corruption.[7] Wherever this powerful and war-like clan went, trouble and violence followed. Another source, however, attributes to the Bow Clan the guardianship of the legendary stone tablets called *owatututveni*, which functioned as a map and the deed to Hopi territory.[8]

One anonymous Hopi medicine man relates the legend of a people who once lived at Mesa Verde. These men became so brave and powerful that they began to think of themselves as gods. The rest of the Hopi built the Sun Temple with two kivas (in the eastern section) connected by a passageway (perhaps the tunnel on the southern side of **Kiva C**). In trying to decide who could make the strongest "medicine" (that is, sorcery), they designated one kiva for the "gods" and the other for the Hopi. When the gods lost, the Hopi would kill them in this passageway. Or so the plan went. However, these god-like men confounded the language of the Hopi (à la the Tower of Babel), so the latter's magic became useless. The displeased "gods" then drove the Hopi out of their homes on Mesa Verde and down the canyons to the desert country in the south.[9] The god-like beings are perhaps a reference to the belligerent and bellicose Bow Clan.

The Bow Clan (*Awata*), together with the Reed Clan (*Paaaqavi*, connected with the making of arrows) and the Greasewood Clan (*Tepi*, connected with making both war bows and arrows), apparently had an intimate spiritual connection with the constellation

Orion. "The Reed-Greasewood-Bow grouping is evidently associated with the fall, with the waxing of Orion and the Pleiades in the night sky, with the onset of cold weather, with hunting (through the use of bow and arrow, and the link with dogs), and, secondarily, with war."[10] With the increase of Orion's presence in the midnight sky, the seasons' requisite ice and snow glittering like stars assure better agricultural growth later in the year.

A little over eighty miles to the south-southeast in Chaco Canyon is another bow-shaped building called Pueblo Bonito. This is the largest structure in the region and had as many as 800 rooms. Unlike the Sun Temple, a substantial number were designed for habitation. Pueblo Bonito is similar to the Sun Temple, however, in that the "bow" is shooting its "arrow" northward along what maverick archaeologist Stephen Lekson has called "the Chaco Meridian."[11] In fact, the former structure's north-south axis is a mere two-tenths of one degree east of true north—a directional accuracy that rivals that of the Great Pyramid of Egypt. Like the Sun Temple, however, the eastern portion of Bonito's southern wall is slightly skewed to the north and, for some reason, does not assume a perfect east-west axis.

Nearby Fajada Butte is famous for its "Sun Dagger" that accurately measures the solstices and equinoxes as it inches across two carved spirals. In addition, a D-shaped petroglyph has been found on the same butte that mirrors the morphology of Pueblo Bonito and may have been carved by the Bow Clan.[12]

In fact, of the dozen major pueblos in Chaco Canyon, half of them are bow-shaped. This clan may have wielded considerable influence here during the cultural apex of the region in the 11th century. After Chaco was completely abandoned by 1150, the Bow Clan's power and prestige shifted—first north to Salmon Ruin and Aztec Ruin during the early twelfth century and finally northwest to Mesa Verde in the early thirteenth century.

In the beginning of this chapter I mentioned Cliff Palace, located just over 300 yards northeast of Sun Temple. The archaeoastronomer J. McKim Malville discovered a circular basin about three inches in diameter and an inch deep pecked into the bedrock at the extreme southern end of the cliff dwelling.

[continued on p. 93]

Cliff Palace, Mesa Verde National Park, Colorado

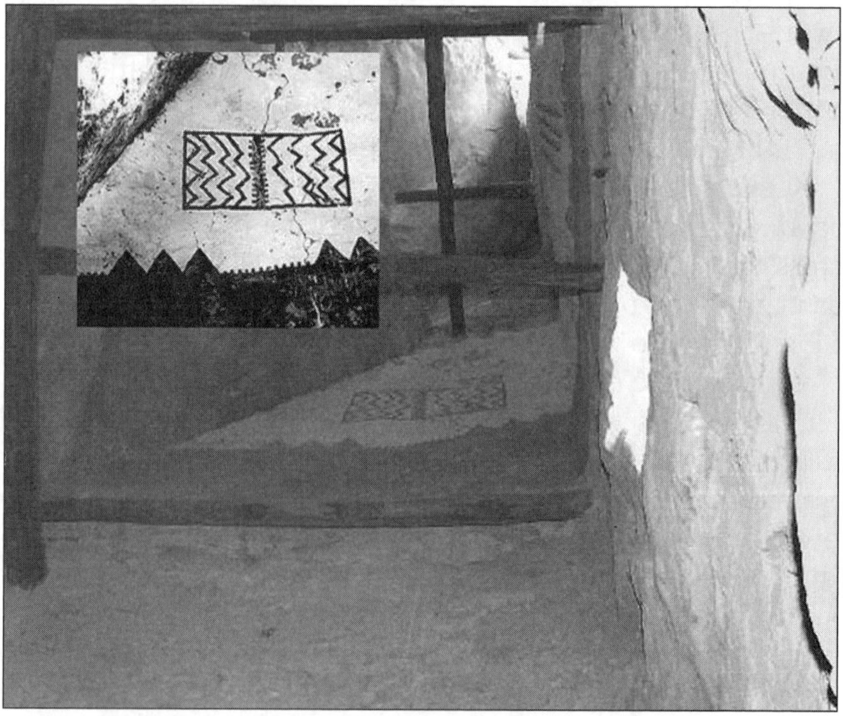

Looking upward inside the square tower, Cliff Palace.
Red pictographs on plaster, blanket shape above triangles.

A line between this basin and the Sun Shrine at the southwestern corner of Sun Temple has an azimuth of 235.5°—close to the winter solstice sunset point (241°).[13]

Even more compelling is a line-of-sight from the T-shaped window in the fourth story of the square tower at Cliff Palace to a tangent between the two kivas (which may have been towers) at the Sun Temple. This arrow-straight line is about 227°2′ azimuth. The "major lunar standstill" at this latitude is 227°9′—nearly the same.

Similar to the Sun's annual cycle, the Moon in its monthly cycle rises and sets at different points on the horizon. However, the Moon also has a longer cycle –18.6 years, to be exact– when its rising and setting points reach extremes on the horizon. Anna Sofaer, who discovered the Sun Dagger at Chaco Canyon in 1977, states that during this period in the major lunar standstill cycle the Moon rises and sets 6.1° north and south of the positions of the rising and setting of the summer and winter solstice suns (at the latitude of Chaco, that is).[14] In other words, at these major lunar standstill times the Moon rises and sets even farther north and south than does the Sun. This fact must have evoked consternation or even awe in the Ancestral Puebloans.

There may be an even more intriguing relationship between the two structures located across Cliff Canyon from each other. The square tower just mentioned also has some pictographs (painted designs) on the white plaster of the interior walls at the third-story level.

The photo (p. 92, looking upward into the tower) shows twelve circles in a horizontal row bracketed on each end by three triangles. (The black-and-white inset unfortunately does not show the third triangle on the right.) The ocher color suggests the depiction of a landscape of sorts, above which is suspended a blanket-like rectangle with designs that resemble traditional pottery. A vertical line with approximately twelve marks on each side divides the "blanket," which has twelve zigzags on each half.

Malville believes this pictograph functioned as a kind of lunar calendar that determined the twelve months or "moons."

> "Such a pattern is not uncommon in Anasazi art, but the recurrence of twelve marks and twelve zigzags is noteworthy because of the twelve 'moons' during the year. In one month, the moon swings from southern extreme to northern extreme and back to southern extreme. That pictograph may be a representation of the changing positions of the rising and setting moons during a one-year period. It is the kind of diagram that an astronomer of today might draw on a blackboard to illustrate the changing positions of the moon or an Anasazi astronomer might have drawn for an apprentice."[15]

It has also been suggested that the triad of pyramid-shapes perhaps depict the peaks of the La Plata Mountains (a sub-range of the San Juan Mountains) about thirty miles to the northeast. Indeed, three primary mountains seem to fit this description. Other mountains higher up in the southern Rockies have greater elevation, but these peaks at the southern end of the San Juans are particularly prominent from Mancos Valley to the southwest.

The Diné (Navajo) tribe considers Hesperus Mountain (13,232 ft.) to be one of the four holy mountains of the cardinal directions. Their language refers to this Sacred Mountain of the North as *Dibé Ntsaa*.[16] About a half mile southeast of Hesperus lies Lavender Peak (13,240 ft.)—about the same elevation. Mount Moss (13,192 ft.) lies about a quarter mile farther to the southeast—all what are called in climbers' jargon "thirteeners." These

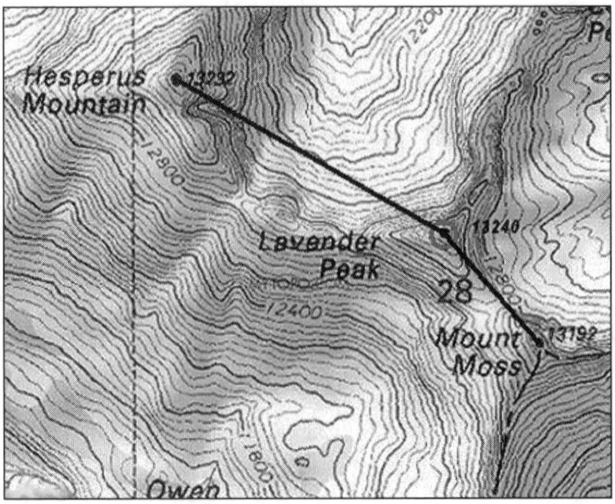

three peaks in a row may be the inspiration for the pictograph inside the square tower at Cliff Palace. A line between Mesa Verde and these three mountains has an azimuth of nearly 60°—or the summer solstice sunrise point. If we look at a topographic map, the three promontories have an almost perfect tetrahedral shape, especially Hesperus and Lavender.[17]

The pictograph shows two sets of three pyramids on either side of the row of twelve dots. Why are these mountains represented twice? Bear with me as I enter a more speculative realm. (Some skeptics would say that I've already been there for quite some time.) If we draw a line southwest from Hesperus Mountain across Mesa Verde, it crosses the Arizona-New Mexico border about six or seven miles south of Four Corners (the point where Utah, Colorado, New Mexico, and Arizona all touch). Continuing southwest along this line, we eventually come to the ancient Hopi village of Oraibi on Third Mesa in Arizona. Extending the same line farther still, we intersect the large Wupatki Ruin, an early twelfth century pueblo located in the shadow of the volcanic Sunset Crater. This line terminates at Humphreys Peak, highest point in Arizona and the Sacred Mountain of the West for the Navajo.

It is about 28 miles from the Mesa Verde cliff dwellings northeast to Hesperus Mountain, whereas it is nearly the same –about 25 miles– from Wupatki southwest to Humphreys Peak. The total distance from Hesperus southwest to Humphreys is about 256 miles. What is quite significant about this northeast-southwest line is its azimuth. From Mesa Verde, the Sun rises on the summer solstice directly over Hesperus. From Wupatki, the Sun sets on the winter solstice directly over Humphreys. Thus, we have a roughly 60°-240° azimuthal line running between these two sacred mountains separated by hundreds of miles.

In my book *Eye of the Phoenix,* I describe Humphreys Peak (12,633 ft.) as part of a triad of pyramid-shaped mountains that includes Agassiz Peak (12,356 ft.) and Fremont Peak (11,969 ft.).[18]

The pictograph at Cliff Palace plausibly represents two triads of mountains: Hesperus-Lavender-Moss in the northeast and Humphreys-Agassiz-Fremont in the southwest. But what about the twelve dots between the two sets of mountains? 256 miles divided by 12 is just over 21 miles. Is it possible that the sacred sun-path was long ago run for twelve days in a row with an average of 21 miles per day traversed?

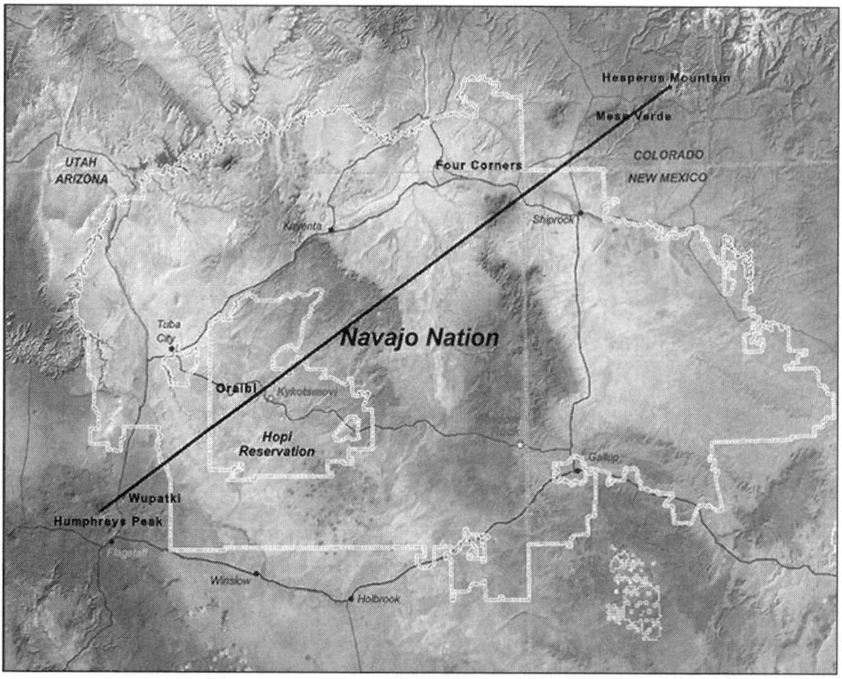

In ancient times the Hopi, the Zuni, and other pueblo groups of the American Southwest, along with the Tarahumara of the northern Sonoran Desert, were renowned for their ability to run great distances at tremendous speeds across extremely harsh landscapes. The purpose was both practical and spiritual.

> "In times of warfare against the Navajos, Hopis runners used to run to Navajo country in order to look for salvia [mint], hair combings, and food in the enemy's hogans. The runners brought back those elements, buried them as bait and ignited a fire above the buried elements so that the Navajo would be weakened before the approaching battle. In such instances, running had a supernatural purpose to it. Hopi running also occurred in conjunction with several ceremonial events. While praying as a group for rain and prosperity during ceremonies like the Snake and Basket dances, running races served as significant ceremonial events."[19]

The sacred tradition of running was carried well into the 20th century. A Hopi named Charlie Talawepi reportedly ran from Tuba

City to Flagstaff and returned to Moenkapi, a total of 156 miles in about 24 hours. He was given a twenty-dollar silver piece.[20] Louis Tewanima also won, coincidentally, the silver medal for the 10,000-meter race in the 1912 Olympics. "Spirit-runs" are held to this day on the Hopi reservation in order to honor the paths of the ancestors and the various sacred sites on Mother Earth.

In this chapter I have confirmed the solar aspect of the Sun Temple by a number of the solstice alignments across various points on the structure. In addition, I have shown how the three kivas of the "Orion Temple" (a.k.a. Sun Temple) directly correspond to the belt of the constellation. It is possible that the isolated kiva near the southeastern corner represented the star Sirius in the overall ground-to-sky template of this solar-stellar temple.

The grand sacred pathway from the Hesperus Mountain triad in the northeast to the Humphreys Peak triad in the southwest may alternately correspond to Orion's belt in its rising and setting positions respectively. The linking of these two tripartite mountain complexes along a major solstice line combines the Sun (*Tawa*) and Orion (*Hotomqam*), ceremonially the most important constellation for the Ancestral Puebloans.

Whether one believes that the Sun Temple at Mesa Verde is primarily a solar structure or a stellar one (or perhaps both), it is hard to deny the exquisite beauty of its architectural design. This is not merely an accident or the result of a talented but uninformed builder. On the contrary, a special type of spiral is incorporated into its very master "blueprint." We recall how the Ancient Ones of the American Southwest were fond of carving spirals into stone to serve as solar calendars.

The specific spiral found within the structure is created in nature according to what is called the Golden Mean, Golden Section, or Divine Proportion, which is simply the ratio (phi) of 1 : 1.6180339... It is derived from Fibonacci's series, or a numerical list whereby each new number is the sum of the previous two numbers: 0, 1, 1, 2, 3, 5, 8, 13, 21, 34, 55, 89, 144... ad infinitum. Regardless of how large the spiral becomes, the ratio of its dimensions remains constant. For instance, the proportion **AB** to **AC** is the same as **BC** to **BD** or **CD** to **CE**. (See next page.)

The growth of many objects in nature is determined by the Golden Mean, including the whorl pattern of sunflowers, the distribution of leaves on a stem, the horn of the bighorn sheep, the individual seeds of pine cones, and even the rotating shape of hurricanes.

In the case of the Sun Temple, a natural aesthetics overlays the complexity of encoded astronomical relationships. Amid the lost echoes of Mesa Verde, it is the soul's task –not the mind alone– to synthesize both the natural and human-made worlds into a sacred cosmology.

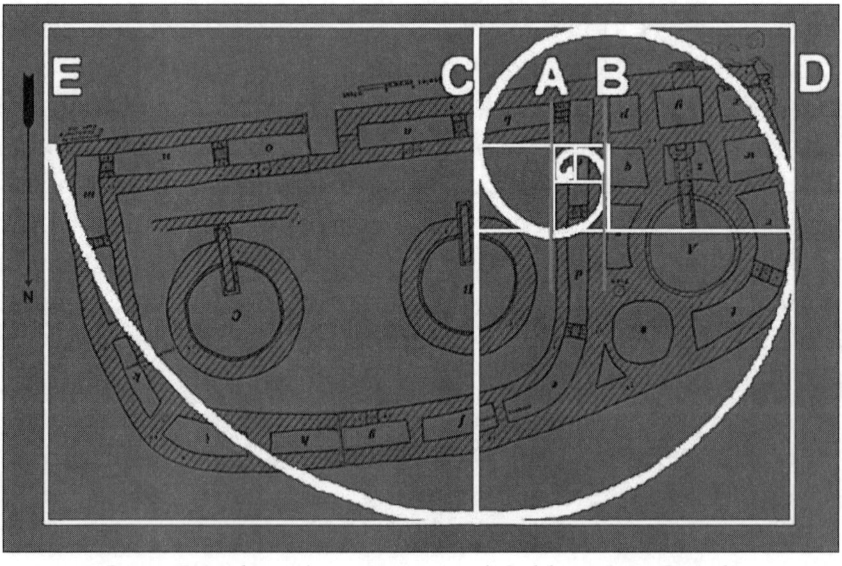

Orion Temple with superimposed Golden Mean Spiral.

Chapter 6
Hopi Flying Saucers Over Arizona

Ancient Aerial Shields and Their Pilots

Ever since pilot Kenneth Arnold sighted nine flat discs erratically skipping across the sky near Mount Rainier in 1947, flying saucers have been firmly fixed in modern consciousness. From the small silver spacecraft in *The Day the Earth Stood Still* to the mother ship in *Independence Day*, the round aerial machine has become one of the primary icons of our age. Flying vehicles could conceivably come in many varieties but the most common seem to be disk-shaped.

This phenomenon is, of course, not restricted to the present. Shortly after the Arnold report and the infamous Roswell UFO crash, the spring 1948 issue of *Fate* magazine carried an article by a Navajo named Oga-Make.

> "Most of you who read this are probably white men of a blood only a century or two out of Europe. You speak in your papers of the Flying Saucers or Mystery Ships as something new, and strangely typical of the twentieth century. How could you but think otherwise? Yet if you had red skin, and were of a blood which had been born and bred of the land for untold thousands of years, you would know this is not true. You would know that your ancestors living in these mountains and upon these prairies for numberless generations, had seen these ships before, and had passed down the story in the legends which are the unwritten history of your people."[1]

Legends from the ancient Hopi Indians also abound with what they call magical flying shields. Although this northern Arizona tribe has traditionally been known as the People of Peace, the warrior shield could be an apt analogy because in Hopi culture the concept of war is inexplicably connected to the stars.

The traditional term used for flying saucer is *paatuwvota*. Since the Hopi word *paa* means water, *paatuwvota* possibly refers to the expanding concentric rings in a lake or pool. This might be a metaphorical description for the way the strange airborne device appears to operate. For a desert people like the Hopi, water is synonymous with wonder—perhaps the type evoked by witnessing these spacecraft.

Many flying shields are piloted by entities commonly called kachinas. (The more correct spelling of the Hopi term is *katsinam*, plural of *katsina*.) Like angels, these beneficent creatures are spirit messengers that act as intermediaries for gods and humans. Although their multicolored masks come in endless varieties, some resemble space helmets. [continued on p. 102]

Aholi Kachina doll, which wears a cloak of many colors representing flowers, the brightness of summer, and germination.

Hu is the name of the Hopi whipper kachina that comes to bring rain to the desert. This ogre has a black mask, goggle eyes, fangs and lolling tongue. It carries a yucca whip in each hand. Sometimes it holds a knife in one hand and a whip in the other.

Hu is also one of the names for the Sphinx at Giza. It acts as guardian of the horizon in the same way that its Hopi namesake is guardian of the kachina dance. Hu is additionally known as the Egyptian god of Taste, springing from the blood of Ra's phallus. *Hu* literally means bad or wicked, and naked, as well as to grieve, to beat, to crush, and to slay. *Huhu* is the primeval watery mass whence came everything. In Egyptian, *Hu* can also mean rain.

In their classic book *Hamlet's Mill,* Giorgio de Santillana and Hertha von Dechend state that *Humeri* is an antiquated Latin word for the constellation Orion, which the Hebrews call Gibbor, or Giant. *Humeri* is also the plural of humerus, the long bone between the shoulder and the elbow.

"I've seen things you people wouldn't believe. Attack ships off the shoulder of Orion…" –Roy Batty, a "replicant" in the movie *Blade Runner*

One handsome kachina named Pavayoykyasi is known to sprinkle the plants with life-giving morning dew. His name, in fact, literally means "moisture tablet." (Again, in the desert, moisture always means amazement.) This finely dressed figure wears an embroidered kilt, a colorful sash, and eagle down feathers in his hair. He also carries a wand in his hand and some sort of backpack.

He refers to his aircraft as "…his pet, a magic flying shield. The shield has two parts, with the lower one spinning and the upper one remaining still. Climbing aboard, Pavayoykyasi rose up into the air and flew off."[2] Because it automatically knew the way to his house, the craft either may have been partially sentient or it employed an ancient version of GPS technology. The use of the term "pet" also implies some sort of flying animal. On the other hand, the description of the lower part spinning and the upper part stationary suggests a machine. Perhaps it was a hybrid of organic and manufactured, similar to Lt. Colonel Philip J. Corso's account of the saucers in his book *The Day After Roswell*.

A very common motif in Hopi legends is one where a kachina mates with a maiden. This echoes the Watchers, the biblical fallen angels who had sexual intercourse with human women in order to produce the giants known as the Nephilim. "There were giants in the earth in those days; and also after that, when the sons of God came in unto the daughters of men, and they bare children to them, the same became mighty men which were of old, men of renown."[3]

Giants, incidentally, also play a large part in Hopi culture and frequently show up at kachina dances. (See Chapter 11.) At one dance I witnessed at the Third Mesa village of Oraibi, for instance, a Hu Kachina, or Ogre, walked within a few feet of me into the plaza, carrying a rusty, foot-long butcher knife. His bulging eyes and fierce teeth even today present a terrifying reminder of the persistent role of giants in the Hopi world.

One example of the unusual union of spirit messenger and Hopi mortal involves an unnamed kachina that took a young woman from Oraibi to the Land of the Cloud People. The girl's father had recently died, causing a hardship for the family. The Cloud People had apparently been watching her and her mother and decided that the kachina should marry her. One day the girl was in the fields picking squash blossoms when "...she heard a roaring sound, a hissing noise like wind coming through a small place, and she wondered what it was." This implies some sort of mechanism rather than either an organic or a metaphysical means of transport. Then she saw the approaching kachina and, like the previous one mentioned, was good-looking with a beautiful kilt and sash and a brightly painted body. He said he wished to marry her and told her he would take her to his home tomorrow. The next morning he returned to the same field.

> "He took her by the hand and walked with her over the hill, and she saw there was something there, something round, and they went straight for the thing and got into it. And when they did that, he did something and there was a big roar and soon they were off the ground. The thing they were in seemed to be spinning, and it streaked off. After a while he said, 'We are here.' They were down on the ground again and the roaring and hissing sound stopped. He took her up to his village, to his home. When they got to his house his mother and father were very happy that he had found the girl they had spoken of."[4]

Another kind of aircraft is called a *tawiya,* or "gourd," which consists of two halves. After climbing aboard, the rider closes the upper half and installs a tightly stretched sinew between the bottom of the gourd and the stem button. He then twists the sinew between his palms, and the flying machine lifts off, making a humming noise.[5] "Hopis say that the gourd is a magic vehicle used by those who have power to use it for travel—something like a spacecraft or flying saucer."[6]

Hopi narratives also describe spinning trays that can transport various beings. A wicker plaque called a *sooyungyapu* has a star design woven on it, thus suggesting its origin. These woven artifacts are perhaps mimetic of the aerial craft.

[continued on p. 105]

Hopi woman making a star plaque (*potayngyapu*) at Shungopovi, 1901.

This petroglyph showing Sótuknang is located on the cliff below the village of Walpi on First Mesa. His face is a crescent moon; above his head is a four-pointed star. His right hand holds a cloud symbol; his left holds lightning. Above the lightning is a symbol for either the four directions or Orion.

One myth incorporating this vehicle describes two virginal sisters from Kawàyka'a (Laguna Pueblo in New Mexico) who constantly resisted the advances of many young suitors in their village. They both finally agreed to marry Tókila, the Night. After going outside the village with him, they found a large "póta," or coiled plaque.

> "So they all took a place on the tray, whereupon they were lifted up and carried through the air to Nuwátok'aovi [also spelled Nuvatukya'ovi, the San Francisco Peaks in Arizona], where they entered a deep canyon or gulch. Here the Night lived. When they came into the house they saw in an inner room a great many human bones. They were the remains of many women whom the Night had stolen in the village, and with whom he had lived a while and then, as soon as they became pregnant, had thrown them into the room to perish."[7]

In this case the entity that piloted the flying shield turned out to be malicious rather than benevolent. Perhaps "Night" is merely the allegorical name for this murderous creature of unknown origin.

In my previous book *Eye of the Phoenix,* I describe, on the other hand, the compassionate Hopi sky god named Sótuknang. His face "shone like a star" and his costume "glittered like icicles." Interpreted metaphysically, this may refer to the glistening aura of a ghostly inter-dimensional being. On a physical level, it may point to some sort of electrically lit helmet and a silvery or metallic spacesuit.

As a primary deity in the Hopi pantheon, Sótuknang had been influencing the people since the beginning of their current epoch on earth they call the Fourth World. In one tale he rescues a young pair of boy-and-girl twins from a deluge, which, by the way, eventually destroyed the Third World (or Era). He takes them up in his flying shield from which they could see the landscape for many miles around.

A craft of this sort would certainly allow the perspective by which one could gauge the accuracy of a star correlation on the ground—that is, the pattern of a constellation such as Orion spread out upon the Arizona desert. (For details of the Arizona Orion Correlation, see my book *The Orion Zone*.) From 175 miles above the earth most of northern Arizona can be seen, from Grand Canyon in the west to Canyon de Chelly in the east, and from Tsegi Canyon in the north near the Utah/Arizona border to the Little Colorado River in the south near the modern town of Winslow. (This altitude is a little less than the lowest altitude for the space shuttle in orbit.)

Like the space flights of Ezekiel or Enoch, a ride on a flying shield would reveal the panorama of the sky-earth correlation and confirm the hermetic maxim "As above, so below."

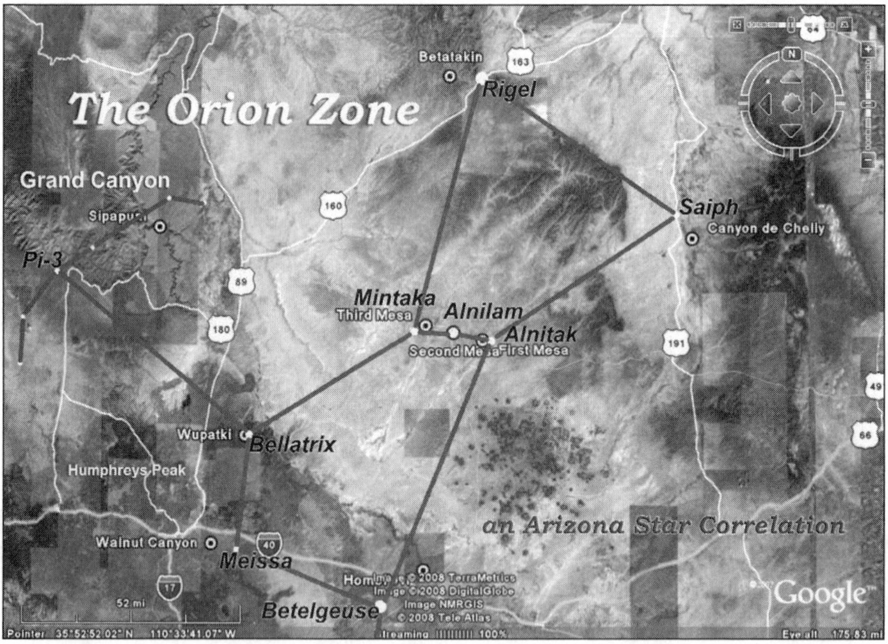

The celestial template of Orion is projected on the high desert of Arizona. A Hopi ruin site or village corresponds to each major star in the constellation. The belt stars (Mintaka, Alnilam, and Alnitak) correspond to Third, Second, and First Mesas respectively. The distance between Betatakin and Canyon de Chelly at the north is slightly stretched in relation to the constellation—about twelve miles. The distance between Walnut Canyon and Homol'ovi at the south is also stretched—about ten miles. Still, this close pattern can not be considered a coincidence. © 2008 Google Earth.

Modern Sightings In the Wild West

In August of 1970 a rash of UFO sightings occurred in the skies over Prescott, Arizona. Over a two-week period many hundreds of flying saucers were seen by hundreds of witnesses. This prompted Chief Dan Katchongva of the Hopi Sun Clan, his councilor, and an interpreter to travel southwest about125 miles from his village of Hotevilla on Third Mesa to Prescott to learn more of the event.

He described to the *Prescott Courier* an ancient petroglyph near the village of Mishongnovi on Second Mesa that depicts a dome-shaped object. "'We believe other planets are inhabited and that our prayers are heard there,' he said. 'The arrow on which the dome-shaped object rests, stands for travel through space,' Katchongva said in explaining the rock carving. 'The Hopi maiden on the dome-shape (drawing) represents purity. Those Hopi who survive Purification Day will travel to other planets. We, the faithful Hopi, have seen the ships and know they are true,' he said."[8] As we have seen, the purity of Hopi maidens throughout the ages has attracted the high-flying kachinas.

Paul Solem, a non-Indian expert on Hopi prophecy and Mormon doctrine, was also key figure during the Prescott sightings. He even wildly claimed to attract the flying saucers by telepathically communicating with them. In one instance he took a group of people outside and then began to mentally focus on extraterrestrial contact. He soon exclaimed: "They are here! I can't see them, but I know they are here. One just said, 'We're here, Paul!' There are several people in the saucer. I can hear them talking." After a few minutes a star-like UFO appeared, halted, then moved first in one direction and then the other.

He believed the entities in the spacecraft were angelic and kind, like the Hopi kachinas, and hailed from the planet Venus. He said that they had shoulder-length hair neatly cut and their voices were musical and androgynous. This sounds like what we would typically describe today as a Nordic ET. He even received the space travelers' proclamations, which he transcribed:

> "We come to lend credence and as a sign or token that the Hopi prophecy was of a divine nature. Great sorrow and fear will be coming to this planet very soon and few will escape it. Our leader as spoken of in Hopi prophecy is already here (on Earth) in mortality and is known as the Apostle John (the same as in the New Testament). The white brother shall be introduced by a huge fire and the Earth shall quake at his arrival. We are of the 10 lost tribes and we will return several nights unless there is contempt for us."[9]

Local UFO researcher Dan Carlson said that the area around Prescott had been a magnet for many of the early important though controversial figures in the field of ufology, including George Adamski, Daniel Fry, George Van Tassel, as well as former Prescott residents Truman Bethurum and George Hunt Williamson. "'If one is to believe Hopi prophecy,' Carlson remarked, 'the reasons the saucers are sighted here most often and contacters seem to be attracted here is that this is a chosen land. Prescott is within the Hopi circle of sacred ground where the beings from another world are supposed to bring about prophecy.'"[10]

Chief Katchongva had been one of the elders most active in bringing the knowledge of Hopi legends and prophecies of End Times to the world at large.[11] He believed that these persistent UFO visitations were among the signs and omens that the Fourth World is about to end. Apparently on the last day of his visit to Prescott an unidentified spacecraft flew in very low—about 800 feet.[12]

Chief Katchongva passed away in 1972 at age 107 under some rather strange circumstances. "When Dan Katchongva 'died', his body was never found. He was last seen walking up a small valley where a UFO had just been seen."[13]

A much more recent sighting of a flying shield occurred on the evening of January 24th, 2007, about 50 miles south of Third Mesa. Sean and Deanna Dover were driving east toward their hometown of Leupp, Arizona, when they spotted a triangular-shaped craft with three lights on it flying an estimated mile-and-a-half above them. The object was moving too fast to be an airplane and was not making any noise whatsoever.

Returning home, they got some night vision equipment that Sean's father owned as a Navajo Nation Police Ranger. That's when they saw (and heard) two jets flying from the southwest intercept the completely silent object, which managed to evade these aircraft. Eventually about 30 witnesses in the small, somewhat isolated town saw the UFO circle the area a total of 15 times over a period of almost an hour before it headed southeast toward Winslow.

They all said the object was triangular with three or four tiers and a pulsating light positioned on a sphere on its underside. A local fifth grade teacher claimed the craft emitted a yellow light and was about twice the size of the school gymnasium.

This amazing sighting, however, did not at all surprise Sean Dover. "'I believe that it really was a UFO because of my family's history. I've seen [UFO's] too many times to remember,' Sean said. 'Leupp is a hot spot for UFO's.'"[14]

The historic relationship between flying shields and the Native Americans of Arizona has become a part of a long tradition. Legends of ancient star beings that pilot spacecraft and sometimes mate with the indigenous people are an accepted fact for the native peoples, not a matter of dispute. Perhaps we should start listening to the deep wisdom and wide experience that the original inhabitants of this continent possess. They've been on the case for ages.

Chapter 7
The Taurus Correlation

Thumbs Up

In my previous book *The Orion Zone*, I suggested that the Orion Correlation in Arizona could be extended to the adjacent constellation Taurus. Projected onto the earth, the stars correspond to the region along the Grand Canyon west of the main part of the park.[1] The Hualapai Reservation near the town of Peach Springs, Arizona, is the site of the Eden-like Havasu Falls at the bottom of the canyon. The main village is called Supai, which literally means "navel."[2]

Cultures worldwide associate either Taurus as a whole or its smaller V-shape called the Hyades with moisture or rainfall. Its brightest star, the orange giant Aldebaran, is 65 light years away and is known as the eye of the zodiacal Bull.

In astrological terms, Taurus is the first of four fixed signs—the other three being Leo, Scorpio, and Aquarius. Aldebaran was known in Persia (modern-day Iran) as one of the four "Royal Stars," or the "Guardians of the Sky"—the others being Regulus in Leo, Antares in Scorpio, and Fomalhaut in Piscis Austrinus (a few degrees south of Aquarius).

The Hebrews conceptualized not Aries but Taurus as the first constellation of the zodiac. The shape of its head mirrored Aleph, the first letter of their alphabet. The Jewish people also sometimes referred to Aldebaran as "God's Eye." The Akkadian name of Taurus was *Gis-da*, literally the "Furrow of Heaven." This signified its dominance at the beginning of the agricultural year during the vernal equinox at least circa 4000 BC and probably even earlier.[3]

[continued on p. 112]

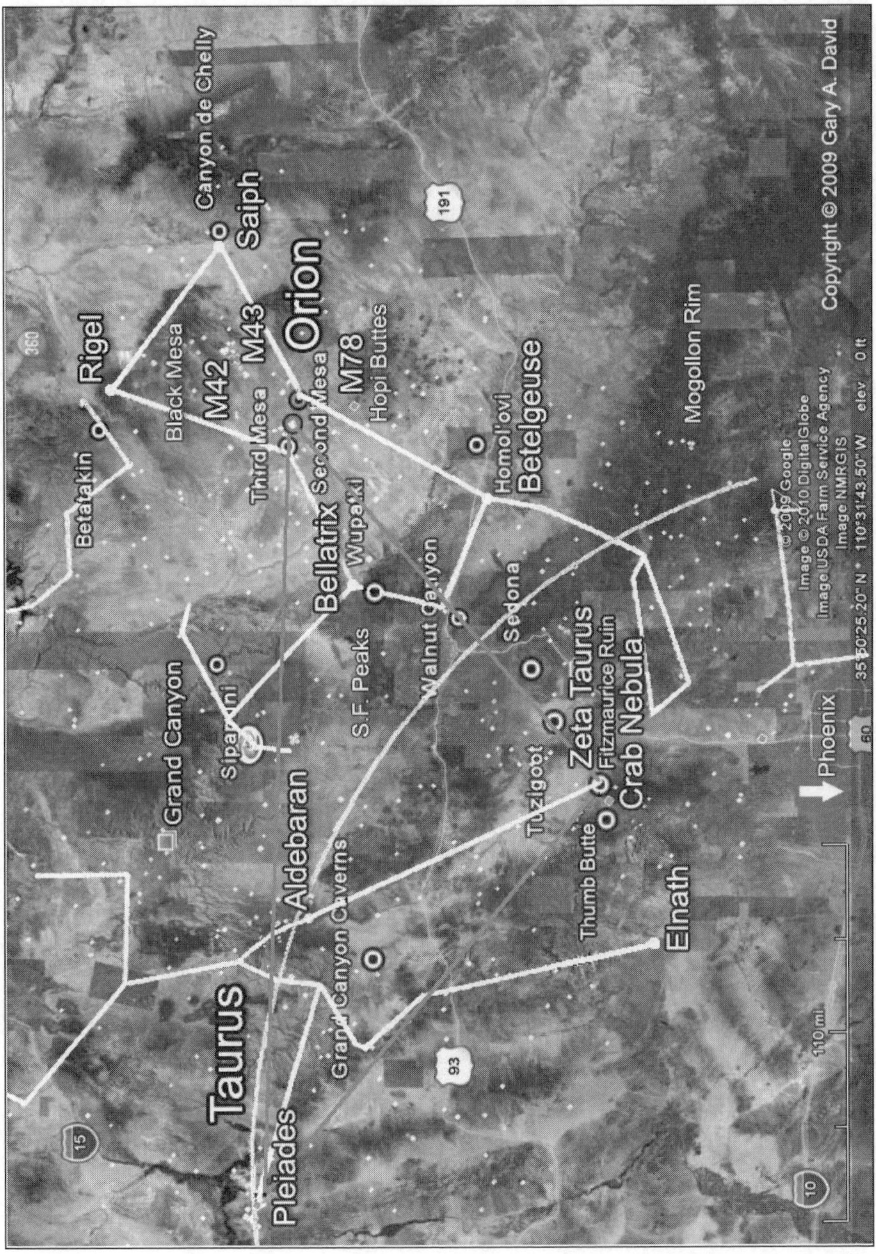

© 2009 Google Earth.

William Tyler Olcott mentions Taurus in terms of one icon from a well known secret society. "The Masonic Tau Cross is an expressive symbol of the vernal equinox and of immortality. The emblem is found on many of the ancient monuments of Egypt, and clearly its astronomical significance can be traced to the constellation Taurus, for... the word 'Tau' is derived from an Egyptian or Coptic root meaning bull or cow."[4]

The Egyptian cross that first comes to mind is, of course, the *crux ansata,* or *ankh.* Another Egyptian example of the Tau is found on the Narmer Palette seen on p. 43. The symbol is located on the upper portion of the palette between two bovine heads, which perhaps represent Taurus in its rising and setting positions. The Egyptian word *tau* means either "bread" or "fire, hot," which are both necessary for life. The same word can also mean "people, folk."[5] On the other hand, the Hopi sun god is named Tawa, equally needed for human survival.

The last letter of the Hebrew alphabet is *tau,* so the pairing of Aleph and Tau has the same sense as the biblical Alpha and Omega. Speaking of the Book of Revelation, we recall that the four beasts of the Apocalypse are: lion, calf (young bull), creature with a man's face, and flying eagle.[6] These correspond to the summer solstice (Leo), vernal equinox (Taurus), winter solstice (Aquarius), and autumnal equinox (Scorpio) respectively. The last sign, Scorpio the Scorpion, has two alternative totems, the eagle and the serpent. I should additionally note that this schema applies to the skies two millennia ago, shifted one sign by the effects of precession.

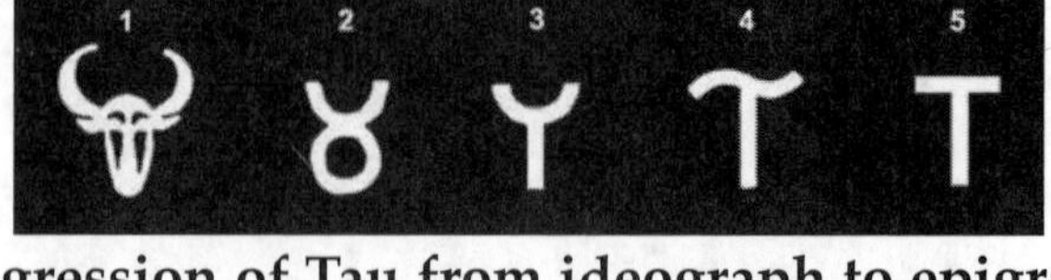

Progression of Tau from ideograph to epigraph.

1. the bull hieroglyphic with crescent moon horns— right side for waxing, left for waning.
2. astronomical symbol of Taurus.
3. & 4. transition from 2.
5. The Greek alphabet letter *tau.*

Astrologer Cyril Fagan describes the beginning of the Age of Taurus. (See my sky chart on p. 35.)

> "Assuming that Aldebaran, in the mathematical center of the constellation Taurus, was the original and hence authentic determinant of the sidereal zodiac, then calculation discloses that the mean vernal point retrograded in the 30th degree of this constellation in April 4152 B.C. when, theoretically, the Taurean Age began. By an astonishing coincidence it almost simultaneously came to the precise conjunction with Gamma [sic Zeta] Tauri, a star of the third magnitude, at the tip of he Bull's South Horn. This star was known to the Chinese by the suggestive title *Tien Kwan*, the 'Heavenly Gate,' and to the Arabs as *Al Hecka* the 'Driver'. The actual date of the conjunction was 4151 B.C., and hence there was just a year between the two phenomena, which is remarkably close. Slowly retreating through the constellation, the vernal equinoctial point, forming its ecliptic conjunction with Aldebaran itself in 3058 B.C., did not leave it until 1955 B.C., when it entered into the 30th degree of Aries."[7]

The ancient Chinese first referred to the constellation Taurus as the "White Tiger" but later called it the "Golden Ox." Olcott also offers, incidentally, a little-known fact regarding cultural diffusionism. "Strangely enough we find that the South American Indians of the Amazon country call this star group 'the Ox.' Here again is further proof that at a very early date there was a transmigration, or a means of communication unknown to us, between the far east and the far west."[8] Incidentally, the Hebrew letter Aleph is most likely derived from a West Semitic word that means "ox."

The previously mentioned Tau cross has had a rich and enduring influence on civilizations and cultures worldwide. My friend and colleague, the late Todd Greaves, who was probably the world's leading authority on this icon, sums up in one sentence the progression of its legacy: "To put it too briefly: the Cow cult already in existence at Çatal Höyük evolved in Sumer into that of the Goddess of the Cattle-byre Hut (Inanna), and in

Egypt into the Hathor/Isis cultus."[9]

The Anatolian village of Çatal Höyük (literally, "fork mound"—in the shape of Taurus, perhaps?) was constructed in 7500 BC (contemporary with Jericho). Relevant artifacts include bucrania (cattle heads) mounted on walls and murals depicting aurochs painted in red.

Shortly before his passing, Todd was in contact with British author Andrew Collins, who was researching Neolithic site of Göbekli Tepe (literally, "hill of the navel") in southeastern Turkey. This may just be the oldest temple in the world, built between 11,500 and 11,000 years ago (middle of the Age of Leo). Of interest here are 20 T- or tau-shaped stone pillars carved with various animals: scorpions (Scorpius?), lions, snakes, boars, foxes, vultures, etc.[10] Between Göbekli Tepe to the east and Çatal Höyük to the west are the *Taurus Mountains*, the source of the Tigris and Euphrates flowing southward to Mesopotamia's Fertile Crescent.

One striking similarity between the village of Çatal Höyük in Turkey and any Hopi village in Arizona is the architecture. A 12th century AD Hopi would feel completely at home in an 8th millennium BC Anatolian domicile. Holes in the ceiling provided access via interior and exterior ladders. Although the Turkish structures were constructed of mud bricks instead of stone, interior walls were plastered in both cases. Flat roofs were supported by large roof beams with smaller timbers perpendicularly placed. Was this design somehow exported to the New World?

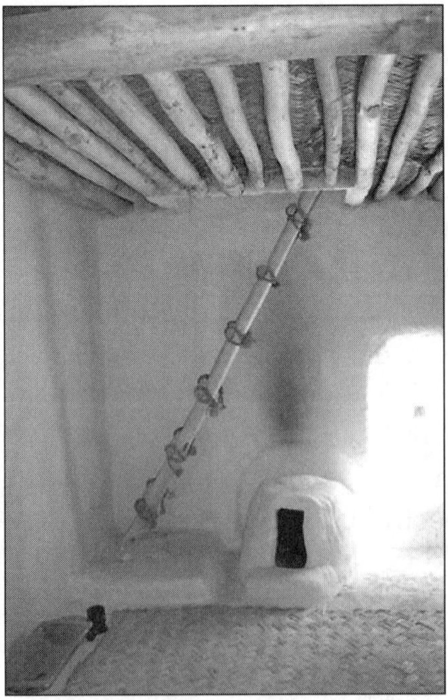
Restoration of interior room with ladder and hearth, Çatal Höyük.

The Hopi most likely call the constellation Taurus *Sootuvìipi*, literally "star-slingshot-pocket." This is a reference to its diamond shape that resembles a slingshot patch.[11] The Hopi know its primary asterism Aldebaran as *Wuyok Sohu,* or "broad star," and associate it with the eye of the "heart-of-the-sky god" named Sótuknang.[12] (See the Hopi symbol on p. 31 identified as "sky window," which is a pottery design that somewhat resembles the lozenge-shaped Ojo de Dios, or "God's eye," that the Huichol tribe of Mexico weaves with yarn.)

I have previously compared the form of Taurus to an ancient Hopi artifact called the *mongko*. This Y-shaped, hand-held object is a male symbol of spiritual authority and power. Both human and supernatural figures carry this potent emblem in their left hand. (For instance, see the kachina doll Aholi, shown on p. 100.)

Frank Waters comments on the significance of the *mongo*: "It gives evidence that each society and the clans comprising it had completed their centuries-long migration."[13] The Hopi societies referred to are: the One Horn, associated with the sky god Sótuknang, and the Two Horn, associated with Alósaka (or Muyingwa, a germination and fertility god). While the One Horn Society may be related to Orion-Taurus region, the Two Horn Society, with their bighorn sheep headdress, may be linked to the constellation Aries, which the Hopi call *Soo'ala,* literally "star-horn." At any rate, if the migrations have been completed, then that fulfills the required number of stone villages built sometime between 1050 AD and 1300 AD in order to establish the stellar template of Orion and Taurus on the high desert.

The *mongko* in turn mirrors the Egyptian instrument known as the *Pesh-en kef,* which was found in 1872 by Waynman Dixon in the north shaft of the Queen's Chamber of the Great Pyramid. It was possibly used for the Opening of the Mouth Ceremony described in the *Book of the Dead*. On the other hand, it was perhaps a version of the *merkhet* ("instrument of knowing"), which was a bar and plumb line, used in conjunction with the *bay,* which was a palm-rib with a V-shape cut at one end. Together they formed a pair of architectural or even navigational instruments.

After reading my book, alternative Christian researcher Roberta Ruth Hill emailed me and suggested that I extend the horns of the terrestrial Hyades to include the Crab Nebula near the star Zeta Tauri—the tip of the constellation's left horn.

I had previously written that the supernova that produced this nebula exploded in the American Southwest in the early morning of July 5th, 1054 AD. It is also called M1—not a semi-automatic carbine but the first astronomical object to be catalogued by Monsieur Charles Messier. At any rate, the anomalous celestial event must have had a profound effect on the inhabitants of the region because rock art from numerous locations supposedly depicts it.

Accounts from other parts of the globe (China, for instance) state that the reddish-white supernova burned in the sky at noon for 23 consecutive days and remained in the night sky for nearly two years. Its pointed rays spreading out in four distinct directions were estimated to be six times as bright as the planet Venus.

I had concluded that the supernova may have been one of primary factors that jump-started a series of migrations in the Southwest, beginning in the mid-11th century and ultimately leading to the projection of the sidereal pattern of Orion, Taurus, and Canis Major onto the Colorado Plateau.[14]

Following Roberta's suggestion, I found that the Crab Nebula directly corresponded –in the sense of "As above, so below"– to a massive geologic formation rising a couple miles west of downtown Prescott, Arizona. This granite upthrust known as Thumb Butte has become an important landmark and logo for the Prescott area.

Thumb Butte is actually a miniature version of Devils Tower, Wyoming, which was featured in the movie *Close Encounters of the Third Kind*. Like the larger geological uplift, it may serve as a beacon for extraterrestrial craft. For instance, during the 1970 Prescott sightings (see previous chapter), Mrs. Irene Wood stated the following: "...we saw a huge brilliant mass of light looking as big as three moons coming very fast over Thumb Butte. It seemed almost over Prescott and went to the east. It halted and a huge mass detached itself and fell straight down behind the hills."[15] Was this a UFO or merely a huge meteor that broke up upon descent?

[continued on p. 118]

Thumb Butte, elevation over 6,500 feet, near Prescott, Arizona.

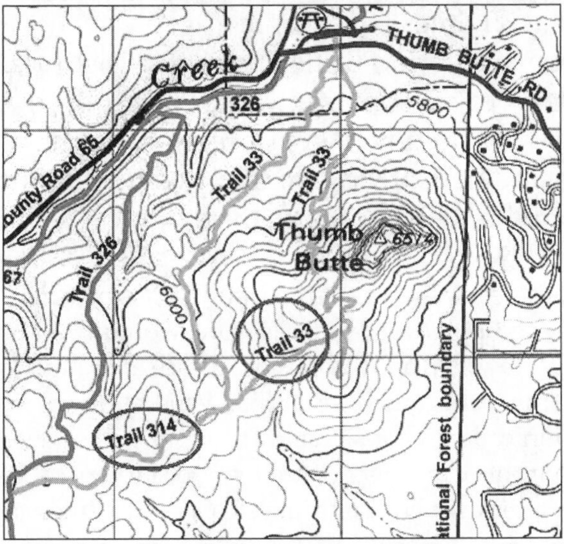

Topographic map of the Thumb Butte area with Forest Service trails. Like Devils Tower in Wyoming, Thumb Butte is a laccolith that may serve as a beacon for UFOs. According to the star correlation theory, this geologic upthrust corresponds to the Crab Nebula. (See Google Earth photo on p. 111.) The Crab Pulsar has a regular period of 33 milliseconds. Trail 33 leads almost to the summit of Thumb Butte. Is this just another "coincidence"? Map courtesy of Roberta Ruth Hill.

As a remnant of the supernova that occurred a little nine-and-a-half centuries ago, the Crab Nebula is 11 light years across and still expanding. I did not know, however, that the Crab *Pulsar*, located 6,585 light years away, had some intriguing properties as well. Located at the nebula's center is a relatively young, relatively rare optical pulsar. This rapidly rotating neutron star has a diameter of only 15½ miles but has a mass greater than that of our Sun. The Crab Pulsar also produces what is called synchroton emission, which is electromagnetic radiation or charged particles moving through magnetic fields at nearly the speed of light. In fact, the pulses are generated from a "hot spot" on its surface, giving off emissions from virtually every part of the electromagnetic spectrum.

In early November of 1968 (about the same time as the annual Taurids Meteor Shower) at Puerto Rico's Arecibo Observatory (the place where Jodi Foster's character searched for ET signals in the movie *Contact*), the 300-meter radio telescope had discovered a regular pulse emanating from M1. Confirmed by a number of other observatories, the Crab Pulsar's period was 33.085 milliseconds, or about 30 times per second.[16]

About one year prior, British astrophysicist Jocelyn Bell had discovered the very first pulsar, which she dubbed LGM1 (Little Green Man1). At that time there were serious discussions among scientists, including Carl Sagan, that this might be proof of ETI (Extraterrestrial Intelligence). Sagan asks:

> "Has anyone examined systematically the sequencing of pulsar amplitude and polarizations nulls? One would need only a very small movable shield above a pulsar surface to modulate emission to Earth. This seems much easier than generating an entire pulsar for communications. For signaling at night it is easier to wave a blanket in front of an existing fire than to start and douse a set of fires in a pattern which communicates a desired message."[17]

Scientists finally came to their senses, at least in their own minds, and proposed that the pulsar's regularity was the result of a naturally occurring "neutron star lighthouse." This model posits two opposed beams of synchroton radiation that form a pair of narrow cones around the star's magnetic axis. When one of the beams sweeps by Earth, we perceive it as a regular pulse, much like the visible beam of a lighthouse.

In the last decade American astrophysicist Paul A. LaViolette, Ph.D., has revived the artificial-versus-natural debate on pulsars in his book *Decoding the Message of the Pulsars*. Author Gerry Zeitlin explains the difference between Sagan's hypothesis and LaViolette's.

> "Unlike Sagan, who accepted the conventional model of a pulsar but wondered if ETI could be adding fine-grained modulation, LaViolette proposes a way in which the steady emissions of stars could be focused into the pulses we see. He explains that ETI might be using a nearly-collimated beam of synchrotron radiation, applying technology that we actually are developing today. This dramatically offsets the effect of distance on the detectability of a beacon over interstellar distances."[18]

LaViolette claims that a series of cosmic ray volleys, which included electromagnetic radiation (radio waves, X rays, gamma rays, etc.), was produced at our galactic core near the end of the last Ice Age. Not merely a flash, this "galactic superwave," as he calls it, lasted a couple thousand years and reached a climax 12,200 BC. As a result, a dense cloud of cosmic dust enveloped the Sun, triggering enormous coronal mass ejections that led to mass extinctions of Late Pleistocene megafauna. *Mas y mas*. And oh, by the way, he also believes that these explosions from the center of our galaxy are cyclic, recurring every 13,000 to 26,000 years—so we may be overdue.[19]

LaViolette further maintains that both the Crab and Vela supernovae were triggered by this most recent galactic superwave.

> "The idea, then, strongly suggests itself that the Crab and Vela pulsars were placed in the heavens as markers to warn us about this past catastrophe. A precisely timed flashing signal is a universal archetype on our own planet for conveying a danger warning (e.g., yellow flashing lights for roadside construction hazards). It arouses attention much more effectively than a constant light source. Consequently, a pulsating beacon would be an ideal signal of choice if a galactic community

wanted to convey a warning to novice civilizations of the existence of a galactic danger."[20]

More recently LaViolette discovered that the three primary pulsars in his proposed system of ET pulsar manipulation have a Golden Mean Ratio or Fibonacci Series relationship. (See pp. 97-98.) As of 1992, the Crab Pulsar with a period of 33.403347 milliseconds corresponds to Fibonacci number **34**; the Vela Pulsar with a period of 89.298530 corresponds to number **89**; and the Vulpecula Pulsar with a period of 144.457105 corresponds to number **144**. As you might have noticed, the Crab Pulsar's period has been slightly increasing since its discovery, and this rate is constant. LaViolette states that its period will exactly equal 34 milliseconds in 2037 AD—a quarter century after 2012. He speculates that an ET civilization is using the universal Golden Mean Ratio to mark a significant event in our future.[21]

The near-Earth asteroid Apophis, named after the ancient Egyptian "serpent of darkness," is due in 2036 or 2037. Acclaimed physicist Dr. Michio Kaku describes how seriously Russian scientists are taking the threat.

> "Anatoly Perminov, head of the Russian Space Agency, caught scientists off guard when he called for a closed meeting of Russian scientists to counter a killer asteroid headed our way. He said that a potential impact from the asteroid Apothis *around 2036* [italics added] could kill hundreds of thousands of people. Immediately this conjured up images of Bruce Willis and his space cowboys riding the Space Shuttle to blow up a comet in the movie 'Armageddon.' Scientists, realizing that the danger is slight but real, have in fact seriously proposed various ways in which to deflect the asteroid."[22]

Is the Crab Pulsar sending us a signal to zero in on this particular time period? One more impending catastrophe to worry about!

At this point let me categorically state what may already be obvious: I do not pretend to be a hard scientist. When viewing photos and a video of this pulsar, I had an intense visceral experience, as if the astronomical object was imbued with some sort of sentience. From one angle it looks like an iris and pupil peering off into space. Watching it in motion, I was reminded of my recent echocardiogram, and the pulsing of a living heart (in that case, mine). The Lakota (Sioux) medicine man Black Elk once used the phrase *Chante ishta*, or "eye of the heart," to describe a visionary way of seeing into the deepest workings of nature. Perhaps this is the natural world being augmented by an advanced ET civilization trying to grab our attention for undetermined reasons.

If the terrestrial correlative to the Crab Nebula was a key locus in the landscape of the ancestral Hopi, we would expect to find some artifacts around Thumb Butte, and indeed we do. Many pottery shards have been found in the area, which were made by both the Prescott culture and the Hohokam. The latter group traditionally lived in the Phoenix Basin to the south and built a massive canal system there. This intermingling of pottery suggests that the two groups were living together. One palette with an incised border was found containing lizard remains. In addition, a number of "circular rooms and human remains" were also discovered, including a cremation burial.[23]

The vicinity of Thumb Butte is also one of the richest petroglyph sites in the Prescott area. Among piñon pine, emory oak, and alligator juniper, rounded granite boulders, pink and tan, provided the rock panels for carving. Icons of the ages include anthropomorphs, zoomorphs, snakes, lightning, concentric circles, spirals, and undetermined artifacts. (See photos on p. 126.)

Roberta Hill offers these comments regarding the Crab Pulsar vis-à-vis Thumb Butte.

> "What I found to be particularly interesting was the fact that this area is also a part of the Prescott National Forest, and that the hiking trail that goes around Thumb Butte has the number 33. Is it a mere coincidence that they picked that number for their trail around Thumb Butte? Well, the fact that the Crab Pulsar pulses at 33.4 milliseconds and that matches the trail number is strengthened by the fact that this would be around the area that the Crab Nebula and Crab Pulsar would be found in the terrestrial Taurus. They are located close to the tip of that horn in Taurus, so this pattern matches everything perfectly."[24]

The sacred masonic number 33, the highest degree a Freemason may attain, is particularly relevant, given Prescott's history in this regard. As I discuss in my book *Eye of the Phoenix*, this frontier Arizona town was the location of the first Masonic lodge in the state. It's name is Aztlan, which means "place of the heron." The heron was the naturalistic version of the phoenix, or the ancient Egyptian *bennu* bird, mentioned in Chapter 2.

Is our era the Age of the Phoenix, embodied by that mythical bird rising from its ashes at the end of the temporal cycle which the Hopi call the Fourth World?

A Village With a View

In addition to the Crab Nebula corresponding to Thumb Butte, I found that Zeta Tauri (one horn of Taurus) corresponds to Fitzmaurice Ruin in Prescott Valley, a little over 10 miles to the east. (See satellite photo on p. 111.) Inhabited between 1140 and 1300 AD, this site was built on a narrow hill situated north-south, which afforded a commanding view of the valley and the Arizona's Black Hills to the northeast. Modest by general standards of pueblos in the Southwest, it is still the largest prehistoric stone "apartment complex" in the Prescott area.

> "In the matter of affluence, the 27-room Fitzmaurice Pueblo gave many indications of such a condition. This pueblo was possibly even more than a cultural center, not only because of the fine construction of the edifice, but also because of the recovery of a large quantity and variety of charms, ornaments, figures and fetishes made of bone, sea shell and many kinds of semiprecious stones. In addition, handmolded items such as beads, spindle whorls, figurines and animal fetishes were included in quantity, as well as miniature ceramic vessels. All of these might indicate a religious as well as a cultural center."[25]

The wealth of material goods was exemplified by the discovery of a burial chamber that obviously contained a shaman or important leader. These included mosaic ornaments made of turquoise and argillite, turquoise beads, and polished turquoise or argillite pieces cut into squares. Four *pahos* (prayer sticks) were also found, two of which had woven basketry sheaths. Six ceramic bowls, both plain and decorated, as well as a decorated pitcher were also among the grave goods.[26]

The majority of the 43 burials found at the site were oriented with their heads toward the east. The skeletal remains average five to five-and-a-half feet in height, except of course for the children.[25] (I will discuss the relative height of the inhabitants of the ancient Southwest in a later chapter.)

Conus shell tinklers, abalone shell ear pendants, and glycymeris neck pendants prove the existence of a trade network with the Pacific coast or Gulf of California. In addition, carved fetishes of macaws were unearthed, and even some actual macaw bones were discovered elsewhere at the site. This indicates the intercultural influence that extended into the territory of the Maya.[27] One of the bird fetishes additionally had an opposing triangle design on its back to represent its wings, simlar to the Hopi warfare symbol seen on p. 31.

Another artifact from Fitzmaurice Ruin may provide a further link to the territory of the Mayan flat-topped pyramids.

> "A piece of jadeite, with six faceted sides and ends, was recovered from Room S-19. The piece measures 1.5 cm long, and resembles, generally a blunted or truncated pyramidal shape. the purpose of the item is not known. Such a worked ornamental stone as jadeite, a complex silicate, could have been used as a charm. It probably was not an item of utility."[28]

One of the world's primary sources of jadeite is the Montagua Valley near the Mayan ruin sites of Quirigua and Copán (the latter discussed on p. 53) along the border of Guatemala and Honduras. Cautious archaeologists such as Franklin Barnett, who excavated the Fitzmaurice site, are loath to hazard a guess at the origin of such an artifact as a truncated pyramid showing up in northern Arizona. He would then have to include the possibility that either the Ancestral Puebloans certainly got around more than academics give them credit for or they had some long-distance

Maya/Toltec visitors, who perhaps traded the tiny jadeite carving for a chunk of New Mexico turquoise or Arizona argillite.

In addition, seven stone spheres measuring five-and-a-half to 16 cm. in diameter were found. The red sandstone, granite, or basalt had been chipped, pecked, and then abraded to semi-smoothness.[29] Did some of the inhabitants of Fitzmaurice ruin make it as far south as Costa Rica, to witness the larger navigational spheres found there?[30] Again, the evidence points in that direction.

As the terrestrial correlative of the eclipsing binary star Zeta Tauri, Fitzmaurice Ruin was also culturally connected to another smaller ruin along Lynx Creek about four miles to the southwest. The eponymous Lynx Creek Ruin was inhabited between 1150 and 1300 AD. This hilltop pueblo contained only about 15 rooms that housed two or at most three dozen people. Perhaps they were all members of a single clan.

Black-on-gray pottery bowls from Fitzmaurice Ruin.

Are these illustrating the wormhole tunnel of a NDE (Near Death Experience)? Or do they show the 1054 AD Crab Supernova? This astronomical event depicted by various petroglyphs in the Southwest occurred almost nine decades before the pueblo was constructed. This is about three average lifespans during this time—someone's great-great-grandfather perhaps?

Left: Three rows of 29 frets (days or years, lunar or solar cycle? Or both?).
If primarily solar, then 29 X 3 = 87. 1054 AD to 1141 AD = 87 years.
(Fitzmaurice construction began in 1140.) Inner zigzags number 20.
Right: The zigzag designs here "coincidentally" number 34. (See p. 120).

Afternoon At Lynx Creek Ruin

Atop a scrub oak knoll at the bottom
of an evergreen bowl of mountains
slow motion dreams
surround, a drowsy image:
a wall of a village builds
from granite blocks, blocks which began
to tumble over over
seven centuries ago. Stop &
smell smoke stalking
from a juniper fire. Hear
laughter of children who dropped
to dust skitter in the dust &
laughter of ancestors
in the sky's breath. Young men go off
to hunt, while elders inside
a kiva stir live coals—unearth
blood-born storm clouds forming
in the ashes. Up from the creek
a woman with bare breasts shining
with sweat slips on the path. Her ocher jar
of water makes a parabolic arc
from her brief epoch, near
perfect in spirit, to ours
enduring the distance forged
tools ratchet inside
our bones. This womb jar catches
& carries to the arid air
we breathe her
                    hoop
                                        of blue sky, smashes
to shards as the village
evaporates time-lapse
in the time we've left
to feel the wet edges.

Petroglyphs near Thumb Butte, Prescott, Arizona.

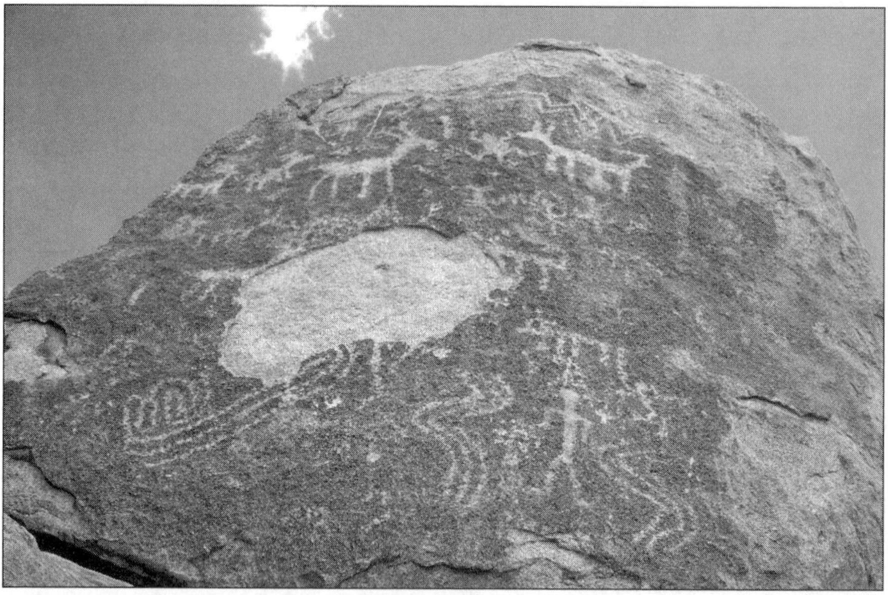

Human figure between two wavy lines, perhaps horned serpent left-below. Animals above. Middle of panel: petroglyph flaked off (or desecrated?)

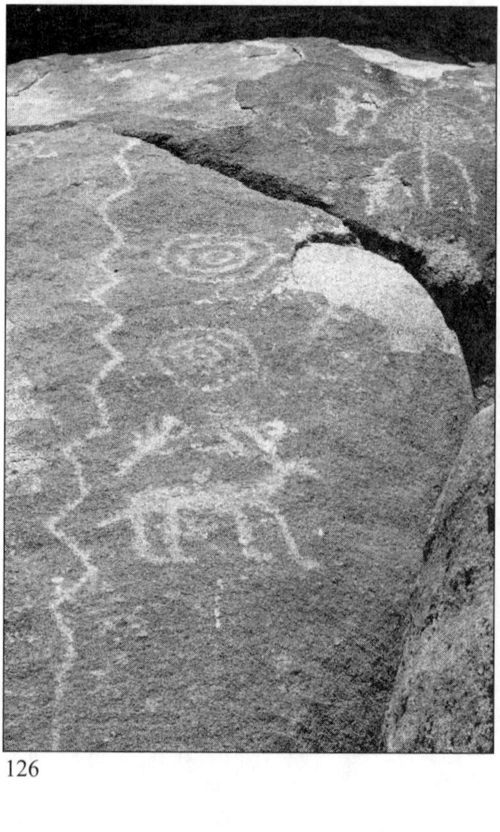

Left: Animal, concentric circles, snake. Artifact at upper-right. Above: spiral, circles, meanders.

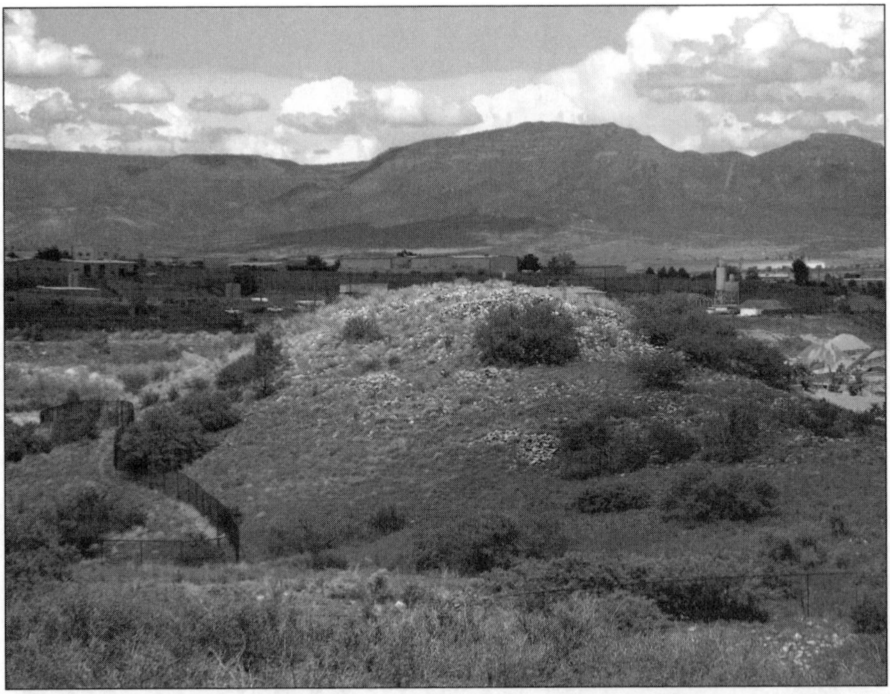

Fitzmaurice Ruin with encroaching modern development, Prescott Valley, AZ

Not much is left of the walls of this 27-room, 12th century pueblo.

Chapter 8
2012 Supernova?

Astronomers Seeing Red

Fierce Orion raises his right arm that holds a warriors' club, ready to strike down his foes. The red supergiant star Betelgeuse (pronounced "beetle juice"), also known as Alpha Orionis, forms his right shoulder. Because of its deep orange or topaz hue, it is called the Martial Star.

Betelgeuse's diameter is 800 times larger than our Sun, and its mass is 20 times greater. It is the 11th brightest star in the heavens, but because it is an irregularly pulsating star called a Mira Variable, its size and magnitude change. At times its diameter equals that of the orbit of Mars, while at other times its diameter is the same size as the orbit of Jupiter. The magnitude of Betelgeuse also varies. Periodically it becomes slightly more brilliant than Rigel, Orion's left knee and the eighth brightest star in the sky. Then for no reason it can reduce in luminosity to approximately the same as Bellatrix, Orion's other shoulder and only the 27th brightest star in the heavens. Clearly Betelgeuse is not a stable stellar object.

Astronomers have recently determined that Betelgeuse is shrinking—in a big way. In the last 15 years it has lost 15% of its diameter! As stated, the size of the star has usually ranged between the diameters of the orbits of Mars and Jupiter, but now it has inexplicably shrunk to the size of the orbit of Venus. Although its size is now smaller, its brightness, oddly enough, did not diminish in the process. In addition, an unusual, large red spot has recently appeared on the star's surface.[1]

All this could be a precursor to it going supernova, when it finally runs out of thermonuclear fuel and ends its 8.5-million-year-old life in a massive explosion. This star would thus become the most luminous object in our sky, much more so than our full Moon. It could even rate as the brightest supernova in history, outstripping those that the Persians, Arabs, Chinese, Native Americans and others recorded both in 1006 AD and in 1054 AD.[2] If Betelgeuse indeed turns into a supernova, it would be visible even during the day and would remain in the night sky for months or even years before fading away—the right shoulder of Orion sadly vanished forever.

Another possible scenario exists: Betelgeuse may have already gone supernova, but we just don't know it yet because its light has not reached us! Scientists have not precisely determined how far the star is from us, although the commonly accepted distance is 430 light years. New measurements taken last year, however, increased the distance to 640 light-years.[3] Let's take a look at these figures.

Suppose we say that the light from the supernova will reach us sometime during 2012, as alternative science researcher Richard C. Hoagland has suggested.[4] This date is, of course, the much-debated end of the current cycle of the Mayan Calendar. It is significant that Betelgeuse achieves midnight culmination (or highest point in the sky when the star crosses the observer's meridian) each December 21st, the winter solstice—the exact date of the calendar's conclusion.[5]

If we assume that the light from the stellar detonation has been traveling for 430 years, it means that the supernova actually happened in 1582 AD—nearly a century after that watershed in history that forever altered the fate of the indigenous peoples of the Americas: that is, the "discovery" of the "New World" by Columbus with all its ensuing misery, enslavement, and genocide.

But what important event occurred specifically in 1582? It was, in fact, the year Pope Gregory XIII rejected the Julian calendar and imposed his Gregorian calendar on the world. According to some scholars of the Maya, the use of this new calendar causes us to be estranged from the natural and spiritual rhythms of the cosmos.

> "The Mayan calendar can be used as a system of divination, but is also an entire cosmology. The Mayan calendar was designed to synchronize life patterns with earth cycles, biological cycles and celestial/galactic cycles. Its use triggers a growth and unfoldment of our personal awareness and potential. The Mayans teach that our current calendar system –the Gregorian system imposed by Pope Gregory XIII in 1582– is out of sync with our biological rhythms, planetary electro-magnetic fields and many celestial cycles. The use of our current calendar system is said to encourage disharmony by throwing humanity out of sync with the living biosphere of the earth. Synchronization with our unnatural calendar has, according to the Mayans, caused humanity to declare war, worship materialism and pollute the planet. We have thus become the enemy of the very biosphere that we depend on for our survival."[6]

The employment of this mechanistic calendar paved the way for the Industrial Revolution and what the prophetic poet and visionary artist William Blake called the "dark Satanic Mills." He also warned against physical cause-and-effect determinism, reductionism, and excessive rationality: "May God us keep From Single vision & Newtons sleep." This clockwork universe brought us into the realm of gross corporeality and linear temporality, where time is money, and, as the bard Bob Dylan has sung, "Money doesn't talk, it swears."

But what if the more recent measurement of 640 light years between Betelgeuse and Earth is actually correct? We would then have to ask: What of any consequence happened in the year 1372 AD? On this particular date, Acamapichtli ("Handful of Reeds") became the first ruler of the Aztecs at Tenochtitlan, now Mexico City.[7] The brutal dynasty he began culminated in political hegemony, military dominance, and the grisly practices of human sacrifice. As we know, this imperious empire met its demise soon after the arrival of Hernán Cortés and his conquistadors in Mexico in the early 16th century.[8]

A subsequent Aztec ruler named Nezahualcoyotl, meaning "Fasting Coyote," was a philosopher and engineer from the city-state of Texcoco east of Tenoctitlan. His life spanned from 1402 till 1472, the date of his death occurring exactly a century after Acamapichtli assumed the throne. Nezahualcoyotl opted for sacrifice of flowers rather than humans in one temple he had built, although he allowed the carnage to continue in the other temples.

Nezahualcoyotl was also a poet, and his corpus was finally published in 1582—the first candidate I discussed for the proposed date of the Betelgeuse supernova. Living in the century before the Spanish came on the scene, he prophesied the obliteration of the Aztec legacy.[9]

> "I foresaw, being a Mexican, that our rule
> began to be destroyed,
> I went forth weeping that it was to bow down
> and to be destroyed.
> Let me not be angry that the grandeur of Mexico
> is to be destroyed.
> The smoking stars gather against it: the one who cares
> for flowers is about to be destroyed.
> He who cared for books wept, he wept
> for the beginning of the destruction."[10]

Is Betelgeuse one of the "smoking stars" to which Nezahualcoyotl referred in his 15th century Aztec prophecy? In the picture on p. 132, his shield possibly depicts one of these smoking stars, perhaps even the red star in Orion. Note that his stance is similar to classic pose of the mythical Orion. Nezahualcoyotl looks like he is just about ready to raise his sword in the position Orion traditionally holds his club. Do the three blue T-shapes (or Tau[11]) hanging near Nezahualcoyotl's belt represent the Zona, or Orion's belt stars? Incidentally, the artist here got the perspective wrong on the toes of each foot—perhaps not a crucial element in codex artwork.

In fixed star astrology, which explores the influences of the major stars on one's natal chart, the keywords of Betelgeuse are:

calamities, danger, and violence. The character is: Mars/Mercury.[12]

> "War and carnage are presaged by Betelgeuse. The star is indicative of great fortune, martial honors and 'kingly' attributes. When rising or culminating the native will be a superior athlete, being endowed with outstanding agility and speed of body. Variable moods and the mind always anxious with the immediate problems of the day. When setting these anxieties may lead to a disturbed mind. Honors and titles will be given the native during his lifetime if the star is rising at birth. If setting, these honors and titles will not come until after death."[13]

Perhaps the end of the Mayan calendar will be accompanied not by huge solar flares as some have claimed (remote viewer Major Ed Dames, for instance, with his "Killshot"), or by an asteroid or comet strike, or even by a major pole shift. We may instead be seeing a massive supernova explosion of the red star Betelgeuse.

Painting of Nezahualcoyotl, Codex Ixtlilxochitl, early 17th century. See teardrop on shield as motif marked "hearthstones" on star ceiling of Senmut's tomb, bottom of p. 357.

If this supernova comes to pass, it probably will not cause any direct physical destruction, due to the great distance between Betelgeuse and the Earth. It may, however, trigger a subtler albeit more profound change—altering both our DNA structure and the vital essence of our etheric bodies. An earlier supernova may provide the guide for what is to come.

The light from the explosion of a blue supergiant named Supernova 1987A left its surface 168,000 years ago and finally reached Earth on February 23rd, 1987—six months before the famous Harmonic Convergence created by alternative Maya scholar José Argüelles. By May of that year it had reached a maximum magnitude of 3, becoming the brightest supernova since the invention of the telescope. This stellar salvo blasted us with neutrinos (chargeless, massless "ghost particles") and bombarded us as well with ultraviolet radiation, infrared radiation, X rays, and gamma rays.[14] We routinely receive such output from the electromagnetic spectrum, of course, but not usually to this degree. Moria Timms in her book *Beyond Prophecies and Predictions* describes its effects:

> "In an instant, quicker than the eye could blink or the phosphene flare in the inner dimensions of the mind, the consciousness of the planet was encoded and imprinted. A superluminal transfer of extragalactic frequencies from deep space impregnated the Earth with the starseeds of neutrinos and radiation. Penetrating to the heart of the Earth's magnetic core, this jump-start of cosmic energy served to accelerate the vibrational frequency of the life force, preparing us for an unprecedented evolutionary leap."[15]

If a supernova 168,000 light-years away could transform us in such a radical manner, imagine the effects of one a mere 430 to 640 light years away. Are we talking about a monumental evolutionary leap forward or a colossal fall into an apocalyptic scenario of world devastation? The spectrum of 2012 predictions includes these two extremes and everything in between.

Hopi Prophecy Seeing Red

Skeptics and debunkers, of course, deride the whole 2012 scenario, chalking it up to pseudoscience, fringe thinking, cyber-fallacies, YouTube lunacy, and other techno-phantasmagoria. However, most of these men (and they *are* mostly men) remain ensconced in the old paradigm, marching in lockstep linear time through the "real world" while sharing the same empirical space with Newton asleep in his grave. A healthy dose of skepticism is good, but a knee-jerk reaction to anything outside the parameters of our sensory perceptions and logic reduces the world to little more than either a three-dimensional prison or a cold laboratory.

Most scientists rarely take the legends of indigenous tribes seriously, unless the latter are the objects of anthropological research. But as far myths or parables that encode sacred universal truths distilled on a subjective level, forget it. The very term myth is synonymous in modern times with "untruth."

Let us, on the other hand, give native wisdom, mythological lore, and the tribal experience of millennia the benefit of the doubt. For instance, the Hopi Indians have foretold that soon after the arrival of the Blue Star Kachina (*Sakwa Sohu*), the Red Star Kachina (*Paha Sohu*) will come and act as the Purifier.[16]

> "The purifier will appear, as the Red Kachina, maybe that means it will appear red in the telescopes that the scientists use. It will remain almost in one place for a long time. Like an eye watching us. That is when Saquasohuh [*Sakwa Sohu*], the one that is called the Blue Star Kachina, will also return. Saquasohuh is benevolent, but the others will not be so. When the others come there will begin the war in the heavens as we have been told."[17]

Hopi spiritual elders say that the Age of Purification is already upon us—signaled by floods, tsunamis, earthquakes, climate change, and environmental degradation as well as social chaos and spiritual confusion. The Blue Star has been variously identified as Comet Holmes (2007), Comet Hale-Bopp (1997), and the heretofore mentioned Supernova 1987A—each a decade apart. Celestial anomalies have always resulted in omens and portents of the end of the world. It is perhaps more than a coincidence, then, that the Hopi word *soto* means "stars," whereas the related word *soti* means "end."

Supernova Betelgeuse may be exactly what the Hopi "Red Star" prophecy was referring to. Unlike a comet, it remains in one place in the sky. In addition, the Hopi characterize this star as malevolent, in contrast to the Blue Star.

The ancient scholars and scribes of India described Betelgeuse in much the same way. In the Hindu epic the *Rigveda*, for instance, Rudra is portrayed as the terrible and awesome aspect of Shiva—"awesome," that is, in the word's original sense. This destructive god of storms and the hunt was the patron deity of Ardra (the "ruddy" Betelgeuse). In one myth he shoots the celestial antelope (the Creator god Prajapati in animal form, represented by Orion's head) with a bow and arrow (the arrow represented by the belt stars).[18]

Hopi legends say that at the end of the current Fourth World, which many Hopis believe is now upon us, a figure called Pahana (also spelled Bahana), known as either the Elder White Brother or the Lost White Brother, will return to Hopiland. He will bear a small corner of a stone tablet that he took back east with him at the beginning of the Fourth World. This piece will match up with the tablet in possession of the Fire Clan, proving his true identity. He is said to arrive wearing either a red cap or a red cloak—metonymic, perhaps, of the exploded star. The late spiritual elder Dan Evehema from the village of Hotevilla, Arizona, enigmatically states: "He will be large in population, belong to no religion but his very own."[19]

Two helpers will accompany Pahana. The first helper will carry two objects: the swastika (Native American, not Nazi), which is a masculine symbol representing purity and the four directions. He will also bring the Maltese cross, a feminine symbol representing virginity and menstrual blood. The second helper will carry merely a sun symbol.

The Fire Clan Tablet shows the corner broken off. In the front we see a swastika at the upper left, a sun symbol wedged into a right angle, a vertical snake-like design, and a V-shape—all overseen by the simple face of Pahana, or possibly that of Masau'u, the Hopi god of death, fire, and the underworld previously mentioned.

The back of the Fire Clan Tablet has a rectangle enclosing a headless figure at the center. Another late Hopi elder named Dan Katchongva (mentioned in Chapter 6 in connection with the Prescott, Arizona, UFO sightings in the summer of 1970) states that during the End Times the evil people will be beheaded and will speak no more. Also within the rectangle are a *nakwatsveni* (friendship symbol) in the middle at the left, a flattened S-shape, and another V-shape (partial cross?) broken off at the lower right-hand corner. In ancestral Hopi rock art, the equilateral cross signifies a star. Outside the rectangle at the top are another V-shape and a half moon. Incidentally, the latter is the Egyptian hieroglyphic for T, or *tau*.

Grandfather Katchongva claims that the swastika is called the "Meha Symbol" and refers to a certain plant with a long root and milky sap, while the Maltese cross is called the "Red Symbol." All three icons could conceivably be associated with the color red: red earth, red blood, and red sun at dawn or dusk.

Of course, many readers probably have already made the connection of the Maltese or Iron cross to World War I, and the swastika together with the Sun to World War II. Mr. Katchongva also predicts a third great tribulation:

> "This third event will depend upon the Red Symbol, which will take command, setting the four forces of nature (Meha) in motion for the benefit of the Sun. When he sets these forces in motion the whole world will shake and turn red and turn against the people who are hindering the Hopi cultural life. To all these people Purification Day will come. Humble people will run to him in search of a new world, and the equality that has been denied them. He will come unmercifully. His people will cover the Earth like red ants. We must not go outside to watch. We must stay in our houses. He will come and gather the wicked people who are hindering the red people who were here first. He will be looking for someone whom he will recognize by his way of life, or by his head (the special Hopi haircut), or by the shape of his village and his dwellings. He is the only one who will purify us."[20]

Here we see a personification of the Red Symbol, which will shake the Earth and make it turn red. Meanwhile the Red Symbol's people carrying out the purification process will swarm over the world like red ants. Filled with blood-red images, this is a dire scenario indeed! Are both Pahana and the Red Symbol a veiled reference to the exploding red star?

Grandfather Evehema sums up the stark dichotomy:

> "The final stage, called The Great Day of Purification, has been described as a 'Mystery Egg' in which the forces of the Swastika and the Sun plus a third force symbolized by *the color 'red'* [italics added] culminate either in total rebirth or total annihilation; we don't know which. But the choice is yours, war and natural catastrophe may be involved. The degree of violence will be determined by the degree of inequity caused among the peoples of the world and in the balance of nature. In this crisis rich and poor will be forced to struggle as equals in order to survive."[21]

Mayan Prophecy Seeing Red

Perhaps the Mayan prophecies were pointing to the same supernova event at the termination of the 13th Baktun, or 13.0.0.0.0—the end of the 5,125-year-cycle of their Long Count calendar. This is, of course, when our Sun will be aligned to the galactic equator due to the precession of the equinoxes—an event that happens only once in 25,920 years.[22]

The Maya specifically refer to the star Betelgeuse as the "red dragonfly" (*chäk tulix*).[23] They also conceptualize the dragonfly (in particular, the Mayan Setwing, *Dythemis maya*) as a positive entity. One legend tells of the moon goddess of procreation named XT'actani (also called Ixchel) and the sun god Kinich Ahau, who were eloping in a canoe. In order to escape a lightening bolt that the rain and thunder god Chac hurled, she changed into a crab (perhaps the constellation Cancer) and he into a turtle (undeniably Orion). Nonetheless she was struck and killed but later revivified with the help of dragonflies.[24] The Hopi also have a positive association with dragonflies, associating them with moisture and fertility.

According to authors Chris Morton and Ceri Thomas, "The Maya considered the dragonfly to be one of the symbols of Kukulcan also known as Quetzalcoatl whose spirit is said to be connected with the fulfillment of the Maya Calendar."[25]

Either Kukulkan of the Maya or Quetzalcoatl of the Aztecs is, of course, the feathered serpent, simultaneously existing on two planes—earth and sky, or physical and spiritual. It epitomizes rebirth and regeneration on both an individual and a global scale. The Hopi figure of Pahana (discussed above) closely resembles this Mayan figure, especially when he proclaimed his own homecoming at the conclusion of the age. Along with their northern counterparts, the Maya still await his return at the end-of-days, perhaps accompanied by the metaphorical red dragonfly, namely, Supernova Betelgeuse.

Aztec god Quetzalcoatl, Codex Borbonicus. This depicts his human form with red skin. His headdress also resembles a dragonfly. In one hand he grasps a serpent; in the other a shield with an equilateral cross (star).

Crop Circle Prophecy Seeing Red

The 2009 crop circle season was a rich and intriguing one, with new formations of complexity and beauty appearing almost daily. On June 3rd, 2009 (less than a week before the news of the potential Betelgeuse supernova hit), a 150 ft.-long dragonfly crop formation was reported in a barley field at Little London near Yatesbury, Wiltshire, England.[26] Incidentally, Orion was known by the ancient Egyptians as "Smati-Osiris," the Barley God.[27] Osiris was generally recognized as the deity of the under-

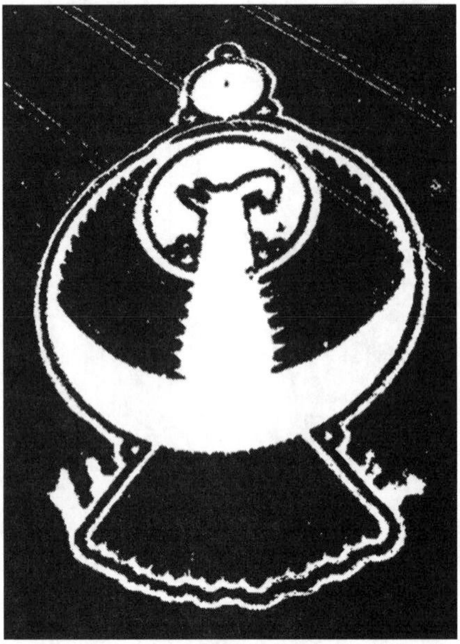

Phoenix, June 12, 2009, Yatesbury, near Cherhill, Wiltshire.

world and death. I believe it is significant that the crop circle dragonfly had the same number of segments on its body as the Mayan Setwing.

Nine days after the dragonfly crop circle appeared, a phoenix 400 feet long with outspread wings materialized in the same field just hundreds of yards away.[28] The bird was contained within a circle, on top of which was another circle, perhaps representing either the Sun, or maybe, just maybe... Betelgeuse.

This phoenix had 16 tail feathers and 12 feathers on each wing. 16 divided by 24 = .666... To claim this as a fractal harmonic of the Mark of the Beast is just too easy. This fraction may instead be a reference to Zechariah 13:8-9 [29], especially given the alchemical dimension of the phoenix. (See discussion below).

A crop circle researcher and astrologer of the Maya named Mark Borcherding has alternately suggested that the three smaller circles arranged in an equilateral triangle around the crowning circle may represent the Mayan "hearthstones," comprised of Alnitak (one of the belt stars), Saiph (Orion's right leg), and Rigel (Orion's left leg). In this case the smoky fire inside the central circle would correspond to the Orion Nebula (M42). This is the Cosmic Hearth established at the creation of the current "world"—that is, the Mayan Fourth Sun, or the Hopi Fourth World. (See bottom of p. 144.)

In the phoenix crop formation, the small circles stacked in triangular patterns –one triad around the crowning circle and one on each side of the phoenix's neck– are also emblematic of the Cosmic Turtle, which the Maya additionally associate with Orion.

[continued on p. 142]

Right: Cosmic Turtle, Madrid Codex. On turtle's back: Alnitak (top stone), Saiph (left bottom stone), and Rigel (right bottom stone), each marked with an X, which is a glyph for "star." Turtle is suspended from two cords, representing the ecliptic.

Below: One Hunahpu, or Maize God, emerging from Cosmic Turtle shell. Temple painting, Palenque, Yucatan, Mexico. Artwork by Linda Schele.

(The Mayan word for turtle is *ak* and the Mayan word for star is *ek'*.) The former triad perhaps shows Orion in its zenith position, while latter two triads show Orion in its rising and setting positions.

In the Mayan epic called the *Popol Vuh*, a figure named One Hunahpu, or First Father, emerges from the cracked carapace of the turtle, flanked and assisted by his twin sons, Hunahpu and Xbalanque. (See drawing on bottom of p. 141.) In the phoenix crop circle, the two small circles flanking the tail feathers may represent this pair. On a mythological level, the cracking open of the turtle's shell refers to the breaking apart of the old world, or era, and the resurrection of the new world (Mayan Fifth Sun). One Hunahpu was also known as the Maize God. The Nahuatl word for 'maize dough' is *toneuhcayotl*, or literally "our flesh," which, in the case of the Maya and other Mesoamerican and North American tribes, is red.[30]

One of the definitions of the word phoenix is "purple-*red*," and the Phoenicians were known as "*red* men." The Egyptians knew the phoenix as the *bennu* bird. (See p. 44.) In Heliopolis (literally "sun-city") it was represented by the conical *benben* stone of meteoric iron located in the Temple of the Phoenix.[31] This avian curiosity is the incarnation of both the heart (or *ab*) of the death-and-resurrection god Osiris and the soul (or *ba*) of the sun god Ra, two primary deities related by this simple word reversal.[32]

The Greek historian Herodotus most notably related the myth of the phoenix. At the end of each temporal cycle (such as the one we are approaching in 2012), this brilliantly plumed male bird with a gold and *scarlet* tail flies to a myrrh tree in Heliopolis, Egypt. There he builds a nest of cassia twigs as a pyre upon which he will be resurrected from the ashes. A new cycle is thereby initiated.

In this regard *Cirlot's Dictionary of Symbols* remarks: "In alchemy, [the phoenix] corresponds to the colour *red* [italics added], to the regeneration of universal life and to the successful completion of a process."[33]

These crop formation creators –whoever or whatever they are– certainly seem to be seeing red in their symbols among the fields of gold. On the other hand, "Successful completion of a process" sounds rather comforting.

Two days later on June 14th, 2009, another enormous crop circle that has been called the Aztec Spirit Bird appeared at Barbary Castle (Iron Age hill fort) near Wroughton, Wiltshire.[34] This bird had eight wing feathers and five tail feathers (total of 13). Its body was comprised of four concentric circles and its head was made of three concentric circles (total of seven). 13 + 7 = 20. The numerals 13 and 20 are the two primary numbers of the Mayan *tzolk'in* calendar of 260 days—coincidentally, the length of human gestation).[35] This crop formation may represent a stylized version of a resplendent quetzal (*Pharomachrus mocinno*), the brilliant bird with a scarlet breast that is related to the Aztec god Quetzalcoatl.

This crop formation might, on the other hand, refer to the Mayan figure of Seven Macaw. Dennis Tedlock, who translated the *Popol Vuh*, states that its Mayan name is *Uucub caquix*, a compound of *cak*, or "red" and *quiix*, or "feathers." He claims this refers to the scarlet macaw (*Ara macao*).[36] The feathers and even whole bodies of his much-revered bird have been found at burial sites as far north as the Hopi territory.

Then on the summer solstice of 2009 an enigmatic crop formation materialized on Milk Hill at Alton Barnes in Wiltshire. (See top of next page.) The central oval or teardrop might correspond to the Hopi concept of the Mystery Egg discussed above. (This ovoid, incidentally, also resembles the shape on Nezahualcoyotl's shield pictured on p. 132.) The egg spawns the five Worlds of Hopi cosmology, corresponding to the five circles attached to five curved lines originating near the center.[37]

The two arms pointing north and east have been likened to both a Freemasonry compass and a sextant. The line running northeast bisects this right angle. However, after it passes the larger circle it jogs a few degrees father northeast. This line just may be an alignment to the rising of the summer solstice Sun on the horizon, which at this latitude (N51°22′) is just a bit over 50° azimuth. (Azimuth is an angle measured in degrees from True North. North = 0°, East = 90°, South = 180°, and West = 270°.)

[continued on p. 145]

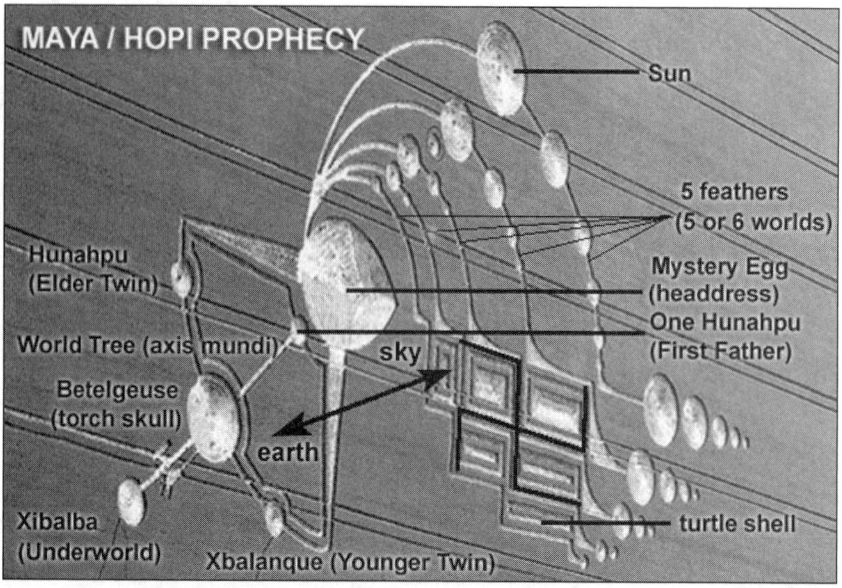

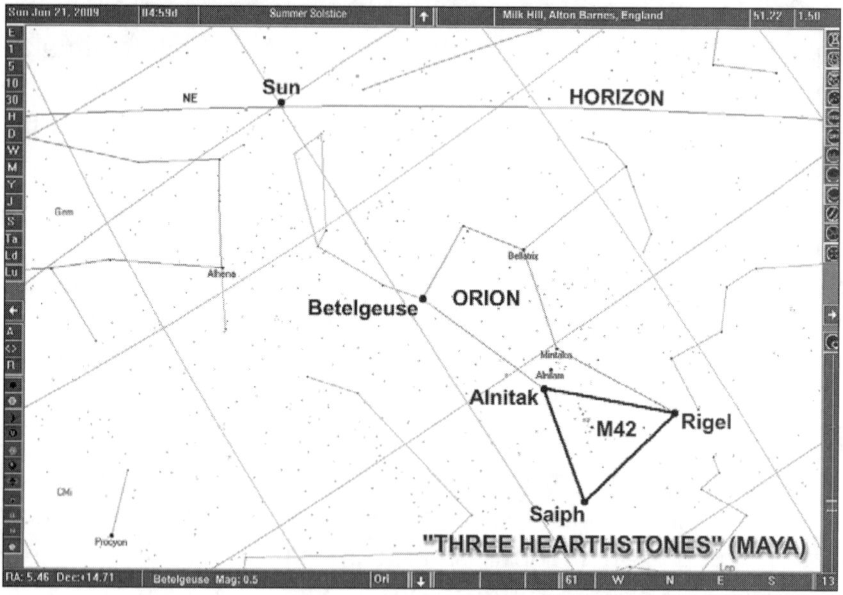

Sunrise on the summer solstice at Milk Hill near Alton Barnes, England. Orion is below the horizon (i.e., in the underworld), with Betelgeuse at -13°. Orion's right arm appears as if it is lifting the Sun above the horizon. The constellation will not be seen for about another six weeks at this latitude, when it achieves its heliacal rising. (The heliacal rising of a star occurs when it first becomes visible above the eastern horizon at dawn, after a period when it was hidden below the horizon or when it was just above the horizon but hidden by the brightness of the Sun.)

By the next day, however, the crop formation had morphed, increasing considerably in complexity. One arm of the compass pointed north toward the White Horse of Alton Barnes. Unlike some of the prehistoric chalk horses found in England, this one made in the late 18th or early 19th century.[38] Nonetheless, those with a biblical mindset might immediately leap to the First Horseman of the Apocalypse, who rides a white horse, wears a crown, carries a bow, and is hellbent for conquest. (Revelation 6:1-2). It is mere fancy, then, that the compass-arms can also be construed as a tightly drawn bow ready to let it arrow fly toward the solstice sunrise? After the white horse, we know that a red horse comes, whose rider carries a greatsword while a terrible orgy of slaughter engulfs the Earth.

I previously discussed the Mayan Maize God's emergence from a crack in the Cosmic Turtle's shell (namely, Orion) as a symbol of the transition between the current age (Fourth Sun) and the forthcoming age (Fifth Sun). The Maya powerfully depicted this mythic event. (Again, see painting on the bottom of p. 141.)

The Maize God known as One Hunahpu, or First Father, is reaching his right hand toward that of his elder son named Hunahpu (left), while his younger son named Xbalanque (right) seems to be pouring water from a pottery vessel. These twin brothers were conceived in Xibalba (the underworld) when the severed head of First Father, which hung like fruit on a calabash tree, miraculously spat into the palm of Xquic (Blood Maiden).

Hunahpu's corpse-like, black spotted skin signifies his dealings there in the netherworld. In other depictions he is frequently portrayed with three dots on his cheek arranged in a triangular pattern, perhaps signifying the Turtle/Orion pattern previously mentioned.[39] Xbalanque has jaguar patches on his arms and non-Mayan whiskers on his chin. After many perilous adventures described in the *Popol Vuh,* the twins were changed into two channel catfish. Finally, they assumed their celestial dimension when Hunahpu was transformed into the Sun and Xbalanque into the Moon.[40]

The Maya defined a 'world' as both an era and what they call *cahuleu*, or "sky-earth"—a combination of celestial and terrestrial.[41] The Turtle shell (Orion) is located at the center of Creation, sometimes conveyed in other artwork of the same event by the World Tree, or *axis mundi*. The flaming skull at the base of the shell is called *K'an-Tok-Kimi,* or "Precious-Torch-Death."[42] The Maize God is struggling to push himself upward through the crack between worlds so that he can initiate the new era.

In the painting, his headdress with a round oval shape on top and five macaw feathers trailing off to the right is particularly interesting. If we look at the new crop formation in the U.K. from a certain perspective (specifically, flipped horizontally and rotated counterclockwise 90°—see upper graphic, p. 144), we find all the elements of the Mayan painting. It's as if we have a modern schematic of the ancient Mayan mythical scene.

We recall that the Hopi prophecy includes the Mystery Egg, where the Earth at the final stage of the Fourth World undergoes a Great Purification with the aid of three elements: the Sun, a swastika, and a red agent (perhaps Betelgeuse). In the Mayan rendition of the scene, a flaming, red skull sits at the base of the "sky-earth," or *axis mundi*. Note the twins Hunahpu and Xbalanque on either side of the back of the Turtle (Orion)/World Tree.

As mentioned in Chapter 3, the Mayan twins also have their counterpart in Hopi cosmology. As key figures at the creation of the First World, these warrior twins are called Pöqanghoya, who is the elder god of solidity and earth, and Palöngawhoya, who is the younger god of sound and air. The former controls the giant serpent at the North Pole, while the latter controls the giant serpent at the South Pole. They also oversee the vibratory centers of the earth, such as the vortex points. Their primary responsibility, however, is to make sure the planet is rotating properly on its axis.

Another crop circle appeared at East Kennett, near Avebury, Wiltshire on the same day, the summer solstice. This dual yin/yang formation possibly reflects the duality of the twins, and the vortex spinning into space above each of the Earth's poles.[43] (See quote about Hopi cosmology on p. 64.)

Crop formations that encode "red" just keep on coming. On June 24th, 2009, a magic mushroom crop circle presented itself at Rough Hill, near Winterbourne Bassett, Wiltshire. The mushroom's pileus (cap) had nine circles, each containing a crescent.[44] The stipe (stem) had three circles, each containing a large crescent. Three spores were located on each side of the stipe. The curve of the pileus echoed the curve of the Alton Barnes Mystery Egg, just as the Mystery Egg's three small circles arranged in a triangle echoed a similar pattern on the crown of the phoenix crop formation.

It is very possible that the mushroom depicted in the Wiltshire field is actually *Amanita muscaria*, or fly agaric. Significantly, this psychotropic mushroom has a brilliant red cap with white spots.

The sacred Soma of the Hindu *Rigveda* may actually refer to this fungus. Because of its hallucinogenic properties, it can be classified as an entheogen. It has been used in a divinatory and shamanic context for millennia from Siberia down into Central America, but it was also known in the Mediterranean as one of the substances ingested at the Eleusinian Mysteries.[45]

The Aztecs called this mushroom *Teonanacatl*, or "flesh of the gods." (Recall that Mesoamericans considered the dough made from maize as the "flesh of the people"—both red.) Although the Maya may have employed an additional genus of psychoactive mushroom (*Psilocybe*), their reverence for both fungi's visionary properties is shown by the carved mushroom stones or mushroom pottery effigies. For instance, a cache of nine phallic mushroom stones dating to about 750 BC was found in the tomb of an elite ruler in Guatemala. (See bottom of p. 148.) Author John Major Jenkins suggests that this represents the Nine Lords of the Underworld.[46] (Thus, the significance of the nine circles on the magic mushroom crop formation. Also, see Chapter 17.)

Another mushroom stone (p. 148) found in El Salvador comes from the Classic Maya period (300-600 AD). Note the nine rays around the figure's face.[47]

Finally, a reputed copy of the whole Fire Clan Tablet (seen above) has been circulating on the Internet. It is in the possession of Grandfather Martin Gashweseoma, the oldest living spiritual leader (*mongwi*) of the Hopi. This tablet differs from the version published in Frank Water's classic *Book of the Hopi*.

[continued on p. 149]

We can readily see why the ancient Maya conceptualized Orion as a turtle shell. The three hexagonal scutes (plates) in the middle of the carapace correspond to the belt stars. 10 scutes surround these central plates and total 13—one of two sacred numbers in the Mayan calendar. The morphology of the shell with its tapered end (right) is similar to what I have called the Mystery Egg. (See top of p. 144).

Magic mushrooms (*Amanita muscaria*), photo courtesy of Onderwijsgek.

Anthropomorphic mushroom stone with nine rays, El Salvador.

Mayan mushroom stones (only seven of the nine shown), Guatemala.

Unfortunately, Waters never actually saw this particular tablet but relied on the description of his Hopi informant. In Waters version, the lower left-hand corner has been broken off; here we see what looks like two fish whose mouths are each connected to a serpentine line that crosses the other. The upper "fish" also looks somewhat like the summer solstice Mystery Egg. These two fish might also be a reference to the Mayan Hero Twins in their catfish form.

Also, in the Waters' version the lower right-hand corner is blank, whereas this version has a nine-pointed star surrounding, surprisingly, the classic Eye of the Pyramid as seen on the dollar bill, which in turn encloses a Christian cross, and what looks like (though probably is not) the numeral 7 rising from an undetermined horizontal shape, perhaps human. This image may or may not be a true representation of the original Hopi Fire Clan Tablet.

In 1963, Grandfather David Monongye, the late spiritual elder of Hotevilla, Arizona, saw a nine-pointed star rising in the sky as a signal of the imminent return of Pahana. Numerology states that 9 is essentially the number of universality, perfection, and the completion of a life cycle, either human or stellar.[48] Does the stone tablet represent the star Betelgeuse going supernova?

[continued on p. 151]

Nine-pointed star, or enneagram, by Athanasius Kircher (1601-1680), *Arithmologica*. The polygon contains the all-seeing Eye of Divine Reason inside the pyramid, similar to shape at the lower right-hand corner of the Hopi Fire Clan Tablet. The wingèd sphere encloses the celestial concentric spheres of the then-known planets. The angel on the right holds a 3X3 "magic square." Ancient Chinese literature describes the great king Yu, who during a great flood tried to channel the waters out to sea. Up from the ocean emerged a turtle with a three-by-three grid pattern that used dots for the numbers on its shell. The sum of the numbers for each row, column, and diagonal equaled 15. The 16th century occult philosopher Heinrich Cornelius Agrippa claimed that this particular magic square was associated with the planet Saturn.

The Navajo (Diné), whose reservation surrounds that of the Hopi, say that at the Time of the End, a nine-pointed star will rise from the East and unite all the races and nations in love and beauty.[49] We recall that the painting (shown on p. 139) of Quetzalcoatl, the Aztec god who had promised to return at the end of the cycle, has nine feathers on his headdress.

The Nine-pointed star is also the symbol of the Baha'i religion, and represents the fusion of the nine major world religions (shown above in clockwise order): Baha'i, Islam, Christianity, Judaism, Jainism, Shinto, Sikhism, Hinduism, and Buddhism.

We are not surprised, then, that a day after the June 24th mushroom crop circle appeared, another formation with nine parts materialized. (See next page.) The larger circle/thin crescent on the left encloses a stagnant pond, followed by nine smaller circles trailing behind that are linked by nine tiny circles in between each. The sandy area around the pond resembles the Mystery Egg of summer solstice crop formation. The present creation is as if some sort of biological creature is pulling a train of circles behind it through either wind or water.

Or perhaps this red energy is even now racing toward us through space as the light and charged particles from Supernova

Betelgeuse that will arrive on December 21, 2012.

Doomsday or New Day? End Times or New Beginning? Death or rebirth? It all depends on your particular character, mindset, and personal life path. One thing is certain though: *Tempus omnia vincit* ("Time conquers all")—at least on the physical plane.

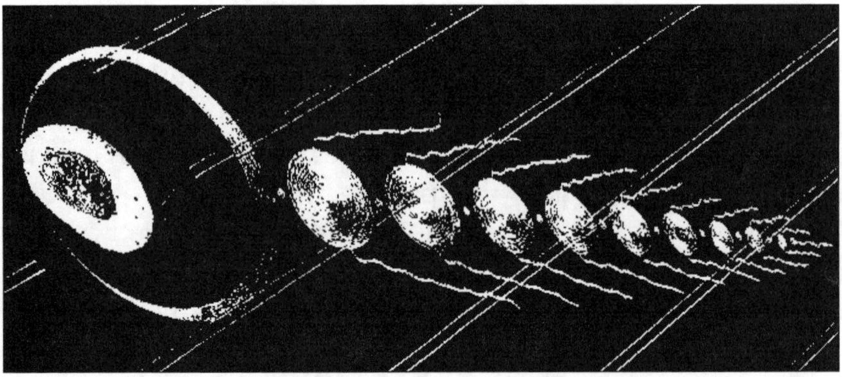

June 25, 2009, Martinsell Hill, near Wootton Rivers, Wiltshire.

Chapter 9
The Wormwood Star

Alpha Orionis to Omega Terra

> "And the third angel sounded, and there fell a great star from heaven, burning as it were a lamp, and it fell upon the third part of the rivers, and upon the fountains of waters; And the name of the star is called Wormwood: and the third part of the waters became wormwood; and many men died of the waters, because they were made bitter." (Revelation 8:10-11)

This famous passage from the Bible identifies Wormwood as a large star that will fall upon the earth in the End Times, poisoning the waters. During the course of this chapter I will explore the possibility that this stellar body may refer to Betelgeuse (Alpha Orionis), the right shoulder of Orion discussed in the previous chapter. In this chapter I will cite examples of its importance in primarily the Mayan, Hopi, Hebrew, Egyptian, Hindu, and Tibetan cultures.

Wormwood is mentioned many times in the scriptures, usually in the context of bitterness, and is frequently linked with gall. This metaphorical meaning refers to the plant *Artemisia absinthium*, the leaves of which are particularly bitter. Thus, wormwood (lower case) signifies bitter sorrow and calamity.

The Hebrew word for wormwood is *la'anah*, which literally means "curse."[1] The Akkadian word *Uri-anna*, or "Light of Heaven," refers, significantly perhaps, to Orion.[2]

Another biblical reference to wormwood includes a reference to Orion in the same sentence. "Ye who turn judgment to wormwood, and leave off righteousness in the earth, Seek him that maketh the seven stars and Orion, and turneth the shadow of death into the morning, and maketh the day dark with night: that calleth for the waters of the sea, and poureth them out upon the face of the earth: The LORD is his name:" (Amos 5:7-8)

In this warning to idolaters, the "seven stars" may be a reference to the northern constellation of Ursa Major, whereas Orion is a southern constellation. Note as well the further reference to waters, a possible flood, and the turning of day into darkness and vice versa.

Another verse continues the motif of Yahweh's admonition to sinners who seek false idols, adding the threat of exile and ultimate annihilation. Note again the reference to non-potable water.

> "And The Lord saith, Because they have forsaken My Law which I set before them, and have not obeyed My Voice, neither walked therein; But have walked after the imagination of their own heart, and after Baalim, which their fathers taught them: Therefore thus saith The Lord of hosts, the God of Israel; Behold, I will feed them, even this people, with wormwood, and give them water of gall to drink. I will scatter them also among the heathen, whom neither they nor their fathers have known: and I will send a sword after them, till I have consumed them." (Jeremiah 9:13-16)

The term *Baalim*, referring to biblical "false gods," is the plural of *Ba'al*, which was the Phoenician god of the rain, thunder, fertility, and agriculture. The name literally means "master" or "lord." Ba'al was also the Canaanite storm god.[3]

In his excellent essay "The God With the Upraised Arm," author Greg Taylor makes the case for the specific physical stance of Orion as being exemplified in artifacts and monuments from Egypt through the Fertile Crescent to Anatolia.[4] The classic pose that we associate with the constellation –upraised weapon in right hand, left foot forward, left arm extended, etc.– was apparently known throughout the Old World (and, as noted in the previous chapter, in the New World as well).

[continued p. 156]

Orion in bronze armor with cudgel and sword. The river Eridanus is at his left foot.

Ba'al stele from Ugarit (Ras Shamra, Syria). 142 cm. high, c. 18th–15th century BC, Louvre.

He raises a club in his right hand and holds a sprouting spear in his left hand instead of a shield or lion's skin like that of Orion. A sword is attached to his belt. Note the waves beneath his feet.

His Holiness the 16th Karmapa bestowing an empowerment. (See p. 159.) His Tibetan hat resembles the headgear on the Ba'al stele.

In the three biblical passages cited above, we see three consistent themes: [1] wormwood (a star or a plant), [2] water (on earth as polluted or in the sky as rain), and [3] the constellation Orion (or its deific variations, such as Ba'al).

As previously mentioned, the right shoulder of Orion is Betelgeuse, which astrophysicists have recently determined may soon turn into a supernova.[5] The Arabic term for the star is *yad al-jawza*, which means either "hand of the central one" or "armpit of the central one"—namely, Orion. Another Arabic term is *Bait al-Jauza*, or "house of the central one."[6]

Astrologer Alan Oken refers to "strong-armed Betelgeuse," which was the primary star in Babylonian constellation *Ungal*, or "the King"[7] This indicates the regal or imperial nature of Orion. The Persian name for Betelgeuse is *Bašn*, or simply "the Arm." The Hindi term for this star, *Bahu*, also means "arm." "In Punjabi, Hindi and Sanskrit languages, the meanings of Bahu are: Arm, Strength, The one who has [the] right. It also contains the meanings of: One who helps and gives support. In Persian language, the meanings of Bahu are: The one who remains with God."[8]

The Sanskrit term *Bahu* denotes "arm" too, but it has a few alternate denotations: "many, abundant, numerous" and also "mighty, large, great." It can additionally refer to the "post of a door" or the "bar of a chariot-pole."[9]

Hindu astrology identifies Betelgeuse as located in the *nakshatra* (lunar mansion) of *Ardra*, literally meaning "moist one," with its presiding deity being Rudra, the red storm god. Its symbol is a teardrop or a human head.[10] Here we see another of our criteria, water.

The particular notion of defiled water can be found in the very name Orion. "It is named 'Orion' from urine (*urina*), that is, from a flood of waters, for it rises in the winter season, and troubles the sea and the land with waters and storms."[11]

As we have seen, many of the terms from diverse cultures referring to the stalwart star Betelgeuse begin with the prefix *ba-*: *Bait al-Jauz, Bašn, Bahu*. It is therefore interesting to see the number of relevant terms in the Mayan language.

Ba-ba-ba, Ba-ba-barann

- *batab* – "chief, leader"
- *bal-kab-winik* – "man"
- *bateel* – "soldier"

These terms are completely consistent with the character of Orion as warrior, giant, and ruler.

On the other hand, a number of other Mayan terms containing *ba* are associated with water, especially in the form of thunderstorms.

- *tzabal-ha* – "to rain"
- *kil-ba* – "thunder"
- *lemba* – "lightning"
- *baab* – "to swim"

Other Mayan words point to a variation of the tool that Orion employs as well as the result of its usage.

- *baat* – "ax"
- *bah-ab* – "hammer"
- *bah* – "to nail"
- *bak* – "bone"
- *baq* – "meat"

The last term here, *baq,* alternately refers to the number 400. This reinforces the Sanskrit term *Bahu,* which means "numerous."

A few other Mayan *ba*-terms seem oddly appropriate in this context.

- *qaba* – "name"—a homonym of the Kaba, the black cube in Mecca, the most sacred site in Islam. (This geometric shape will be discussed in the next chapter.)
- *bal-kah* – "world," which is sometimes represented by a

square.

- *balam* – "tiger" or "puma"—more specifically, a jaguar.[12]

It is worth remembering that the ancient Egyptian word *ba* meant "soul." In addition, the name Ba referred to the Ram-god of virility.[13] Note the ram horns on the stele of Ba'al pictured on p. 155. *Bar* is the actual name the Egyptians used for the Phoenician god, who was sometimes identified with the Egyptian god Set.[14] Furthermore, Ba alternately designated the Leopard-god[15], which resonates with the Mayan term for feline, *balam*.

The Egyptian word *bah* referred to "phallus of a man or animal."[16] The word *bahu*, homonym of the Hindi/Sanskrit term for Betelgeuse, meant "men" or "people."[17] The word *baba* meant "drink" or "liquid"[18], while the word *båh* referred to both "flood, inundation" and "lion"[19]—the latter again being associated with the Mayan word *balam*.

The syllables *ba* and *pa* are very close linguistically and are sometimes interchangeable. Two Mayan *pa*-terms denote the male and highlights Orion's extreme masculinity.

- *pal* – "boy"
- *tepal* – "ruler"

The Mayan word *paak*, which means "square things, things with four edges," corresponds to the Arabic term *Bait*, or "house." The Mayan term *pakab* refers to "lintel."[20] This may obliquely correspond to the Sanskrit *Bahu* in its definition as "door-post."

In the ancient Egyptian lexicon, *pa* meant "to exist,"[21] while *pa* (long "a") meant "ancestor."[22] It also had the meaning of "flame, fire, spark"[23]—the scintillation of the star mentioned in Revelation, which will burn like a lamp. On the other hand, *pa-t* referred to "liquor, drink,"[24] which, depending on the potency, can also burn as it goes down the hatch.

Considering the Tibetan *pa*-words, we find that the term for "wormwood" is *khan-pa*.[25] The Red Hat sect of Tibetan Buddhism is headed by the Karmapa (*karma-pa*, as opposed to the Yellow Hat sect headed by the Dalai Lama).[26] In 1974 the 16th Karmapa, Rangjung Rigpei Dorje (1924-1981), visited the United States, including the Hopi Nation in Arizona, where he performed a number of sacred rituals.[27] (See his photo on p. 155.)

He was fulfilling an 8th century prophecy given by Padmasambhava, founder of Tibetan Buddhism. (Note the first syllable of his name.) "When the iron bird flies [airplanes] and the horse runs on wheels [cars], the Tibetan people will be scattered like [red?] ants across the face of the Earth, and the Dharma [doctrines and teachings of Buddhism] will come to the land of the red men." We don't need to be reminded of the repression and exile that the Tibetan people have suffered at the hands of the Communist Chinese since the 1950s. The phrase "red men," of course, refers to Native Americans.

The Hopi elder Grandfather Martin Gashweseoma recently adopted a Cherokee woman named Kymberlee Ruff into the tribe and assigned her the role of "Hopi/Tibetan Prophecy Carrier." She describes a Hopi prophecy, which is almost exactly the same as the Tibetan one. "'When the Iron Eagle Flies and the Horses Run on Wheels...' The Hopi Prophecy begins this way and goes on to describe in detail how people will come from the East wearing red robes with wisdom that will help in The Time of Purification."[28]

A few Hopi words are also relevant in our Betelgeuse/Wormwood connection. *Paakungya* is the term for wormwood (*Artemisia glauca* or *Artemisia dracunculoides*), literally meaning "water-mountain-sagebrush."[29] Mountain Sagebrush (*Artemisia frigida*) is frequently attached to a type of Hopi prayer stick called a *paho*.[30]

Pahu is the word for "water" (in nature). The prefix *pala-* means "red" (the hue of Betelgeuse), while the suffix *-pala* means "moisture" (a traditional attribute of that star). *Paalata* means both "shine a light" and "to make moist." Is it any wonder, then, that the Hopi syllable *pa,* in addition to meaning "water," also refers to "wonder, surprise"? [31] Furthermore, would we really be surprised to discover that the same Sanskrit syllable, *pa,* means not only "the act of drinking" but also "guarding, protecting, ruling"?[32] The color red, water, a shining light, wonder or awe, and kingship or leadership—these are all characteristics of Betelgeuse in Orion.

Sage or Sap?

In addition to *ba* and *pa,* the syllable *sa* can be added to the linguistic nexus of our discussion. The ancient Egyptian word *sam* referred specifically to the plant wormwood, which was used medicinally as a vermifuge (a medicine that expels intestinal worms).[33] However, the word *såm* meant "darkness" or "rainstorm,"[34] and *såms* meant "club, cudgel,"[35] an accouterment of Orion. In addition, the distinguished co-authors of the classic book *Hamlet's Mill,* Giorgio de Santillana and Hertha von Dechend, state with confidence that the biblical Samson (Sam-son) is an analogue of mythical Orion.[36] Both Samson and Orion, incidentally, had the misfortune of being blinded during their lifetimes.

Having the same prefix, the Egyptian word *Sahu* referred to the "star-gods in the constellation Orion"[37], while *sahu* meant an unspecified "plant"[38]—another term for wormwood, by any chance?

In Gnostic literature we find that the evil Demiurge named Ialdabaôth has a few alternate names that are relevant here. He is also known as either the first Archon Samael or Sacla—names that resonate with the Egyptian prefix *sa* just discussed. He is also identified with both the god Osiris (Orion) and the planet Saturn. (Sa-turn? In the following chapter, this planet will be discussed.) Furthermore, Ialdabaôth is also called Ariael, which literally means "lion of God"—reiterating the feline motif. In fact, he appears in a monstrous physical form with the body of a snake and the head of a lion—the latter, of course, being another attribute of Orion.[39]

Among the Hindu legends compiled in the *Rigveda,* the figure of Prajapati (Praja-*pa*-ti) is associated with Orion. "Prajapati, as represented by Orion, may also be naturally supposed to commence the year when the vernal equinox was in Orion [4000–2500 BC]. Rudra [the storm god mentioned above] killed Prajapati, and as I have shown before, Prajapati, *Samvatsara,* and *Yajna* were convertible terms. Rudra therefore killed Prajapati or Yajna at the beginning of the year; and Yajna also meant sacrifice."[40] Here we see one alternate name for Orion, *Samvatsara,* echoed by the Egyptian syllable *sam* or *såms*. The similar Sanskrit term *samsara* means either "the world of illusion" or the "cycle of rebirth." Prajapati was also god of the dead who lived in the mountains.

Rudra presides over *Ardra,* or Betelgeuse, the right shoulder of Orion. The fact that Rudra, the bowman, slays Prajapati (Orion, the hunter) demonstrates an element of self-sacrifice. What prompted the killing was that Prajapati, in the form of either a stag antelope or deer, desired his daughter Rohini, in the form of a doe (Aldebaran, in Taurus); his murder was thus the result of that incestuous impulse. Orion's belt stars represent the three-jointed arrow shot at him.

The Sanskrit meanings for the name Prajapati are varied: "lord of creatures; creator; supreme god above or among the Vedic deities; Time personified, the sun, fire; a king, prince." "Prajapati's world" is "situated between the sphere of Brahma and that of the Gandharvas."[41] The Sanskrit *praja* means both "people, offspring" and "wisdom."[42] The Sanskrit *pa,* as we have seen, means both "to drink" and "to protect." Most of these semantic variations could, in one way or another, refer to the constellation Orion.

Prajapati is also directly identified with the god Soma and his divine potion of the same name. Soma is the copper-colored god of the Moon, who rides through the sky, trailing a red pennant from his chariot that is drawn by either a pair of antelopes or ten white horses.[43] He had 27 wives—all sisters, which correspond to the 27 *nakshatras,* or lunar mansions. However, he began to lose interest in all of them except one, Rohini, whom we previously encountered. Their father, King Daksha, decided to kill him due to his spousal neglect, but his wives interceded in order to allow him to wither and then be reborn every 28 days—just like the waning and waxing of the Moon.

The libation *soma* is known as the elixir of the gods. Bestowing immortality and supreme power, this divine nectar is made by pressing the stalks of a certain plant between a pair of millstones in order to squeeze out their juice. Opinions vary as to what the actual species is. Some believe it was cannabis or ephedra, while others claim that it was certain psychoactive mushrooms such as *Amanita muscaria* (see p. 148) or *Psilocybe cubensis*.[44]

The terrestrial aspect of *soma* by other accounts is considered to be a plant with golden flowers—perhaps even wormwood, a species commonly found in the mountainous regions of Kashmir and Tibet, just the sort of place Prajapati inhabited. Scholar R. C. Zaehner remarks on the legendary properties of *soma*.

> "From the texts it appears that the plant was of a yellowish colour and that it was to be found in the mountains : from its juice an intoxicating liquid was prepared which was believed to give strength and long life to gods and men : it was the drink of immortality. In the hymns to Soma the pressing of sacred juice through a woollen filter into a vat containing milk and water is likened to all manner of celestial phenomena with which it would appear to have nothing to do."[45]

The last sentence of this quote can only be true if we forget the hermetic dictum: "As above, so below."

A majority of the hymns from Book Nine (also called, incidentally, Mandala Nine) of the *Rigveda* is devoted to Soma Pavamana (Pa-vamana, "purified Soma").

> "In the stream's wave wise Soma dwells, distilling
> rapture, in his seat,
> Resting upon a wild cow's hide.
> Far sighted Soma, Sage and Seer, is worshipped
> in the central point
> Of heaven, the straining-cloth of wool.
> In close embraces Indu [the Moon?] holds Soma
> when poured within the jars,
> And on the purifying sieve."[46]

If Prajapati is another version of Orion, which according to Hindu astrology is located at the most auspicious portion of the heaven, then it also makes sense that Soma would reside at the navel of the sky. The woolen cloth through which the liquid is purified may be symbolic of clouds. Some claim that the celestial aspect of *soma* is the "seed (semen) of Prajapati," which formed a giant lake we know as the Milky Way.

According to the *Puranas,* Soma was born from what was called the "Churning of the Milky Ocean," or *Samudra manthan.* (NB: Here we find another *sam* word, like those discussed on the top pf p. 160. In this case, *samudra* refers to both a geographic and an atmospheric ocean. It is also interesting to note that the term "semen" is etymologically related to the O.H.G. *samo.*[47])

Although this legend is too complex to describe here in depth, the king of serpents named Vasuki served as a churning rope that was wrapped around a churning dasher, or vertical pivot (*axis mundi*), which was in fact Mount Mandara (Mt. Meru?). The gods grabbed the snake's tail while the demons grabbed his head, and they alternately pulled, thereby producing the celestial nectar in much the same manner that earthly *soma* was produced.[48]

However, the mountain soon began to sink into the sea, causing a deluge. To remedy this, the mountain had to be placed on the back of the turtle or tortoise named Kurma (a variation of *karma*), whose name refers to "the earth considered as a tortoise swimming on the waters."[49] This reptile is especially significant due to fact that the Maya considered the turtle/tortoise as a celestial representation of Orion.[50] (See discussions of the Pueblo People's Turtle Dance in Chapter 2 and of the Cosmic Turtle in Chapter 8.)

In addition, the ancient Egyptian word *Abesh* referred to "one of the seven stars of Orion" (which one, we are not sure), as well as to "a benevolent serpent-god." On the other hand, Apesh was the name of the Turtle-god.[51] Hence, we find three elements of the Hindu scenario –Orion, turtle, and serpent– in these two linguistically similar Egyptian terms.

In the process of producing the sacred *soma* by churning the sea, the serpent –due to all the tugging on his body– spewed forth poison upon the waves, which was consumed by the Hindu god Siva and thus rendered harmless. Again we find the theme of poisoned waters.

[continued on p. 165]

Yellow-flowered wormwood (*Artemisia absinthium*)

Bas-relief depicting the Churning of the Milky Ocean, Angkor Wat, Cambodia. Vishnu the Preserver (center) is seen similar to his central place in the Hindu Trinity. As Vishnu's incarnation, the turtle Kurma is at the bottom submerged in milky fluid. Asuras (gods, on the left) and devas (demons, on the right) pull upon the snake.

The Mythological Obsession with Precession

The co-authors of *Hamlet's Mill* are convinced that this myth from India joins a multitude of others from all over the globe to function as an allegory of the precession of the equinoxes.[52] If we reduce the concept to its most basic sense, the gradual shifting of the sunrise point of the vernal equinox backward through the constellations of the zodiac at the rate of one degree every 72 years causes the stars of the uranography, or "skyscape," to alter their positions basically once every 2,160 years—one-twelfth of the Great Year (25,920 years). This is universally depicted in various mythological systems as world cataclysms at the conclusion of each Age or Era—for instance, the transition from the Age of Pisces to the Age of Aquarius. (Some predict mass destruction in 2012, for instance. See Chapter 17.)

The wheeling heavens are conceptualized as a colossal mill, revolving around the Pole Star. In his book *Heaven's Mirror*, Graham Hancock describes the inexorable grinding of this cosmic mill of time: "The prime image used by these as yet unidentified archaic astronomers 'transforms the luminous dome of the celestial sphere into a vast and intricate piece of machinery. And like a millwheel, like a churn, like a whirlpool, like a quern, this machine turns and turns endlessly'."[53]

Long ago this celestial mill had ground out gold, then in the next age it produced salt, but now it only grinds sand and stones. "That things are not as they used to be, that the world is obviously going from bad to worse, seems to have been an established idea through the ages. The unhinging of the Mill is caused by the shifting of the world axis. Motion is the medium by which the wrecking is brought about."[54] When this mill is finally wrecked, it is cast into the sea, where it keeps spinning uselessly as a massive whirlpool. Only after a new Pole Star is chosen as the fiducial axis can the mill begin to function properly again.

One example that Santillana and von Dechend provide to make their case comes from the national epic of Finland called the *Kalevala*. In this tale, the mill is named Sampo (Sam-po), which rested inside a Mount of Copper. (In regard to this metal, see the following chapter.) In the context of either churning or grinding, the syllable *sam* seems to recur—this time derived from the Sanskrit *skambha,* which means "pillar" and "pole"[55] but also "prop" and "Fulcrum of the Universe."[56]

The *Rigveda* uses that exact term to refer to the god Soma.

"The lake is brightened in the floods.
Soma, our Friend, heaven's prop and stay,
Falls on the purifying cloth."[57]

Like the Egyptian phoenix that cyclically rises from the ashes of the past epoch, the world must be reborn after each of these "End Times." The *Egyptian Book of the Dead,* Chapter 83, contains a "Spell for becoming the Benu Bird [that is, the phoenix]." In it *ba* (the soul) proclaims:

"I flew up as the Primeval God and assumed forms—
I grew in the seed and disguised myself as the Tortoise,
I am the seed corn of every god,
I am yesterday . . .
I am Horus, the god who gives light by means of his body . . .
I come as day, I appear in the steps of the gods,
I am Khons (the moon) who proceeds
through the universe."[58]

This resonates with the Prajapati (Orion) *cum* Soma (Moon god) *cum* Turtle (cosmic tortoise) complex of Hindu mythology. For instance, in the *Rigveda,* Prajapati is referred to as a "Golden Seed" (*Hiranyagarbha*) or "Mystery Egg"[59]—the latter reminiscent of not only the Primal Egg of ancient Egyptian cosmogony but also, as I mentioned in the previous chapter, an icon of Hopi prophecy regarding the End Times. As a personified universal germ, Prajapati is accompanied by a fiery seed (Agni) that vivifies the primeval waters and allows for the creation of all material forms. The concomitant heat may be the result of the friction caused by the revolving quern-stone.

If we consider both the terrestrial and celestial forms of *soma,* or "...in earth, as it is in heaven" (Matthew 6:10), problems might arise. In some cases what is ambrosia to the gods is poison to humans.

> "We must remember that Soma as the nectar of the Gods can be poison to mortals. Mortals who are not prepared can be killed by drinking Soma, which is a force that the ordinary human nervous system cannot handle, like the awakening of the Kundalini that requires a high power of awareness to endure. Therefore, the Soma-poison opposition reflects a meaning everywhere in the Milky Way which as the milk of heaven is a drink that mortals are barred from taking, unless they develop special divine qualities within themselves."[60]

In beginning of this chapter, I used the biblical Wormwood as a starting point in order to discuss how the syllables *ba* and *pa* correspond in many cultures across the globe to either Betelgeuse in particular or Orion in general. I also noted that the syllable *sa* is associated with Orion. In addition, I talked about the constellation's connection to both the potentially destructive capacity of water and the possibly tainted aspect of the liquid. The feline concept also seemed to recur in the context of Orion. The bitter quality of wormwood was a further dimension of a complex semantic constellation of concepts, as I considered its relationship to the Hindu god Prajapati (Orion) and the nectar *soma*. In the next chapter, I would like to explore the relationship between Betelgeuse and a particular metal. . . copper.

Chapter 10
Orion's Copper Connection

Pennies From Heaven

Although Arizona's gold and silver mining has historically gotten all the glory, copper mining has been the more enduring and trustworthy industry. It was **Cu**, not **Au** or **Ag**, that forged the destiny of the state. Unfortunately, it has also left scars, in the form of huge, open-pit strip mines.

At the center of the Arizona state flag is a five-pointed (i.e., Egyptian-style) copper star. The lower half of the flag is midnight blue, while the upper half is comprised of 13 rays: 6 yellow rays and 7 red rays, which suggest the seemingly endless sunset skies in the pristine air of the American Southwest.

I mentioned in the previous chapter that the Tibetan Karmapa came to the Hopi of Arizona in 1974 in order to fulfill a common prophecy. It not so surprising, then, that the flags of Tibet and Arizona are similar in form and color. The six rays of both red and blue on the Tibetan flag reflect the six yellow rays of the Arizona flag. (Red and yellow are also the colors of the robes of Tibetan monks.) The white pyramid on the Tibetan flag represents the Himalayas with the pair of snow lions facing the middle. The yin-yang symbol is rendered in copper. The central flaming jewels correspond to the three objectives of Buddhist refuge: Buddha, Dharma, and Sanga.[1] The triad, however, could just as well correspond to copper-colored Betelgeuse, white Alnilam (middle star of the belt), and blue Rigel (the left foot) of Orion.

[continued on p. 170]

State flag of Arizona.

Flag of Tibet.

The Hopi term for constellation is *Hotòmqam*, literally "beads on a string," which may refer not to his belt but rather to the three stars in Orion: Betelgeuse, Alnilam, and Rigel. This star pattern ranks as the most important in the Hopi ritual system.

I have previously written that the star Sirius in the constellation Canis Major was traditionally associated with copper.[2] However, both red Sirius (the Egyptian goddess Isis) and red Betelgeuse (right shoulder of the Egyptian god Osiris) are connected to the heretofore mentioned Hindu lunar mansion of *Ardra* [3], so it is likely that both stars are associated with copper.

Scientists have, in fact, recently determined that almost all of the copper on Earth originated from stars like Betelgeuse. "Most of the copper in pennies and pipes arose in supergiant stars like Rigel and Betelgeuse, say astronomers in Italy. The stars then exploded, casting the copper into space. The new finding means that gold, silver, and copper all owe their existence to massive stars."[4] Thus, red giant stars and the red metal are causally linked.

The crystal structure of copper is technically called a face-centered cubic[5], which recalls the Mayan word *paak*, or "square things."

Hexing Saturn

Astronomer, mathematician, and mystic Johannes Kepler (1571-1630) claimed that each of the Platonic solids corresponds to one of then-known planets as well as to one of the classical elements. To the cube, he assigned the planet Saturn and the element earth.[6]

Saturn is also variously known as Kronos (Chronos), Father Time, the Grim Reaper, and Lord of Karma. Sharing the first syllable of his name, he was furthermore associated with Satan, Lord of the Earth. Saturn was also deemed Lord of the Mill, as discussed in the previous chapter.

Although the planet is sometimes associated with lead, it is interesting to note that Saturn's orbital period averages 29.5 years. In the periodic table [7] the metal copper is, coincidentally (*not!*), number 29.

[continued on p. 172]

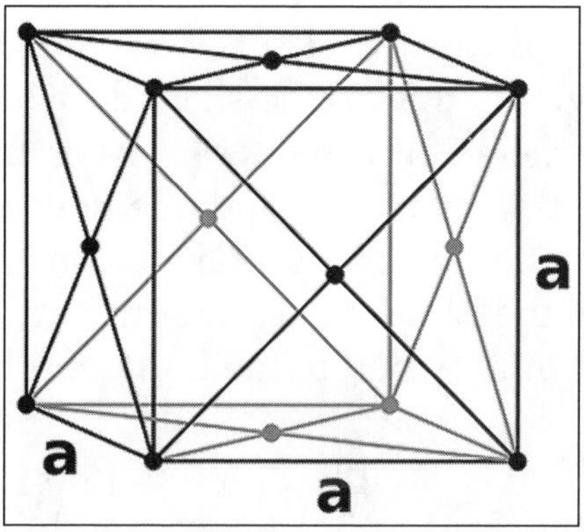

Left: face-centered cube: the crystal structure of copper.

Below: Platonic solids model of the solar system, from Kepler's *Mysterium Cosmographicum.*

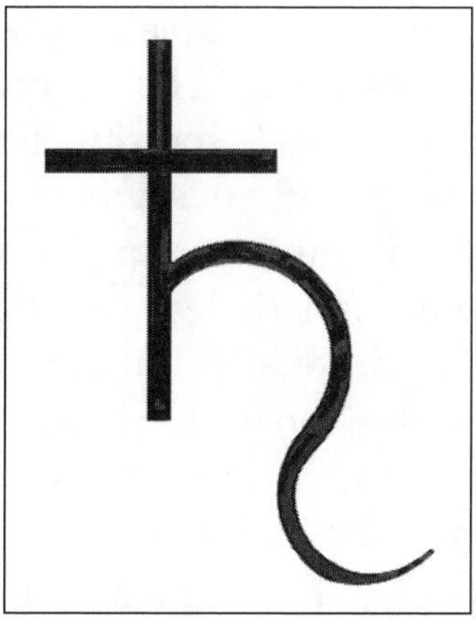

Astrological symbol of Saturn

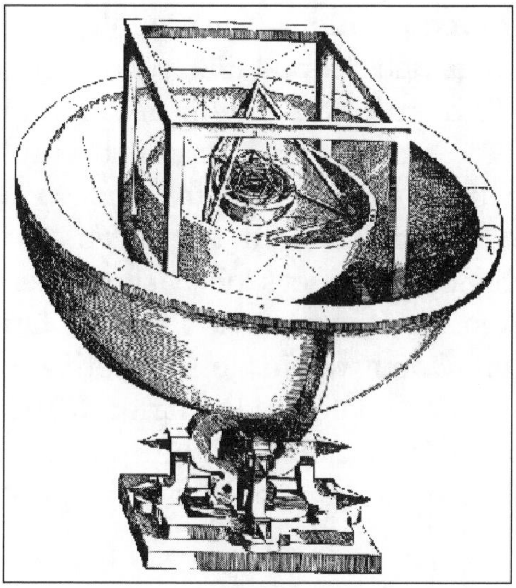

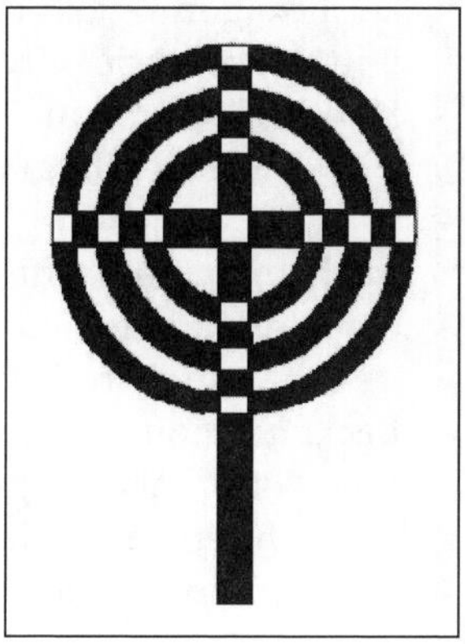

Left: seal of Atlantis, showing bridge and concentric rings of canals. *Orichalcum* (Greek, *orei-chalkos,* literally "mountain copper") was a copper-gold alloy that reputedly covered the walls of Atlantis.

The name Orion, or Oarion, may derive from the Greek word *oros,* "mountain." The English word "ore" comes from a conflation of numerous older words meaning brass, copper, bronze, or brazen.

Anthropologist Francis Huxley makes a direct correlation between Saturn and Orion. "He [Saturn] is also to be found in the constellation Orion, who wields that sickle-shaped sword called a falchion and which farmers call a billhook.... For the Egyptians Orion was associated with Horus and the soul of Osiris; in the Hindu Brahmanas he is seen as Prajapati in the form of a stag; several nations in the Middle East refer to him as the Giant, or the hunter Nimrod mighty before the Lord; and he was Saturnus to the Romans."[8]

The 19th century poet identified as simply T. S. (not Eliot, of course) evokes the presence of the Trojan hero Aeneas, with his curved falchion. "Meanwhile, Aeneas, shining / In martial trappings rich, / Stood like a god, reclining / In some temple's niche : / His mantle was the lion's, / In all its tawny bars, / His falchion, like Orion's, / Was gemmed with golden stars. / Upon his lofty helmet, / A brazen Terror rode ; / No sword could overwhelm it / When in the fight it glowed..."[9] Not the most moving verse (hence the poet's obscurity), these lines nonetheless associate Aeneas' weapon with that of Orion, additionally linking this renowned warrior to the motifs of both the lion and bronze.

Also related to the Grim Reaper, the sickle, when affixed to a cross (a variation of the square), is the astrological symbol for Saturn. (See the middle of the previous page.)

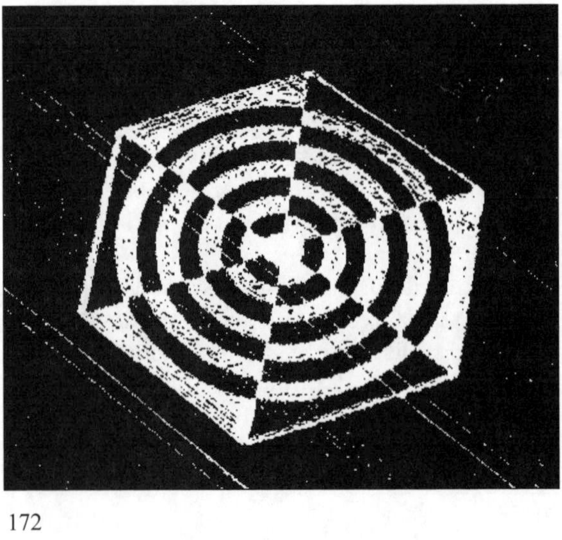

2D hexagon or 3D cube with concentric circles, Knoll Down, June 28, 2009, Wiltshire, England.

In the stunning series of crop formations of 2009, a cube appeared near Beckhampton, UK, on June 28th. This brings to mind the sphere within a cube of Kepler's model.

In addition, the three-dimensional cube can also be seen as a two-dimensional hexagon due to the fact that a cube is a six-sided polyhedron. It is interesting, then, that astronomers have recently discovered a counterclockwise rotating hexagonal wave pattern in the atmosphere above the northern pole of the planet… Saturn. This mysterious cloud-hexagon measuring 8,575 miles on each side is surrounded by a number of huge concentric circles.[10]

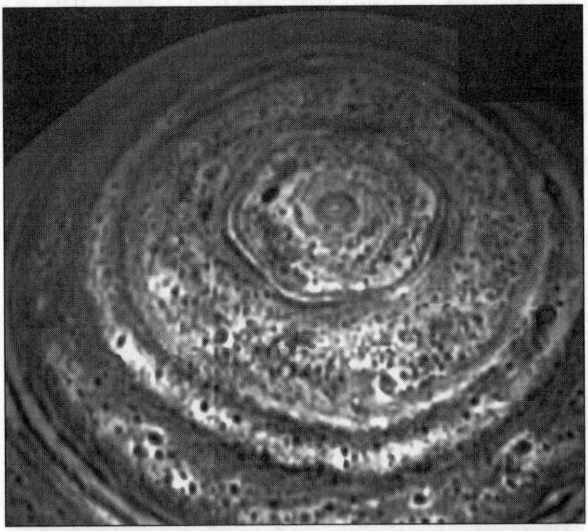

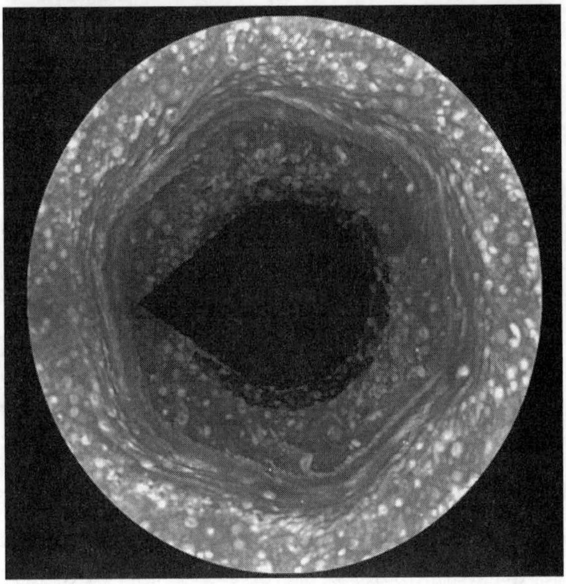

Above: Infrared image taken by NASA's Cassini spacecraft of a polar vortex cloud over Saturn. Below: Closeup of the hexagonal orifice 60 miles deep.

As mentioned in the previous chapter, Orion's name may derive from *urina,* or "urine." One version of Orion's birth involves the three Greek gods: Zeus, Hermes, and Poseidon. While traveling together on Earth, they were warmly greeted by Hyrieus, King of Boeotia, oldest city in Greece. This childless widower, however, desired to have a son. In gratitude the gods proceeded to urinate on the hide of a bull (Taurus?) –or in some versions the hide of either a heifer or an ox– and then buried it in the ground. Nine months later the newborn Orion emerged.[11]

In this context it interesting to note the morphology of copper ingots, which were traditionally formed like a animal skin.[12] The shape –also hexagonal– additionally reflects that of Orion.

The Greek trinity of gods previously mentioned may correspond to the Hindu Trimurti: Brahma, Vishnu, and Siva. Some Vedic scholars claim that Betelgeuse is the abode of the third deity, Siva (Shiva)—a later and less violent form of Rudra, referred to above. "Orion was supposed to come into being when Shiva assumed the form of a hunter and took out one of Brahman's heads with his arrow."[13] Given the Greek myth just cited, it is noteworthy that another aspect of Rudra is "Lord of Cattle." In addition, we recall from the *Rigveda* the passage cited on p. 162 that Soma was seen sitting on a wild cow's hide.

The Sanskrit word for "copper," *ambaka* –note middle syllable, *am-ba-ka*– is also called Siva's Eye—corresponding to his Third Eye, or pineal gland.[14] "In Siva temples, a pot made up of copper or brass, with a hole in the centre, is kept hanging over the image or Linga [phallus] of Siva, and water is falling on the image throughout day and night.... Lord Siva drank the poison that emanated from the ocean and wore the Ganga and moon on His head to cool His head. He has the fiery third eye."[15] This quaffing of toxic liquid took place during the Churning of the Milky Ocean, described in the previous chapter. Here we are back to the motif that began Chapter 9: a poisoned ocean. We also recall that the moon god Soma, who was born during this process, had copper-colored skin.

Incidentally, the Hopi word for copper is *sivapala* (*Siva-pala*), literally "metal-red." In addition, one of the ancient Egyptian terms for copper is *båa* [16]—another *pa / ba* variant discussed in the first part of Chapter 9.

[continued on p. 176]

Copper ingot from Crete.

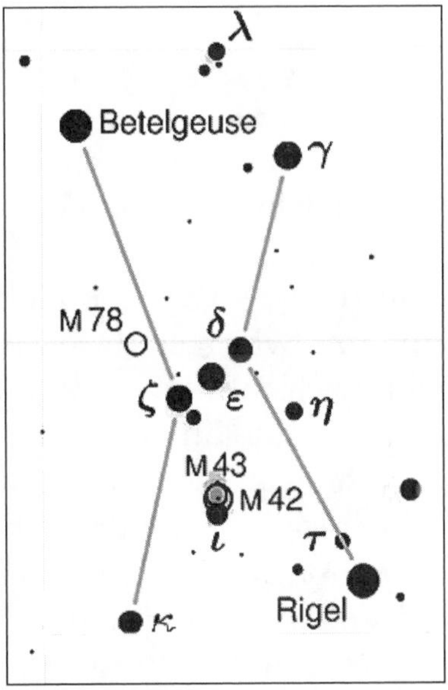

Orion constellation.

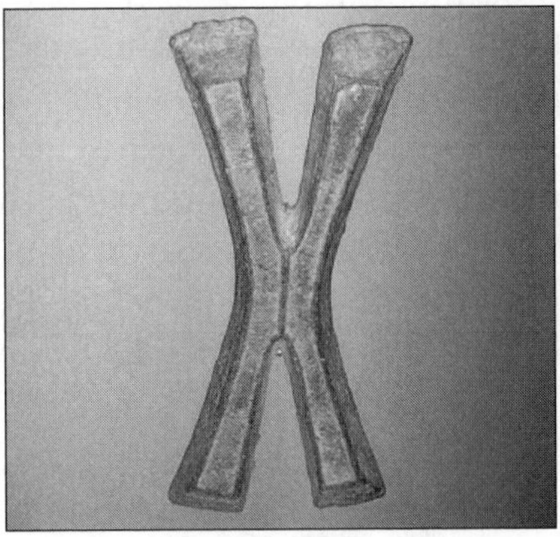

Orion-shaped copper ingot
from Zimbabwe,
National Museum, Bloemfontein,
South Africa.

A phallic Shiva Linga shrine, India. The copper-colored "eye" looks somewhat like the vortex at the North Pole of Saturn.

In Homer's epic *The Odyssey*, Odysseus witnesses the shades in the underworld:

> "...I was aware of gigantic Orion
> in the meadow of asphodel, rounding up and driving together
> wild animals he himself had killed in the lonely mountains,
> holding in his hands a brazen club, forever unbroken."[17]

In other words, the club that Orion holds in his upraised right arm, which starts at his shoulder (Betelgeuse), is made out of bronze, an alloy consisting of copper and tin or zinc. But another connotation of "brazen," of course, is boldly impudent, which the giant Orion certainly was.

We recall as well that the biblical giant Goliath had a helmet and armor made of brass.[18] In addition, the Book of Revelation describes the wrathful, fiery presence of the Redeemer: "And his feet like unto fine brass, as if they burned in a furnace; and his voice as the sound of many waters. And he had in his right hand seven stars [the seven churches? the seven stars of Orion?]: and out of his mouth went a sharp twoedged sword: and his countenance was as the sun shines in his strength."[19]

The Koran also describes the sky and earth on Judgment Day: "On that day the sky shall become like molten brass, and the mountains like tufts of wool scattered in the wind."[20] This parallels the Old Testament passage that conveys the consequences of disobedience to Yahweh: "And thy heaven that is over thy head shall be brass, and the earth that is under thee shall be iron."[21]

Regarding the 28th degree of Scottish Rite Freemasonry, the Masonic writer Albert Pike comments on what is called the "Brazen Sea," which refers to a laver (a large basin for ablution) located in the original Temple of Solomon. In this degree a series of "operations" strive to bring forth the alchemist's hermetic gold. The fourth operation deals with the "Cubical Stone," which is submitted to the "third Degree of Fire." This recalls the face-centered cubic crystal structure of copper and the planet Saturn as designated by Kepler. Then, the fifth and final operation incorporates the "Flaming Star."

> "In the Brazen Sea we are symbolically to purify ourselves from all pollutions, all faults and wrongful actions, as well as those committed through error of judgment and mistaken opinion, as those intentionally done; inasmuch as they equally prevent us from arriving at the knowledge of True Wisdom. We must thoroughly cleanse and purify our hearts to their inmost recesses, before we can of right contemplate that *Flaming Star*, which is the emblem of the Divine and Glorious Skekinah, or presence of God; before we may dare approach the Throne of Supreme Wisdom."[22]

At this point the process of spiritual purification of all earthly pollution is a familiar theme. Although the Masons sometimes refer to the "Blazing Star" as Sirius, in this case the "Flaming Star" may in fact refer to the cleansing aspect of Betelgeuse as it goes supernova—the possibility I discussed in Chapter 8.

In the context of alchemical *calcinato* (purification by burning)[23], it is interesting to note that the word "wormwood" (see previous chapter) comes from the Old English *wermod*, which literally means "man-courage."[24] Another connotation of "mettle" (homonym of "metal") is courage or fortitude—a requisite for the forthcoming global trial-by-fire. This word *wermod* is similar to the German *Wermut* and is related to the English "vermouth," an absinthe-flavored liquor.

The plant wormwood is used to make absinthe. Due to the green hue of the herb's chlorophyll, this dangerous alcoholic drink has been called the Green Goddess. Because the particular color is similar to the oxidized state of copper, disreputable manufacturers, especially in the 19th century, tried to fabricate the green coloration more cheaply by adding copper sulfate. "...symptoms of absinthism include; delirium, nausea, hallucinations and epileptic attacks. Many of these absinthism symptoms are identical to the symptoms for copper toxicity, and were possibly signs of poisoning from the various colorants used."[25] Again we see the apocalyptic motif of poisoned liquid.

The genus of wormwood is *Artemisia*, which refers to the venerable Greek goddess Artemis, the virgin huntress. She became a hunting companion of Orion, whom she eventually shot dead with an arrow –as one legend goes– for brazenly trying to violate her or, in another version, her attendant Oupus. (His death by an arrow seems a constant theme across different cultures.) In effect, Artemis (or *Artemisia,* wormwood) causes the demise of Orion on Earth, allowing for his resurrection as a constellation in the sky.

As we saw in Chapter 9, the syllables *ba* and *pa* are a universal currency that refers either specifically to Betelgeuse or generally to the bellicose character of Orion. Astrophysicists have recently speculated on the imminent possibility of a "Supernova Betelgeuse."[26] This copper-colored star, which along with other supergiants created the copper deposits on Earth, serves as the house of the Hindu Destroyer and Transformer, Siva/Rudra. Recalling one of the Arabic terms for Betelgeuse (namely, *Bait al-Jauza*), we might ask: Is this the "house" of the biblical star Wormwood?

Hopi Coppertone

According to author Frank Waters, the previous Hopi Third World (Era), which they call Kuskurza, has east or southeast as its symbolic direction, red as its color, and *copper* as its metal.[27] Due to human iniquity, sorcery, and both social and spiritual chaos, this age was destroyed by a flood of biblical proportions—the same sort that destroyed Atlantis. The Third World may correspond to the Greek notion of the Bronze Age, the third successive stage of humankind. The Hopi also conceptualize the Third World as being spatially located below the current Fourth World—our earth plane. In other words, the Third World is a subterranean underworld to which departed spirits journey after death.

Pahana (Pa-hana, also spelled Bahana) is the name for the Lost *White* Brother or Elder White Brother who will return at the end of the current age, much like the Mayan Kukulkan or the Aztec Quetzalcoatl. Most Hopi spiritual elders say that the conclusion of the Fourth World is imminent. Hopi prophecy predicts that at the end of this age, the Red Star Kachina –perhaps Supernova Betelgeuse– will act as the Great Purifier of Planet Earth.[28]

Wearing a red hat or red cloak (like the Tibetan Karmapa previously mentioned), Pahana meanwhile will arrive from the East to the homeland of the Hopi (Arizona) with two helpers, who among them carry a total of three symbols: the Native American swastika, the Sun, and a Red Symbol—the last one listed being the agent of purification. One Hopi spiritual elder, the late Grandfather Dan Evehema, enigmatically says that Pahana's population is great[29], which reinforces the Sanskrit definition of *Bahu* as "numerous."

The red-garbed Pahana (with all his *pa* and *ba* permutations), the Red Star Kachina, and the Red Symbol may be different manifestations of the same force. In any event, this crimson or copper-colored agent might trigger the harrowing process of spiritual cleansing that will ultimately allow transition to the new, pristine Fifth World.

One of the Arabic names for Betelgeuse is *Mirzam*, the Roarer or the Announcer[30]—the exact meaning of the name of the Hindu god Rudra, who rules over it. At the End of Days perhaps this star will roar like a lion to announce the passage from one age to the next. May the bitterness of Wormwood transubstantiate to the sweetness of "a new heaven and a new earth." (Revelation 21:1)

Hexing the Hopi

In this chapter I have discussed the hexagon as a form of the two-dimensional cube, as if the latter were viewed at an angle. (For instance, see the crop formation on p. 172.) I stated that the character of the constellation Orion has historically corresponded to both the Roman earth god Saturnus and the planet Saturn. Kepler claimed that this planetary body, located farthest from the Sun of the originally known planets, is associated with the six-faced cube.

On the other hand, Orion can be conceptualized as a variation of the hexagon: namely, a six-sided figure shaped like an hourglass—Chronos, the Bringer of Old Age. As lord of the world and temporal cycles, Saturn rules the domain of sensory perception and physical manifestation.

In an astrological sense, he is a no-nonsense guy who whacks us on top of the head when we are influenced by too much Neptunian dreaminess. "Pay attention!" he admonishes. "You have duties and responsibilities. Get with it!" He is a stern taskmaster, whose persona is basically melancholic, patriarchal, and unyielding. Dickens' character Scrooge must have had a major Saturnian aspect in his natal chart. Under his authoritarian eye, we must show patience and fortitude when thwarted by life's material blockages or limitations. Pragmatism, frugality, and clear-eyed reality are his positive hallmarks. Parsimony, bitterness, and blind cynicism are his downfall. He displays all the psychological traits of the chronic (*chronos* again?) skeptic.

Raising the negative aspect another notch, we recall from the TV program *Star Trek: The Next Generation* that the fictional Borg was a malevolent collective of cybernetic species that assimilated rather than conquered their victims and navigated the Delta Quadrant of the galaxy in millions of immense cubes. These synthetically supercharged drones produced sheer hormonal terror in anyone who had the misfortune to confront their impersonal "hive mind." Of course, beehives are also constructed of contiguous hexagons.

The Borg cube from *Star Trek* is the ultimate "hex symbol."

And as I previously stated, astronomers have more recently discovered that a revolving hexagonal cloud has remained stationary about Saturn's North Pole for over three decades. This perfectly geometric cloud, a complete anomaly in our solar system, has baffled scientists. If we looked downward at the pole, we would see this hexagonal vortex, which could fit nearly four Earths inside it, encircled by the wider rings of Saturn.

Both the 2D geometric form –the hexagon– and the Platonic solid –the cube– are apparently relevant to the Hopi culture in particular. Archaeologist Chris Hardaker has discovered that the hexagon is encoded in the landscape of the American Southwest at a very specific latitude: roughly between 35° and 36° North. He targeted his research by using as a primary example the ancient ceremonial city of Chaco Canyon, New Mexico, located at N 36° 30′. His theory is also valid, however, for the area I have designated as the Orion Zone. (See Google Earth screenshot on p. 106 and table below.)

Other Hopi Ruin or Village Sites in Arizona
Betatakin (Navajo National Monument) = 36° 41′(Terra Orion's left leg)
Shungopavi (Hopi Second Mesa) = N 35° 48′(Terra Orion's middle belt star)
Homol'ovi (near Winslow) = N 35° 01′ (Terra Orion's right shoulder)

At all of these latitudes the various azimuths for the four solstice sunrise and sunset points on the horizon form axes, whose angles when combined with the north-south axis make up a hexagon. Hardaker found that this geometric form is mirrored in the architecture of the great kivas as well as that of the smaller clan kivas.

> "After a review of geometric design types found in Chaco Canyon kivas, a rather remarkable coincidence between design and astronomy is discussed. Classical, or sacred, geometry can construct the perfect hexagon from the radius of a circle. A six-fold division is common among the smaller 'clan' kivas. The 60-degree central angle of the hexagon mirrors the 60-degree azimuth of the Winter and Summer Solstices in Chaco Canyon. The ramifications of these two facts play themselves out in the dynamic symmetry of the great kiva of Chetro Ketl."[31]

[continued on p. 183]

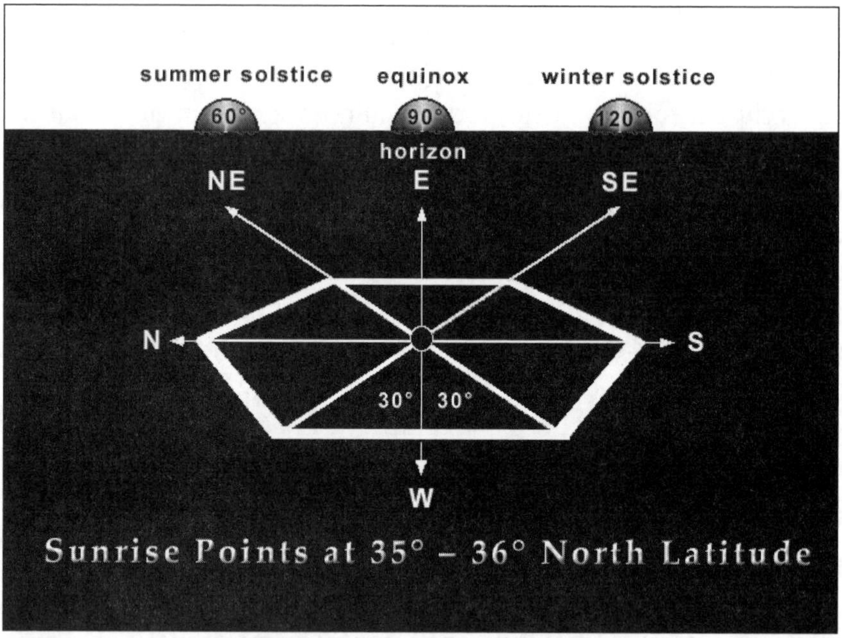

Both diagrams on this page adapted from drawings by Chris Hardaker.

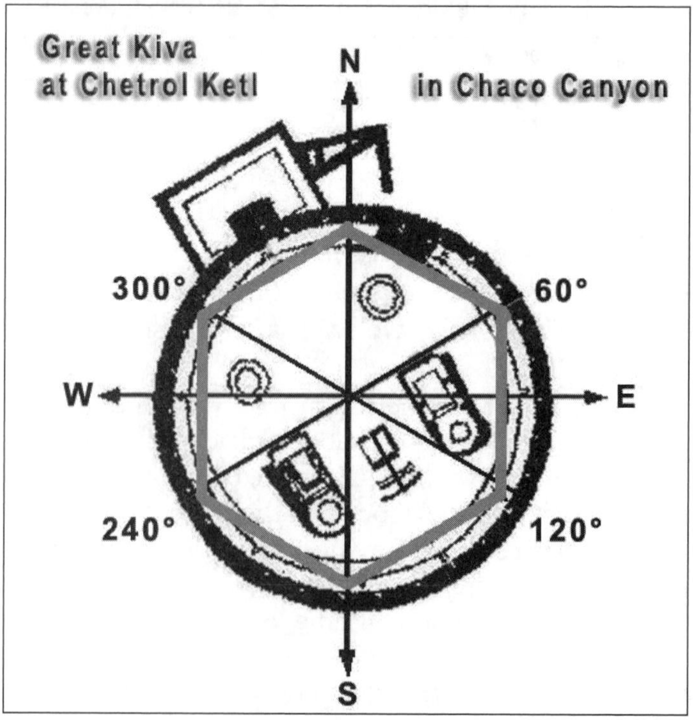

Overhead view of architectural features: solstice sunrise and sunset points.

In the case of clan kivas, the six evenly spaced pilasters used to support the roof form a hexagon. (See diagram on p. 17 and drawing on p. 75.) On the other hand, the interior vault and post holes used to support the massive roof structures of the great kivas form square relationships. In the pueblo of Chetro Ketl in particular, an axis made along the northern face of a pair of vaults constructs a summer solstice sunrise / winter solstice sunset line. This, when combined with a north-south axis, forms the ever-present hexagon.

Hardaker calls this "solstitial symmetry," as opposed to the bilateral symmetry of cardinal directions. The former is also seen, he says, in the great kiva more than 50 miles due north of Chaco Canyon at Aztec National Monument, located at 36° 50′ latitude—nearly the same as Betatakin Ruin in Arizona, which corresponds to the left leg of the terrestrial Orion.

In both examples –small clan kivas and great kivas– we see how ancestral Hopi architecture at a specific latitude reflects the astronomy of that latitude—specifically the solstice sunrise and sunset points on the horizon. Again, "as above, so below."

Cubing the Hex

In nature the hexagon is found snowflakes, quartz crystals, and honeycomb cells. Despite its name, the Western Diamondback Rattlesnake (*Crotelus atrox*) has also dark hexagonal blotches along it body. As we saw in Chapter 8, the plates on a turtle's shell are hexagonal as well. I previously stated that the Maya associated the turtle with Orion. In addition, Puebloans of the American Southwest once did and still do perform the Turtle Dance on the winter solstice when Orion is the most prominent constellation.

On the northeast coast of Northern Ireland the so-called Giant's Causeway was volcanically formed some 50 million years ago into thousands of interlocking hexagonal columns, the tallest being over 35 feet high. The legendary hunter-warrior Fionn mac Cumhaill (Finn McCool) supposedly built these steppingstones to Scotland in order to battle his Scottish counterpart Bennadonner. Fionn mac Cumhaill may correspond to Lugh, Cúchulainn, or even the sky giant Orion himself.[32]

The celestial manifestation of this geometric shape is called the Winter Hexagon. Except in the very southern portions of the southern hemisphere, it is visible not only in winter but in any season when the following constellations can be viewed: Canis Major, Canis Minor, Gemini, Auriga, and Taurus—all surrounding the figure of Orion. The polygon's six vertices are comprised of the following respective stars: Sirius, Procyon, Pollux, Capella, Aldebaran, and Rigel.

Connecting the alternate vertices of a hexagon will give you a hexagram—that is, a Star of David or Solomon's Seal (see facing page). In addition, an equilateral triangle (outlined in gray) is formed with Betelgeuse at the apex and Procyon and Sirius at the base .

The apex of one triangle resting on the horizon is Sirius, the brightest star in the heavens. It achieved its heliacal rising in the predawn hours of July 26th (New Years Day in the Mayan Calendar, by the way), 850 AD—about the time when major construction began at Chaco Canyon. The Hopi know this star in the Greater Dog as *Ponótsona,* literally "sucks from the belly," or mammal. This triangle's base formed by Pollux and Aldebaran is very near M1 (Crab Nebula), discussed in Chapter 7. The base of the other triangle making up the Star of David is formed by Procyon and Rigel, while its apex is Capella. The Greeks knew this star as Amaltheia, the she-goat who suckled Zeus. (In the sky chart, Jupiter just happens to be on the ecliptic near M1.)

Orion's club forms one corner of this sky cube. (Technically, it is a rhombohedron, or stretched cube.) In *The Orion Zone,* I made the case that Orion served as the celestial version of the Hopi god Masau'u, who rules the earth plane as well as the underworld and death. He also wields a short club called a *maawiki.* (See picture on p. 247.)

[continued on p. 186]

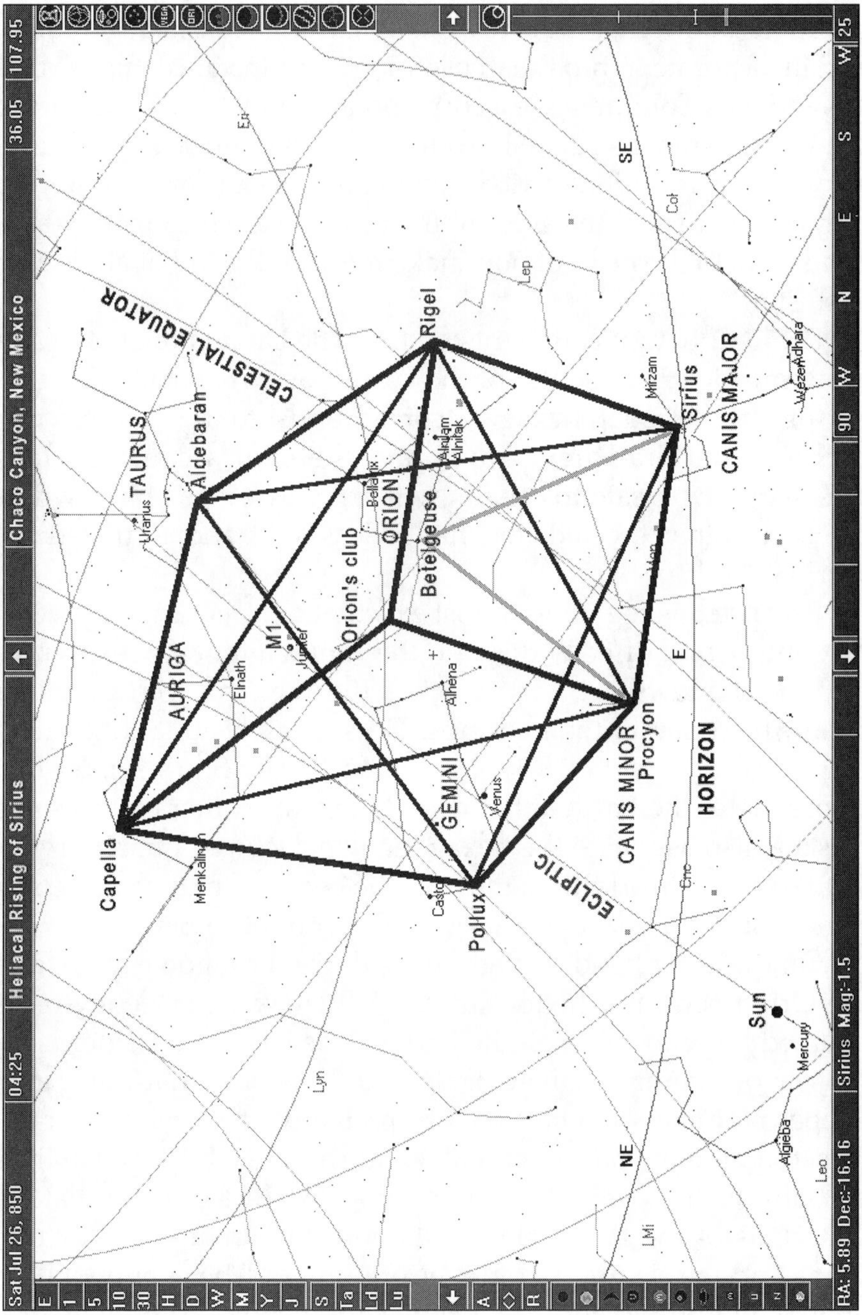
Sat Jul 26, 850
04:25
Heliacal Rising of Sirius
Chaco Canyon, New Mexico
36.05
107.95
CELESTIAL EQUATOR
TAURUS
Aldebaran
Uranus
Rigel
ORION
Orion's club
Betelgeuse
Bellatrix
Alnilam
Alnitak
Lep
Col
SE
Mirzam
Sirius
CANIS MAJOR
Wezen
Adhara
AURIGA
Elnath
M1
Jupiter
Alhena
Capella
Menkalinan
GEMINI
Venus
CANIS MINOR
Procyon
HORIZON
E
Mon
ECLIPTIC
Castor
Pollux
Cnc
Sun
Mercury
Lyn
NE
Algieba
Leo
LMi
RA: 5.89 Dec:-16.16
Sirius Mag:-1.5
N
W
S
90
25

Hexing the Equator (A Brief Detour)

Some aboriginal cultures recognize this celestial geometry and incorporate it into their cosmology. For instance, the Desana of southeast Columbia see a correspondence between the stars of the Winter Hexagon and six waterfalls that delineate the boundary of their traditional tribal homeland. Living in a rainforest, they conceptualize the sides of the polygon as six giant sky-anacondas, with the head of one snake meeting the tail of another at each star.

Dr. E. C. Krupp comments on how the Desana relate to what they consider their Center of the World, or *axis mundi*. "The center of the celestial hexagon corresponds to the intersection between the Pira-Paraná River and the earth's equator. Here, where the sky is said to cohabit with the earth, is the place where the Sun Father erected his shadowless staff and fertilized the world."[33]

Because this region is almost exactly on the equator, the equinox Sun passes directly through the zenith at noon, when virtually no shadows are cast. During the day this vertical pillar forms the center of their cosmos. Thus, a ray of sunlight coming from directly overhead is believed to be the Sun's semen that impregnates the Earth at her core. Like many other cultures, the Desana also associate the hexagonally structured quartz crystal with semen.[34] In addition, they see the bee as a solar creature and honey (stored in hexagonal cells) as a form of semen.[35]

On the other hand, at night the sidereal hexagon encompassing Orion becomes the focal point. Whereas the ancient Greeks deemed this constellation the Hunter, the Desana consider it the Master of Animals named *Vaí-mahsë*. This supernatural gamekeeper maintains the balance of procreative energy in the rainforest's game (mostly mammals) and the rivers' fishes. He lives on both the hills or rocky outcroppings of the former and at the waterfalls of the latter. He assists both the fluxing life-force of fauna and the slaying techniques of hunters. The energy of both animal and human fertility is thus kept in a biotic equilibrium.

In addition, he resembles the Hopi god Masau'u in a number

of ways. He takes a sexual interest in human females. He also sends illness or dangerous animals when hunting protocols or general cultural mores have not been correctly followed. And, like Masau'u, he carries a magic club, without which he loses all his power. Note as well the similarity of the two names.

> "*Vaí-mahsë* is a jealous guardian of his flock, and, moreover, he is directly their procreator. He takes a personal sexual interest in the fertility and multiplication of the different animal species, mainly in the deer and the tapir. But at the same time he is a hunter and even helps other hunters in their task. As a weapon, *Vaí-mahsë* possesses a short wand that is highly polished and red in color; when he leaves his moloca [house] and sees an animal that attracts his attention as prey, he takes his wand and points it. With just this gesture the animal falls dead."[36]

The Desana conceptualize the cosmic *moloca* as the World House, through which flows the Milk River from the eastern Water Door to the western Door of Suffering, the latter leading to the underworld.[37] The river runs directly through the center-place, where the staff of *Vaí-mahsë* was implanted at the cosmogony as a tripartite *axis mundi* (sky, earth, and underworld). In the east is a large lake of life, which is the source of the Milky Way flowing east to west above the earth with a turbulent current known as a "wind skein." It is interesting to note that the Desana call themselves *wirá-porá*, or "sons of the wind."[38] They metaphorically describe the Milky Way as fibers of the *cumare* palm but symbolically see it as an immense seminal reservoir.

It is significant that the cosmography of the Desana was probably informed to a great degree by the traditional use of the hallucinogen ayahuasca (yagé). Another divinity known as *Vihó-mahsë*, who controls all psychotropic substances of the rainforest, lives in the Milky Way and wanders over his "road" there. The main objective of the *payé*, or shaman, in consulting *Vihó-mahsë* is to take him to the abode of *Vaí-mahsë*, the Master of Animals.[39]

Maya scholar John Major Jenkins briefly describes the incredibly complex world of this tribe, which is much too detailed to explore in depth here.

> "The Desana envision space as a great hexagon bounded by six stars centered upon Epsilon Orionis, the middle star in Orion's belt. Desana shamans also perceive this six-sided shape in the structure of rock crystals and honeycombs. The Milky Way is an important celestial dividing line for the Desana, and the entire celestial vault is envisioned as a cosmic brain, divided into two lobes by the great fissure of the Milky Way."[40]

The Desana of the Columbian rainforest inhabit rectangular *molocas*, which are surrounded by magically protective circular fences [41], which in turn are encompassed by the tribal boundary marked off by the six sacred waterfalls—ultimately forming a giant terrestrial hexagon that reflects the celestial one.

It is possible, then, that the Hopi of the Arizona high desert recognize a giant terrestrial *kiva,* also formed like a hexagon.

Hexing Arizona

Copper has been mined in Arizona in both prehistoric and historic times. The map on the facing page is marked with **Cu** to represent the original *six* mining districts. These were all underground operations, whereas today there are many more open pit mines in the state extracting low-grade ore.

In central Arizona we find the Jerome district in the Verde Valley near Tuzigoot Ruins, Globe-Miami near Besh-Ba-Gowah Ruins in the eastern Superstition Mountains, and Morenci-Clifton just north of the Gila River near the Arizona-New Mexico border. In the north copper was mined from White Mesa on the Navajo Reservation west of Betatakin and Keet Seel. In the south we find the Ajo district west of the Tohono O'odham Reservation and the Bisbee district (Warren) district in the Mule Mountains of the southeastern part of the state.[42] Although gold and silver was also present in some cases, it is clear that ultimately copper was king.

The Winter Hexagon can be overlaid upon an Arizona map, showing all six constellations with some overlap in both California and New Mexico. If we take the 3:10 to Yuma located on the Colorado River, we find Auriga, the Charioteer or Reinholder. The Hopi most likely call this *Soomalatsi*, literally "star finger," because of its pentagonal (five-fingered?) shape. It encompasses the Kofa, or "King of Arizona" gold mining district.

Unlike both the Hohokam and the Hopi who lived or still live in fixed settlements made of adobe or stone, the Yuma (Quechan) and Cocopah (Kwikapa), two warlike tribes of the harsh desertscrub landscape along both banks of the "Nile of Arizona," inhabited instead mud-and-brush wickiups along the river bottoms and wove fine basketry. Archaeologists call the ancestors of these tribes Lowland Patayan, who may have lived in semi-subterranean pithouses and made buff-colored pottery. If there were once sedentary villages, however, the river silt has claimed them.[43] One important religious component may have been the "dream song," accessed by means of the halluncinogenic plant jimsonweed (*Datura*).[44] (See more in Chapter 12.)

In my two previous books I have written about the Blythe geoglyphs, or intaglios, made in this area by the ancestral Mohave and the other tribes I just mentioned. These were constructed exactly like the famous Nazca lines of Peru by removing the upper layer of "desert varnish" –that is, the small darker pebbles that have been oxidized over the ages– in order to reveal the lighter soil underneath. These anthropomorphs, zoomorphs, snakes, circles, stars, crosses, tracks, or geometric designs are actually not very impressive on the ground, at least in a physical sense.

Geoglyphs are ideally viewed from a hot air balloon, an ultralite aircraft, or powered paraglider (or, per Chapter 6, a Hopi flying shield), but they are certainly meant to be viewed from the air—by some sky god perhaps. Or, high above the terrestrial manifestation of the Charioteer constellation, from the vantage of the chariots of the gods themselves.

An interesting intaglio has been constructed about 13 miles north of the town of Blythe, California. This male humanoid is 95 feet long and oriented on an exact north–south axis. Located 145 feet to the southeast is a zoomorph with its head pointed southwest. 45 feet father southeast of this animal is a spiral.

The male figure is thought to represent the creator-god Mastamho, who created the world atop Avikwa'ame, Spirit Mountain (or Newberry Peak near Grapevine Canyon and Laughlin, Nevada). The tribes once performed four-day ceremonial pilgrimages from the point of creation in the north to Avikwal (or Pilot Knob near Yuma), the dwelling place of the dead in the south. This longitudinal trail along the Colorado River is perhaps similar to the ancient transit along the Nile between the northern Mound of Creation at Heliopolis and the southern necropolis of Osiris at Abydos. The name of the primordial deity Mastambo is similar to the Hopi god Masau'u, who –like Osiris– rules over death and the underworld.

[continued on p. 192]

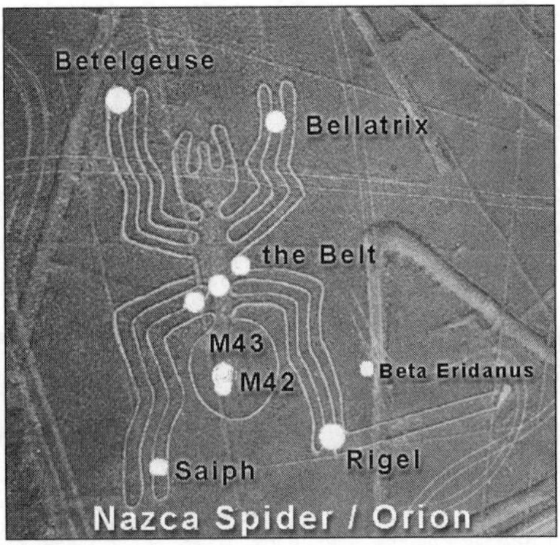

Above: The 150-ft.-long Spider in the Altacama Desert of Peru may represent Orion.

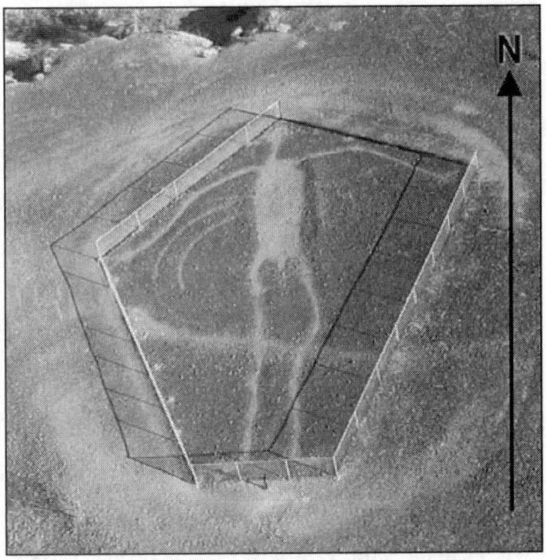

Right: This male anthropomorph near Blythe, California, depicts Mastamho, creator of the Earth. He is positioned north-south to reflect his ritual pathway.
Coordinates: 33° 48′ 02″ N,
114° 31′ 56″ W.
Photo © by Bob "Bubba" Peters.[45]

Below: This human figure to the west of the first figure near Blythe is aligned southwest–northeast, which is the orientation of the Orion template in Arizona.

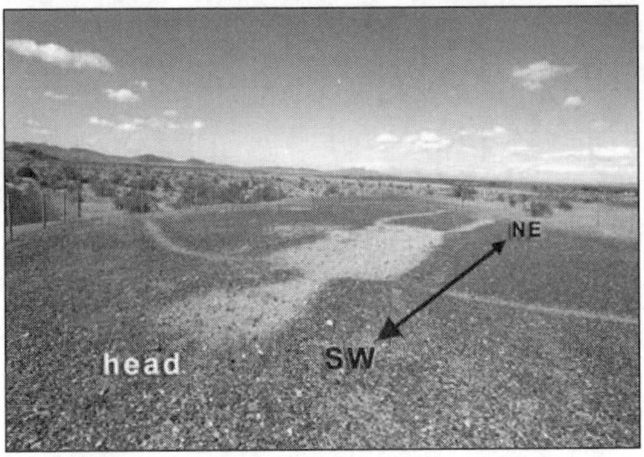

Another anthropoid geoglyph is found 1,850 feet nearly due west of the aforementioned human figure. Its head is pointed southwest—the same as the Arizona Orion Correlation.

Returning to the map on p. 189, we see Taurus corresponding to the Hualapai Reservation along the Colorado River. Aldebaran correlates to Grand Canyon Caverns. (See Chapter 7.) In my book *The Orion Zone,* I have written extensively how the Orion star pattern is mirrored on the earth. Here, the double star Rigel corresponds to the cliff dwellings of Betatakin and Keet Seel in Navajo National Monument. In addition, my two previous books have described the connection between Sirius in Canis Major and the massive pueblo complex of Chaco Canyon in New Mexico. (See the next chapter for the darker side of Chaco.)

Moving in a clockwise direction, we come to Gila Cliff Dwellings National Monument. Located in the rugged Mogollon Mountains of west-central New Mexico, these ruins are comprised of 40 rooms distributed in five of the seven volcanic caves located 180 feet above the canyon floor. These structures have been tree-ring dated to the 1280s and were abandoned by 1400. The Mogollon people (also known as the Mimbres), who once inhabited the site, are known for their exquisite black-on-white pottery that uses realistic though stylized designs. (See e.g. on p. 199.)
Gila Cliff Dwellings correspond to Canis Minor's brightest star Procyon, known by the Babylonians as the "Water-dog"[46] because it borders the river of the Milky Way, which on our map corresponds to the Mogollon Rim. The ruins are indeed located near the headwaters of the Gila River and a hot spring. The Babylonians also saw Procyon as the "scepter of Bel"[47] (or Ba'al), whom, as noted in Chapter 9, is a variation of Orion.

The Belgian scholar Dr. Antoon Leon Vollemaere believes that the site was the legendary Chicomoztoc, or the Seven Caves—an important stopping place for the proto-Aztecs during their migration to the Valley of Mexico.[48] I have previously made the case that one of the tribes that later helped to form the Aztecs was called the Chichimecs, literally "Sons of the Dog," who lived for a time at Chaco Canyon, which corresponds to Sirius, the Dog Star. (See more about this on pp. 228-230.)

[continued on p. 194]

Interior of one of the caves at Gila Cliff Dwellings National Monument.

Pictographs (rock paintings) of three birds atop step pyramids, near Gila Cliff Dwellings. The pyramids are similar to petroglyphs on p. 59. Does this represent Orion's belt and star-birds?

Gila Cliff Dwellings are located nearly on the 33rd parallel. Looking again at the map on p. 189, we see what I call Orion's chakra line that extends from Mesa Verde in southwestern Colorado through Hopi Second Mesa, traversing the ruins at Walnut Canyon/Meissa, passing by Thumb Butte/M1 (see Chapter 7) and ending up near Capella at the mouth of the Colorado River. The angle between this diagonal and 33° north latitude is 52°—which (by chance?) is approximately the same as the angle of the slope of the Great Pyramid at Giza (51.5°).

An interesting longitude line appears in the middle of the map. The Tohono O'odham (formerly known as the Papago tribe) consider Baboquivari Peak near the Mexican border as the navel of the world, the place where the people emerged from a subterranean existence. Their creator god I'itoi, or Elder Brother, lives in a cave just below the summit. This mountain is actually the central one in a triad of peaks. Baboquivari (elevation 7,740 ft.) is in the middle, while to the north lies Kitt Peak (6,875 ft.), upon which an astronomical observatory has been built. At the southern end of the range is Caponera Peak (4,885 ft.).

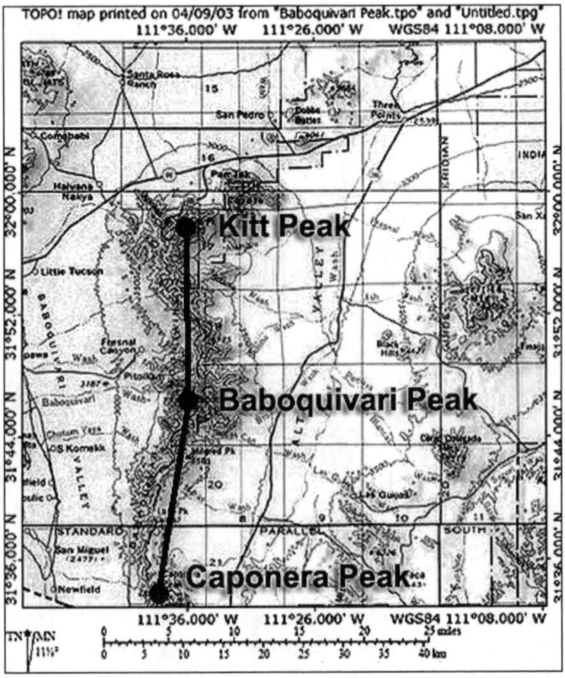

A similar triad of mountains exists nearly 238 miles to the north. Humphreys Peak (12,633 ft.), the highest mountain in Arizona, is flanked by the slightly lower Agassiz Peak (12,356 ft.) and the still lower Fremont Peak (11,969 ft). These northern sacred mountains are the winter home of the Hopi kachinas. The three mountains mirror the three Hopi Mesas where this tribe has lived for over a thousand years. In turn both the tripartite mountains and the tripartite mesas reflect the belt stars of Orion.

Surprisingly, Baboquivari and Humphreys are on an exact north-south meridian.

Baboquivari: 111° 35′ 44″ west longitude
Humphreys: 111° 40′ 42″ west longitude

In the O'odham language, Baboquivari is known as *Waw Kiwulik*, meaning "narrow about the middle." Maybe it is merely a coincidence that the figure of the Orion constellation is also "narrow at the middle." Or considering all the other Orion lore in Arizona, maybe not.

The last constellation on our tour of the Arizona Star Hexagon is Gemini, the Twins. Like Taurus, it is part of the zodiac, so the ecliptic passes through both. On our map (p. 189) the pathway of the Sun, Moon, and planets can be imagined to go from the southeast to the northwest. Castor and Pollux rest on the Arizona-Mexico border, while Alhena at the opposite end of the constellation overlays the Superstition Mountains.

This is the territory where abound the so-called trincheras, or *cerros de trincheras,* "hills with entrenchments." At the summit of numerous volcanic hills in Arizona, Sonora, and Chihuahua, complexes of megalithic, dry-laid masonry walls and terraces were constructed. They were used between 1100 and 1300 AD, but some may be as old as 1000 BC. Their purpose? Theories include terraced agricultural plots, fortified villages, hilltop communication points, and public ceremonial sites. Ultimately they remain a mystery.

Norwegian explorer and ethnographer Carl Lumholtz during his foray through the *Papagueria* in the early 20th century described one site three miles west of the mission of San Xavier.

He reported two rows of stone walls on the northern side of the hill. They were four feet high and 10-15 feet wide at the base, extending some 200 yards. The Tohono O'odham referred to the trinchera as *tjuk*, or "black," inferring a volcanic hill. In fact, the name of the city of Tucson comes from the word *Tjukson*, which means "at the foot of the black hill." Lumholtz saw other larger trincheras farther south of the border and concluded that their main function was not defensive or agricultural but religious.[49]

The 3,000-year-old trinchera named Cerro Juanaqueña in northern Chihuahua contains 100 rock rings and 468 terrace walls totaling five miles in length. These arc-shaped terraces made of piled basalt cobbles are more than a yard high and three to six yards wide. An estimated 22,000 tons of rock and soil were used to construct the site—a prodigious effort for a supposedly semi-nomadic people in the Late Archaic period.[50]

My friend Jack Andrews of Tucson explored one trinchera named Nachi Kulik (el. 3096 ft.), also called La Ventana, located seven miles northwest of the previously mentioned Caponera Peak. (Nachi Kulik coordinates: 31° 36′ 01″ N, 111° 42′ 30″ W.)

> The walls are massive and there are what appear as circular low rock walled 'rooms' on the north end of the mountain (outcropping). I climbed up to the top and sure enough there was what appeared to be a 'natural water tank'... The last wall on top (last of several) has large and thick vertically pointed upright megalithic boulders spaced at intervals of fifteen or so feet, evenly across the length of the wall. They actually scared (startled) me when I first glanced up at them, looking like guardian sentinels. At the east side of the top there is another large craggy outcropping which has a large natural hole through it horizontally. (La Ventana or 'window'.) The wind constantly roars through the 30-or-so-foot hole. Both times I visited the site, there was a large eagle circling overhead like another spirit guardian.[51]

About 45 miles south of Ajo, Arizona, on the U.S.-Mexico border is Vertex 17 of the Becker-Hagens "Earthstar" Planetary Grid System. This grid point is one of 62 major vertices of the mercator-based hexakis icosahedron projected on the Earth globe.[52]

[continued on p. 198]

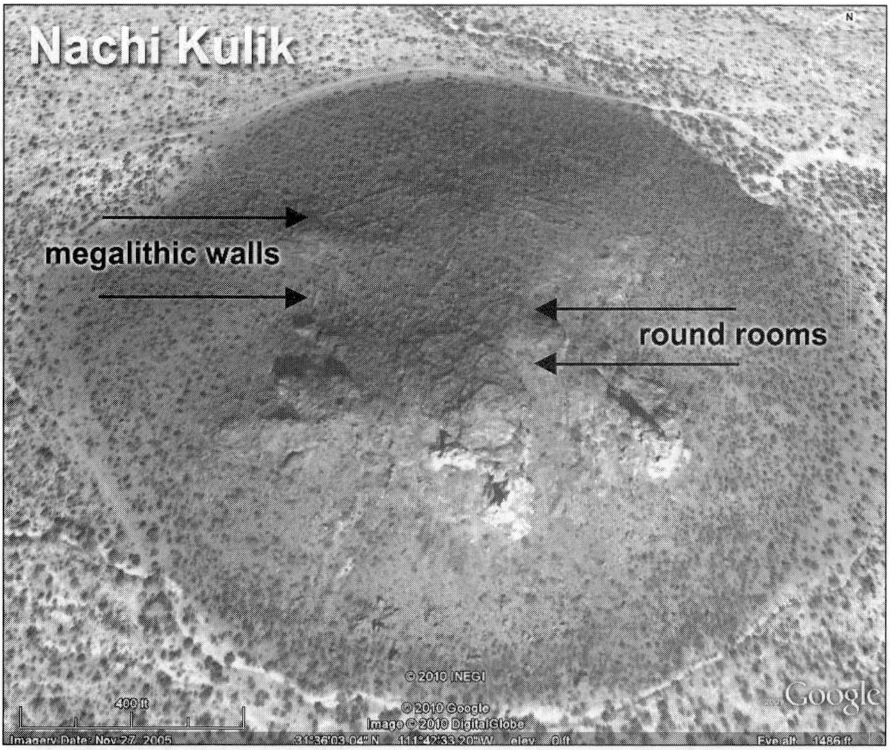
Nachi Kulik
megalithic walls
round rooms
© 2010 INEGI
© 2010 Google
Image © 2010 DigitalGlobe
400 ft
Imagery Date: Nov 27, 2005
31°36'03.04" N 111°42'33.20" W elev 0 ft
Eye alt 1486 ft
Google

PLANETARY GRID SYSTEM
Hovenweep
Mesa Verde
Betatakin
Aztec Ruins
Salmon Ruins
Las Vegas
Sipapuni
Taos P
Canyon de Chelly
Second Mesa
Chaco Canyon
Puye
First Mesa
Grand Canyon Caverns
Wupatki
Tyuonyi
Pecos
Walnut Canyon
Casamero
Kuaua
Homol'ovi
Albuquerque
Tuzigoot
Sedona
New Mexico
Fitzmaurice Ruin
Arizona
Blythe geoglyphs
Phoenix
Mesa
Gila Cliff Dwellings
Tucson
UVG 17
El Paso
Cerro Cubabi
© 2010 Europa Technologies
© 2010 Google
Image © 2010 DigitalGlobe
© 2010 INEGI
169 mi
31°39'05.73" N 112°46'18.94" W elev 0 ft
Eye alt 555.41 mi
Google

The area between the Colorado River and Sonoyta, Mexico (across from the U.S. town of Lukeville, Arizona) is known as Camino Del Diablo, the "Devil's Highway." The only water sources are the *tinajas*, or mountain water tanks cut into solid rock in order to hold the scarce, precious rainwater. Gold treasure and artifacts are said to be hidden in the desert sands, but few are brave or foolish enough to linger in this area, especially in the summer.[53] Over 200 undocumented immigrants perish annually due to dehydration, heat stroke, or hypothermia while trying to cross over to the "broken promised land" of El Norte.[54]

There have always been more copper pennies than gold nuggets, I'm afraid—even in antiquity. Classical Chinese documents, for instance, describe a trans-Pacific journey to the American Southwest in the late 5th century AD. Scholar Henriette Mertz believes that Hwui Shan, a Chinese explorer and mendicant Buddhist priest along with five or six others landed at Point Hueneme near present-day Los Angeles. They then traveled 350 miles inland to the Kingdom of Women, which Mertz says refers to the matriarchal Mogollon people of east-central Arizona and west-central New Mexico.

Among other oddities, he writes about the minerals of this land he calls Fu-sang: "The ground of the country is destitute of iron but has copper. Gold and silver are not valued."[55] He also said the people lived underground in round houses with entrances like burrows (pithouses or kivas.) The women were normal humans but sometimes took serpents as husbands (the Snake Clan). Curiously, the men had human bodies but the heads of dogs, and they made barking noises (the Chichimecs—see p. 227 and following.)

The canine motif is repeated in an Akimel O'odham (Pima) myth:

> "In the *261h Annual Report of the Bureau of American Ethnology*, 1904-05, Frank Russell related a myth held by the Pima Indians: To the daughter of Si'al Teu'-utak Si'van [a chief] was born 'a strange-looking creature. The people wanted to destroy it, but the mother said it was her child and she wished to care for it. The people wished to destroy the child, because it had long claws instead of fingers and toes; its teeth were long and

sharp, like those of a dog. They gave it the name of Hâ-âk, meaning something dreadful or ferocious. This female child grew to maturity in three or four years' time. She ate anything she could get her hands on, either raw or cooked food. The people tried to kill her, because she killed and ate their children. She went to the mountain Ta'-atûkam [Picacho Peak] and lived there for a while in a cave. Then she went to Baboquivari for a time and then to Poso Verde [near Sasbe, Arizona], where she was killed by Elder Brother.... When he killed Hâ-âk a great feast was made.' To commemorate this entire event, the Pima built a shrine—about five miles north of Sacaton, Arizona. 'The people formerly placed offerings within the enclosure to bring them good luck .... The place is yet visited.'"[56]

Dog-headed men? Women with serpent spouses? There is even a town in southern Arizona named Patagonia, which means "land of mythical giants." The ancient Southwest is full of them. This is the subject of my next chapter.

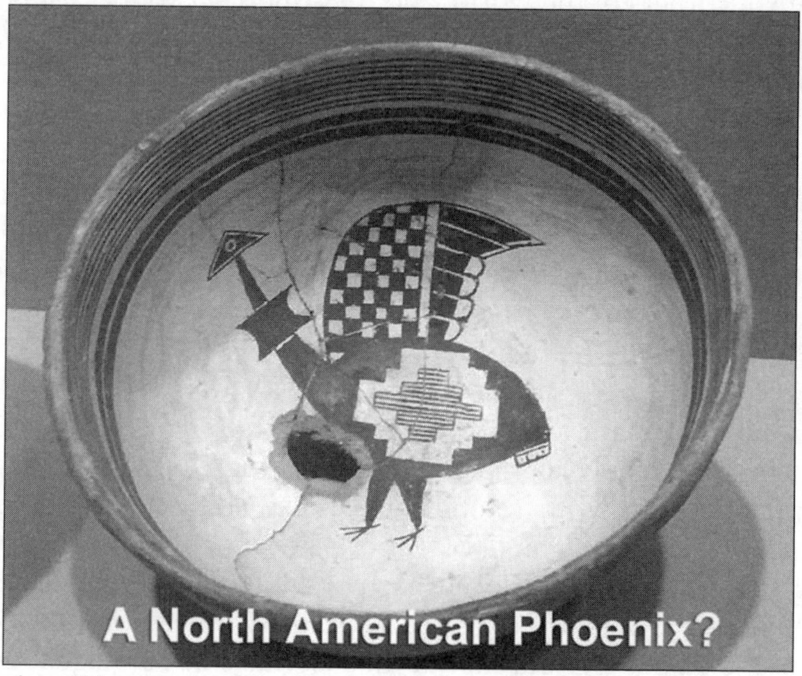

Mimbres (Mogollon) pottery bowl, c. 1000–1150 AD, Dallas Museum of Art. Pyramid-shaped head with "eye." Checkerboard on wing represents the Milky Way. Double step pyramid inside body signifies mountain or cloud.

Chapter 11
Ancient Giants of Earth and Sky

Native American Tall Tales

"There were giants in the earth in those days..." (Genesis 6:4)

Legends of giants are found not only in the Bible but also from all corners of the world, and the American Southwest is no exception. It seems natural that a land of such immensity would spawn creatures of comparable size.

Most tribes of this region have some collective memory of giants. Diné [Navajo] legends, for instance, refer to the *anáye,* which literally means "alien gods" but also implies those who speak a non-Navajo language. These ogres attained great stature, sometimes "half as tall as the tallest pine-tree." Although not particularly fast or smart, they were connoisseurs of human flesh. The fiends were even known to consume each other.

One giant with the difficult name of Tse'*tahotsiltá'li,* which means "He Who Kicks (People) Down the Cliff," was struck between the eyes with a stone knife and killed by the Navajo culture hero Nayénezgani, or Slayer of Alien Gods. His corpse was beset upon by his 12 children, each of which ravenously desired a choice piece of their father to consume. Nayénezgani then slew 11 of the 12 giant-children, but the last one was so disgustingly filthy and ugly that the Navajo took pity on him and sent him away. "The boy [a cannibal monster, really] went to Natsisaán

[Navajo Mountain, elevation 10,388 feet on the Utah-Arizona border], as he was told, and there he became the progenitor of the Puhutes [Paiutes], a people ugly, starved, and ragged, who never wash themselves and live on the vermin of the desert"[1]

The Navajo account is somewhat confusing because the Paiutes themselves, who lived mostly in Nevada and Utah, have legends of fierce battles with red-haired giants. Add to this another twist: Members of the Hopi *Ko'kop* (or Fire) Clan, who once lived in the vicinity of Navajo Mountain, were traditionally known as the "redheads." (The Hopi name of the mountain is *Toko'navi,* literally "flesh in abundance.") This most aggressive of clans was first to emerge from the underworld at the beginning of the current era (Fourth World) but declined a leadership role because its members wanted to stay by themselves. The *Ko'kop* founded the presently extinct Warrior Society named *Mòmtsit,* or *Mots,* meaning "disheveled hair." As the legendary enemy of the Aztecs, the *Ko'kop* is actually a phratry, or grouping, that includes a number of other clans: Masau'u, Coyote, Cedar, Pinyon, and Yucca.[2] (The related Hopi word *motski* refers to the narrow-leaf yucca, *Yucca angustissima.* I will briefly take up the relationship between the death-and-underworld god Masau'u and the yucca plant in Chapter 14.)

Sarah Winnemucca Hopkins, a Paiute who lived during the latter half of the 19th century, was the first Native American woman to publish in English. Her 1883 autobiography titled *Life Among the Paiutes* describes, among other things, her tribe's adversaries. These were a fierce group of as many as 2,600 people who once lived by Nevada's Humboldt Sink, an intermittent dry lakebed 11 miles long and four miles wide. They hunted and fished the marshy area in bulrush canoes made of tule grass.

The barbarians were called *Say-do-carah,* which means "conqueror" or "enemy." A lesser-known source spells it *Side-okahs,* which, Mrs. Hopkins claims, more specifically denotes cannibals.[3] She said that they even engaged in necrophagy—or digging up and eating human corpses.

A three-year war fought with bow-and-arrows raged between these despicable creatures and her tribe. The brutes escaped to Lovelock Cave, where Hopkins' kin piled and ignited sagebrush and firewood at its mouth, finally smothering them.[4] "My people say that the tribe we exterminated had reddish hair. I have some of their hair, which has been handed down from father to son. I have a dress which has been in our family a great many years, trimmed with this reddish hair. I am going to wear it some time when I lecture. It is called the mourning dress, and no one has such a dress but my family."[5]

In 1911, miners were extracting bat guano from this cave located 22 miles southwest of Lovelock, Nevada. The horseshoe-shaped cavern sits atop a high hill and is about 45 feet deep and 160 feet wide. Out of the guano that measured six feet deep, numerous Native American artifacts were unearthed. These included woven basketry and mats, sandals, fishnets, fishhooks, arrows and atlatl darts, fur or feather blankets, textiles, moccasins, stuffed birds' heads and ceremonial feathers as well as worked pieces of stone, bone, horn and leather. They even found finely crafted duck decoys made of reeds, which, along with the fishing equipment, remind us that a huge lake once occupied this arid region in ancient times.

A probable calendar stone was also discovered. This torus-shaped object had 365 notches on the outside rim and 52 notches on the inside rim.[6] (Read more about torus stones in Chapter 16. The numeral 52, incidentally, was used as a primary number in the Mayan calendar system.)

Most surprising, however, was the discovery of a mummy six-and-a-half-feet tall with bright red hair. The miners, in fact, uncovered 13 mummies before two University of California archaeologists named Llewellyn Loud and Mark Harrington were called in. Unlike the Egyptian variety, these bodies were naturally mummified due to the arid climate. By the time the excavations were completed, the skeletal remains of nearly 60 individuals and over 10,000 artifacts had been recovered. The scientists estimated that the cave had initially been inhabited between 3,000 and 4,000 years ago. It should be noted that the average height for a person living in the American Southwest at that time was between five and five-and-a-half feet.

Later archaeological research at the site pushed back the initial period of human habitation to about 2700 BC with a total of 20,000 specimens found. One "large femur" was radiocarbon-dated at 1450 ± 80 BC. What exactly 'large' means, the report does not say.[7]

Like a lot of the anomalies in the American Southwest, much of the physical evidence of the Lovelock Cave giants has been misplaced, simply lost, or intentionally hidden. Unconfirmed rumors persist of large skulls or bones gathering dust in the basements of museums in Lovelock, Carson City, or Winnemucca. Some even say that the tall, red-haired stranger referred to above was absconded by the local Masonic organization for its initiation rituals.

A recent issue of *Ancient American* magazine published color photos of four skulls housed at the small museum in Winnemucca. The skull size is somewhat larger than modern skulls but the jaws are significantly larger. The curator there claimed that additional mummies, skulls, and artifacts were shipped to Berkeley, California, but "…that the state will not recognize those bodies & that they are not allowed to display them."[8] This may be either a cover-up or just an attempt to avoid relinquishing them to American Indian tribal groups due to NAGPRA (Native American Graves Protection and Repatriation Act).

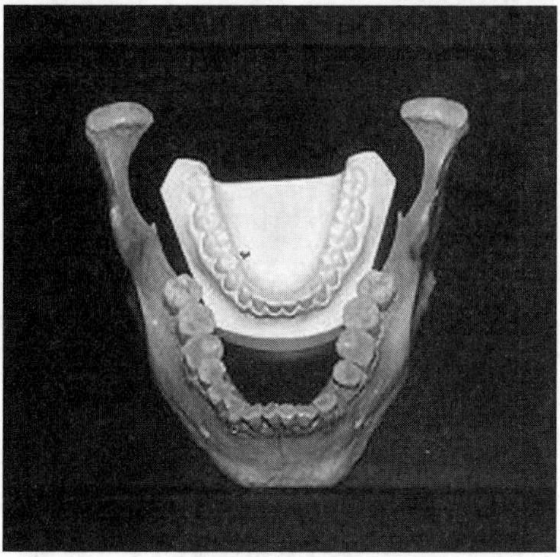

Plaster caste of modern jaw next to large jaw in the collection of the Winnemucca museum. Photo courtesy of Stan Nielsen, © 1995-2010.

Discovery of giants in the Southwest continued well into the 20th century. In Brewer's Cave on Temple Hill near Manti, Utah, a pair of mummified giants, both about nine feet tall, were found inside two stone coffins. One body had red hair and the other blond hair. They were both wearing crowns and breastplates.

A set of stone steps led to the burial chamber, whose dimensions were about 14 by 20 feet. It also supposedly contained ten stone boxes, five of which held small metal plates of bronze or even gold engraved with an unknown script. A few of the indecipherable icons on the plates resembled, some say, modern computer schematics. Other artifacts included shields and a sword.[9]

These archaeological discoveries seem to corroborate numerous Native American legends of giants. From the San Ildefonso Pueblo in New Mexico comes one account of a man-eating giant who lived underground. "...in the great cave on the north side of the mesa there once lived (they said) a cannibal giant. His cave was connected with the interior of the vast, house-like mesa by tunnels which took him to his rooms. His influence on the surrounding country was heavy. Persons did the proper things to avoid being caught and eaten by him."[10]

The Hopi also share this idea of giants disciplining people –especially children– lest they become a meal. For instance, Nataska, or Bigmouth Ogre, wears a black mask with goggle-eyes, large crocodile-like jaws that clack together, sharp teeth, and a green crows-foot painted on his forehead. A curved horn rises on each side of his head. In one hand he carries a saw, in the other either a hatchet or bow-and-arrows. He supposedly has the ability to swallow children whole. Another version of this bogeyman is called Tseeveyo (also spelled Chaveyo), literally "Giant Kachina."

The So'yoko Mana, or Ogre Woman, is also an awesome (read "bad") creature that haunts the Hopi territory. Her dark mask has stringy black hair and a protruding tongue. In one hand she might carry a bloodstained butcher knife, in the other a long crook to snag misbehaving children. On her back is a large burden basket (*hoapu*) with which to carry off naughty kids.

[continued on p. 206]

Above: So'yoko Taqa, Hopi painting from Fewkes, *Hopi Katcina.* This male version of the So'yoko Mana also carries a burden basket to abduct children. He carries a saw, perhaps to cut off his victims' limbs.

Right: Nataska, or Bigmouth Ogre, is a chief kachina who in this case carries a bow. He ususally appears with his twin during Powamuya, or the Bean Ceremony in February. Waiting impatiently to be fed, they threaten the children by saying they will chew their bones and no one will ever see them again.

The young boys' task is to catch mice or other rodents, while the young girls' job is to grind corn as offerings to the threatening beings. If these monsters come growling and stomping into the village without the children having done their duties, then they are abducted. The terror these creatures instill certainly seems unduly harsh by modern standards of child rearing.[11]

One scholar named Susan E. James has even compared the Hopi Purification ceremony in February, which includes these intimidating giants, to the Aztec rite of child sacrifice.

> "...during the Hopi Powamu, children are of featured importance and offer a sacrifice of tears (and sometimes blood) in the whipping rites conducted at this time in the kivas. An apparent mimetic reenactment of the Aztec sacrifice of children occurs on the fourteenth day of the celebrations with the arrival at the mesas of the kachina Soyoko accompanied by the kachina He'e'e and the ogre-kachinas, generally known collectively as Nata'askas [or Nataskas]."[12]

The tears of the terrified children produce a sympathetic magic that causes abundant rainfall in the coming year. At Second Mesa the ogres are accompanied by Masau'u, the Hopi god of death and the underworld. Physical contact with Soyoko is thought to actually bring about death. Although the Hopi probably never actually performed child sacrifice like the Aztecs did, the parallel rituals induced the same outcome of agricultural fertility. After the giants depart, taking their chaos and violent behavior with them, the "purified" village reverts to its natural harmony and balance for yet another year.

One legend from Wupatki tells of a So'yoko Taqa, or Ogre Man, who was constantly killing and eating people in the village. An unfortunate teenage boy out hunting in the foothills of the San Francisco Peaks was caught and held captive by this giant with buggy eyes, large snout, and wild hair. The boy managed to escape only with the help of Old Spider Woman –a recurrent aid to Hopis in distress– and an immense rattlesnake. The reptile spat venom on the boy's arrows, with which he shot Ogre Man dead.

His wife, So'yoko Mana, then sought revenge, but this time

the boy was assisted by a billy goat. In addition to a mean streak, the female ogre curiously possessed a "vagina dentata," or sharp teeth inside her privates.[13] Luckily, after the goat smeared a magically protective sumac berry potion on his member, he tupped her with such ferocity that she died in the process.[14] The Hopi certainly do not bowdlerize their legends.

Even from as far away as China, we find ancient tales of giants living in the American Southwest. Compiled at the amazingly early date of 2250 BC, *The Classic of Mountains and Seas* states:

> "In the Great Waste Beyond the Eastern Sea there is a mountain which by hyperbole is called 'the Place where the Sun and Moon Rise.' It has rolling valleys and mountains. This is the Great Man's Country... A man by the name of Cheu-Fu-Chang picked up a wooden arrow with an iron point which was six feet and a half long. Reckoning from the length of the arrow, the shooter must must been a rod and five or six feet tall."[15]

Giant Steps: Evidence of Six-toed Giants in the Southwest

Other fragmentary tales from the Southwest describe prehistoric gigantism—except with an added element. In 1891 in Crittenden, Arizona, which is north of the village of Patagonia mentioned at the end of the previous chapter, workmen excavated a massive stone sarcophagus buried at a depth of eight feet. Inside was a granite mummy case designed for a human body that was once about 12 feet tall but had since turned to dust after being buried for hundreds or perhaps thousands of years. The carving on the granite case curiously indicated that the giant had six toes on each foot. That certainly rings a biblical bell.[16]

> "And there was yet a battle in Gath, where was a man of great stature, that had on every hand six fingers, and on every foot six toes, four and twenty in number; and he also was born to the giant." (2 Samuel 21:20)

What is called polydactyly (or sometimes hexadactyly—that

is, possessing six digits on each hand or foot) was, in fact, not uncommon in the American Southwest. For instance, a six-toed foot bone was unearthed at Sand Canyon Pueblo, a dozen miles west of Cortez, Colorado. Petroglyphs of human figures with six toes and/or six fingers have also been discovered 50 miles west of Sand Canyon along the San Juan River in southeastern Utah.

From what the Hopi call Nuvakwewtaqa, or Chavez Pass Ruins in Arizona, archaeologists also found a foot bone of a juvenile that exhibits a left fifth metatarsal with a lateral branch, making it essentially a six-toed foot.[17]

Perhaps the most compelling evidence, however, occurs at a huge 10th century AD ruin, where we have both rock art depiction and skeletal evidence. Paleopathologist Ethne Barnes writes:

> "At the base of the cliff face behind Pueblo Bonito in Chaco Canyon in northwest New Mexico, there is a rock art panel depicting a set of three vertically placed human footprints carved into the rock face. They are directed upwards in a normal gait pattern with a right, left, right foot print. All three foot prints have six toes. The extra digit clearly appears adjacent to the fifth toe (little toe) on the lateral side of the foot."[18]

The petroglyphs showing the six-toed person are surprisingly corroborated by the discovery of a six-toed foot bone. Specifically, in Room 330 of Pueblo Bonito a bifid fifth metatarsal from the right foot of an adult was found. This proves that the rock carving was just not an artistic expression as we conceive it today but an actual description of a physical condition of one or more of the inhabitants of Chaco Canyon.

In brief, it seems that more than one person with six toes on each foot was walking around the American Southwest. Far from being seen as having a deformity, though, he or she may have even achieved a ritual status seemingly bequeathed by the gods. But with more than a thousand years separating our society from theirs, fleshing out the specific role of those blessed (or cursed) with four-and-twenty digits is –forgive me– a rather tall order.

[continued on p. 210]

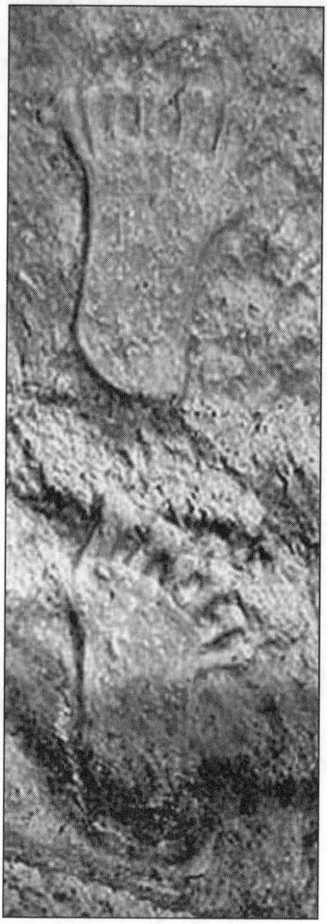

Above: Petroglyph of six-fingered handprint below snake figure, Three Rivers Petroglyph Site, New Mexico.

Right: Petroglyphs of six-toed footprints on the cliff behind Pueblo Bonito in Chaco Canyon.

Photo © by Scott Catron. Pictographs (rock paintings) of giant red figures in The Great Gallery, Horseshoe Canyon, Utah (part of Canyonsland National Park). The panel is 200 feet long, 15 feet high, and the figures are about 7 feet tall—or lifesize?

The Colossi of Chaco Canyon

Let's recap the major traits of giants in order of importance. First of all, they are –obviously– tall, or at least taller than average. Secondly, they might have a proclivity for cannibalism. Thirdly, they may have six fingers on each hand and/or six toes on each foot.

Ugliness or freakishness, however, may or may not be present. We recall that the biblical giants, those "men of renown" (Genesis 6:4), were not described as grotesque but just aggressive or violent. If we met a giant on the street today, we might find him rude, crude, or even lewd but certainly not inhuman.

The three criteria of giants seem to come together, fortuitously, at Chaco Canyon. In the previous section of this chapter, I discussed the third trait, polydactyly, there and elsewhere in the Southwest. Now let me address the first attribute of height, saving the most controversial one, cannibalism, till last.

Chaco Canyon is the largest complex of prehistoric sites in the Southwest, and one of the most archaeologically important. The dozen large pueblos in the canyon exhibit exquisite architectural style and craftsmanship. More than 200,000 pine roof beams were used in their construction. With an average of 15 feet in length, seven inches in diameter, and 60 pounds in weight, they were hauled from the Chuska and San Mateo Mountains over 50 miles away. Was this the work of giants? If not, then it was at least a gigantic feat.

The "great house" later named Pueblo Bonito was erected from 30,000 tons of shaped sandstone blocks quarried in the canyon and 25,000 imported roof beams. This D-shaped prehistoric "apartment building" contained immense plazas and over 650-800 terraced rooms, some of which were four to five stories tall. The complex covered two-and-one-half acres and had 40 kivas.

A number of "high status" burials have been discovered at Chaco. A generally greater variety of grave goods of higher quality workmanship are associated with Pueblo Bonito than almost anywhere else in the Southwest. These artifacts include thousands of turquoise beads, *Olivella* and *Haliotis* shells, crystals, and worked pieces of hematite, azurite, malachite, galena, gypsum, kaolin, and iron pyrite. Also discovered were numerous adornments such as pendants, necklaces, bracelets, earrings, and copper bells—this last artifact perhaps originating in Arizona. One necklace found at Pueblo Bonito had over 2,500 tiny, finely crafted turquoise beads and four turquoise pendants.

Woven items included baskets, yucca and bulrush mats, cotton cloth, and feather robes. Archaeologists also uncovered sandstone tablets, mortars and pestles, bone awls, bone scrapers, bone dice, obsidian projectile points, reed arrows, leaf-shaped stone knives, pipes, throwing sticks, ceremonial sticks, clay plume holders, wooden flutes, and shell trumpets.

Artistically rendered ceramics painted mostly black-on-white were also unearthed: bowls, jars, pitchers, ollas, mugs, ladles, and unique cylinder vessels. One frog effigy carved from jet was inlaid with turquoise, while other effigies of mountain lions and birds had been crafted as well. A cylindrical basket was also beautifully inlaid with a turquoise mosaic.

In other words, the standard of living was fairly high for the people who used these items. Rather than an egalitarian model for Pueblo Bonito, an authoritarian hierarchy probably existed here. In comparison to the smaller surrounding pueblos, this great house must have been the seat of imperial power and prestige. In all likelihood the high status was hereditarily ascribed rather than individually achieved. The reigning polity was thus both an oligarchy and a plutocracy, and probably a theocracy as well. In other words, a few rich priests had ruled.

The valuable ornaments and ceremonial paraphernalia, which were stored primarily in the northern section of the pueblo, suggest the presence of this priesthood. The burials are located within rooms rather than outside, which implies, paradoxically, both a respect for the rulers and a need for protection of their graves from pilfering.

These sociopolitical leaders were apparently healthier than the rest of the inhabitants of Chaco Canyon, and thus achieved greater stature—both literally and figuratively.

> "Perhaps the best evidence of better health over a number of generations is attained growth, or stature, because this is one of the more sensitive indicators of nutritional status. It is particularly significant for Pueblo Bonito, where both males and females from the northern room clusters are *the tallest reported for Southwestern populations*. [italics added] Femur lengths for the northern cluster burials average 44.5 cm [17.5 inches] for males and 41.6 cm [16 inches] for females."[19]

The average length of the femur of a modern human is 48 cm (19 inches), so this elite group of religious cultists had long bones only one-and-a-half inches shorter than ours. They were certainly not giants per se, but they may have seemed that way to the shorter populace at Chaco, especially if other methods of intimidation were employed. (More on this aspect later.)

Mug and olla, Chaco Canyon black-on-white pottery.

In this region the average lifespan was a mere 27 years, while no more than 15 percent lived to age 50.[20] This older minority of the population achieved its longevity in part by a lower rate of iron deficiency anemia. "When compared to other Southwestern populations, the Pueblo Bonito rates for porotic hyperostosis (25% for infants and children) indicative of iron deficiency are among the lowest reported and lower than for the small-site population (83%)."[210]

These statistics are a rather sad proof of the quotidian suffering that the lower classes endured in the *Hisatsinom* social system. In the "suburbs" and smaller villages outside of what archaeologist Stephen Lekson has called "downtown Chaco," the inhabitants fared much poorer in terms of diet and lifestyle. Archaeologist Steven A. LeBlanc, who more than anyone else refuted the stereotype of the peaceful Anasazi, writes:

> "...one thing about the Chaco Interaction Sphere is remarkably clear: This is the only time in the entire Anasazi sequence when there is striking evidence for distinct classes of people. The people who lived in Great Houses inhabited structures very

> different from the rest of the population. Great House rooms were several times larger and taller than those in the surrounding room blocks. Great Houses were high and massive, whereas the room blocks were low and small. Anyway else in the world, such a dichotomy of living arrangements would be seen as an elite/nonelite duality. These differences did not occur earlier in the Southwest, and they were gone by the beginning of the 1200s."[22]

Were the rooms of the elite larger simply because of social status? Or were the ceilings higher because of physical stature? It might have been a case of both.

The normal Ancestral Puebloans, due to their corn-based, high carb diets, were shorter than, say, the normal Plains Indians who feasted on protein-rich buffalo. Still, the taller upper-class that lived at Pueblo Bonito must have gotten their meat from somewhere. Once the human population of Chaco Canyon reached a certain level, the wild game resources such as antelope and deer began to be depleted. The problem of how to obtain dietary protein remained, however.

Adventurer and author Richard D. Fisher proposes a radical theory regarding the kivas in Chaco Canyon and at other prehistoric villages of the Southwest. He believes that the smaller ones did not function as sacerdotal structures but were actually corn silos, whereas the Great Kivas served as communal kitchens. He also claims that the Chacoans used "fertilizer dehydration basins" in order to provide soil nutrients to produce spectacular bumper corn crops.

One would think this food surplus would be advantageous, but unfortunately it had some unintended negative consequences. *Zea mays* (corn) has the essential amino acids for growth but lacks proper iron levels needed for robust health. Hence, the seeds of the culture's destruction were planted in its maize mounds. Fisher concludes:

> "This naturally occurring resource [namely, fertilizer] allowed the Chaco Canyon Anasazi to fill their massive system of granaries, increase population densities and create monumental archi-

tecture that had a practical and spiritual use such as Pueblo Bonito, the hundreds of other Great Houses and the extensive 'road system.' With the surplus corn that they were able to produce, however, came increasing anemia and depletion of regional wildlife populations which provided the essential dietary iron, leading in turn to increased warfare and even cannibalism."[23]

Whether or not Mr. Fisher is correct in his assumption about the ultimate role of the kiva in Anasazi life, his theory points to a society based on dual stratification: the corn-eaters versus the meat-eaters. Now the legends of cannibalistic "giants" are starting to make sense.

Cannibal Canyon?

Some archaeologists believe that a ritual terror campaign of fear and retribution centered at Pueblo Bonito developed during Chaco Canyon's dominance between about 900 and 1200 AD. David R. Wilcox from the Museum of Northern Arizona posits the existence of a relatively small but well-trained military force that would travel to outlying areas in order to demand tributes of food or valuable items for the great houses, including Pueblo Bonito.[24] If this is the case, then the despotic governing body resembled the Roman Empire more than the Catholic Church.

An even more controversial scenario, however, has been proposed. Christy G. Turner, the regents' professor of anthropology at Arizona State University, caused a furor both in academic circles and among modern Indian tribes when his book *Man Corn* was published in 1999. The title comes from a Nahuatl (Aztec) term *tlacatlaolli,* which means "sacred meal of sacrificed human meat, cooked with corn."[25]

Turner found evidence of at least 38 episodes of cannibalism in the Southwest between 900 and 1300 AD, involving the consumption of at least 286 individuals of all ages and both sexes. And this is a conservative estimate.[26]

The extensive forensic and osteological evidence gathered at various archaeological sites includes fracturing, chopping, sawing, cutting, and breaking of human bones consistent with food preparation. Some bones were also split lengthwise, apparently to extract the marrow. Others, especially skulls, had "anvil abrasions" received when they were put on an anvil-like stone and then bashed apart with a club or another stone.

Turner claims that the overall bone damage due to butchering and cooking can be distinguished from non-cannibalistic bone damage or traditional mortuary practices. A portion of the skeletal material he examined had polished tips, which suggest that they rubbed against the interior surface of cooking pots in the process of boiling that he called "pot polish." Burn marks on some of the bones indicate that the flesh was still on them when it was roasted. Burns at the back of numerous skulls indicate that they were placed in the fire, effectively simmering the brains in their own brainpans. A grisly kitchen indeed!

Less than 10 miles northeast of Four Corners (the geographic point where Utah, Colorado, New Mexico, and Arizona meet), a very important piece of archaeological evidence was discovered in the year 2000. Specifically, a piece of fossilized human feces called a coprolite had been deposited in the hearth of a pit house (a single-room, semi-subterranean dwelling) built in Cowboy Wash in about 1150 AD. This coprolite unexpectedly contained the residue of human myoglobin, a protein that occurs solely in human muscle or heart tissue.

Anthropologist Brian R. Billman of the University of North Carolina–Chapel Hill found the bones of seven people at the site, both male and female of all ages, that exhibited incisions typical of butchering. Defecation in the ashes of the fire that cooked this meal was probably one attacker's final act of disdain. Other hacked and battered skeletal remains at adjacent sites suggest that as many as 35 people may have been killed and consumed in the assault.[27]

This evidence along with Turner's work suddenly altered the archaeological paradigm used for decades to describe the Anasazi. Over night the peaceful, cooperative, humble agrarian had become a violent, vindictive, bloodthirsty cannibal. This reactionary characterization was not quite accurate, though, since Turner's scenario assumes that one or more bands of Mesoamerican warrior-cultists migrated into the American Southwest, radically changing the tenor of the existing cultural landscape of the indigenous Puebloans.

The epicenter of the cannibalistic practices, however, appears to be Chaco Canyon's great houses—characteristically un-Anasazi in the monumental scale of their architecture. Turner comments:

> "Southwestern cannibalism seems to be explainable, at least for the moment, by a hypothesis that combines social control, social pathology, and ritual purpose within the Chacoan sphere of influence. Each of these classes of explanation is evident as well in the intertwined Mesoamerican psychosocial, economic, and cosmological beliefs that were acted out through interminable warfare, unimaginable amounts of human sacrifice, and centuries of cannibalism—all carried out on the orders of tyrannical rulers with unlimited authority over the lives of their people. It appears to us that this harsh, totalitarian, and fatalistic Mesoamerican worldview was carried to the San Juan basin by actual immigrants from Mexico and imposed on a resident population that earlier had received only bits and snatches of Mexican culture from itinerant traders, explorers, and wanderers."[28]

A few of the Hopi, who are among the descendants of the Anasazi, claim that if cannibalism had indeed taken place, the perpetrators had never been formally accepted into the Hopi clan system and were basically *qahopi,* or non-Hopi. In other words, the cannibals had been interloping foreigners migrating northward from southern Mexico.

Rina Swentzell, who grew up at Santa Clara Pueblo in New Mexico, believes that the great villages of Chaco Canyon, unlike other pueblos of the Southwest, were informed by a uncompromising sensibility that was contrary to the spirit of her own people. Rather than showing oneness with the earth and all of its creatures, the stern patriarchy was basically anthropocentric and, to use a contemporary term, "left-brained." The Chaocans, whoever they were, apparently instituted a paradigm of command and control over both human and natural resources.

> "The Chaco great houses projected a different sensibility. The finished product was very important. Skill and specialization were needed to do the fine stonework and lay the sharp-edged walls. I concluded that the structures had been built by men in the prime of life with a vision something beyond the daily life and the present moment. These were men who embraced a social-political-religious hierarchy and envisioned control and power over place, resources, and people."[29]

Even Swentzell, however, admits to hearing stories about her pueblo ancestors who resorted to cannibalism during times of extreme stress.[30]

Remember Room 330 in Pueblo Bonito, where the six-toed foot bone was found? This square room with a central fire pit and a solitary access via a ceiling hatchway may have functioned as a council chamber. At one time some very dark rituals must have taken place there. In fact, Charles Manson couldn't have dreamed a more gruesome helter-skelter.

Located on the western side of the pueblo, the room contained between 23 and 32 individuals. An accurate number is difficult to obtain due to the smashed and disjointed condition –technically called "disarticulation"– of all but four of the skeletal remains. The mid-20th century archaeologist Neil M. Judd in his excavation of the site described the bones as "callously pulled and kicked about."

Skulls were smashed, crushed, or suffered other blunt force trauma. They were sometimes ritualistically arranged in clusters of two or three. Violently mutilated and dismembered, the bodies were haphazardly dumped, giving the impression of sacrificial killings. An arrowhead was embedded in a lumbar vertebra of one individual. Intentionally chipped teeth were found in others. One individual had its vertebrae positioned in a ring as if they had been strung together with a string and then laid down in a circle. One teenage female had a blown-out alveolar socket of an upper incisor. Another individual had a deep gash in the pubic bone.

Photographs of Judd's archaeological dig, Turner says, show that "...skeletons [were] wildly scattered, awkwardly positioned, and sometimes face down."[31] Unlike other Anasazi burial sites, this charnel certainly does not show a respect for the deceased.

Many of the skeletons Turner examined displayed evidence of perimortem breakage—that is, fractures occurring before, at, or just after the time of death. This suggests a brutal regime that employed ritualistic torture as a comprehensive strategy for absolute psychological and political control bordering on sociopathy.

Clearly, an evil wind blew through this great house.

Human head on an effigy pottery vessel, Pueblo Bonito.
Note tattoo-dots on chin and tear-dots streaming from the eyes.

Giants in the Sky

The Hopi word *Hopqöy* refers to Chaco Canyon as "a mythical place in the northeast where marvelous building was accomplished by *powaqam*, 'sorcerers'. The suggestion has been made that this may have to do with the Chacoan ruins."[32] In other words, Chaco was the regional center of witchcraft, by which its monumental architecture was to a great extent achieved.

The Diné (Navajo) also possess memories of the imperious culture that once terrorized this dry, desolate basin. Douglas Preston's influential article was published in the *New Yorker* about the time the "cannibal controversy" first hit the popular culture. "Chaco, some older Navajo say, was a place of hideous evil. The Chaco people abused sacred ceremonies, practiced witchcraft and cannibalism, and made a dreaded substance called corpse powder by cooking and grinding up the flesh and bones of the dead. Their evil threw the world out of balance, and they were destroyed in a great earthquake and fire."[33]

In modern times the Diné are famous around the world for their turquoise and silver jewelry. This exquisite craftwork more or less epitomizes the Southwest. Archaeologists believe –and it *is* just an educated guess– that the Navajo migrated from the north into the Four Corners region about 1500 AD. However, it is curious that this tribe possesses legends regarding Chaco Canyon, which was abandoned over three centuries before this tribe supposedly came into the area.

One story involves an evil gambler named Nááhwíilbiihí (also known as No*h*oílpi or Noqoilpi), which means "He Who Wins Men At Play." Originating from a place far to the south, he began to manipulate the indigenous population soon after his arrival in the Four Corners region. He also had the bad habit of chewing the narcotic gum resin from wire lettuce (*Stephanomeria pauciflora*) as a sedative.[34] The use of mind-altering plants was not traditionally a part of Hopi practice.

This Gambler challenged the men at Chaco Canyon to various games and contests, in which they wagered their property, their wives, their children, and even themselves as slaves. Then he said he would give them back everything if they would build him a palace, so the people of Chaco begin to do his bidding in hopes of regaining their former lives.

Richard M. Begay, a Diné from New Mexico, has written about some of the information that was passed down by his family and community in regard to Chaco.

> "Through Navajo oral traditions, we know that hundreds, if not thousands, of people labored to build the structures we see today. Chaco was also a center of economical and social activity. At Pueblo Bonito, one could trade for anything: pottery, all types of food, clothing, ceremonial items, turquoise. The oral histories also tell us that the canyon was a place of many vices. It was the place for prostitution, sexual deviancy, and incest. Gambling was a common pastime; indeed, it was through gambling that Nááhwíilbiihí was able to enslave people. He was a preeminent gambler, and in the end each challenger has nothing left but himself or herself to wager. Thus, slowly, all challengers and their families became spoils of gambling and pawns of the Gambler."[35]

Navajo stories also talk about settling near a pueblo called Kinteel (Kîntyél), or Broad House, which, they say, was in the process of being built but not yet finished. One source identifies this as Chetro Ketl, a 500-room structure that was completed in 1054 AD. This, coincidentally, is the same year as the massive supernova explosion that was depicted in pictographs (rock paintings) on the walls of Chaco Canyon. (See p. 116.)

Yet another story describes the Gambler as coming not from the south but from the sky. "Some time before, there had descended among the Pueblos, from the heavens, a divine gambler, or gambling-god, named No*h*oílpi, or He Who Wins Men (at play); his talisman was a great piece of turquoise."[36] This celestial origin makes sense because in the complex cosmology of Chaco Canyon, north is associated with the nadir or underworld, whereas south is associated with the heavens.

One young Navajo man, the son of *H*astsé*h*ogan, was selected and prepared by the gods to confront the Gambler and beat him at his own game. (The elder *Hastséhogan*, literally "House God," was a beneficent divine being, or *yéi*, who lived in caves or cliff dwellings. He was also god of evening, who wore a black shirt adorned with four star-designs.)

Using supernatural assistance, the younger Navajo eventually triumphed. Finally, with a "Bow of Darkness" he shot the Gambler into the sky like an arrow. It is significant that Pueblo Bonito is architecturally bow-shaped with its arrow pointing northward. (Both of my books, *The Orion Zone* and *Eye of the Phoenix*, detail numerous connections between the bow-and-arrow motif and Chaco Canyon.)

Before being hurled skyward, the Gambler prophesied that his children would one day return. This may indeed have come to pass in the form of gambling casinos on Indian reservations. In November of 2008, for instance, the Navajo Nation opened its first gaming establishment called Fire Rock Casino near Church Rock, a few miles east of Gallup, New Mexico.[37]

Some accounts describe the Gambler as being aerially projected due south into Mexico.[38] Other versions even claim that he himself was an Hispanic from Mexico, who, while sojourning in the sky world, received a new kind of wealth: horses, sheep, pigs, goats, and chickens. He later would return to earth with these animals, thereby beginning to dominate the American Southwest during the mid-16th century.[39]

On the other hand, the Great Gambler may have been a magician or sorcerer with a non-Indian hooked or crooked nose—at least that's what Navajo archaeologist Taft Blackhorse claims. (Thus, he may have even been of Semitic origin!) Blackhorse also believes that the great house in Chaco Canyon called Kin Klizhin, literally "Black Charcoal," had a "barbecue pit" inside its tower kiva, which functioned as an altar for ritual cannibalism. "According to Blackhorse, the Gambler rode out to Kin Klizhin in a large reptile that was his guardian. His priests sacrificed humans at the site, and the Gambler, says Blackhorse, came here 'to swallow their souls.'"[40]

What was that giant reptile, anyway? A type of chariot or perhaps even some sort of flying serpent-machine?

The early 20th century ethnographer Alfred Tozzer states that Navajo myth equates the Gambler with Orion. This sky-giant, however, is the reverse of the Old World one: Rigel is his left hand instead of his left foot, whereas Betelgeuse is his right foot rather than his right shoulder.[41]

The oral tradition provides slight variations in the basic narrative. One version includes an interesting detail. Just before the winner of the contests, *H*astsé*h*ogan Jr., was to kill the Gambler with an ax, the Sun exclaimed:

> "'Wait a minute, do not kill him, *he is your elder brother* [italics added]. Why kill him when he has nothing but his life on the earth?' The Sun laid the Black Bow down and told the young man to stand the Gambler on the top of it, and to stretch the cord and let go. It threw the Gambler up into the air. He went up a little way and called out: 'Long ago I died in the center of the earth.' He went up still farther and called down: 'Long ago I died in the center of the earth. My spirit will want to return there. My spirit will want to return to the center of the earth.' He went still farther up in the sky and all that they heard was: 'Adios.' He was gone. He went to the upper worlds."[42]

In its day, Chaco Canyon would have certainly been considered the cosmological center. And use of the Spanish word confirms Turner's hypothesis that the "bad guys" originated in Mexico. The fact that the Gambler was apparently the older brother of the Navajo man that beat him points to a common mythological theme found in the Southwest and Mesoamerica.

My friend, the diffusionist scholar Gene Matlock, comments on this duality: "...the Phoenicians and the Hebrews, who always traveled together, were known throughout the world, in every culture, even in the Americas, as 'twins': Gemini twins, Castor and Pollux; the Warrior Twins (among American Indians); the Asvin brothers or Nasatyas Twins in India. Wherever these myths of 'twins' can be found, we know automatically... that the Phoencians were once there."[43] Thus, this may explain the distinctive nasal feature that Mr. Blackhorse pointed out. (For the Gemini region of Arizona, see the map on p. 189.)

Salako kachina doll.

Another Hopi name for Chaco Canyon is Yupköyvi, or literally, "the place beyond the horizon." According to Leigh J. Kuwanwisiwma, director the Hopi Cultural Preservation Office, the Bow Clan once moved to Chaco Canyon from Hoo'ovi (literally, "arrow-up place"). Today the site is known as Aztec Ruins National Monument, located about 55 miles due north of Chaco in extreme northern New Mexico. The name perhaps refers to the symbolic archery-energy that bow-shaped Pueblo Bonito shoots to the north. Its semicircular "bow" faces northward, while its "string" runs precisely east-west along the southern side. Its south-north axis is, in fact, just .2° east of true north—an accuracy comparable to the geodetic measurements of Egypt's Great Pyramid.

This clan settled in the canyon and began performing the Salako (Shalako) ceremony. The traditional purpose of the ritual dance is to attract what the Hopi call the Cloud People. Kuwanwisiwma comments on the clan's migrations: "The Bow clan members stayed at Yupköyvi for a long time, performing their dance four times every sixteen years. Then they returned to Hoo'ovi, from where they carried the ceremony to Awatovi and later Orayvi [Oraibi]. The many kivas at Pueblo Bonito are seen by Hopis as Salako kivas, because every time the ceremony was performed, a kiva 'home' had to be constructed for it."[44]

Oraibi, founded about 1120 AD, is one of the primary towns still inhabited on the Hopi Third Mesa in Arizona. The village of Awa'tovi ("bow-up place") located on Antelope Mesa was established even before the other villages on the Hopi Mesas. Members of the spiritually important Bear Clan saw the smoke of its hearths to the east when they first arrived at Third Mesa.[45]

Awa'tovi was destroyed and abandoned in 1700 AD. It is the only known instance of major intra-tribal violence in Hopi history, and even today they are loath to talk about it. To briefly summarize the event, the Warrior Societies from the villages of Walpi on First Mesa and Oraibi killed all the men of Awa'tovi and took the women and children prisoners. The cause of the massacre was that fact that most of Awatovi's population agreed to be converted to Catholicism and had been baptized. As in many other cases regarding the Pueblo people of the Southwest, the intrusion of Spanish missionaries had threatened the survival of traditional Hopi religion.[46]

The most distinctive feature of the Salako kachina is its height. Rising seven to eight feet above the plaza, it towers over the other kachinas. A white shawl and a long, eagle-feathered dress cover its slender body, which is armless or even shoulderless, resembling the pictographs seen on p. 210. Its mask has horizontal slits for eyes, in most cases no nose, and a rainbow-colored chin beneath a red mouth shaped like an inverted U. The figure sometimes wears gaudy, multi-strand turquoise necklaces—perhaps symbolic of Chaco's role as clearinghouse for the blue stone in the American Southwest. The Salako kachina's headdress, or tablita, adds additional height, with its stepped-cloud icons and eagle plumes.

Author Frank Waters has called the Shalako ceremony the "Zuni Book of the Dead." Both the Shalako and the ceremony described in *The Tibetan Book of the Dead* take place over a period of 49 days.

> "For above all, the Shalako is a ceremonial for the dead. The process of death, the return of the dead, the ritual feeding of the dead, the long recitals of the spirits of the dead, the psychological preparation for death—these combine into the one underlying motif of the complete ceremonial. This is what makes it one of the greatest Pueblo ceremonials and one of the unique rituals in the world. To understand its meaning we

> must bear in mind all that we have learned of Pueblo and Navaho eschatology and its parallels found in *Bardo Thodol, The Tibetan Book of the Dead,* in *The Secret of the Golden Flower,* the Chinese *Book of Life,* and in the Egyptian *Book of the Dead.*"[47]

In that vein the Hopi definition of the word *sa'lakwtimayto* is revealing. It means "go to see the Shalako ceremony (usu. in ref. to the Zuni Shalako). Also said as a euphemism for 'die.' He went to see the Shalako ceremony. (could mean: He died.)"[48]

These imposing Salako figures eerily floating across the plazas of Pueblo Bonito must have instilled an uncanny sense of fear mingled with reverence. Rudolph Otto has deemed this phenomenon *mysterium tremendum,* the "Wholly Other," or a paradoxical feeling of numinous dread.[49]

In addition to mythological evidence from Aztec Ruins, where the Salako ceremony originated, we have archaeological evidence of giants living there. In one of the rooms the bones of an obviously high-status man nicknamed "the Warrior" was found, wrapped in a turkey-feather blanket. His skeleton measured 6'2" tall, making him at least a foot taller than the average height of males at that time.

A Mesa Verde kiva jar was broken over his skull. On top of his body was found a large woven-basketry shield measuring three feet in diameter. The center of the shield was painted blue-green, and the dark red band on its rim was speckled with selenite, or moonstone, which has a pearly blue luster. Placed on this warrior shield were several curved sticks that may have served as either swords or long throwing sticks (i.e., boomerangs). When the discovery was made, newspapers called him "a veritable giant" and "the emperor of the Aztecs of the village."[50]

In our journey to seek evidence of giants in American Southwest, we have spent a lot of time in Chaco Canyon. This erstwhile nexus of gigantism included ghastly tales of cannibalism and aberrations of both body and spirit. Archaeologists have proven that the individuals living in Pueblo Bonito were the tallest in the Southwest. This is the mainly result of a protein-intensive and iron-rich diet, though distinctive genetics may have also play a part.

The irony is (no pun intended), the San Juan Basin where Chaco lies has never been replete with big game animals such as the elk, moose, bighorn sheep, and bear that are found in the mountains. In addition, buffalo herds were restricted to the plains of eastern New Mexico. The pronghorn or mule deer are rarely seen now, but if they ever lived here at all in substantial numbers, they were probably hunted out in the first century or so of Chaco's existence. This left only smaller game such as rabbits, squirrels, raccoons, and wood rats—hardly enough protein to produce the domineering height of the rulers. The only reasonable explanation is anthropophagy—or, to use the emotionally charged term, cannibalism.

And emotion –primarily terror– was the paramount means of control. Did crypto-zoological giants akin to Bigfoot actually walk across the American Southwest? And did they have six toes on each foot? Or did unusually tall humans don gruesome masks to make their appearance even more fearsome? Whatever the case, these imposing figures endure.

Legends of giants are still dramatically represented in various Hopi sacred rituals. As I previously mentioned, at one kachina dance in the late 1990s at Oraibi, I saw a Hu Kachina, or Ogre, walk into the plaza, carrying an imposing butcher knife. (See photo and description on p. 101.) His fierce presence even today is a terrifying reminder of the persistent role of giants in the Hopi world, whose ancestors once either migrated to or inhabited Chaco Canyon.

Canine Coda

Mainstream archaeologist Brian Fagan asks the same question that anyone who has ever visited Chaco Canyon poses: in essence, why here? "By any standards, Chaco Canyon is a place with unpredictable water supplies. Herein lies the question of questions. How did people manage to build numerous large pueblos in a place where water supplies were at best exiguous, the growing season relatively short, and the temperature contrasts enormous? The question has exercised some of archaeology's best minds for more than a century."[51]

Few academics, however, would attribute the positioning of the particular locus of the "Chaco-plex" to a grand celestial schema. According to the basics of the star correlation theory, this is yet another template of constellations projected upon the Earth. (See maps on p. 189 and p. 326.) Egypt was apparently not the only ancient land that lived by the maxim "As above, so below."

Chaco/Sirius was the first in the series of sites that mirrored the heavens, beginning construction about 850–900 AD. Next was Canyon de Chelly/Saiph in Orion, where cliff dwellings were built—starting in about 1050. The Hopi Mesas/Orion's belt were settled in 1100 AD or so, and Wupatki/Bellatrix was developed about two decades later—thereby completing the east-to-west axis. The pueblos at Homol'ovi/Betelgeuse and the cliff dwellings at Betatakin and Keet Seel/Rigel were constructed at the same time, circa 1250 AD. Both sites on the north-south axis are equidistant from the Hopi Mesas. Thus, it took a total of about four centuries for this sky-to-ground pattern to be completed. The *Hisatsinom* were a patient people.

It is my contention that a group of proto-Aztecs called the Chichimecs, or "Sons of the Dog," directed building of the monumental architectural structures in Chaco Canyon—the place of the Dog Star. This tribe of erstwhile hunter-gathers who settled into the decadent urban life at Chaco had a primary symbol: the bow. The Chichimecs may in fact have also been called the "Sons of the Bow," for it was they who eventually introduced this formidable weapon to Mesoamerica. British scholar Gordon Brotherston comments:

> "Along with the spear-thrower [atlatl] came the bow and arrow. As developed by peoples north of Mexico, it was brought south by the Nahua-speaking Chichimec and played a big role in Mesoamerica in the centuries immediately prior to the Spanish conquest. Because of its range and accuracies, this weapon was frequently related to the very notion of restless ambition and military expansion, and to what the Aztecs called the 'acquisitions of the hunt'."[52]

The Chichimecs may also have had associations with the Hopi Bow Clan. On the top of p. 91, I quoted another British scholar, Richard Maitland Bradfield, on the character of the Reed-Greasewood-Bow phratry, which includes the Bow Clan. He claims that it is inherently associated with the stars, especially the winter constellations of Orion and the Pleiades. This clan grouping is also connected with warfare, and, of course, hunting with the bow-and-arrow.[53] The phratry is furthermore linked with the Ko'kop-Coyote clan grouping. "Wolf and coyote... are sources of *duhisa,* witch power. So also are dogs *(po'ko)* and owls *(moñwu),* both of which figure among the clan names of Reed-Greasewood-Bow."[54] Many of these dark themes have already been dealt with in this chapter.

One funerary practice highlights the canine. Hundreds of dogs were ritually buried between 400 BC and 1100 AD in northern New Mexico and on the New Mexico-Arizona border. This suggests that canines "…played a key role in the spiritual beliefs of ancient Americans…" These grave dogs, which in the arid climate became naturally mummified, served as escorts in the spirit's afterlife journey through the underworld.

Dody Fugate, an assistant curator at the Museum of Indian Arts and Culture in Santa Fe, New Mexico, remarks: "All of that area was full of doggy people."[55] If we consider the possible presence of the Chichmecs in the San Juan Basin, then Fugate is correct in more ways than one.

The ancient Egyptian jackal-headed god Anubis and the Aztecan dog-headed god of death Xolotl are just two examples of the same meme found all over the world. This canine psychopomp, or spirit guide, is perhaps suggested by the sidereal presence of two dogs, one large and one small, at the feet of Orion.

In the Southwest this tradition goes back at least to the late Basketmaker Period (450–750 AD). For instance, the mummies of a collie and a short-haired terrier were found in a Basketmaker cave in northeast Arizona. Dogs were not generally used as food because very few of their bones are found in refuse heaps.[56] In some cases the interred dogs were in fact given other bones to chew on in the afterlife.

In a small pueblo (Site 1360) north of Fajada Butte in Chaco

Canyon, quite a large kennel must have existed because the remains of more than two dozen small dogs were found—both puppies and adults.[57] At the former Bow Clan stronghold of Awa'tovi village (mentioned on pp. 224-225), murals of the Poko (Dog) Kachina were also discovered .[58]

One Hopi legend describes the quest of a Reed Clan member named Sikyá-tsi-tiyo, or Yellow Bird Youth, to find a pet dog. He journeyed to the home of the Dog People, the entrance of which was guarded by a huge snake named Káytoye (or Káto'ya, black Guardian Snake of the West and night), whom he placated with a *paho*, or prayer feather. At the top of a mountain he saw a large space flooded with water from which protruded a ladder. He descended the ladder to the Dog People's kiva and saw dog-skins hung on the wall. Humans donned these skins and began to dance, turning into dogs in the process. He then selected one male and one female puppy to take back home with him on Second Mesa.[59]

In the next chapter we turn from Dog People to Mothman.

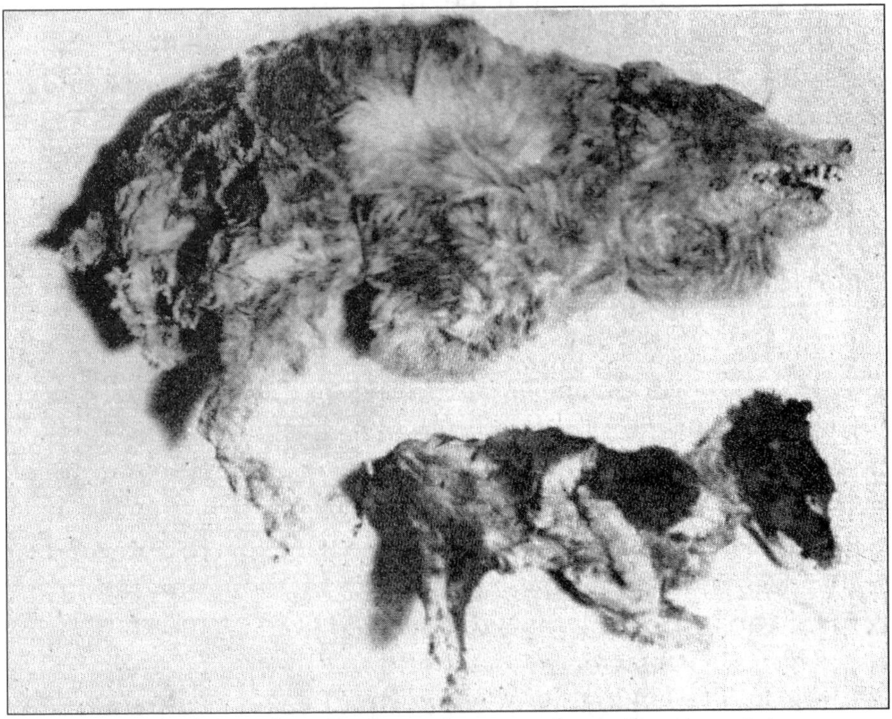

Mummified dogs from Basketmaker caves in northeastern Arizona.

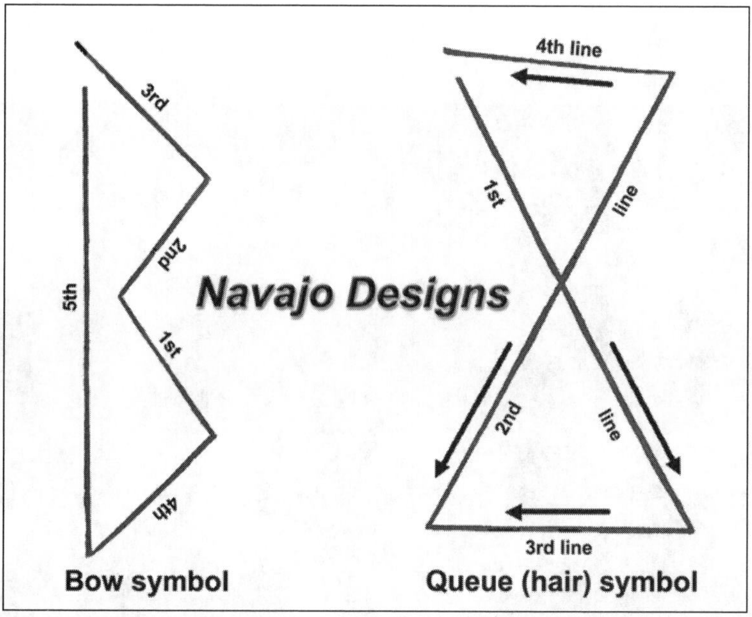

Left: The symbol worn during the Night Chant on the left leg by the impersonator of Nayénezgani, Alien God Slayer or Monster Slayer, who was mentioned on p. 200 in connection will the killing of the Piute giant. He was born after Estsánatlehi, or Changing Woman, was impregnated by a ray of the Sun.

Right: During the same ceremony this symbol is worn on the left leg by the impersonator of *To'*badzists*í*ni, Child of the Water, who was born after Yo*l*kaí Están, or White Shell Woman (Changing Woman's younger sister), was impregnated by a waterfall. The queue symbol resembles Orion, the pattern of which is found in Arizona. In rock art, opposing triangles designate warfare.

The elder Nayénezgani and the younger *To'*badzists*í*ni together form the Hero Twins, or warrior twins. The former is associated with light and heat, whereas the latter is associated with darkness and moisture. As noted on p. 223, this duality is omnipresent in myths around the world. Nááhwíílbiihí (the Gambler, who is sometimes seen as Orion) and the son of *H*astsé*h*ogan, the Navajo younger brother who defeated him in a series of contests and shot him into the sky with a bow, may also be connected with this sibling pairing.

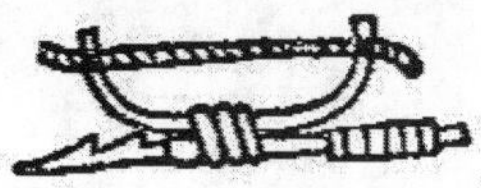

Symbol of the Chichimecs, "Sons of the Dog"

Left-below: Bow symbol of the Chichimecs who inhabited Chaco Canyon, which corresponds to Sirius, the Dog Star. The Hopi word *poko* means "dog." The Hopi elder twin is named Pokonghoya which is the Reed-Greasewood-Bow phratry's clan deity.

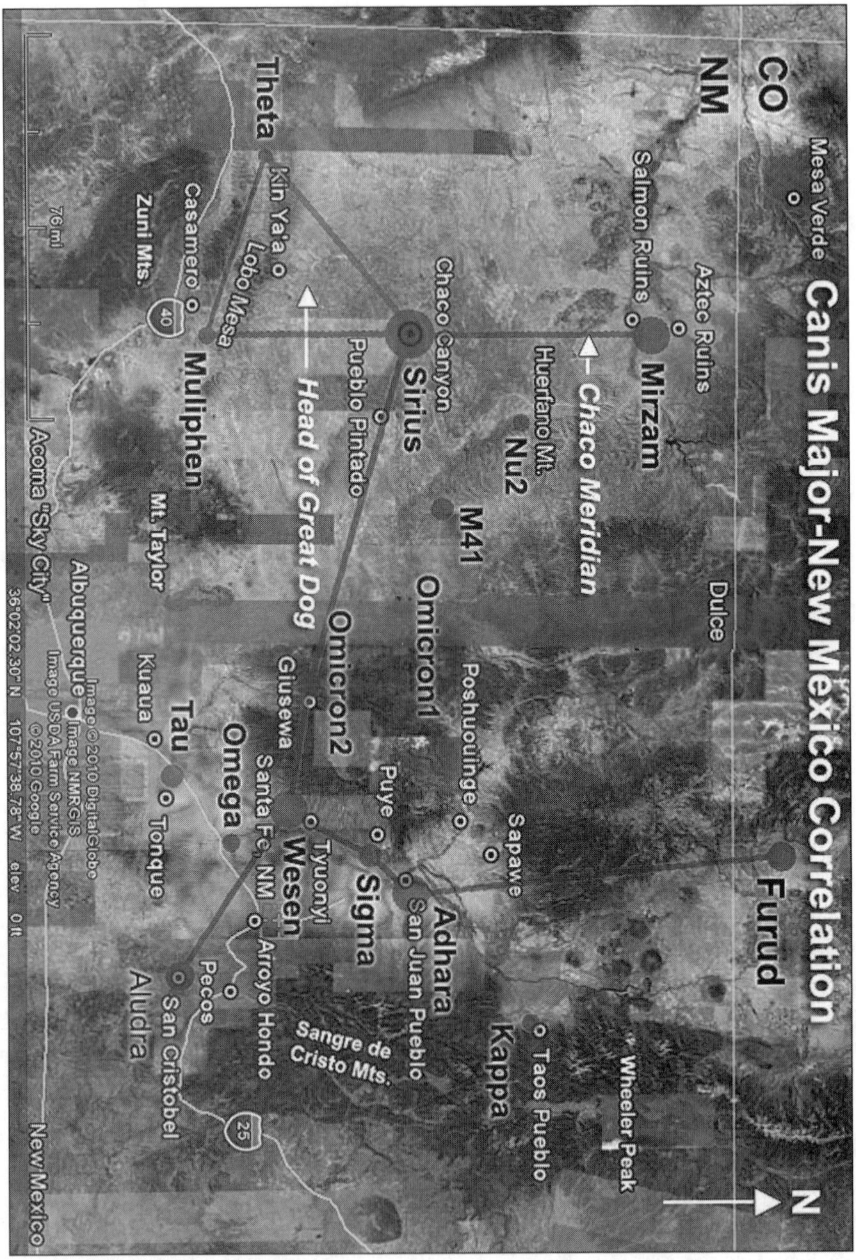

© 2010 Google Earth.

Chapter 12
Indian Mothman and Sacred Datura

From late 1966 though late 1967 the small town of Point Pleasant, West Virginia, along the Ohio River was terrorized by a series of sightings of an uncanny creature that became known as Mothman. He was typically described as a broad-shouldered black or gray humanoid at least seven feet in height with moth-like wings that extended about ten feet. His glowing red eyes seemed to have a hypnotic effect. Sometimes the creature appeared headless, with his round, reflective eyes set down in his shoulders.

The eerie entity would reportedly swoop down on people or cars and chase them at very high speeds. Sometimes it would suddenly shoot straight up in the air and completely disappear. During the same period accounts of luminous balls or other UFOs and unexpected appearances of Men In Black increased.

Were all these sightings of Mothman and other anomalous incidents just a weird precursor to the brief psychedelic era in popular culture when hallucinations became the norm? Or are there precedents for this phenomenon in the distant past?

Cut to the high plain of central New Mexico in about the middle of the 14th century. On the western bank of a turbulent, muddy river we see a flat-topped pyramid where a bizarre ritual is taking place. It involves a ring of elders wearing feathered head-dresses, geometric medallions, white sashes, and brightly painted capes. Some are holding round shields and eagle-talon staffs.

At the center stands a tall being with the gray wings and

coiled proboscis of the night flying hawk moth. One of the elders raises a woven plaque heaped with tiny yellow and black seeds and brown spiny pods. The participants begin to eat the seeds, while low chants punctuated by a lone cottonwood drum rise into the endless desert night.

An uncertain period passes as dizzy heads spin in swirling silver smoke. The creature then extends his massive wings and rockets high above the lone pyramid. He soars over whispering cornfields and circles the bulwark of the pueblo. Suddenly in a burst of purple light the Mothman disappears into gauzy clouds, while moths flutter gently over jimsonweed blossoms glowing ghostlike in silent moonlight.

Located about 12 miles southwest of the modern town of Los Lunas is the ancient village where this ritual took place. Archaeologists know it as Pottery Mound, named for the profusion of polychrome potsherds. In fact, a greater variety of pottery styles were found there than at any other spot in New Mexico, with culturally distinctive ceramics coming from the Zuni and Acoma regions to the northwest and the Hopi region even farther northwest. About 90 percent of the pottery retrieved from the site is non-utilitarian or decorative, so in its heyday the place was probably a major ceremonial center.

Frank C. Hibben, the head archaeologist who initially excavated the site, writes: "The Rio Puerco Valley at the site of Pottery Mound is wide and almost level. In the whole region there is no place where a flat-topped structure of even modest dimensions would appear more imposing than at this spot. It is easy to see why the original builders constructed a pyramid there."[1]

The pyramid itself, technically called a "platform mound," was constructed of puddled adobe and trash fill. As Hibben suggests, it must have dominated the expansive landscape, although it once rose only about 13 feet above the plain. Its sloping sides were originally coated with a smooth caliche surface. The mound was built on two levels with the upper one covering about 215 square feet.

Surprisingly, three pueblos, each three or four stories high, had been constructed at different times –one above the other– on top of the pyramid, with additional buildings extending down the sides and around the base. Perhaps these were added at a later stage. Also unearthed were four plazas and 16 rectangular kivas (subterranean ceremonial prayer-chambers) that were roughly 30 by 30-some feet in size plus one round kiva 22 feet in diameter.

The flat-topped structure was similar to those found in Mexico, especially at the major settlement of Paquimé (also called Casas Grandes) in Chihuahua. It may even have had an affinity to the larger stone pyramids farther south, for which the Toltec, Maya, and Zapotec are renowned. A sunken edifice that looks like a ball court located just south of the mound also points to Mesoamerican influences.

The most spectacular feature of Pottery Mound, however, is not either the pyramid or the pottery. Instead we find the walls of every kiva covered with lavishly painted murals depicting a variety of social and spiritual motifs.

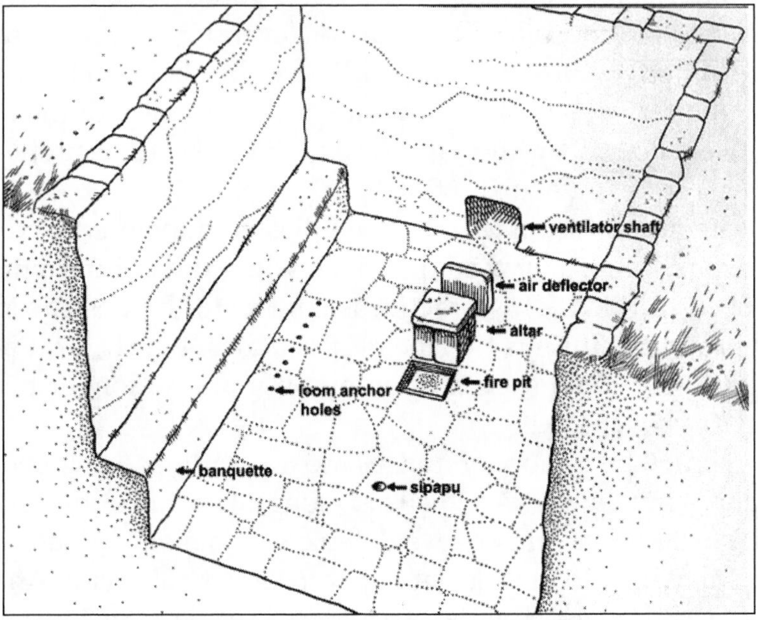

Typical rectangular kiva at Pottery Mound. The access was via a ladder through an overhead hatchway. Colorful murals covered all four walls. The *sipapu* (hole in the floor) is conceptualized as a portal to the underworld.

Rock art expert Polly Schaafsma defers in this case to the subtler visual medium by stating that these murals were essentially the "apex of Pueblo art":

> "The mural art consists of bold, dynamic design layouts adapted to the entire wall surface. Border and framing lines are often used to break up the wall surface, or the whole wall may be treated as a single, unbounded, integrated composition. Subject matter consists of ceremonial and ritual themes into which elaborately attired humans, animals, birds, and abstract designs are incorporated. Shields, feathers, baskets, pots, jewelry, textiles, miscellaneous ceremonial items, food, and plants are also pictured. While this is a highly meaningful art, full of graphic portrayals and symbolic content, it is, at the same time, very decorative. Colors are highly varied and sensitively juxtaposed. Areas of flat solid color contrast with those broken into intricate patterns or bold designs."[2]

One of the most striking aspects of the murals is the variety of brilliant colors: eight shades of red, three of yellow, two of green, two of blue, as well as purple, lavender, maroon, orange, pink, salmon, white, gray, and outlines of black. From three to 38 layers of plaster, each one providing a visual space for the paintings, were found on the kiva walls. Thus, the total prehistoric murals numbered about 800!

Some murals seem to have been plastered, painted, and then re-plastered after just a couple days when their ritual purpose had been fulfilled. This practice is similar to the destruction of Navajo sand paintings or Tibetan mandalas, which form a crucial part of a given sacred ceremony but are no longer needed when it is concluded.

Among the plethora of images are non-indigenous green parrots and scarlet macaws, which also suggest a wide trade network with Mexico. One fresco even depicts a jaguar and an eagle, which may refer to the ancient Mexican jaguar-eagle cult. Another shows a rattlesnake superimposed on an "eagle-man." Just add a cactus and you'd have the traditional symbol for Mexico.

One disturbing image shows an unfortunate man painted

purple with a red equilateral, outlined cross on his chest being eaten by a horned serpent with sharp teeth and a feathered ruff. This creature is, of course, the archetypal plumed serpent Quetzalcoatl, also called Awanyu by the ancestral Puebloans of New Mexico. Another mural shows a horned serpent with a zigzag body cradling a four-pointed star with a circular face at the center. This star-face (which, by the way, is frowning) supposedly signifies a "soul-face," possibly the soul of a warrior killed in battle. (See painting on p. 241.)

Some of the most unusual murals, however, are those that depict what today we call the Mothman. One shows the creature with a red body, white sash, black kilt with geometric designs, and a red headdress. His translucent wings are cross-hatched and painted with a few lavender spots. One wing's lower edge has three red spots on a white jagged background. (See top of p. 238.)

The other figure in basically the same pose has a yellow body and a brown and yellow headdress. This one has star symbols on his wings and a couple of dragonfly symbols beneath him. (See top of p. 239.) With his left hand he is grasping a lightning bolt emanating from a bowl balanced on a maiden's head. (She is not seen in this picture, but she is, by the way, holding a macaw in each hand.) Both of the Mothman figures have a coiled or curved proboscis.

What prompted the depiction of this strange insect-human hybrid? One of the archaeological interns who originally excavated Pottery Mound and helped to copy its murals has put forth an intriguing theory. In a poster presentation at the Society for American Archaeology conference, March 2005 in Salt Lake City, Utah, independent researcher and anthropologist Paul T. Kay provided some interesting links between the night flying hawk moth (*Manduca sexta,* also called sphinx moth) and the Datura plant. "There exists a mutualistic relationship in nature between the hawk moth and the Datura plant. ALL of this is related to the widespread ritualistic use of Datura during SHAMANIC practices…"[3] The pink-spotted hawk moth (*Agrius cingulata*) may also have been intended.

[continued on p. 240]

Mural of Mothman with red body at Pottery Mound, New Mexico.

Pink-spotted hawk moth (*Agrius cingulata*) on a jimsonweed bloom.

Mural of Mothman with yellow body and star symbols on wings.

Sphinx moth (*Manduca sexta*) with yellow on wings.

Datura wrightii is known as devil's weed, thorn apple, or jimsonweed. The latter term is a corruption of Jamestown weed, after the Virginia colony where Europeans first unwittingly ingested a similar species. This perennial grows throughout the American Southwest in open land with well-drained soil. Its nocturnally blooming, white trumpet-shaped flowers are pollinated by the hummingbird-sized hawk moth, which inserts its long proboscis into the fragrant flower tube to reach the profuse nectar.

Kay furthermore believes that the classic plumed serpent traditionally depicted on ceramics, murals, and rock art is actually the instar, or larva, of this moth. The only problem with this part of Kay's theory, however, is that the 'horn' is at the posterior, not the head. Ancient Pottery Mound inhabitants would surely have known this.

Datura is a powerful and dangerous hallucinogen.[4] It has been used both medicinally and ritually for at least 4,000 years in the Southwest. Ground-up portions of the plant were sometimes employed as an anesthetic or as a salve for wounds or bruises. The Aztecs called it *toloatzin*, or "nodding head." This refers to the seedpods but may as well mimic the unconscious head of one who has ingested the psychotropic plant. The Navajo have a folk adage regarding this poisonous tropane alkaloid of the nightshade family: "Eat a little, and go to sleep. Eat some more, and have a dream. Eat some more, and don't wake up."

Symptoms of Datura intoxication include dizziness, flushing, fever, dilated pupils, temporary blindness, dry skin and mouth, difficulty swallowing, tachycardia, heightened sexuality, restlessness, inability to concentrate, idiosyncratic or violent behavior, delirium, visual and auditory hallucinations, sometimes terrifying phantasmagoria, inability to distinguish fantasy from "reality," and amnesia.

Ethnobotanist and health guru Andrew Weil highlights the negative aspects of the plant: "*Datura* is not a nice drug. Although sometimes classified as a hallucinogen, it should not be confused with the psychedelics. It is much more toxic than the psychedelics and tends to produce delirium and disorientation. Moreover, *Datura* keeps bad company. All over the world it is a drug of poisoners, criminals, and black magicians."[5]

[continued on p. 242]

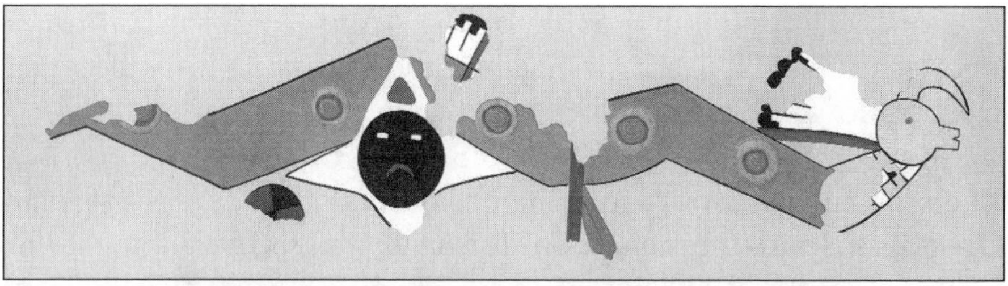

Mural of star-face and horned serpent with feather ruff.

Hawk moth larva.

Above: Egyptian hieroglyphic for "star."

Right: Blossom of *Datura wrightii*.

Various species of Datura grow in Egypt. Is the morphology of the night-blooming "moonflower" the source for this hieroglyphic? *Duat*, the Egyptian word meaning "underworld," was also spelled *Dat*, the root of the word Datura.[6]

For the indigenous people of the Andes in Peru, Datura is known as *yerba de huaca*, or "herb of the graves." This is because its use allowed communication with the spirits of ancestors.[7]

Many tribes of the western U.S. have traditionally incorporated the Sacred Datura into their religious rites. "Societies in the Great Basin and in much of California also used the plant, where it was commonly employed in vision quests for spirit helpers and in boys' initiation rites… Ritual uses include initiation, divination, good luck, and transport to the spirit world for other purposes. Shamanic healers have exploited the plant's mind-altering qualities to diagnose illnesses in patients."[8]

Zuni priests of New Mexico used Datura to communicate with birds and petition them for rain. "In 1879 the writer discovered that the Zunis employed a narcotic… found to be *Datura stramonium* or jimson weed… when the rain priests go out at night to commune with the feathered kingdom, they put a bit of powdered root into their mouth so that the birds may not be afraid and will listen to them when they pray to the birds to sing for the rains to come."[9]

Extracts or derivatives of Datura mixed with the fat of a wild boar are sometimes used in a paste known as a "flying ointment." Anthropologist and author Carlos Castaneda, during his tutelage with the Yaqui shaman and *diablero* don Juan Matus, recounts his teacher's intimate knowledge of Datura to accomplish psychic flight:

> "The second portion of the devil's weed [the root] is used to fly… The unguent by itself is not enough. My benefactor said that it is the root that gives direction and wisdom, and it is the cause of flying. As you learn more, and take it often in order to fly, you will begin to see everything with great clarity. You can soar through the air for hundreds of miles to see what is happening at any place you want, or to deliver a fatal blow to your enemies far away. As you become familiar with the devil's weed, she will teach you how to do such things."[10]

In this case the plant itself is referred to as a feminine ally who is actually conscious. Castaneda asks whether his own body actually flew like a bird, and don Juan replies:

> "A man flies with the help of the second portion of the devil's weed. That is all I can tell you. What you want to know makes no sense. Birds fly like birds and a man who has taken the devil's weed flies as such [*el enyerbado vuela así*]."
>
> "As birds do? [*Así como los pájaros?*]."
>
> "No, he flies as a man who has taken the weed [*No, así como los enyerbados*]."[11]

Several jimsonweed seeds were actually found in a deeply buried room floor at Pottery Mound. In addition, small ceramic effigy vessels have also been discovered in the region. Conical bumps on their outer surface resemble the spiny seedpods. They may have been used either to store the seeds or as a cup for the Datura brew.

A menacing anthropoid painted on the interior of a different type of flat pottery bowl has a body that resembles the plant's round, prickly seedpod. (See middle photo on p. 244.) He has half-moon eyes, a rectangular mouth with teeth, and red hair or headdress. This last feature may correspond to the red headpiece of the first Mothman mural shown above.

As mentioned in the previous chapter, members of Hopi Fire Clan (*Ko'kop*) were also known as "the redheads." Perhaps this aggressive clan, which also founded the Warrior Society named *Mòmtsit*, is depicted on the pottery bowl.

The Fire Clan is furthermore associated with an ominous being named Masau'u, the Hopi god of death, war, and the underworld. The figure depicted on the ceramic resembles some of the Hopi rock art renditions of this god. Interesting in this context is the Hopi word for moth: *masivi*. This word has the same root as the name of the Hopi death god, which literally means gray—the color of moth wings.

[continued on p. 245]

Spiny seedpods of the Datura.

Red ceramic bowl with "Datura Man" painted in black and red.

Pot with painted moth from the ruins of Puaray, located near Bernalillo, New Mexico, a little over 40 miles north of Pottery Mound. Occupied between 1300 and some time prior to 1680 AD, Puaray was known as the pueblo of the Worm or the Insect, which may refer to the hawk moth larva.[12]

One Hopi synonym for "moth" is even more intriguing: *Tsimonmana* specifically refers to "a type of moth attracted to jimsonweed." This word literally means "jimsonweed maiden"[13], thereby echoing the feminine designation of Datura that we find in Yaqui culture. Some Hopi legends do indeed describe pairs of licentious young femme fatales who wear Datura blossoms in their hair while they seduce and harm unsuspecting males. We thus have the moth and jimsonweed contained in the single Hopi word, *Tsimonmana*.

One Zuni legend describes a girl and boy who dwell in the underworld but suddenly find a trail that leads to the bright earth plane. On their heads they wear garlands of Datura blossoms, which allow them to put people to sleep and or make people see ghosts. This sorcery alarms the gods, so the children are sent back to the dark realm. The beautiful but deadly white flowers remain, however, and are soon spread far and wide across the desert.[14]

The Zuni are culturally related to the Hopi, so it is interesting that the Hopi *puvuwi* is another word that means moth, but has an alternative meaning of "someone who sleeps all the time."

Other peculiar creatures depicted at Pottery Mound seem to resemble those far to the south. Fortean researcher John A. Keel describes a number of cryptozoomorphs in his book *The Mothman Prophecies*, which ignited the initial frenzy surrounding the modern Mothman sightings. He specifically refers to Mexican tales of black flying entities called *ikals* that live deep in caverns like bats.[15] The Mayan word *ik* means air or wind and *ikal* means spirit, while *ek* means black.

These hairy humanoids are on the average of three feet tall, and they have human hands but horse hooves on their feet. They are mostly nocturnal and spheres of light sometimes accompany them. The Tzeltal Maya of Chiapas try to fight off these ugly creatures with machetes when they fly down and attack them. They can paralyze humans and are known to kidnap and rape women.

One Pottery Mound mural seems to portray this figure precisely. The short, dark figure with piercing brown eyes and a frowning red mouth is suspended upside down in the air over a red slab that designates the earth. His left hand has two curved lines instead of fingers. This may correspond to the hooves of the Mayan version, though they are on his hand instead of his foot.

The Mothman's flight patterns seem to range extensively through space and time. Just as he was seen along the Ohio River in recent times, he haunted the Rio Puerco Valley of New Mexico 700 years ago. The range of Datura is equally extensive, from the East to the West Coasts of the United States and from Canada down to southern Mexico. Perhaps this potent psychoactive plant merely opens a dark doorway through which the inter-dimensional Mothman flies toward the light. Whatever the reality, this wingéd wraith has taken hold of our modern imagination just as surely as it must have moved those pueblo people at Pottery Mound so long ago.

Pottery Mound mural of a creature that resembles the Mayan *ikal*. It also is similar to the Hopi death god Masau'u mentioned above.

Right: Grapevine Canyon in the southern tip of Nevada. Datura plant (foreground-left) in front of boulder with abstract petroglyphs, possibly depicting entoptic imagery.

Below: Collage of the Hopi god Masau'u and Orion near Oraibi, Arizona.[16]

Chapter 13
Arizona's Psychic Archaeology

Mainstream academics said no artifacts would ever be found there, but Jeffrey Goodman, a Ph.D. archaeologist and geological engineer, proved them wrong… with the help of a bona fide psychic! His stunning discoveries were made during the 1970s along a dry creek bed high in the San Francisco Peaks near Flagstaff, Arizona.

The Hopi consider this area to be the home of the kachinas (also spelled *katsinam*). These spirit messengers live in the sacred mountains from July until December and spend the rest on the year on the Hopi Mesas about 75 miles to the northeast.

At an elevation of 8,000 feet, the excavation was no Sunday picnic. Goodman dug a shaft five feet square and, eventually, thirty-five feet deep. He used a boom and winch to extract rocks and soil from the hole, and wooden beams to reinforce it. He gradually had to switch from shovels to chisels and sledgehammers and finally an air hammer and compressor. At a couple points he even had to dynamite large boulders that impeded his downward progress. Late in the dig, Goodman tunneled horizontally into the shaft for fifteen feet, shoring up the sides and roof.

This project becomes even more interesting when considering its unorthodox methodology. An aeronautical engineer named Aron Abrahamsen, who also happened to be a psychic, told Goodman exactly where to dig. He assisted him both long-distance from Oregon and on-site in Arizona by using what is known as psychic archaeology.

[continued on p. 250]

Schultz Pass in the San Francisco Peaks in northern Arizona, where extremely ancient artifacts were found. From the Hopi Mesas on winter solstice, a Sun Chief watches the sun set on the horizon near the pass. This area in the Coconino National Forest was burned by a 15,000-acre fire in the summer of 2010.

Probable site of Goodman's archaeological excavation with metal doors over hole. Photo taken in about 2000—over 25 years after the dig.

This discipline is basically defined as the employment of a psychic's skills to locate archaeological sites and identify their artifacts. The psychic uses clairvoyance and retro-cognition (seeing into the past) or other techniques to assist in the progression of an archaeological dig.

Abrahamsen's abilities included psi-mediated mental imagery –what today we would call technical remote viewing– along with discarnate spirit guides, or channeling. Although discounted by nearly all professionally trained archaeologists, psychic archaeology nonetheless appears to have unearthed some intriguing evidence.

Out of this psychic's 57 archaeological and geological predictions, 50 proved correct, which is an 87% success rate. These results verified Goodman's own precognitive dreams, which set him on his wild quest in the first place.

In one dream Goodman was searching for the archaeological remains of ancient hunters who used head deformation. Believing he would find blackened skeletons together with some sort of jewels, he lifted up one creek bank like a trap door and discovered bones resting in strange black soil. Then he woke up.

But regarding what would become the real dig, Abrahamsen gave Goodman much detailed information. This included the type of specific artifacts that would be found at given geological levels. At the 27-foot depth in the shaft, for instance, Goodman discovered chert or basalt tools such as choppers, hide scrappers, hammerstones, and flaked blades—all corresponding to a level at least 100,000 years old!

He additionally found an "Apache tear" that came from at least 75 miles away. This teardrop-shaped piece of obsidian used by the Ancient Ones as an ornament was found at the 16-foot level corresponding to 25,000 years old.

These dates, of course, are way outside the traditional paradigm for habitation in the American Southwest. Most academics claim that Paleo-Indians did not live in the region much before 14,000 years ago, although that timeframe is constantly being pushed backward. Bucking the standard line of thinking in his field, George Carter, Ph.D. of Texas A. & M. University, was "tremendously excited" over the artifacts that he examined from Goodman's site. Carter was not at all troubled by their 100,000-year-old date.

Dr. William Kautz of the Stanford Research Institute was also impressed with the project. In addition, John White, director of the education at The Institute for Noetic Sciences, gave Goodman's grant application high priority. But due to tough economic times, the money never materialized, and further expansion of the initial test site came to a halt.

Abrahamsen predicted, however, that many other artifacts would eventually be found, such as woven fabric, potsherds, and even human bones. His clairvoyance included a scene of a mother and her two children who had perished at the site 100 millennia ago, when the ice flows from an avalanche quickly buried them along with their horse.

Goodman in his book *Psychic Archaeology* writes of the potential discoveries that still lie waiting:

> "Aron's readings on the hypothetical full-scale excavation said that we would find evidence of other sophisticated practices as well-carvings, paintings, wooden ankhs, cured leather, and parchment scrolls with hieroglyphic writing. He even cited a mysterious underground tunnel system. This had also been predicted by a number of other psychics who gave me information about the site. (Underground tunnels play a key role in Hopi mythology.)"[1]

The Hopi have lived in the same stone villages in northern Arizona since at least 1100 AD. Legends describe how members of their tribe survived two different world cataclysms by taking refuge in caverns or tunnels. They even state that the destruction of the Second World was caused by ice, perhaps a glacial ice age triggered by a pole shift—thus confirming Abrahamsen's psychic vision of people perishing in the area 100,000 years ago by an avalanche.

The Hopi furthermore say that the people once lived below Grand Canyon in the Third World and emerged to the present Fourth World by climbing up a large tunnel called the *Sipapuni*.

[continued on p. 253]

Satellite photo of the *Sipapuni* on the Little Colorado River, a travertine dome near Grand Canyon. Hopi legends claim this is the actual "Place of Emergence" from the previous Third World, destroyed by a great flood.

Left: The circumpunct. This universal symbol variously represents the sun, gold, the heart, the sacred center, or the creative spark of divine consciousness.

Below: It is highly probable that the three intersecting lines forming the star were human-carved. Is this some sort of star map?

Goodman also contacted a few other psychics to verify Abrahamsen's predictions. These included an anonymous woman associated with the Michigan Metaphysical Society. He sent the subject a map of the Flagstaff area to "psychometrize." (Pyschometry is defined as the handling of relevant objects in order to receive psychic impressions.) The woman visualized a small colony of artists who had come to live by the creek that then flowed like a river. Upheavals in the landscape, however, eventually caused the stream to shrink. She also saw a "black race of people," which long ago traveled through the region on their way to South America.[2]

Goodman speculated that this might be a reference to the Olmecs of Mesoamerica, who created colossal sculptured heads with undeniably African physical characteristics. It is interesting in this regard to note that the Crow Clan, which founded the Hopi village of Mishongnovi on Second Mesa, once lived in the San Francisco Peaks. No one knows why members of this clan generally have darker skin than most Hopis, but they may have mated with this migrating group of blacks.

Incredible as it may seem, Abrahamsen stated that human habitation of the mountainous region reached as far back as 500,000 years ago. Using his psychic insight, he saw communal bands of peaceful people from both Atlantis and Lemuria (Mu) living where tourists now drive their campers. These ancient immigrants cultivated crops and domesticated livestock while possessing an advanced yet non-intrusive technology.

In the subsequent excavation of the same site, University of Alberta archaeologist Alan Bryan, Ph.D., found a geometrically engraved, flat piece of volcanic ash at the 23-foot level. This four-by-six inch stone was incised on both sides, one of which shows a star-like pattern. (See picture on lower part of facing page.)

Goodman in his sequel *American Genesis* writes: "There was no way nature could score such a small stone with so many absolutely straight lines at such angles—on one side, three lines crossed at a single point in a kind of asterisk near the center of the stone and this pattern was repeated near the edge of the stone. Here, finally, was the conclusive piece we had all hoped for. It was as if a Paleo-Indian had left his irrefutable signature for us."[3]

As reported in Goodman's later book *The Genesis Mystery*, Dr. Thor Karlstrom, senior geologist with the U.S. Geological Survey, believed the zone from which the engraved stone came was at least 70,000 years old, making it an interglacial artifact.[4] This scientist's estimate, though not as old as Abrahamsen's, still predates by tens of thousands of years the chronology accepted by most of his colleagues.

On the reverse side of the Flagstaff Stone, a "twinned line" consisting of two lines side by side is seen. This was probably made when an engraving tool jumped out of its track and made an adjacent line. In other words, the lines on the stone were not just naturally scored.

Upon examining this stone in 1980, Alexander Marshack of Harvard's prestigious Peabody Museum said that the engraved lines were similar to those found on stones carved by the Cro-Magnon people in Europe.

The specific location of Dr. Goodman's site in the San Francisco Peaks is also particularly synchronistic.

> "One day as we were setting up at the site, some Hopi Indians came by. One of their religious leaders told us that they had come to gather spruce boughs for the upcoming ceremonial dance *Niman Kachina* from the very slopes on which we were digging. At this dance the Hopi bid farewell to the *Kachinas,* spiritual beings who since the beginning of the world of the Hopis come to help them for part of each year. When not assisting the Hopi, the *kachinas* reside in the mountains outside of Flagstaff. We were digging on the very slopes the priests believed they favored. So if the parallel between Aron's readings and Hopi mythology was correct, we could rest assured that we had good ethnographic control on the location we were digging."[5]

The kachinas migrate from the San Francisco Peaks to the Hopi Mesas after the first day of winter. They return home in July after the *Niman* (Home-Going Dance), the last ceremony in the annual kachina cycle.

The Hopi men gathering spruce for the last dance of the annual ceremonial cycle of the kachinas were not arbitrarily collecting from just any spot on the sacred peaks but were focused on a region near what is called *Luhavwu Chochomo*—literally, Testicle Hill, which looks like what it describes. This is aligned to Schultz Pass, an alpine meadow less than 500 feet wide.

Nearly 80 miles to the northeast is the Hopi village of Walpi on First Mesa. For centuries each *Tawa-mongwi,* or Sun Chief, has stood during the winter solstice on the roof of the Bear Clan House at the very southern tip of the mesa. From this expansive vantage he watches the Sun set in a notch on the horizon directly over this Schultz Pass at an azimuth of precisely 241.83°.[6] (See diagram on p. 71. "Azimuth" is the arc of the horizon measured in degrees from the north point, or 0°. East = 90°, south = 180°, and west = 270°.)

The first day of winter signals the opening of the kachina (or *katsina*) season. That is the date when these spiritual intermediaries of humans and gods begin their return from the mountains in the southwest to the Hopi Mesas.

The shortest day of the year also culminates in the sacred fertility and purification ceremony called the *Soyal*. This annual rite lasting about two weeks is performed in part to turn back the Sun as it moves southward along the horizon from the summer to the winter solstice. The final portion of the ritual takes place on December 21st in a kiva. It paradoxically begins at night during the precise moment that Orion appears in the overhead entryway. This constellation thus synchronizes one of the most important events in the Hopi ceremonial calendar.

As we have seen, Goodman's archaeological dig was described beforehand in detail by the process of psychic archaeology. Skeptics scoff, but this site may go back as far as Atlantean or Lemurian times. Just a mile-and-a-half to the west is a certain natural spring, the name of which seems more than a coincidence. It is located five miles southeast of Humphreys Peak, the highest point in Arizona (12,633 ft.), where a major Hopi kachina shrine is located.

We can find the name of this effluence on any U.S. Forest Service map of Coconino National Forest. It is called "Orion Spring."

Stock tank at Orion Spring just west of the Goodman site. The Spanish misnamed these peaks Sierra Sinagua, or "mountains without water."

Chapter 14
Hopi Kachinas and Egyptian Stars

Kachina Dancing with the Stars

In both of my previous books I have written about kachinas, but they are so essential to Hopi spiritual life that a brief review of the basic concepts connected with them is warranted.

In the simplest sense the kachinas (also spelled *katsinam*, plural of *katsina*) are intermediary spirits that can take on the shape of any physical object, creature, or phenomenon. Distinct from the Hopi pantheon, these spiritual go-betweens are not actually worshipped, though certain deities (such as Masau'u, god of death and the underworld) can alternately appear as kachinas. Representing the spirit beings, the familiar kachina "dolls" (*tihuta*) are carved to instruct children about the spirit world, and in modern times to sell to tourists.

When a man puts on a kachina mask, he does not simply impersonate or mimic the particular kachina spirit, but he actually becomes that spirit. It is a total transformation from human to spirit during the duration of the dance. (And kachina dances, like the original Shakespeare plays, can only be performed by men, even though they may represent female kachinas.) It is said that the kachinas originally came as physical beings, but now, due to human decadence and failure to live according to the precepts of the Creator, the kachinas arrive only in non-material form.

The masks come in many forms: cylindrical, circular, square, dome-shaped. Some have horns, feathers, or black hair; others have brightly painted tablitas that symbolize clouds rising like stepped pyramids from the tops of their heads. Some appear goggle-eyed, others simply have painted slits for eyes, while still others have no eyes at all. Several display squash-shaped or tube-shaped snouts, while some exhibit sharp fangs or protruding tongues. A few have ears but many lack noses. Unless they are clearly representing animals or birds, some kachinas even wear helmets that look uncomfortably extraterrestrial.

The costumes for the various dances greatly differ, but they include clan kilts, sashes, bandoleers, turquoise pendants, and moccasins. The dancers might add eagle or turkey feathers, fox fur, evergreen ruffs, willow bows, yucca whips, gourd rattles, and knee bells or turtle shell leg-tinklers. During each particular dance, however, the majority of the participants has the same masks, dress, and accouterments.

The Hopi cosmological model shows that when it is day on the earth plane, it is night in the underworld; when it is summer above, it is winter below. The kachina season lasts from about April until July, a few weeks after the summer solstice—the period when the sowing and most of the hoeing occurs. During the non-kachina season (July until the winter solstice in December), the kachinas inhabit the nether realm in order to help its chthonic denizens in their agricultural pursuits—non-material though they are. Physical life and ethereal afterlife thus mirror each other in perfect symmetry.

During spring planting season the constellation Orion disappears altogether from the sky. The Hopi, like the ancient Egyptians, conceptualize him as descending to the underworld in order to act as a catalyst for the subterranean forces of plant growth, ushering corn and other crops toward the sunlight. Orion's absence lasts about 70 days, which incidentally was the embalming period of Egyptian mummies. At the very moment the kachinas are dancing on the summer earth of the upper world, Orion is rising in the winter sky of the lower world. (See pp. 67-69.)

Although the Hopi have hundreds of kachinas, one in particular pertains to Orion. The most prominent feature of Sohu, or

Star Kachina, is the three vertical four-pointed stars arranged horizontally in a row across the top of his head. These bring to mind the "belt stars" of what is the most important constellation in Hopi cosmology. These stars are interspersed between four vertical eagle feathers.

This kachina has dark straight hair, goggle eyes, and diamond-shaped teeth. On his right cheek is painted an equilateral cross (i.e., a star), on his left a crescent moon. He wears a fringed buckskin shirt and a kilt made of turkey feathers, both of which are odd attire for a kachina. The 19th century archaeologist Jesse Walter Fewkes observes that Sohu has equilateral crosses painted on his forearms and legs. He holds yucca whips in both hands and a fox skin trails behind him. As scholar Barton Wright succinctly notes: "He does not resemble the usual Hopi Kachina."[1]

The Hopi word *sohu* (or *soohu*) simply means "star," but in their belief system stars are conceptualized as supernatural entities, with those of Orion being ritually paramount. For instance, Orion synchronizes both the "New Fire and manhood initiation" ceremony (*Wuwtsim*) in November and the winter solstice ceremony (*Soyal*) in December. For the latter the constellation achieves the highest point in its arc across the southern sky at midnight. When the "belt" of Orion appears in the overhead hatchway of the kiva, this is a signal for the ceremonies to begin. The constellation's stellar trio is thus an astro-chronometer for the Hopi ceremonial cycle.

Hopi drawing of Star Kachina from the village of Walpi on First Mesa.

Egyptian Nights Tales

Now let's turn to Egypt in roughly the period that most archaeologists believe the major pyramids were built. In the pristine air of the Sahara Desert the constellation Orion shines with extraordinary brilliance. The word "Sahara" comes from the Arabic word *çahra,* which itself means desert. One of the Egyptian Pyramid Texts –some of the world's oldest funerary literature– states that the word *Sahu* (or *Sah*—the first syllable of "Sahara") refers to "the star gods in the constellation Orion."[2]

The pharaoh was the divine embodiment on earth of Sah/Orion in the sky.

O King,
you are this great star, the companion of *sah,*
who traverses the sky with *sah,* who navigates
the *Duat* [or *Tuat,* "underworld"] with Osiris;
you ascend from the east of the sky,
being renewed at your due season
and rejuvenated at your due time.

Utterance 466, *The Pyramid Texts*

Hieroglyphic for *Sah.* Note triad ("belt") and sash ("sword," or Orion Nebula).

Like the Hopi Star Kachina (*Sohu*), the triadic "belt stars" on Egyptian representations of Orion are instead positioned on the crest. "Since Sah represented in hieroglyphic was positioned above the head, the Orion's Belt was assumed to be a crown on the head of Sah."[3] So the belt is really a crown!

"Sah (Orion) in the southern sky was one of at least two distinctive star patterns the ancient Egyptians recognized and incorporated into their funerary ideology. In the earliest surviving royal funerary texts inscribed within the pyramids from the end of the Fifth Dynasty, Sah was the 'father of the gods'—the gods referred to were probably the *akhs* (spirits) of the dead kings, who became 'Imperishable Stars' or gods/great ones."[4]

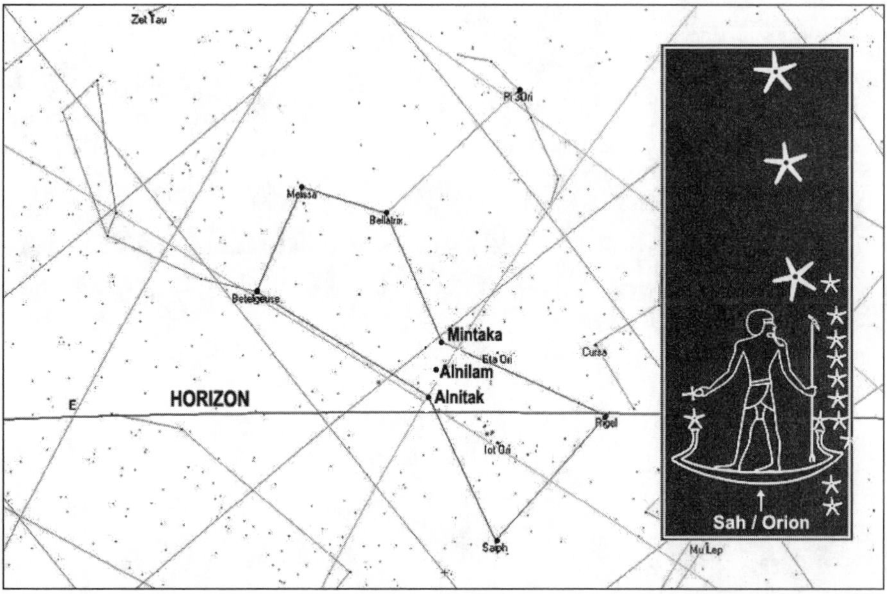

Heliacal rising of Orion's belt, 4:00 a.m. on June 21st, 2500 BC, Giza Plateau.

From the Pyramid of Unas (circa 2375 BC), we find the following: "He [the deceased king] is given the arm (power?) as the Great Sekhem, the star Sah (Orion), the father of the gods. He renews his risings in the sky, the *flesh of the Crown* [italics added], as Lord of the horizon."[5] Utterance 216:151 of *The Pyramid Texts* states: "Orion is encircled by the Duat, when *the One-who-lives-in-the-Horizon* purifies himself."[6] By the way, at Saqquara the Pyramid of Unas, on whose walls the Pyramid Texts are inscribed, lies to the south of the Step Pyramid of Djoser. (See photo on p. 59.)

In the sky chart above, the inset on the right is found on the ceiling of Senmut's tomb, circa 1475 BC. We see the predawn "belt" stars rising perpendicular to the horizon, positioned in much the same way as in Senmut's tomb. Note the top star on the panel in his tomb is offset—like both Mintaka and the smaller Menkaure pyramid at Giza. (See full panel on p. 357.)

Is "the flesh of the Crown" a reference to the stellar trinity that rises above the eastern horizon to renew itself as lord of the earth?

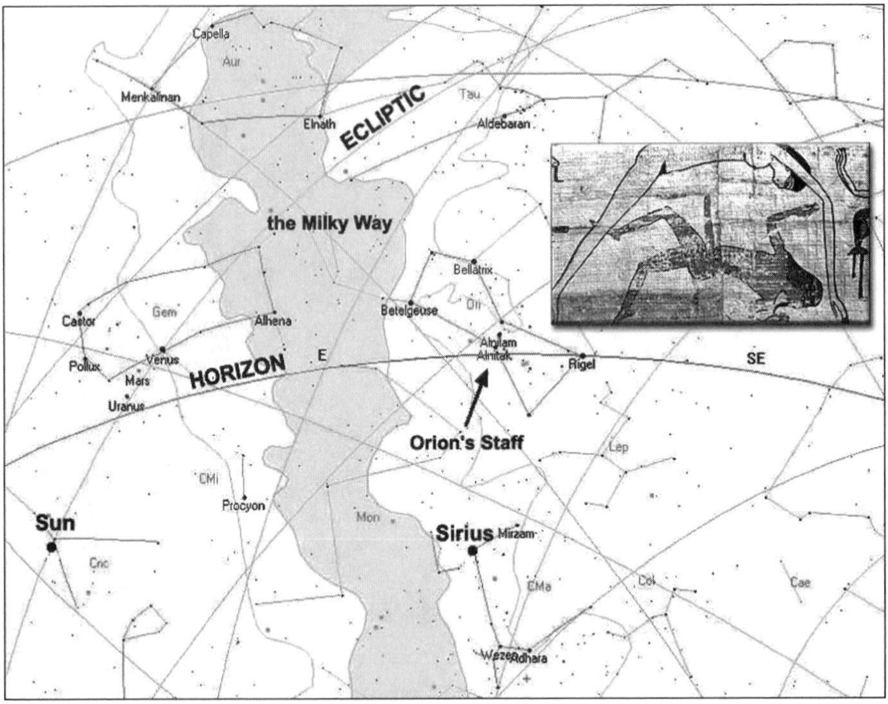

Geb (see inset at the upper-right), who lies supine upon the earth and whose green body represents vegetation, is also known as the father of the gods.[7] He is usually portrayed as ithyphallic—metaphorically, "the flesh of the Crown"? The goddess Nut –metaphorically, the Milky Way– arches above him with star-seed glistening on her breasts, belly, and thighs. The union of Geb and Nut, earth and sky, produces the brothers Osiris (Orion) and Seth, as well as the sisters/wives Isis and Nephthys.

In this mythological nexus, Geb is conflated with Osiris, Nut with Isis. A celestial layer of further complexity shows Osiris associated with Sah/Orion and Isis with Sirius. "Behold, he has come as *sah*, behold, Osiris has come as *sah*..."[8] Pun intended?

In the *Egyptian Book of the Dead*, we find the following: "Prepare a path for me, O you who are at peace; see, I enter into the Netherworld, I open up the beautiful West, I make firm the staff of Orion..."[9]

Most appellations for Orion have a masculine connotation, but the three stars in a line are specifically called "Jacob's Rod," a reference to the virile forefather of biblical twelve tribes of Israel.

"Sahû and Sopdît, Orion and Sirius, were the rulers of this mysterious world. Sahû consisted of fifteen stars, seven large and eight small, so arranged as to represent a runner darting through space, while the fairest of them shone above his head, and marked him out from afar to the admiration of mortals."[10]

From the drawing below it is difficult to identify the "belt stars," though they could be the two stars at belt-level on the left and one on the right. The horizontal curve of these three stars corresponds to their position when Orion is at its culmination, or meridian passage. The one star at head-level on the left and the two on the right are also horizontal. This, we recall, reflects the orientation on the headdress of the Hopi Sohu Kachina. Sahu/Osiris wears the white crown of Upper Egypt.

Plutarch remarks on the concept of stars as souls: "...their souls shine in heaven as stars; and that of Isis so called by the Greeks the Dog-star, but by the Egyptians Sothis; that of Horus, Orion..."[11]

Behind Orion/Sah/Osiris, Sirius rests in her barge as the cow Hathor with the star between her horns. Hathor and Isis are sometimes conflated. The sparrow hawk on the papyrus column, or *axis mundi,* represents their son Horus, which sometimes is also identified with Orion.

ORION AND THE COW SOTHIS SEPARATED BY THE SPARROW-HAWK.

Scene from the rectangular zodiac of Denderah, drawn by Faucher-Gudin.

As a sky god, Horus wears the red crown of Lower Egypt. If the positions of the deities on this vignette suggest a celestial map, then the tip of Horus' crown reaches above Orion's upraised arm to an area known as the northern stargate. (See Chapter 2.)

NÛÎT THE STARRY ONE.

"The celestial portal to the horizon
is opened to you,
and the gods are joyful
at meeting you.
They take you to the sky
with your soul, you having been
endowed with a soul
through them.
You will ascend to the sky
as Horus upon the *sdsd* of the sky
in this dignity of yours
which issued from the mouth of Ra
as Horus, who is at the head
of the spirits, you being seated
upon your iron throne.
May you remove yourself
to the sky, for the roads
of the celestial expanses
which lead up to Horus
are cleared for you.
Seth is brotherly toward you
as the Great One of On,
for you have traversed
the Winding Waterway in the north
of the sky as a star crossing the sea
which is beneath the sky.
The *Duat* has grasped your hand
at the place where *sah* is.
The Bull of the Sky has given you
his hand and you eat of the food
of the gods..."[12]

Above: Nut, drawn by Faucher-Gudin, the painted inner lid of a coffin from the XXIth [sic., or XIXth?] dynasty in Leyden. The stars on her body and limbs represent the Milky Way. See more about Nut and Geb on p. 40.

In this passage from *The Pyramid Texts,* the word *sdsd* is a standard identified as a *Wepwawet,* also *Upuat,* or "opener of ways." Ra is the Egyptian sun god. Seth is the brother of Osiris. On, or An, is either a form of Osiris or Horus the Warrior. The Winding Waterway refers to the Milky Way. The Bull of the Sky is, of course, Taurus.

In addition to *Sah* denoting the "soul of Orion," we find an important verification for the sky-ground dualism of the Orion Correlation Theory (OCT).[13] The Egyptian homophone *sahu,* for instance, means property, and its cognate *sah-t* refers to "landed property," "estate," "site of a temple," "homestead," or "environs."[14] Because the term *sahu* simultaneously refers to both stars and ground, this conceptual mirroring aligns the two realms, or "...on earth as it is in heaven."

Why the close parallel between *Sahu* of the ancient Egyptians and *Sohu* of the ancestral Hopi? These and other linguistic correlations corroborate if not a Hopi migration from the Old World, then at least a pre-Columbian contact with Middle Eastern or North African mariners, perhaps Phoenician or Libyan.[15]

The following native quotation suggests a transoceanic connection: "Then we who are called Hopi came to inhabit this place. We were the first to set foot on this earth. For this reason Maasaw [also spelled Masau'u, a complex deity whose dominion includes the earth], the god who lives invisibly, transferred this land to us. He gave us not only this land here, but also that which lies beyond the oceans."[16]

Unlike some constellations, Orion (*Sah*) can be seen from anywhere on earth. Is it merely a coincidence that *Soh,* the Hopi word for star, and *Sah,* the ancient Egyptian word for Orion, are similar? Variants of this word have, in fact, made the rounds all across the globe.

Scholar Ralph Ellis makes the case for the universality of *Sah.*

> "As the result of this intimate association between the pharaoh and Sah (Osiris), the name *sah* has become a royal appellation, not just in Egypt, but all over the world. It has been transliterated into nearly every language in the western world and used as the title of nearly all our kings. The Israelites took the name with them during the exodus, and *sar-hair* was the name given

> to their tribal kings, while the word *sar* still means 'prince' or 'ruler' in Hebrew. *Sah* was seen as a sacred title by the Magi and used in Persia, where it became the royal title *shah*. Further eastwards, in India, it became *sahib*. In the greatest of all ancient empires, Rome, they chose the appellation *caesar*. The Saxon tribes also inherited the title, but by the looks of the spelling it somehow arrived in Saxony via Greece; it appears that the Saxon tribes have taken the Greek rendition of *caesar*, *kaisar*, and transliterated it as *kaiser*. In the frozen wastes of the north, in Russia, they inherited the same tradition and the title became *tsar*. Word of the power of such a sacred name spread far and wide and so, in the damp north-west of Europe, in Britain, the royal appellation became sire. For lesser nobles here, the title became sir, but in the military world the tradition remains and this is always pronounced as 'sar'! Such was the power and influence of ancient Egypt."[17]

It is interesting to note that the Hebrew word *sar* is made of the letters *sin* or *shin* ('s') and *resh* or *reysh* ('r'), with the vowel 'a' being implied. Of course, Hebrew is read from right to left, so the tripartite letter *sin* is on the right here, where the letter *resh* is on the left.

שׁר

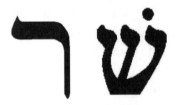

The shape of the letter *sin* somewhat resembles the Egyptian hieroglyphic for *Sah*, depicted on p. 260. The Hebrew *resh* looks like some sort of curved club, perhaps like the one Orion wields.

The Egyptian word *hemt* means "copper." The hieroglyphic also has a tripartite shape. This is particularly relevant when we remember Orion's link to copper. (See Chapter 10.) The word *Khemt* (which contains the word *hemt*) means both "three" and "trident."[18] (See discussion of the trident on pp. 65-66.)

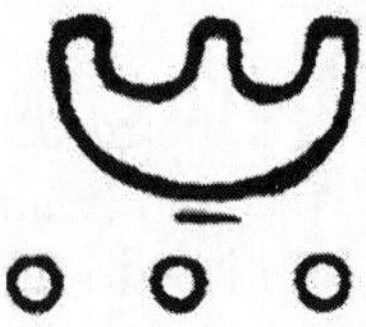

Khemet is the ancient word for Egypt itself and literally means "black"—either the black mud of the Nile or the black people of Africa. The word "alchemy" is derived from the Arabic word *al-kimia.* The first stage in the alchemical process is called the *nigredo* (blackening) or *putrefactio* (corruption and dissolution).[19]

At any rate, the masculine *Sah* has literally walked (or sailed) his way around the world. (It would not be going too far, then, to relate that the Hopi word *saha* means "calf of the leg.") The Greeks believed that Orion, because he was the son of Euralye (which literally means "broad, far-ranging") and Poseidon (god of the sea), had the miraculous ability to walk on water. Is this just a metaphorical description of seafaring? Or is this the origin of the power attributed to Jesus? It is also interesting to note that the "belt stars" are also known as the "Three Kings," namely, the Magi. These wise men (read "magicians" or "sorcerers"), of course, made the long journey to Bethlehem from the East, probably either Persia (Iran) or Babylon (Iraq).

THE WAR-DANCE OF THE TIMIHU AT DEÎR EL-BAHARÎ.[1]

These warriors hold curved clubs or bommerangs. The Hopi also use curved throwing sticks, or "rabbit sticks," which they call *putskoho.* The warriors' headdresses shown here have three feathers. French Egyptologist Gaston Maspero claims the Timihu were Berbers from the Sahara region.[20] (See the end of Chapter 1 in my book.)

Star-Studded Orion Set In Stone

Many examples of this constellation's stellar trinity can be found in the rock art of Four Corners region of the U.S. These are portrayed both in the vertical (Orion-on-the-horizon) and the horizontal (Orion-at-culmination).

In Hopi culture the One Horn society is called *Kwan*, which refers to the agave, a type of cactus. Members of this fierce para-military group act as village guardians, possessing the absolute authority even to execute anyone caught trespassing upon sacred ceremonies. *Kwan* additionally plays a large role in the *Wuwtsim* ceremony previously mentioned, which somewhat resembles the Mexican *Dia de los Muertos*, or "Day of the Dead." This society also pays homage to the warlike sky god Sótuknang, who has one horn as well. One-horns incidentally imported the cult of the horned or plumed serpent from Mesoamerica to the Southwest.

"Also in front of the One Horn altar in the Lance Kiva is planted a six-foot lance with a flint point sharpened for destruction or for correction of world evils."[21] The One Horn shamans thus warn us of impending doom on the earth, or, as the Hopi say, the ultimate destruction of the current Fourth World.

The single horn of the Hopi Kwan society as well as the staves that its members hold morphologically echo both the scepter of Sah/Orion/Osiris and the phallus of Geb. Also, the stiff yucca whips of the Star Kachina remind us that the spiny leaves of the yucca plant poetically resemble the scintillations of stars across the desert sky.

On the facing page at the top-left is a one-horned shaman with spear or arrow. The ancestral Hopi designated stars in rock art by equilateral crosses or plus signs instead of the Egyptian five-pointed asterisims. This carving perhaps shows anthropomorphic Orion on the eastern horizon. At the bottom of the page is another one-horned shaman with rectangular body and spear. At lower right are either three "crows-feet" or three stars—both symbolic of warfare. If stars, then they could represent Orion at its culmination, or the point when it crosses the meridian.

[continued on p. 270]

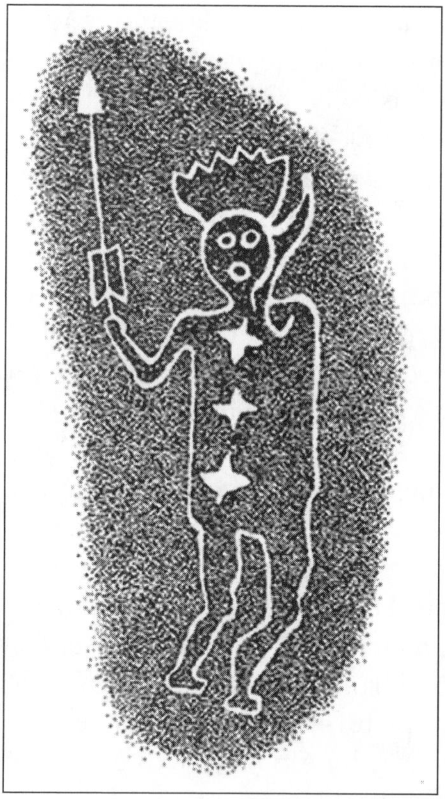

Left: Drawing of One Horn petroglyph, San Cristobal, New Mexico. Above: Painted with the finger instead of a brush, these dolls are given as gifts to adolescent Hopi girls. Attached to the figure is a sprig of rabbitbrush. The belt line may represent the Orion triad.

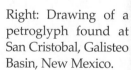

Right: Drawing of a petroglyph found at San Cristobal, Galisteo Basin, New Mexico.

One of the primary roles of *Kwan* is to serve Masau'u, god of the underworld, fire, and death but also of the earth. (See collage on p. 247.) This Hopi god can basically be correlated to the Egyptian god Osiris/Orion. In my book *The Orion Zone* I extensively present the case that Masau'u is in fact a terrestrial equivalent of Orion. He is, for instance, the sole nocturnal god in the Hopi pantheon, who travels across the entire earth before morning comes. What better way to express Orion's movement from the eastern to the western horizons during the course of the night?

Although Orion's shape is frequently conceptualized as an hourglass, it can also be seen as a giant rectangle in the sky. Rectangles or squares iconographically signify the earth or place, not only in the rock art of the American Southwest but in many cultures around the world. As mentioned, Masau'u is the primary Hopi god who rules over the earth plane. In rock art he is sometimes depicted with a rectangular torso. His form as a kachina is frequently embodied in flat, rectangular dolls crudely painted with dark colors as distinguished from the vivid colors of most other kachina dolls. (See top-right picture on previous page.)

Masau'u is traditionally seen as a lone figure with a sack of seeds and a dibble, traversing the vast desert mesas. Like the spear, the planting dibble is essentially a male symbol. After being used throughout his life as an agrarian tool, it is finally planted upon a man's grave. In this way his spirit can climb down to the subterranean realm of the afterlife.

Another version of Masau'u (also spelled Maasaw) shows him wielding a club in his right hand, similar to Orion. "People claim that the inside of Maasaw's club is filled with planting seeds. He is reputed to be an excellent farmer. For this reason he has within his club every variety of planting seeds."[22] As this quotation implies, Masau'u additionally shares the fecund aspects of the Egyptian god Geb. These include both the vegetable and animal kingdoms. If one dreams of Masau'u, for instance, an abundance of crops and livestock will result. Masau'u paradoxically uses this club as a lethal weapon or to induce unconsciousness in anyone touched by it.

Masau'u is even responsible for human procreation. If a

women wishes to bear children, she paints a decorative circle on the neck or brim of a ceramic vessel but leaves a half-inch gap called a "gate of breath." This she dedicates to Masau'u.[23]

Masau'u is related to another kachina, the first syllable of whose name is the same: Mastop, or Death Fly Kachina. His body is painted black, and either one or two white handprints are painted on his chest, with other smaller handprints on his legs and upper arms. He carries a short black-and-white striped staff in his right hand (like Orion's club) with which he beats away the village dogs. His black, cylindrical helmet has a rounded crown, and on each side of the mask are painted white dots representing stars. These wedge-shaped star groupings on each side of his head might signify Orion's "belt" in both the rising and setting positions, together with his "sword." Trailing down from Alnitak, this celestial weapon contains Iota Orionis and the fertile star-seeds of the Great Nebula, M42 and M43. Given the virile aspect of Mastop, Orion's phallic sword is an appropriate mask decoration.

Mastop Kachina doll, Museum of N. Arizona. Note dot inside triangle for mouth. (See same symbol: photo, p. 199.)

Always arriving in pairs, dark Mastop and his twin appear on the second to the last day of the *Soyal* (winter solstice) ceremony. They approach from the northwest, the direction of Grand Canyon, where departed spirits go to exist in a subterranean afterlife. Antically leaping about, each Mastop dashes up to a crowd of females, grabs one of them by the shoulders from behind, and makes a series of short hops that mimic copulation. Fertility and death are thereby inextricably linked.

This contrasting light-and-dark nature can also be applied to Orion. Another name for the constellation is *Jugula*. The term possibly derives from the Indo-European root *yeug-*, which means "to join" or "to yoke," thus reinforcing the conjugal meaning suggested by the Orion's sword within its sheath. On the other hand, the word may refer to the slayer who severs the jugular vein with his sword.[24]

If one reviews Orion's influence throughout a number of cultures, a composite picture emerges: warrior, hunter, hero, giant. The warfare and hunter qualities of Orion can also be attributed to Masau'u. Prayers for victory in battle, for instance, are offered to this fierce god, but only at night. A warrior about to embark on the warpath will make prayers feathers as offerings to the shrine of the deity.

Masau'u is also associated with success in hunting, especially small game such as rabbits. "Maasaw's special relation to rabbits is manifest from the very fact that he constantly pours their blood over his masked head in order to protect his face from the intensive heat of the fire by which he sits. In this context the god is actually characterized as maakya, the Hopi term for 'a successful hunter.'"[25]

In many diverse folklores the rabbit is connected not only with fecundity but also with the Moon, reinforcing the nocturnal nature of Masau'u. More obvious, perhaps, is the fact that beneath his feet Orion hunts the hare in the form of the constellation Lepus.

In the ever-complex mythology of the ancient Egyptians, Osiris/Orion is also bound up with the Moon and the hare: "Osiris represented Lunar Light in his character of the Hare-headed Un-Nefer, the up-springing Hare in the Moon."[26]

As mentioned above, the sparrow hawk is the totemic form of the Egyptian god Horus. He represents the living pharaoh on earth, whereas his father Osiris represents the dead king "risen" in the underworld. These two concepts may ostensibly seem contradictory, but both the cosmology of the Egyptians and that of the Hopi conceive the underworld or afterlife as co-extensive with the celestial realm.

Also previously mentioned, the Hopi *Wuwtsim* ceremony links the worlds of the living and the dead, somewhat in the manner of our Halloween. It occurs in early November, the month that the Hopi designate as the "sparrow hawk moon." The word *kyeele*, or "sparrow hawk" (*Falco sparverius*), has a alternate meaning of "neophyte," "novitiate," or "a boy who is initiated into manhood,"which is part of the purpose of the ceremony.[27] This raptor is a symbol of bravery, since it attacks birds larger than itself, but its main diet is rodents such as rabbits.

This secretive ritual is not for the faint-hearted. As anthropologist Mischa Titiev has written:

> "Let us recall that on the fourth day of the proceedings, visitors are barred from the pueblo and all the trails are closed. This is a night of mystery and terror. People are forced to remain indoors and are forbidden even to glance outside, and patrols of Kwans [the Agave, or One Horn, Society] and Horns [the Al, or Two Horn Society] rush madly through the village, constantly challenging each other and maintaining a dreadful din. Concurrently, in the kivas underground, a most esoteric and awe-inspiring ritual is being performed which no white observer has ever glimpsed."[28]

All the roads leading to the village have been closed with lines of cornmeal by the fierce and autonomous *Kwan* society, the only exception being the road from the northwest where the *Maski*, or House of the Dead, is located and along which the spirits may proceed. This is, of course, the direction of Grand Canyon—the place of the initial Emergence of the Hopi from the Third World as well as the current home of ancestor spirits. Around sundown great quantities of food had been set out on the western side of the village of Oraibi for the visiting spirits to consume.

Just when Orion, his brilliant stellar trinity blazing, reaches the top of his parabolic journey across the night, the spirits throng the village and enter the kivas with which they were connected while still alive. In the pandemonium that results from the mingling of life and death, Orion looks down in the dead of night from his most commanding position in the firmament, observing the ceremony expressly dedicated to Masau'u—the underworld god who can only walk nocturnally with the living upon the face of the earth.

On the petroglyph panel below we see a possible depiction of the "belt stars" in the context of a bear. This figure at center-right contains three horizontal stars inside its body—perhaps Orion's triad when it is high in the sky. Hopi cosmology does not associate the bear with Ursa Major (the Big Dipper). Instead the high-ranked Bear Clan is primarily concerned with spiritual matters and healing. The bear is additionally associated with warfare. After the killing of a bear, for instance, its dead body is treated as if it were a dead human enemy, and its slayer is called a *kahletaka*, or "war chief." Eaters of bear meat also have to paint their faces black.[29]

Above the bear is juxtaposed a rabbit and a four-pointed "soul-face" star surrounded by three or more Masau'u-faces. This panel also possibly depicts a one-horned shaman, a pair of two-horned shamans, three serpents (horned or plumed), another four-pointed star, an equilateral cross, a handprint, two birds, a couple lizards, and a naturalistic corn stalk.

Thus, we have seen the same Orion motifs displayed in Hopi kachinas and rock art as well as in Egyptian gods and paintings. The next chapter shifts the focus from northern to southern Africa.

Petroglyphs from the Galisteo Basin, New Mexico.

Although they look fierce, these Apache dancers on this old postcard are not devils but are invoking *gan,* or "mountain spirit beings." Note tripartite headdresses and four-pointed stars painted on chests. The Apache *shigan* means "hand."

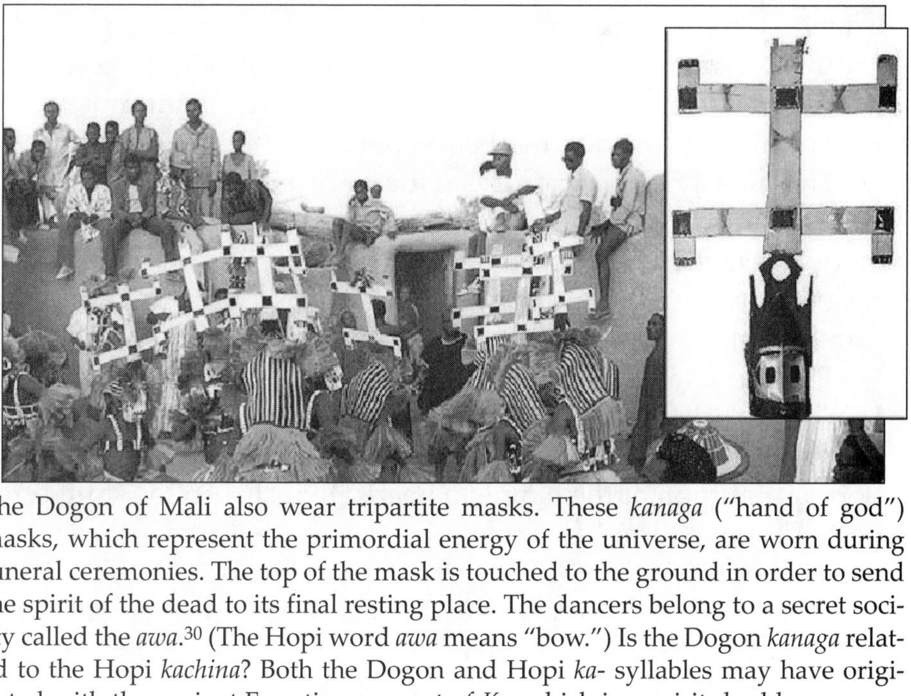

The Dogon of Mali also wear tripartite masks. These *kanaga* ("hand of god") masks, which represent the primordial energy of the universe, are worn during funeral ceremonies. The top of the mask is touched to the ground in order to send the spirit of the dead to its final resting place. The dancers belong to a secret society called the *awa*.[30] (The Hopi word *awa* means "bow.") Is the Dogon *kanaga* related to the Hopi *kachina*? Both the Dogon and Hopi *ka-* syllables may have originated with the ancient Egyptian concept of *Ka,* which is a spirit-double.

Chapter 15
Under South African Skies

From the High Desert to the Upper Karoo

In the central part of the South African subcontinent, equidistant from the Indian Ocean and the Atlantic, lies a high plateau known as the Great Karoo. This arid landscape of scrubby thornveld, grassland, and savannahs is dotted with occasional umbrella and camel thorn trees (*Acacia tortilis* and *Acacia erioloba* respectively). The northern part of the semi-desert region lies north of the Orange River near the city of Kimberley, although it does not extend all the way up to the Kalahari Desert.[1] The Karoo ranges southwest and ends near the town of Calvinia. With an average elevation of about 4,000 feet, the temperatures in summer can reach well over 100 degrees Fahrenheit.

This unforgiving territory is the ancestral homeland of the San (sometimes known as Bushmen) and the Khoe (or Khoi, the erstwhile Hottentots). In fact, the word *karoo* is a San word that means "land of great thirst."[2] The former tribe was basically hunter-gatherer, whereas the latter herded sheep and cattle.

The late summer monsoon rains drawn from the Indian Ocean sometimes briefly collect in the salt pans spread across the barren plains, then dry up. Rainfall averages nearly eight inches in the northern portion of the biome to nearly 16 inches in the southern part. Thunderstorms are violent but patchy, with rain streamers sometimes evaporating before reaching the ground—much like in the deserts of the southwestern U.S. However, the rainfall was once enough to support a rich diversity of wildlife: giraffe, zebra, wildebeest, hartebeest, eland, springbok, buffalo, and ostrich.

Along riparian areas were rhino, hippo, and elephant. Predator species included lion, leopard, hyena, and wild dog.

On the distant horizon flat-topped hills ("koppies") of sandstone and shale are also reminiscent of the mesas in the American Southwest, while dark dolerite outcroppings strewn with heavily patinated, igneous boulders were perfect for carving petroglyphs, or, as they say in South Africa, rock engravings. In September of 2009, I had the opportunity to travel to that country in order to assist my friend and colleague Rob Milne with his rock art research.[3] I will describe in detail a couple of the sites we visited shortly.

The pristine skies above this vast, expansive terrain played an equally expansive role in lives of its inhabitants. In a poem about the Anglo-Boer War (1899–1902), English author Thomas Hardy describes a naive, rural soldier who had fallen in battle so far from home. Both the landscape and the skyscape that cradle his unmarked grave are foreign, and yet his "Northern" dust forever mingles with this strange "Southern" milieu.

The Dead Drummer

They throw in Drummer Hodge, to rest
  Uncoffined—just as found:
His landmark is a kopje-crest
  That breaks the veldt around;
And foreign constellations west
  Each night above his mound.

Young Hodge the Drummer never knew–
  Fresh from his Wessex home–
The meaning of the broad Karoo,
  The Bush, the dusty loam,
And why uprose to nightly view
  Strange stars amid the gloam.

Yet portion of that unknown plain
  Will Hodge for ever be;
His homely Northern breast and brain
  Grow up a Southern tree.
And strange-eyed constellations reign
  His stars eternally.

[continued on p. 280]

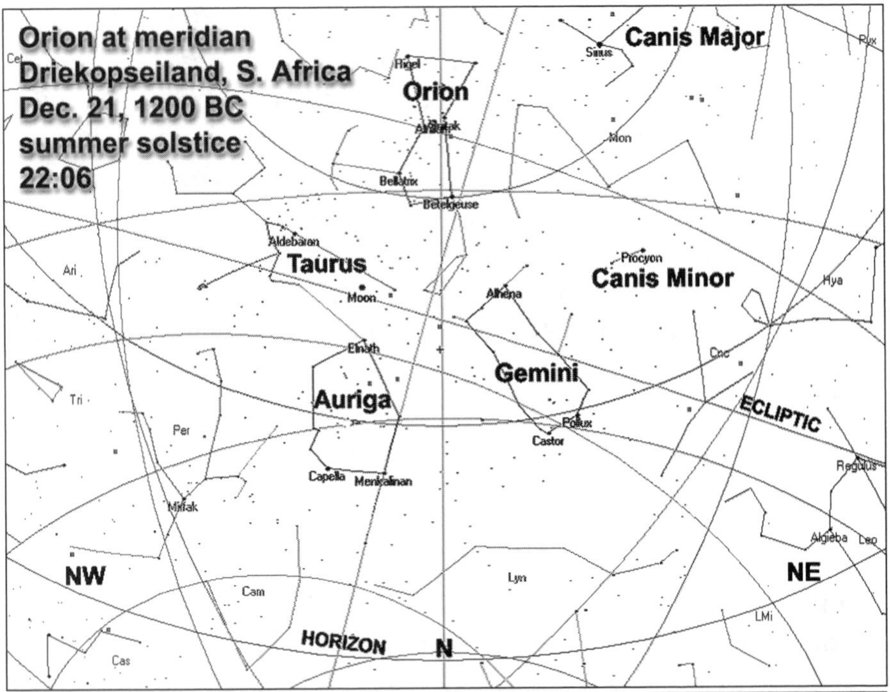

View from a koppie with salt pan at Wildebeest Kuil Rock Art Centre near Kimberley in the northern Karoo.[4] The site has over 400 petroglyphs, mostly zoomorphs. Barely visible on the horizon is Platfontein, one of the final relocation sites of the Khoisan. A giant anthill is seen in the foreground.

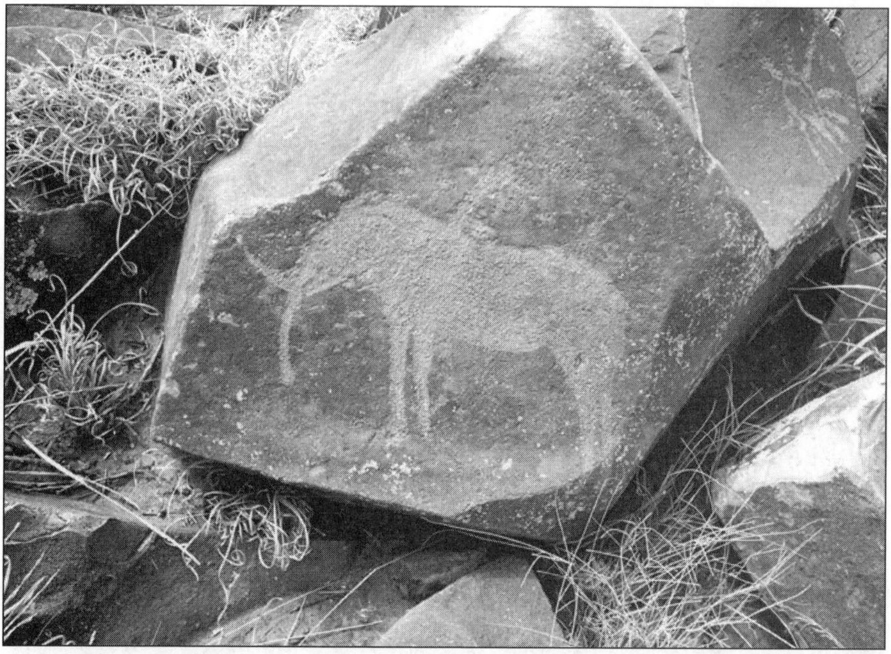

Petroglyph of elephant, starburst (upper-right corner), Wildebeest Kuil.

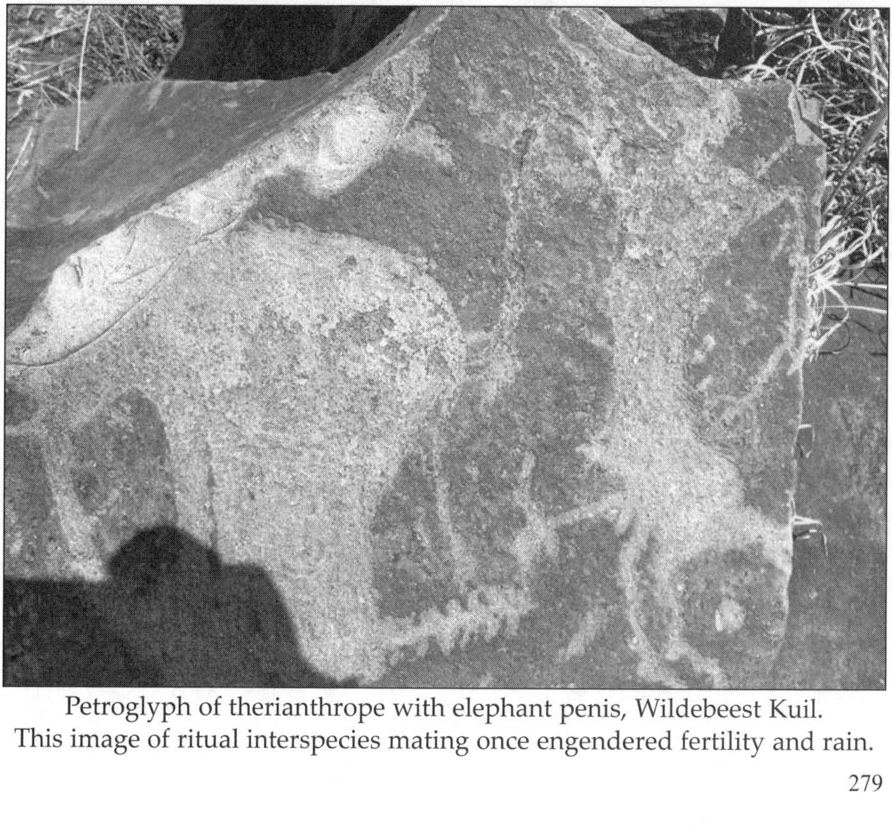

Petroglyph of therianthrope with elephant penis, Wildebeest Kuil.
This image of ritual interspecies mating once engendered fertility and rain.

The constellations do indeed look upside down from the perspective of one accustomed to the heavens of the northern hemisphere. For instance, if one looks north, Orion's head points downward. (See sky chart on the top of p. 278.) This, incidentally, is the way Orion appears in both the Giza and the Arizona Orion Correlations. The prototype of the sky-ground Orion template may thus have originated in southern Africa.

Carving the Back of the Water Snake

In addition to visiting the Wildebeest Rock Art Centre, Rob Milne drove me and his wife Slava to a petroglyph site near Kimberley called Driekopseiland, literally, "three hills island," located on a working farm along the Riet River in Northern Cape Province. We arrived on the vernal equinox (September 22) at about 5:00 a.m., when Orion was just reaching its meridian. Getting out of the car to open the farm gates, I saw the brilliant star Canopus for the first time—the second brightest star in the night sky after Sirius. The San consider Sirius to be the Grandmother of Canopus.[5] A number of rabbits and a steenbok (antelope) darted across the dirt road as we made our way to the site in the predawn chill. (Later in the day we saw a warthog dash across the road and a troop of mongooses scampering about and chattering. Surely a cobra must have been nearby.)

The Riet ("reed") River, a tributary of the mighty Orange River that flows into the Atlantic, is lined with non-indigenous eucalyptus trees and reeds 20 feet high. As a wrote in my book *Eye of the Phoenix*, the reed is a universal symbol of civilization, high culture, education, writing, and even celestial significance.[6]

Driekopseiland contains over 3,500 engravings pecked or chiseled into a glaciated andesite "pavement" that parallels the river. The main part of this blue-gray slab is cut by natural fractures, thin and straight, that divide the horizontal rock expanse into various sections or panels. The whole area is at least 150 yards long and 75 yards wide.

[continued on p. 282]

Dawn along the Riet River, South Africa. The damn (seen in the background) was built upstream from the petroglyphs in the 1920s.

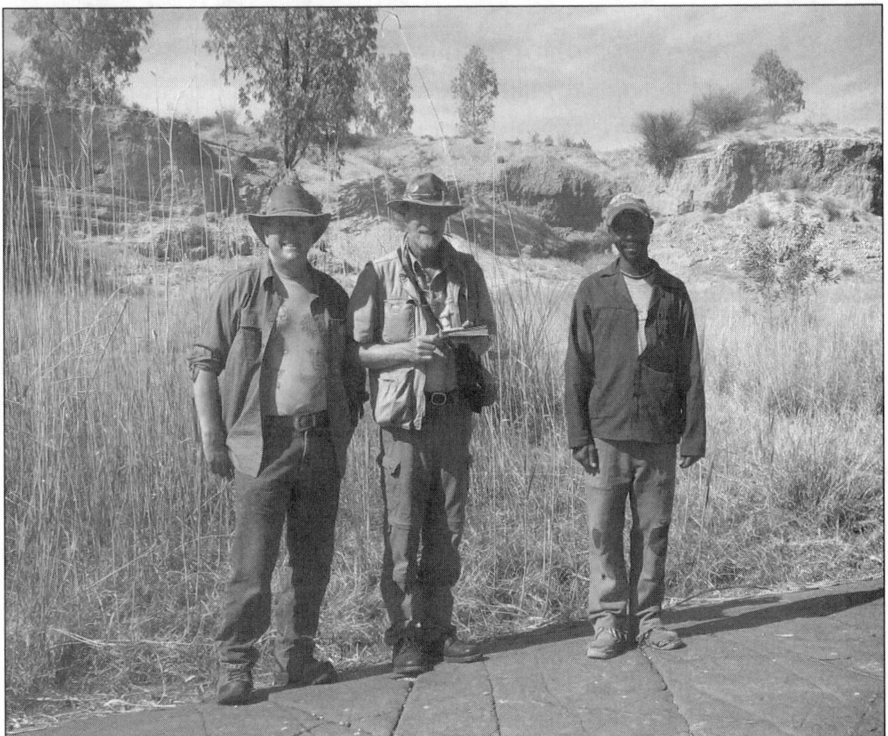

The author, Rob Milne, and San guide Adam. Photo © by Bronislava Milne.

According to anti-diffusionist archaeologist David Morris, whom we later met at McGregor Museum in Kimberley and who autographed his new book for us, over 90% of the petroglyphs are geometric, abstract, or nonrepresentational: grids, meanders, dots, hatches, zigzags, concentric circles, ovals, spirals, star shapes, sunbursts, nested figures, and calendar wheels. Some of the shapes resemble paramecia, with interior cross-hatching.

We even found a great number of Celtic crosses! (A Celtic cross is an equilateral cross inside a circle. See photo on the top of p. 287.) South African scholar Brenda Sullivan comments:

> "This symbol has many names. It has been called the five-fold bond, the tree of life enclosed within the circle of eternity, and more commonly, the Celtic cross. Well, the Celts may claim pride of name, but this most ancient symbol has been associated with the isangomas [medicine people] of Africa for millennia, and is still one of Africa's most powerful signs of protection and communication with the Creator through the Shades."[7]

On a panel downstream from the main section of the site, however, we found petroglyphs that represented zoomorphs: eland, elephant, rhino, baboon, anteater, and warthog. We also encountered a few anthropomorphs. At any rate, every foot or so we came across some bewildering design deeply carved into stone so smooth it almost looks polished. Ranging in size from a few inches to a few feet, these perplexing petroglyphs were rarely superimposed.

The dating of these engravings is all over the map, so to speak, and is anybody's educated guess. Estimates range from 1200 BC to the end of the first millennium AD. One cation-ratio dating study of the nearby site of Klipfontein, however, has found engravings as old as 8000 BC.[8] Joseph Campbell states that rock art pecked on diorite and basalt fragments in the vicinity of the Orange River and Klerksdorp are similar to Capsian artifacts.[9] This is a Mesolithic culture that existed between 10,000 and 6,000 BC in Ancient Libya and modern Tunisia and Algeria. Yet another link to northern Africa.[10]

Incidentally, Michael Cremo has noted that the museum in the town of Klerksdorp houses a number of synthetic-looking, metallic spheres with three parallel grooves along the equator. Cremo argues that these are not limonite concretions, as some claim, because, unlike limonite, they are extremely hard and cannot be scratched with a steel point. Most baffling, however, they were found in a Precambrian strata that is 2.8 billion years old![11]

Whenever the Driekopseiland glyphs were incised, they certainly took a long time to make. In other words, these labor-intensive markings were no idle doodling to wile away a hot afternoon. Andesite is a fairly hard mineral, and is rated 6 on the Mohs scale. Granite is perhaps a bit harder at 6.5 and quartz is only 7. Diamond is the hardest mineral and rates 10 on the scale.

Brenda Sullivan believes that diamonds have been mined for thousands of years on the subcontinent. She should know, because her late husband was a diamond-buyer in the region; thus, she had firsthand knowledge of the business and actually discovered some prehistoric mines –both diamond and gold– herself. (My friend Rob has also found the same.) She claims that in antiquity, diamonds were valued not in the monetary sense we think of today but were instead worshipped as "Stones of the Sun."

> "The Dreikops Eiland site is a massive slab of striated amygdaloidal diabase. The rock is hard—incising the surface takes time, strength, and a writing tool with a point considerably harder than the rock. Perhaps, and because they were in a region rich in alluvial diamonds—Driekops Eiland is only about fifty kilometers from the diamond centre of Kimberley—like the Biblical prophet Jeremiah, they too used a diamond-tipped pen to inscribe their message (Jeremiah 17:1)."[12]

In historic times, diamonds were first discovered in 1866 downstream from the confluence of the Orange and Vaal Rivers; and, of course, Kimberley is the home of the world-famous De Beers company, whose "Big Hole" and museum we later visited.

But what is the meaning of these enigmatic dream-symbols carved into the bedrock? Aye, there's the rub. David Lewis-Williams, cognitive archaeologist and specialist in South African rock art, posits that these rock engravings (and also the San rock paintings for which South Africa is renowned) are not merely static stone whereon, like the modern artist's canvas, representations of the natural world or abstractions of inner space are rendered. No, they are instead "windows on other worlds," veils between the physical world and the spirit world, like the interactive screens of a sacred video game. Older than we can imagine, the engravings were also "reservoirs of potency" that came alive in the moment when people trance-danced in front of them.[13]

Lewis-Williams is also the major proponent of the theory that the geometrics found at Driekopseiland are a depiction of the entoptics created by the optic nerve in the initial stages of an altered state. The shaman experiences these varied abstract shapes via intense drumming and dancing, sometimes in conjunction with hallucinogens. Just rub your eyes hard to get a sense of this phenomenon. (For a possible example of this in the petroglyphs of the American Southwest, see photo on the top of p. 247.)

Even the academic David Morris admits to sacrosanct function of the engravings. "As a powerful portal between spiritual realms, a point of breakthrough perhaps second to none in the area, Driekopseiland would have been the kind of place where !Khwa was appeased, where protections were sought, so that 'the rain comes down gently.'"[14]

Like the Pueblo people of the American Southwest, the San distinguish between (1) "male rain," or lightning, fierce winds, and thunderstorms that pummel the earth, causing floods; and (2) "female rain," or gentle rains that slowly soak into the earth.[15]

Morris believes that the ancient people who made these carvings conceptualized the river as the mythic Water Snake named *!Khwa,* so prominent in San mythology. (See photo top of p. 281.)

> "The regular emergence and submergence of images from the waters of the Gama-!ab [San term for Riet River] seems to us a crucial element in the power of the engravings and, arguably, a key to their meaning. Like the body of a large beast living in the depths of the river, the rock surfaces appear to rise from one medium to another, glistening, striated and engraved. Using a related analogue, the artist Walter Battiss spoke of 'great whales lying in the mud' of Driekops Eiland, their backs 'decorated with innumerable designs.'"[16]

[continued on p. 290]

Phallic engravings with dots next to river, Driekopseiland, South Africa.

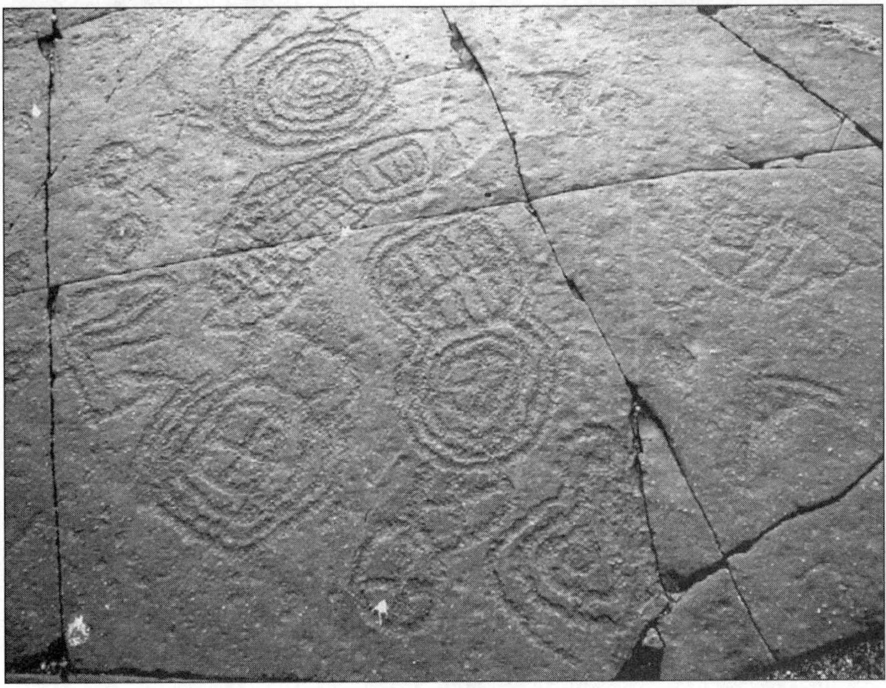

Geometric petroglyphs at Driekopseiland. Photo © by Bronislava Milne.

Lunar calendar with 13 lines inside inner circle and 27 or 28 lines in outer circle.

Oval with interior lines.

Parallel lines form a chevron inside a shield, plus geometrics.

Engravings from Driekopseiland, South Africa.

Left: Paramecium shape with interior parallel lines, plus abstract designs.

Imagine the number of hours it would have taken to engrave these petroglyphs into the flat, hard andesite "pavement."

Celtic crosses (upper-left), sunburst, abstracts. Photo © by Bronislava Milne.

Profile of creature, Dreikopseiland. Photo © by Bronislava Milne. Curved headdress framed by triangular fractures resembles both the Phrygian cap and the crown of Iyoba, the Queen Mother of Benin, Nigeria (see next page). It also looks like the curved horn of the Hopi sky god Sótuknang. (See p. 99 of my book *Eye of the Phoenix*.)

Anthropoid figure with staff and striped helmet, Driekopseiland.

Hopi Corn Kachina doll, Kriss Collection, Museum of N. Arizona.

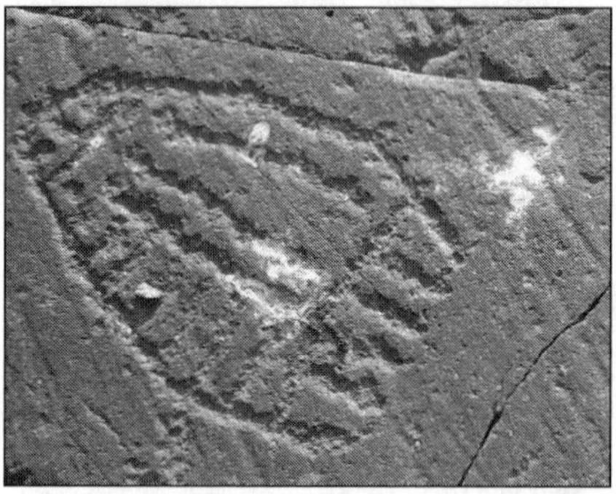

Above: Petroglyph of cone-shaped rocket (?), Driekopseiland. It is found in the vicinity of "the Spaceman" pictured above. Photo © by Bronislava Milne.

Right: Bronze sculpture of Iyoba, early 16th century AD, Nigeria, University of Pennsylvania Museum.

More engravings from Driekopseiland.

Above: Petroglyph of flying saucer ascending (?).

Right: Space platform (?) with six legs carved a yard or so to the left of "the Spacemen" shown on the facing page. Photo © by Bronislava Milne.

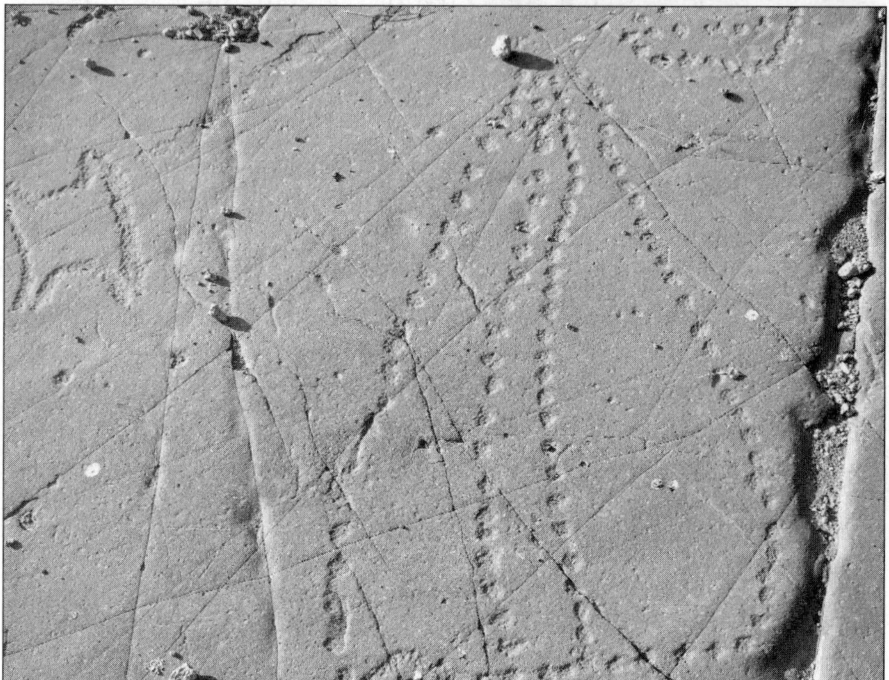

Dot-cone space capsule (?). Ingot (upper-left) is one of a group here. (See p. 175.)

Arching its engraved back, the giant Snake breaks the surface of the water, then plunges back into the stream. This vertical undulation has cosmological significance due to the fact that "to go under water" is a San trance metaphor for "to die," or death.

The Water Snake may also be linked to a non-species "rain-animal" or "rain-bull" called *!Khwa-ka xoro*.[17] Lewis-Williams comments: "Shamans could calm a rain-animal of either sex by allowing it to smell the scent of the aromatic herbs known as buchu. After the shamans-of-the-rains had captured a rain animal by throwing a thong over its head, they led it across the countryside to their territory where they wished the rain to fall; there they killed it so that its blood and milk would fall as rain."[18] Hence, these mythical creatures had a very real impact on the survival of the San.

Morris further suggests that the petroglyphic imagery may be connected to menarcheal (or first menstruation) rites. These carvings may even have been representations of tattoos or scarification made during female puberty rituals.[19]

Sullivan notes that a large quantity of hematite was found on the hill above the site. Red ochre, of course, was ritualistically known all over world in ancient times as the menstrual blood of the Earth Mother.[20] Sullivan also suggests that the people who made the engravings here were probably women, most likely priestesses or female *Sangomas*. She reminds us that it was the Berber women, also famous for their facial tattoos, who were the ones that made rock engravings in northern Africa.[21] (Read about the Hopi-Berber connection at the end of Chapter 1.)

On the other hand, the number of phallic symbols adjacent to the river suggest that males may also have carved the rock, perhaps in association with the puberty ritual of a young hunter's first kill. (See photo on the top of p. 285.) South African author Laurens van der Post remarks on the unique physiology of the San, both female and male:

> "The women were born with a natural little apron, the so-called *tablier égyptien*, over their genitals; the men were born, lived, and died with their sexual organs in a semi-erect posi-

tion. The Bushman found dignity in this fact and made no attempt falsely to conceal it. Indeed he accepted it so completely as the most important difference between himself and other men that he gave his people the name *'Qhwai-xkhwe'* which openly proclaims this fact."[22]

In other words, the term by which the San identify themselves refers specifically to their genitalia. In the case of the male, they are apparently ithyphallic.

The late epigrapher Barry Fell had interpreted some of the more abstract symbols at Driekopeiland as Libyan inscriptions written in Ogam script, one translation of which is as follows: "Under constant attack we have quit this place to occupy a safe stronghold." Brenda Sullivan amplifies Fell's rendition: "'People suffering. A time of death and suffering. People were forced to abandon the place, and seek protection elsewhere'—either because they were attacked, or because of violent storms and flooding."[23] If Fell is correct (and he may or may not be), then we have one more link of South Africa to the Maghreb.

Although I am not psychic, as I sat in the midday sun at this site, a vague sense of malaise and subliminal tension pervaded the atmosphere. Even my South African friend Rob admitted he would not camp overnight here, due not to the dangerous wildlife but because of the evils spirits that potentially inhabit the place even today. Maybe we were simply experiencing, to again quote van der Post, "...the ghosts of Africa which, as we all knew, walked not at midnight but noon."[24]

What can we make of the engravings of humanoids with their bizarre paraphernalia? The "rocket," the "flying saucer," and the "platform" shown on pp. 288 and 289 are all located the general vicinity of this "Spaceman" anthropomorphic petroglyph. Note that the protrusion from his helmet is somewhat similar to the cone-shaped nose on the kachina. (This is also similar to the petroglyphs of the one-horned shamans shown on p. 269.)

Are these carvings in stone merely projections, à la Erich von Däniken and Zecharia Sitchen, of the paradigm of modern technology upon an ancient culture? Are these South African petroglyphs representative of the same sort of spirit messengers that the Hopi of the American Southwest believe in? Are they inter-dimensional beings or extraterrestrial entities originating from somewhere far away in our physical universe? Like most rock art, these engravings at Dreikopseiland generate more questions than answers.

Crypto-Creatures from "Strange Stars"

I can already hear the snickers and see the sneers on the faces of those traditional archaeologists who by some small chance might be reading this. In his essay on "off-beat conjectures" and "loony claims" from the "fringes of archaeology," Professor Morris cites Canadian archaeologist Bruce Trigger:

> "Archaeologists cannot rule out the possibility that extraterrestrial visitors have influenced the course of human development to some degree, any more than they can exclude the biological existence of purple unicorns. Yet, clumsy, inadequate, and uncertain as our present scientific understandings of cultural change may be, they account for what is observed in the archaeological record in both its totality and individual features, while extraterrestrial salvationism keeps alive only by making speculative and always inconclusive claims about isolated phenomena."[25]

Maybe Dr. Trigger has jumped the gun here. In the *anthropological* record, plenty of evidence indeed exists that African tribes in the past interacted with entities not from this Earth.

For example, Henri A. Junod was a Swiss ethnographer and Protestant missionary who studied the Tsonga (or Thonga, a branch of the Bantu) of South Africa in the late 19th and early 20th centuries. His two-volume magnum opus titled T*he Life of a South African Tribe* was published in 1912 and 1913—35 years before Roswell and the modern wave of UFO sightings.

One of his informants, whom he describes as "a thoughtful and intelligent person" and who was a counselor for one of the sub-chiefs, earnestly remarked: "Have you not heard that in Maputju two dwarves (psimhu-ñwanyana) fell from Heaven ; a little man and a little woman. They came to say to the people : 'Do no kill the grasshoppers! They belong to us!'"[26] These ecologically sensitive "inhabitants of Heaven" were called *balungwana*. In the Tsonga language, Black people were called *banhu*, whereas White people were called *balungu*.[27] Thus, the diminutive *balungwana* that originated in the sky might have had lighter skin.

Henry Callaway, another anthropologist-cum-missionary, did fieldwork in South Africa even earlier than Junod. Publishing a couple important volumes in 1868 and 1870, Callaway found that the Zulus conceptualize the heavens as a blue rock dome, inside of which are the Earth, Sun, Moon, and stars. One of his informants said: "And the men who, we suppose, are on the other side of the heaven, we do no know whether they are on the rock, or whether there is some little place which is earth on the other side; we do not know that. The only thing which we know is this, that these heavenly men exist. Therefore there is a place for them, as this place is for us."[28] In other words, this particular Zulu confirms the existence of ETs.

This tribe also believes in "...*heaven*-descended unkulunkulu; and there is, so far as I know, every where, among the people of all tribes, a belief in the existence of *heavenly* men (abantu bezulu); and a king of *heaven*, whom they suppose to be the creator of lightning, thunder, and rain."[29]

The word *uNkulunkulu* literally means "the old, old one" and refers to the first man and ancestor of all. He sometimes is paired with a woman named uThlanga. The demigod uNkulunkulu appeared from a huge marsh of *reeds* –recall the Riet River– and brought the fruits of civilization to the Zulu. Sometimes also known uKqili, or "the wise one" and "the great one," he taught people how to hunt, make fire, grow food, and raise cattle. This scenario greatly resembles the early legends of the Nommos, or "instructors," of the Dogon in Mali (see the bottom of p. 275) and the amphibious god Oannes of the Babylonians in ancient Iraq. When uNkulunkulu's lightning struck cattle, it meant that he was hungry.[30] This relationship with cattle is somewhat akin to the modern cattle mutilation phenomenon. After the influence of Christian missionaries, however, uNkulunkulu became associated with the creator God.

Junod proclaims that the Tsonga possessed only a paucity of information regarding the stars. "These few superstitions and observations comprise all the Astronomy of the Thongas. The sidereal world is almost entirely outside the range of their preoccupations."[31] On the contrary, I suspect that his informants thought that their great wealth of star knowledge was too secret and too sacred to share with some mere White missionary.

The intimacy that many African tribes have with the celestial realm is presently confirmed by a world-renowned Zulu *Sangoma* (medicine man) and *High Sanusi* ("uplifter of the people") whose name is Vusamazulu Credo Mutwa.

> "I learned astronomy from Swazi healers who said that the stars were very important to the welfare of humans and animals on earth. They taught me that all knowledge that we humans possess comes from the stars above. They told me something that my Christian mind refused to mind to believe; namely that there were creatures among the stars who sometimes visited us, bringing us knowledge. They are the ones who brought us the laws that we now have. They are the ones who gave us our belief in God."[32]

Baba (an honorific Zulu term meaning "father") Mutwa was born in 1921 as a Roman Catholic in the KwaZulu-Natal province of South Africa. After trying in his youth to become a school teacher, he suddenly and inexplicably became very ill. Seeing this as a sign of his future vocation, he then undertook an arduous and sometimes harrowing apprenticeship from a number of shamans, both male and female. Eventually becoming a world traveler, he spread the wisdom of the pan-African culture to many countries. Unlike most academicians who seem to put up barriers between peoples and compartmentalize them for study, Baba Mutwa continuously shows us the enduring but dynamic connections between continents. For instance, he sees direct parallels between Native American and African tribes.

> "There is not a single nation among Native American peoples whom I visited in my journeys to the United States that does

> not have cultural and linguistic links with Africa. Among the Hopi Indians of the American Southwest, I found a custom where masked people, who are called *Kachinas*, come at certain times during the year and conduct sacred ceremonies and bless the people. In the African country known as Zambia, there is a group of people who practice what is called *Mackishee*. People wearing elaborate masks, which refer to certain spirits, visit villages at times and listen to confessions of the villager's sins. These 'spirits' bless the people for the coming period of time and go on their way again."[33]

In contrast to the informants of the early ethnographers, Baba Mutwa is eager to share the starlore and ET stories of many African nations. He writes that the historic Zulu King Shaka, for instance, had gone out to battle the Mapepetwa people. Camped at the foot of a great mountain, the king saw in the night sky three gigantic shields of fire hovering over the opposing armies. After these shields had flown around the mountain three times, both sides agreed to put down their weapons.[34] It is interesting to note that the Hopi also refer to flying saucers as "shields," or *paatuwvota*—literally, *pa-* = "water" or "wonder" and *tuwvota* = "warrior shield."

The San (Bushmen) have a god named Nxunxa, who flies through the sky in a giant ostrich egg. He supposedly even brought people to Earth in this aerial egg. [35]

One incredible Zulu legend with a definite sci-fi aura involves a Firebird's egg but also corroborates Dogon mythology. Humans once lived on a Red World (Mars?) close to Earth. On this world women ruled, and a war between the sexes eventually erupted. This strife unleashed "star-eating demons," which all but ravaged the planet. A culture hero named Moromudzi took his wife Kimanmireva and a chosen few into a "gigantic iron dragon that was capable of flying between stars." They navigated to a star called Peri Orifici, which Baba Mutwa identifies as the "Star of the Wolf," or Sirius.

One planet that revolved around this star was a Water World where an amphibious creatures lived and a king named Nommo ruled. (Sound familiar?) Soon one of the humans killed and ate one of the Water People, so all of the former had to leave.

Wowane and Mpanku, twin sons of Nommo, loaded the people in a Firebird's giant egg and sailed past the Red World to eventually arrive at Earth, slamming into the sand and burrowing deep underground. The humans emerged from the subterranean level and finally populated the planet.

The Water World twins rolled the pocked egg back up into the sky, where it became the Moon. The Firebird, discovering its loss, flew through vast space to the Earth and tied Wowane to a stone, where the bird proceeded to tear out his bowels—much like the Greek myth of Prometheus. Wowane had not stolen fire but rather the *Fire*-bird's egg.

Mpanku, however, dove under the ocean and soon married a mermaid, producing the race of dolphins. Baba Mutwa says the Zulu name for these intelligent creatures is Hlengeto, or "one who saves." Legends worldwide relate that the compassionate dolphins will back you back to dry land if you fall into the sea.

Baba Mutwa added that after many centuries, the immortal Nommo came to Earth with 12 amphibian counselors. These benevolent creatures bestowed upon humans all the knowledge of civilization and some of the wisdom of the stars.[36]

> And they created a lake around their sky ship and every morning they used to swim from their sky ship to the shores of the lake and there preach to the people who assembled in large numbers around the lake. It is said that before the Nommo departed, returning with a great noise back to their home star, they first chose one of their number, killed it and cut its body up into little pieces and then gave these pieces to the assembled people to eat in the first sacrificial ritual of its kind on earth. When the people had eaten the sacred flesh of the star creature and drunk its blood mixed with water, the Nommo took the lower jaw of their creature and by some incredible fact of magic brought the whole creature back to life again. We are told that this is the way that the Nommo taught our people that there is no death and that behind every death there shall be a resurrection.[37]

Other African tales involve space flight. The hunter-gatherer Pygmies of Zaire also have a legend of a knowledge-bringing figure named Kani or Kahani, who came to Earth in a great swing.[38] The glowing swing or golden basket, Mutwa says, is an ancient metaphor for the flying saucer. The term *Kahani* may be linguistically related to the Hopi *kachina*. (For a full discussion of the global implications of the *ka-* syllable, see Chapter 16 in my book *Eye of the Phoenix*.) In particular, one kachina named Káhayle (also spelled Káhayla or Kahaila) is alternately known as the Hunter Kachina, the Mad Kachina, or the Turtle Kachina.[39] (For the Turtle-Orion connection, see Chapter 2, Chapter 8, and Chapter 9 of the present volume.)

The tall Massai warriors of Kenya speak of a wise god with a long white beard named Uru-Wantayi, who once descended from the heavens in a "canoe" made of gold and iron to give the people herds of cattle.[40] It is interesting to note the linguistic parallel between the name of this tribe and the Hopi figure of Masau'u, tall gray god of the underworld and death, and, as I believe, also the terrestrial equivalent of the constellation Orion. (See picture of Masau'u on p. 247.)

Baba Mutwa claims that creatures from a star in Orion once lived in pre-human times on the Earth and built a huge subterranean metropolis in the heart of Africa. He also states that many generations ago a group of Tibetans in colorful robes and hats went in search of this mysterious city of copper, but were never heard from again.

> "Before human beings were created on this planet, there had existed a very wise race of people known as the Imanyukela. These people had come from the constellation known to white people as Orion, and they had inhabited our earth for thousands and thousands of years. And that before they had left our earth to return once more to the sacred Spider constellation, they made a great evacuation under the earth, beneath the Ruwensory [Rwenzori] Mountains—the Mountains of the Moon. And deep in the bowels of Mother Earth, the Imanyukela built a city of copper buildings. A city with a wall of silver all around it. A city built at the huge mountain of pure crystal. The mountain of knowledge. The mountain from which all knowledge on earth comes. And a mountain to which all knowledge on earth ultimately returns."[41]

Perhaps these entities manufactured the metallic spheres of Klerksdorp previously mentioned. At any rate, the Africans call the spider Anansi, and he is known as the Trickster. He taught people weaving and is the repository of wisdom.[42] (See photo of trapdoor spider engraving on the top of p. 300.)

The Hopi also have a spider figure named Kokyangwuhti, or Spider Woman, who usually assists people in their quests and was present during the origin of humankind. The Hopi, incidentally, acknowledge four races of people. Kokyangwuhti gathered four colors of mud –black, white, yellow, and red– and mixed them with her saliva in order to create these four races, each with its own basic language. Humans were, by the way, created in the image of the sky god Sótuknang.[43] (See photos on p. 307 and p. 343.)

It is interesting to note that Orion is designated as the spider constellation, since the people who created the Nazca lines in Peru probably had the same belief. (See photo on the top p. 191.) The Nazca Spider depicted on the desert is, in particular, the genus *Ricinulei*—an extremely rare spider found only hundreds of miles away in the inaccessible portions of the Amazon rain forest.[44]

Baba Mutwa also claims that the shy Bantwana tribe, or "children of the stars," who live near the Zambezi River in northern Zimbabwe, originally came from the planet Mars, which they call Liitolafisi, or "eye of the brown hyena." They also know of bird-like creatures that once came from a certain star in Orion. These strange ET humanoids had 10 fingers, but only two large toes on each foot. They mated with people of the tribe to replicate at least their bizarre podological condition, which Mutwa witnessed.[45]

Credo Mutwa is not without controversy, and he has his detractors, who call him a South African fraud or a New Age charlatan. On the other hand, he also has ardent supporters, such as the late psychiatrist and Harvard professor Dr. John Mack, who did research on the transformative and spiritual aspects of the alien abduction phenomenon.

Baba Mutwa himself has even admitted to being abducted and examined by the typical grey aliens he calls *mantindane*, or "sky monkeys," aboard a metallic craft shaped like a round water tank lying on its side. These hairless beings were three feet tall and had large black eyes, white-clay faces with an oily sheen, small jaws, tiny nostrils, no ears, lipless razor-cut mouths, and on each hand two, three, or four thin fingers, each with an extra joint. He said the creatures staggered about in a jerky way as if they were "powered by batteries." They all wore seamless, shiny silver-gray uniforms that crackled. The room had an electric smell of copper and rotten fish. At one point an instrument was inserted into his nose that made his brain explode with pain.

He was then forced to have sex with a cold, doll-like female humanoid with polished skin. When she mounted him like "a crazy Zulu girl," he said it felt like making love to a machine or a dead body. This traumatizing experience left sores burning on his penis, blood oozing from his pores, and a half-inch scoop mark on his thigh. When he was returned in a mental fog to the Inyangani Mountains of Zimbabwe where he had originally been, he found that he had been missing for three days. He was close to madness, and it took him several months to recover.[46]

Baba Mutwa attributes to the *mantindane* many baneful effects, such as wars and manufactured diseases that test human resistance to sundry strains of bacteria. On the positive side, though, he claims that they taught the Zulus how to drill through stone (perhaps with diamond-tipped tools) and showed the Egyptians how to cut the huge blocks used to construct the pyramids.[47]

Mack describes Mutwa's work as a bridge between ancient lore and modern meme:

> "Credo links the *mantindane* to the *wanddinja*, the sky-gods of the Australian aboriginals [see photo on p. 62 of the present volume], which are depicted in cave drawings with startlingly large black eyes, and to ancient Sumerians, whose drawings showed bald heads and faces with unusually large eyes, small chins, and rudimentary noses. He also relates them to other nonearthly creatures and events like Sasquatch sightings, animal mutilations resembling those documented in Western accounts, and the mysterious, intricate 'crop circles' seen in fields, especially in southern England. Credo himself has made many drawings and paintings of variously shaped spacecraft, most of which look familiar to anyone who has studied the subject carefully."[48]

[continued on p. 301]

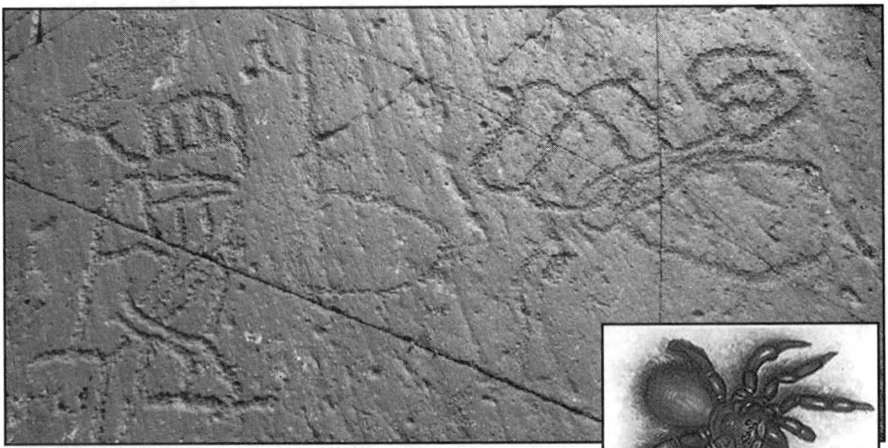

Driekopseiland "Spaceman" engraving next to trapdoor spider and burrow. Rob Milne believes that the depiction of the eight legs would be superfluous, because the spider is stationary.

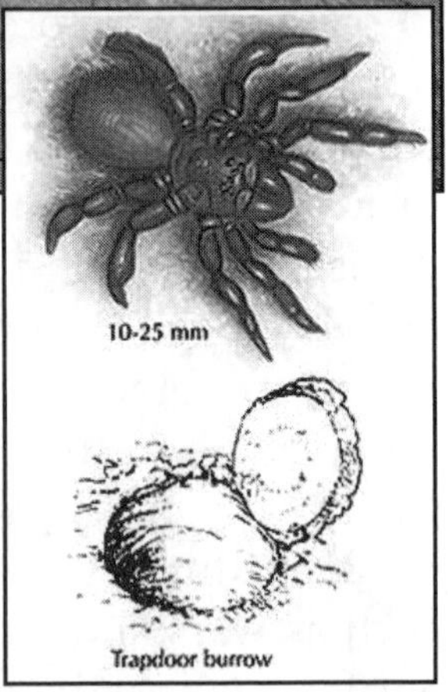

The trapdoor spider is a nocturnal insect. Credo Mutwa claims that Orion is the Spider constellation.

Photo above © by Bronislava Milne.

Left: Drawing by Credo Mutwa of metallic space being, courtesy of Rob Milne.

Note Third Eye motif. Tripartite headdress is like that worn by women of the Herero tribe of Namibia and Botswana.

The Zulu healer Mutwa has also encountered at least 10 different types of cryptozoological entities in his shamanic journeys through inner space, but it is difficult to distinguish between subjective and objective realities from his accounts. One more example will suffice, though, to illustrate how radically different the *Sangoma*'s reality is from our contemporary Western existence.

> "The Mutende-ya-ngenge is known in Botswana, South Africa as *Sekgotswana,* "the short one," or sometimes as *Puhwana*. I have seen some of these. They are quite humanoid in shape, with light skin and with long eyes that make it seem as if they are wearing large goggles. The eyes go from the nose almost to the temple, and are covered with a kind of horny black layer. Its ears are very tiny and set low. Where human beings' ears are set high, this creature's ears are set almost where the point of the jaw would be on a human being, and they have tiny little mouths. They have got dirty grayish white skins, and very beautiful, unusual hands. Their hands have six long fingers, with their index finger and the finger next to it unnaturally long. They have two thumbs, not where my thumb is. When the creature grabs something, the second thumb assists the first thumb grabbing. One thumb is set in the center of the hand. It is very long. This creature is also very thin in body, almost as if it's got tuberculosis."[49]

A few points need explanation. Baba Mutwa says that these creatures are about three feet in height, so perhaps they are the same as or similar to the "dwarves" that Henri Junod's informant witnessed falling from the sky in the early 20th century. (See pp. 292-293.) It is also interesting to note that the alternate name Puhwana sounds a lot like the Hopi figure named Pahana, or "the Elder White Brother." This entity once lived among the Hopi in Arizona, but then retreated to the east, much like Quetzalcoatl. At the end of the Fourth World he will return both to purify the wicked ones and to assist the virtuous Hopi in surviving the cataclysm. (See pp. 135-136.)

In addition, the goggle eyes, gray skin, and thin frame of Mutende-ya-ngenge resemble those of the Hopi god of death, fire, the underworld, and the earth named Masau'u. (See picture on p. 247.) Finally, this African creature has six fingers on each hand. Engravings of six-toed footprints have been found in southern Africa, much like those in the American Southwest. (See pp. 207-209.)

The Bakwena tribe of southeastern Kalahari Desert believe that Metsing was the place of Creation. This was a round hole with the spring at the bottom, out of which in succession came: all the animals, a one-legged giant eponymously named Metsing, the San, and finally the first ancestors of the Bakwena named Bakalahari (after which the desert was named). "Among the engravings on the rocks at Metsing are images of footprints showing large feet with six toes. Believe it or not, this gives credence to the Bakwena and San tales of an early race of giants, because records of six-toed giants actually exist."[50] Brenda Sullivan then cites the biblical passage of 1 Chronicles 20:6: "And yet again there was war at Gath, where was a man of great stature, whose fingers and toes were four and twenty, six on each hand, and six on each foot: and he also was the son of the giant."

The San (Bushmen), as Sullivan mentions, also share this belief in a primal giant race. (See Chapter 11 of the current volume.) J. C. Hollmann comments on the San's "Astrological Mythology":

> "In the mythical past the sun, moon and stars, and all the animals (and many insects too) were people. They were *!xwe-/na-se!ke*—the 'first-there-sitting-people'—a phrase that Lucy Lloyd translated as 'The Early Race'. These folk looked human and lived much as |xam hunter-gatherers did, but possessed simultaneously attributes that made them unique and different from people. It was this formative and unstable combination of human and non-human qualities that eventually caused the collapse of the Early Race 'society' and the subsequent establishment of an order in which the planets, humans and other organisms became the distinct entities we recognize today."[51]

The idea of these entities "sitting there" corresponds to one conception of the Hopi kachina as "...a 'sitter.' i.e., one who sits with the people (and among other things, listens to their petitions for rain and other spiritual and material blessings.)"[52] In other words, they listen to human entreaties and bestow the necessities for a bountiful and felicitous life. This parallels the rare beneficent aspects of the *mantindane* as experienced by Credo Mutwa.

These "sitters" are also known as the Watchers. "I saw in the visions of my head upon my bed, and, behold, a watcher and an holy one came down from heaven..." (Daniel 4:13) The primary Hopi "watcher" is named Sótuknang, the sky god. In one legend the warrior twins named Pöqanghoya and Palöngawhoy (see pp. 63-64) were mischievously stealing from the Flute priests and Snake priests a number of items: a lightning frame, a thunder board (bullroarer), a netted water jug, and a bull snake.

> "When they arrived at the Corn-Ear Bluffs they found a great many báhos [*pahos,* prayer feathers], little artificial melons, watermelons, and peaches which the Hopi had made and deposited in the different niches, cracks, etc. They had been deposited here by the different societies in their different ceremonies as prayer-offerings, that they might have an abundance of these things. On top of the rocks they saw the Watcher (Tû'walahka), who owns this rock. It was Cótukvnangwuu [Sótuknang], who was sitting there in the form of an old man."[53]

Tû'walahka, or Tuuwalaqa, is the guardian kachina, who in this case is synonymous with an elderly form of the celestial deity Sótuknang. The elder brother Pöqanghoya oversees the earth's solidity and is associated with the North Pole, whereas the younger brother Palöngawhoya controls air and sound vibrations and is associated with the South Pole.

It is interesting that these three figures from Hopi mythology can be directly compared with three figures from Sumerian mythology. Zecharia Sitchin points out that Anu, the sky god (who is analogous to the Hopi Sótuknang), was in charge of the middle celestial band called the "Way of Anu," which included the zodiac and extended 30° on either side of the equator.

The elder Enlil, lord of wind, ruled over the northern band. It was called the "Way of Enlil" and ranged from the North Pole to 30° north latitude. (In Akkadian religion, his name was Bel or Ba'al.

See photo on p. 155.)

The younger half-brother Ea (otherwise called Enki), lord of earth or water, reigned over the southern band. It was called the "Way of Ea," and ran from the South Pole to 30° south latitude.[54] By the way, 30° north latitude is the location of pyramids of Giza, the sacred city of Lhasa in Tibet, and the ancestral Hopi pueblo town of Casas Grandes in Chihuahua, Mexico. 30° south latitude is in the heart of South Africa's Karoo.

The only difference between the Hopi and Sumerian scenarios is that in the former the northern realm is connected to earth while in the latter it is connected to wind. Likewise, the Hopi southern realm is associated with air while the Sumerian southern realm is associated with earth.

Similar to Credo Mutwa's visitors, the Watchers can seem totally terrifying and the embodiment of absolute evil. The Dead Sea Scrolls from Qumran provide a graphic description of reptilian or serpent-like creatures—the ophidian element contained as well in the Hopi legend (on p. 303) of the encounter with the sky god. From the Testament of Amran, one fragment reads:

"I saw Watchers
in my vision, the dream-vision. Two men were fighting
  over me, saying . . .
and holding a great contest over me. I asked them, Who are you,
  that you are thus empowered over me?' They answered me, 'We
  have been empowered and rule over all mankind.'
  They said to me, 'Which of us do you choose to rule you?'
  I raised my eyes and looked.
One of them was terrifying in his appearance, like a serpent,
  his cloak many-colored yet very dark . . .
And I looked again, and . . . in his appearance, his visage like a viper,
  and wearing . . .exceedingly, and all his eyes . . .

. . .empowered over you . . .
I replied to him, 'This Watcher, who is he?' He answered me,
  'This Watcher . . .
and his three names are Belial,
  and Prince of Darkness and King of Evil." I said, 'My lord,
  what dominion . . .

'and his every way is darkened, his every work darkened.
In Darkness he . . .
You saw, and he is empowered over all Darkness, while I am empowered over all light.
. . .from the highest regions to the lowest I rule over all Light, and over all that is of God. I rule over every man..."[55]

Belial, of course, is simply a variation of the name Ba'al. Like stories of the Hopi Twin Warriors and the Sumerian half-brothers, we also see in the Dead Sea Scrolls the motif of two male figures who dominate opposing aspects of reality.

In Egypt the Watchers were referred to as the Urshu. "The Urshu, i.e., the Watchers, of Pe and Nekhen may have been groups of well-known gods, who were supposed to 'watch over' and specially protect cities; but, on the other hand, they may only have been the messengers, or angels, of the souls of Pe and Nekhen."[56] Falcon-headed Pe of Buto, capitol of Lower Egypt in the north, and jackal-headed Nekhen of Hierakonpolis, capitol of Upper Egypt in the south, were alternately seen as a pair of stars that formed a ladder whereon the dead pharaohs rose to heaven.[57] ("As above, so below.") Again we see a north-south duality of influence. The prefix *Ur-* means "earliest" or "original," thus signifying something very old. It is, of course, also the name of a primary city of ancient Sumer. The Akkadian name for Sumer is *Shumer,* which means "Land of the Guardians."[58] Shu (the syllable found in Ur-shu) is the Egyptian god of air and dryness.

The Egyptian word *Uru* means either "the great chiefs of heaven" or "a group of gods who lightened the darkness."[59] We recall as well one of the sky visitors of the Massai, Uru-Wantayi (p. 297). Sitchin defines the Egyptian word *Ntr* as:

> "...'Guardian, Watcher'. They had come to Egypt, the Egyptians wrote, from *Ta-Ur,* the 'Far/Foreign Land,' whose name *Ur* meant 'olden' but could have also been the actual place name—a place well known from Mesopotamian and biblical records: the ancient city of Ur in southern Mesopotamia. And the straits of the Red Sea which connected Mesopotamia and Egypt, were called *Ta-Neter,* the Place of the Gods, the passage by which they had come to Egypt."[60]

Budge, on the other hand, defines *neter* as "God" or "a god" in general and the proper noun *Neter* as "a serpent-god who bestowed godhood on the dead."[61] One cylinder seal from Sumer depicts Ea (or Enki, the earth god previously mentioned) with his lower body as a serpent.[62]

The Sumerian term NFL (not the American football league, but "Nefilim") means "to be cast down" and refers to "*...those who were cast down upon the Earth!*"[63]—namely, fallen angels. "...a fundamental tenet of Sumerian history and teachings was that Kingship was *actually*, and not just figuratively, brought down to Earth from the heavens—that the **Anunnaki** (= 'Those who from Heaven to Earth came') actually began their civilized presence on earth in five settlements..."[64]

However, according to *Peake's Commentary On the Bible*, the Aramaic word *nephîliâ* also refers to beings from a specific constellation: "those that are *of Orion* [italics added]."[65] Chief of the Nephilim was the great hunter Nimrod, who, according to some Jewish traditions, is equated with the constellation Orion.

"And there we saw the giants, the sons of Anak, which come of the giants: and we were in our own sight as grasshoppers, and so we were in their sight." (Numbers 13:33) The giants, or Nephilim, are the sons of Anak (or Anakim, literally, "long-necked"), or the Annunaki. Sitchen emphatically states: "The *Anakim*, we suggest, were none other than the *Anunnaki*."[66]

The so-called Early Race of titans that lived contemporaneously with the San Bushmen might be synonymous with the gargantuan Nephilim of the Bible (Genesis 6:1-4). According to the San Bushmen, the creatures of the Early Race were cannibals, like many giant races of old. They possessed characteristics both human and animal, and the delineation between the two was sometimes blurred. They were in fact the same sort of figures that the San painted in their rock art, namely, therianthropes. These eerie beings were sometimes portrayed as antelope-headed men in the same way that ancient Egyptians conceived of falcon-headed or jackal-headed humans.

[continued on p. 308]

Sótuknang, Hopi kachina doll, Museum of Northern Arizona.

Benin bronze plaque, Nigeria.

Victory Stele, Naram-Sin, King of Akkad, 2190–2154 BC, Louvre. Note his horns.

In the late 19th century, one of Lucy Lloyd's San informants cryptically stated: "The lion goes, for he goes above in the heaven. Therefore he stands firmly above in the sky. He is a lion who talks, he eats people, he talks. He is a lion, he is a man, he has hair, he is a lion, his hands are a man's."[67] The two pointers stars to the Southern Cross (Alpha and Beta Centauri) were believed to be male lions. Two brothers of the Early Race –a reprise of the twin motif– hunted lions (not a current practice) with throwing sticks, or "knobkerries." The elder made his weapon from an elephant bone, while the younger made his from an ostrich bone. We recall that this method of hunting was also used by the Hopi of Arizona and the aborigines of Australia.

The primary deity of the San was /Kaggen, conceptualized as both a trickster and the Creator. He was also a shape shifter, who had possessed the ability to change into an eland (his favorite animal), a hartebeest, a snake, an eagle, and even a louse. Oddly enough, his name literally means "mantis." This insectoid anthropomorph was also a culture-bringer, teaching humankind about fire, clothing, and tools. Joseph Campbell remarks:

> "...the folktales of living Bushmen represent the eland as the first and favorite creation of their principle divinity: a god variously named, in the various Bushmen areas, as Gauwa, Hishe, Kaggen, Dxui, Gao na, and so on. Kaggen means "mantis," and it is in this character that the god commonly appears—not exactly as an insect, but as an ambiguous, manlike figure in the Mythological Age of the Beginning."[68]

In San cosmology the temporal concept of the past is actually a spatial dimension that you can visit by performing the trance dance. This directly parallels the Hopi notion of the subterranean Third World, or previous era, a watery world located below Grand Canyon. Virtuous spirits journey there after they have passed on from the material life. The San frequently located this sacred space-time at waterholes. "Once you were dead and buried you walked the path of the !Khwe //na s'o !kwe, the People of the Early Race, to this great hole where you would live and walk around, while your heart went into the sky and became a star."[69]

For the San, the death of an eland, either in a literal or a figurative sense, generates *!gi*, or potency, which propels the shaman into the spirit world during the trance dance. In the thrall of its halluncinatory frenzy, he essentially *becomes* the eland. This is exactly what the Hopi kachina dancer experiences in the process of the dance, becoming basically the kachina spirit itself, and not merely a masquerade of it. The eland also symbolizes rain, rain making, and water in general in the same way that the bighorn sheep does in Hopi religious thought.

The San (or /Xam) specifically conceptualize Orion's belt as "Three Female Tortoises (hung on a stick)," while his sword is seen as "Three Male Tortoises (hung on a stick)." (Confusion exists re. gender, as statement on p. 53 shows.) The star Betelgeuse was also sometimes considered to be a Tortoise.[70] As I have shown in this book, many cultures associate the tortoise or turtle with Orion.

The !Xu Bushmen saw Orion's belt as "a Man, a Dog, and a Buck," while the !Kung Bushmen knew it as "Three Zebras," a male flanked by two females.[71] The Namaqua people imagine a whole hunting scenario. My friend Rob Milne comments: "The husband of the daughters of the Sky God, Aldebaran, shot his arrow (Orion's sword) at three zebras (Orion's belt) but it fell short. Afraid to retrieve his arrow because of the lion (Betelgeuse) and not wanting to go home empty-handed, the husband sits in the cold watching the zebra with his wives (the Pleiades) behind him."[72] The Songye of Zaire conceptualized the belt as "a Hunter with a Dog and an Animal," presumably his quarry.[73] This reflects the Greek uranography of Orion the Hunter, Canis Major the Great Dog, and either Lepus the Hare or Taurus the Bull as his game.

In addition, the San considered that Procyon in Canis Minor was a Male Eland, and Aldebaran in Taurus was a Male Hartebeest.[74] A girl of the Early Race created the Milky Way by grabbing a handful of white ashes from the fire and hurling it into the sky. She dug up red and white roots of a plant and threw them upward, where they because red and white stars.

Archaeoastronomer Richard Wade describes the southern African practice of human sacrifice connected to Orion's belt.

> "It appears that the three stars of Orion called 'Rhinoceros', 'three wild pigs' and the 'For God I Cut You' stars are amongst those chosen for a most sinister event, for at this exact time when The 'Giraffe' [Southern Cross], Pleiades and moon form a conjunction marking the 'New Year's Day', the three stars of Orion will ascend on the eastern horizon and are hailed with fires. The rainmaking ceremonies then commence with the words, 'For God I Cut You!' or 'Mademba-Ndikuteme!' and a sacrificial victim was chosen at this stage to be cut at the throat and then thrown on a fire to coax the rain – and 'the rain would always fall when the entrails burst forth'."[75]

In this chapter we have learned that the ancient tribes of southern Africa, far from being indifferent to the stars, had an intimate and enduring relationship with the celestial realm. "Above" and "below," reflecting the hermetic maxim, were seamlessly connected in a holistic cosmology. In the earliest era –what the ancient Egyptians called *Zep Tepi* and the Hopi call *Tokpela,* (literally, "night-flat area," or "sky")– the San Bushmen were springboks. The San also call Orion's belt the springbok stars.[76] This possibly indicates their interstellar origin.

The people spent countless hours carving sacred symbols into obdurate stone. These inner visions of the spirit world had been received from both cathartic trance states and quiescent deep meditation. The veil between the physical and non-physical universes was extremely thin, and in many cases the interaction between the two occurred right at the rock surface, which appeared as a translucent and permeable membrane.

Beyond the two worlds merging like dual circles of the vesica piscis were myriad realities, world upon world. Some of these were stars with revolving planets inhabited by entities whose technologies may be millions of years ahead of ours. Others worlds were purely inter-dimensional, with completely different laws of physics and ontological paradigms. As postmodernists thousands of years removed from San sensibilities, we must in the end admit that we are nothing but Horatios confronting this "wondrous strange." At the end of the 19th century, one San informant reported: "We do not utter a star man's name."[77]

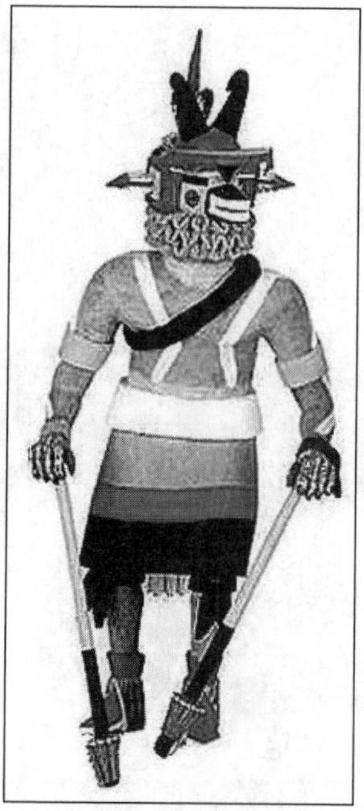

Left: Hopi Antelope Kachina. This kachina promotes rainfall. Like the eland, the pronghorn is associated with precipitation.

Above: Rock painting of a therianthrope (antelope, probably an eland), bent over with sticks in hands, made by Maluti Bushmen, Melikane Rock Shelter, Lesotho. Three vertical lines were incised, apparently at a later date.[78]

Therianthrope with flywisks, swimming turtles, fish, and snakes. /Xam painting from the Northeastern Cape Province. One researcher speculates that the figures at lower right are magic mushrooms (*Psilocybe cubensis*).[79] (See p. 148.)

Some tribes see Orion's belt as a rhino. Engraving at Wildebeest Kuil.

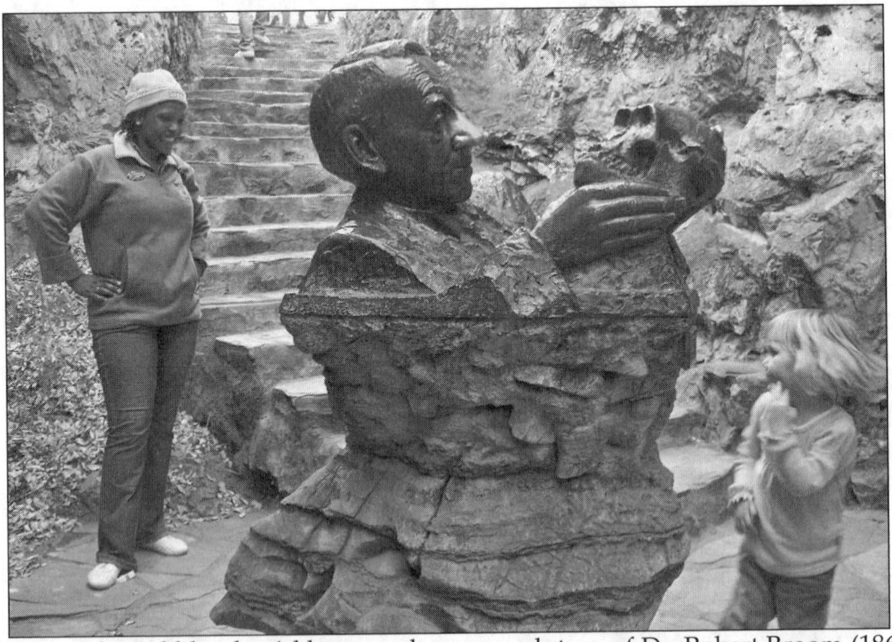

Tour guide and blonde girl between bronze sculpture of Dr. Robert Broom (1866 –1951). He is inspecting "Mrs. Ples," an *Australopithecus africanus* skull 2.1 million years old that he and Professor Raymond Dart of the University of Witwatersrand found in 1947 at Sterkfontein Cave, South Africa. Incidentally, Brenda Sullivan mentions Dart's assertion that "the nearest serological relatives" to the Auen and Kung of Namibia are the Douiret, a Tunisian Berber tribe of northern Africa.[80]

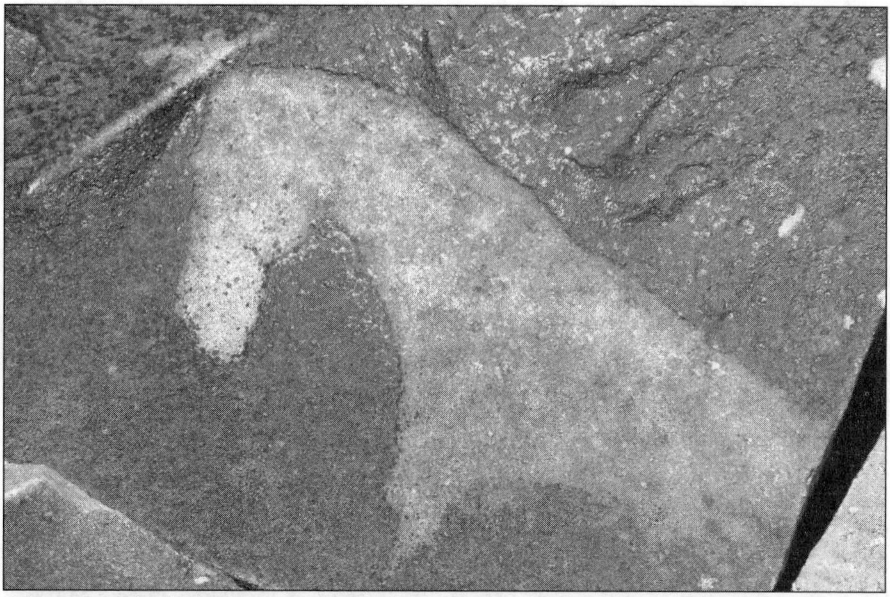

Others see the belt stars as zebras. Engraving of head, neck at Wildebeest Kuil.

Above: sun symbol (?) engraving at Wildebeest Kuil. Sullivan claims this is a double cross sacred to the twins Castor and Pollux. She also says that it is the sign of Tanit, Phoenician fertility goddes and patroness of sailors.[81]
Left: pottery sun symbol from Zia Pueblo. It has also become the emblem of the New Mexico state flag.

Right: Solar flare with dots (stars or planets?) Engraving at at Wildebeest Kuil.

Below: Polished calendar stone, Mpumalanga Province, South Africa.

Concentric circles: raindrops in pools? configurations of stars? Mpumalanga.

Polished stone with grooved top and hyrax engraving, Mpumalanga Province. The trance dance was perhaps performed in a ring around this rock. The mythological hyrax, or dassie, was named Coti, wife of Kaggen, who had two sons, Cogaz and Gewi. His adopted daughter !Xo, Porcupine, married Kwammang-a, Meerkat. Another of Kaggen's daughters married "snakes who were also men," namely, the Nagas.[82]

Are the "Lydenburg Heads" evidence of an ET presence in South Africa?

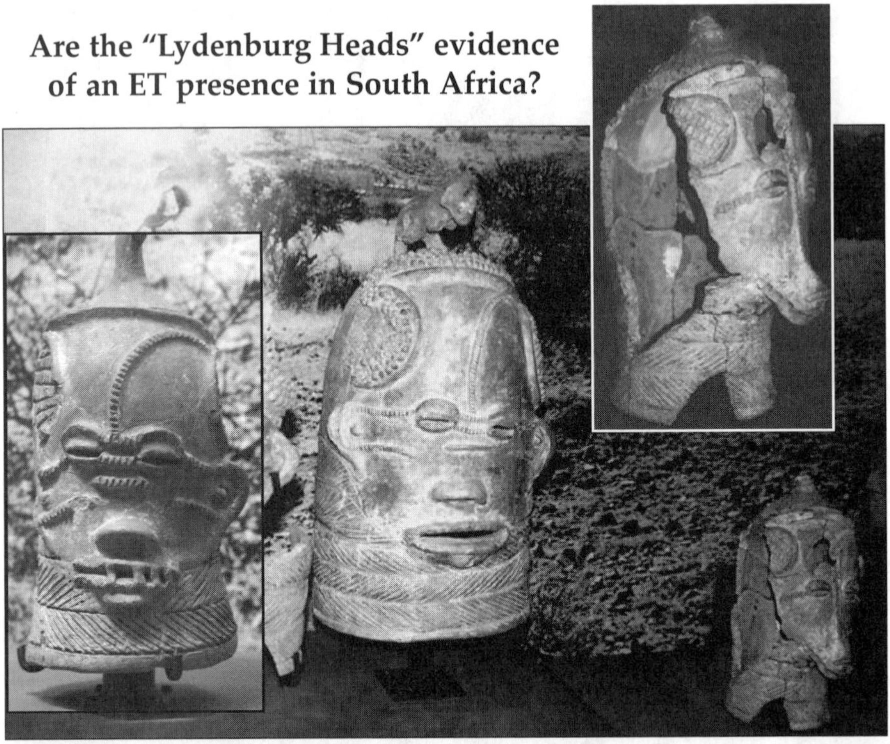

Seven terracotta heads found near Lydenburg, South Africa, were radiocarbon-dated to 490 AD. Two were large enough to be worn by children as ceremonial helmets. A dinosaur-like creature is located on top of one of the two larger heads (upper-middle). Their dome-shape resembles some Hopi kachina masks. (See photo on p. 288, for instance.) Therianthrope head on upper-right. Middle head below is pictured at upper-left. The smaller heads may have been attached to a pole. National Museum, Cape Town, South Africa. Photos © by Rob Milne.

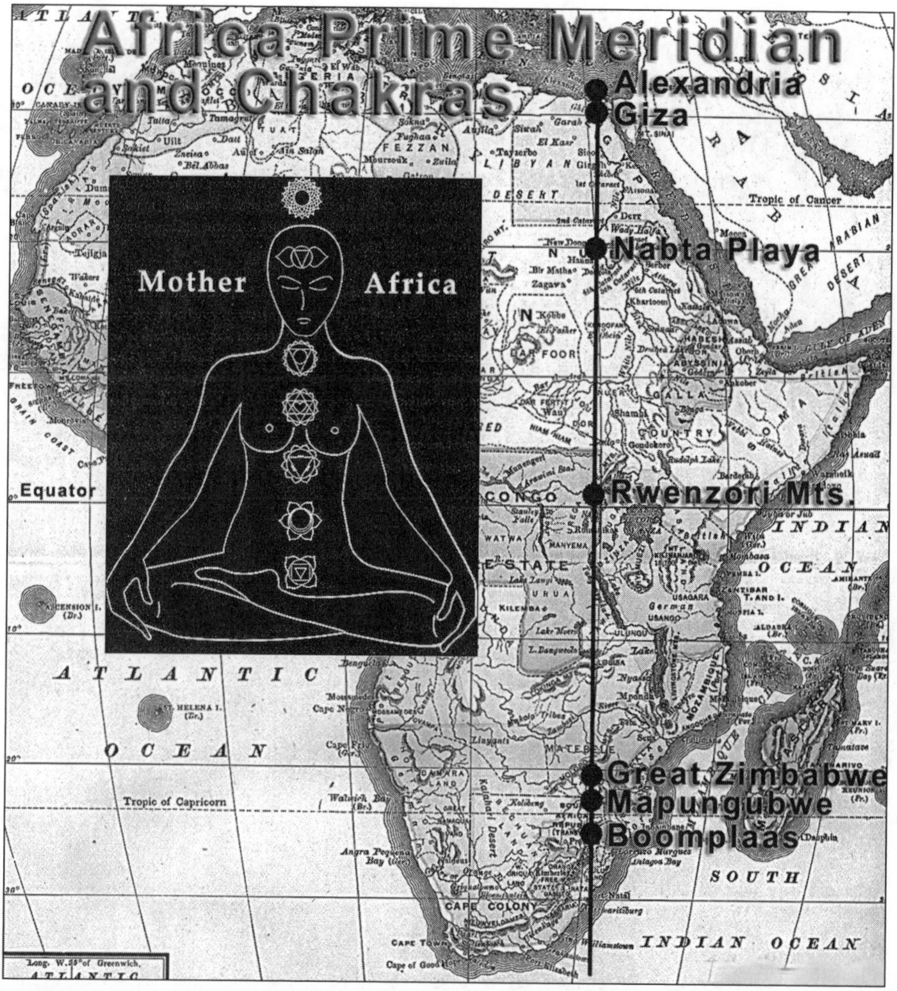

Crown:	Alexandria (Pharos Lighthouse)	29° 53′ E
Third Eye:	Great Pyramid, Giza, Egypt	31° 09′ E
Throat:	Napta Playa, southern Egypt	30° 42′ E
Heart:	Rwenzori Mountains, Uganda	29° 57′ E
Solar Plexus:	Great Zimbabwe, S. Rhodesia	30° 56′ E
Sacral:	Mapungubwe, S. Africa	29° 22′ E
Root:	Boomplaas, S. Africa	30° 24′ E

Prime Meridian: about 30° east longitude. Distance between Giza and Boomplaas: over 3,800 miles!

For a description of Napta Playa, the world's oldest astronomical observatory, see Thomas G. Brophy, *The Origin Map*. For a mention of the ancient city in the Rwenzori Mts., see Credo Mutwa quote on p. 297. Great Zimbabwe is 320 miles south of Zambezi R., 1270 – 1550 AD, pop. c. 18,000. Mapungubwe on Limpopo R., 900 – 1300 AD, pop. c. 5,000. For a description of Boomplaas ("Tree Farm") Petroglyph Site, see Appendix 1 by Rob Milne in my book *Eye of the Phoenix*.

The 6" X 9" gold-anodized aluminum plaque (above on the facing page) shows the position of the sun with respect to the center of the galaxy and nearby pulsars. Carl Sagan and Frank Drake created it in an attempt to communicate with extraterrestrial life somewhere in the far reaches of outer space. Launched in 1972, the Pioneer 10 and the Pioneer 11 were the first spacecraft designed to leave the solar system, and both carry duplicates of the plaque. It displays the then-nine planets, including Pluto, which was discovered at Lowell Observatory in Arizona. It also shows the Pioneer spacecraft's planet of origin, its trajectory past Mars and Jupiter, and its slingshot past Saturn outward from our helio-heart. The radial pattern consists of 14 lines made up of long binary numbers that represent the periods of the pulsars. The horizontal line that extends past the humans represents the Sun's relative distance to the center of the galaxy. A silhouette of the spacecraft in scale is juxtaposed to the humans so that relative size can be determined. The two circles at the top represent the fundamental state of the hydrogen atom, which acts as a universal clock. The regular decrease in the frequency of the pulsars will enable ETs to determine the time elapsed since each spacecraft was launched. In about 2 million years the plaque should arrive at Aldebaran, 68 light-years away. Let's hope that whatever intelligence retrieving this message in a bottle is not reading an elegy to an extinct civilization.

Thirty-three years ago, Voyager 1 and 2 spacecraft, also designed to escape the gravity of the solar system, were launched with a more complete and complex array of information about the Earth and its inhabitants etched on a gold-plated copper disk. This included recordings of greetings in 55 different languages as well as nature sounds, the music of Bach, Mozart, Beethoven, Stravinsky, and Chuck Berry. Diagrams and photographs of DNA, human anatomy, food, architecture, the planets and solar system, and other salient scientific facts were incorporated into this time capsule. Printed messages of politicians and world leaders were also included. However, the same pulsar map and hydrogen molecule found on the Pioneer plaque were also integrated into this interstellar "barbaric YAWP." In 40,000 years Voyager 1 will be within 1.6 light-years of a star in Ophiuchus, the Serpent Handler. Voyager has just exited the solar system. Just after this happened, the spacecraft inexplicably began to send back data in an altered format that scientists have been unable to decode. Paleo-SETI expert Hartwig Hausdorf speculates that the spacecraft might have been hijacked and reprogrammed. Motive? Unknown. It seems we can create codes but we can't crack them.[83]

Below on facing page is an engraving from Driekopseiland, South Africa, with a radial pattern similar to that of the Pioneer Plaque. Photo is rotated so the natural rock fracture bisecting the circle is horizontal. There are seven rays in each hemisphere of the circle, corresponding to the pulsars. At the upper-right is a circle that contains two lines, corresponding to the hydrogen molecule. The outer circle may contain 33 rays, but it is impossible to tell because the rock surface is flaked to the immediate right of the circle.

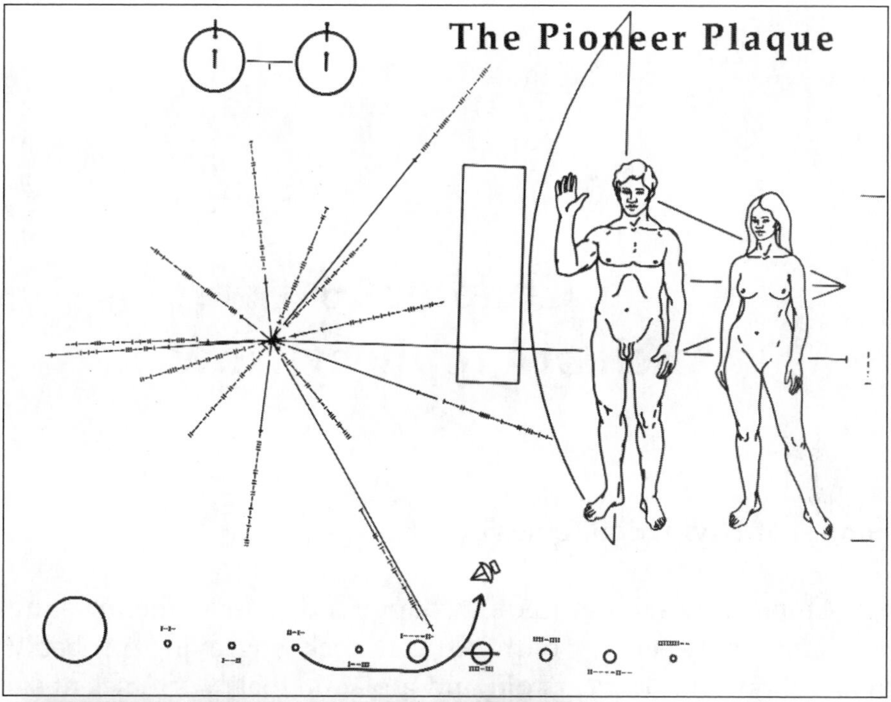

Did the people who made this rock engraving in South Africa 3,200 years ago or more actually "remote view" the future and glimpse this image we created in the late 20th century which is now bound for the stars? Were they in contact with an intelligence that knew about the Pioneer Plaque from their journeys through space and/or time and wanted to convey its significance to indigenous tribes?

Or is this all just a big "coincidence"?

Chapter 16
Ancient Prophecy Now

Stones of Divination, Lines of Fate

At the end of the preceding chapter, I discussed the uncanny similarity between a South African rock engraving probably many thousands of years old and a plaque that NASA scientists recently launched into space. Other than coincidence (which clumsily tries to dismiss the inscrutable), the only plausible explanation is that these ancient people were using what we might today call "remote viewing" of the future. By using unspecified paranormal techniques, they somehow received the image of a group of symbols from the psychic ether that for some reason they considered significant. Another word for this is prophecy.

All cultures in all ages have used prognostication. It is humankind's valiant attempt to pierce the mysterious veil of temporality. The *Sangoma* Baba Credo Mutwa, whom I discussed in Chapter 15, is pictured in one book holding an imposing bronze staff surmounted by a doughnut-shaped stone.[1] He specifically calls these "stones of prophecy."[2] The indigenous tribes of South Africa used to beat the ground with them in order to call up the spirits of the ancestors. Of course, materialist archaeologists attribute a utilitarian function to these stones—namely, a weight for a digging stick. For ancient cultures, the physical and spiritual realms interpenetrated each other to a degree we can hardly comprehend, so it's probably not strictly a case of "either/or."

Dr Cyril Hromník is a diffusionist archaeologist at odds with the mainstream, especially in regard to these circular ring stones. "Hromník says the stones (called *!kwe* by the Quena and Soaqua) are common in Hindu temples, where they are called *yoni* stones and represent Siva's female energy. This position brought Hromník in very direct conflict with the South African Archaeological Society, whose newsletter is called *The Digging Stick,* and has a drawing of this implement –complete with stone– in its masthead!"[3]

Born and bred in South Africa, rock art investigator Rob Milne comments on the significance of the round stones to the indigenous tribes. "The Tswana people in Botswana say that these are 'The Stones of the Gods'—they were handed down by the Gods from the skies in very ancient times. The Tswana beat these stones on the ground near the graves of their ancestors and in this way are able to communicate with them. I also heard another angle from someone who spent a lot of time working on the diamond mines in Botswana. He said that some of the Medicine Men hang them in a tree and look through them whilst meditating. This enables them to communicate with other Medicine Men who may be many miles away, and also to see into a different dimension."[4]

Bored stone, dug up from a garden in Machadodorp, South Africa. Weight: 5.2 kg. Diameter (not perfectly round) maximum = 17.5 cm.; minimum = 16 cm. Thickness: (width of wheel) 12 cm. Hole diameter: at top end 5 cm; in middle 2.5 cm. Estimated age: circa 12,000 BP or older. Photo by © Rob Milne.

In Botswana these bored stones were also called *Lentswe la Badimo,* or "stones of the ancestors." The Ancient Ones looked through the hole in these stones to see what the people were doing in the village. Occasionally these sky-beings would drop one from the heavens, so now they sometimes can be found in the veld. The !Xam Bushmen used the unique stones to communicate with deceased sorcerers or even Kaggen, the creator god mentioned in the previous chapter. Some researchers speculate that in the sacred cosmology of the San, the stone's hole represents the vortex that shamans have to pass through in order to communicate with the spiritual realm. The Bantu tribe of the central Transvaal made offerings to the ancestors by pouring boiled grain or beer through the hole before the rest was consumed. The Dodomo tribe of Tanzania connected the bored stones with a certain rainmaking ceremony. This was done, however, only in conjunction with phallic stones, which tends to corroborate Hromník's theory of *lingam* (male) and *yoni* (female) stones. "These accounts all support the concept that bored stones, irrespective of their possible mundane uses, were also regarded by various communities as communication channels with the spirit world. Thus, the term 'Lentswe la Badimo' is regarded as inordinately appropriate for these unique southern African artefacts."[5]

However, they are not quite exclusive to Africa. This same sort of worked stones has been found in the American Southwest as well. Made from basalt, diorite, or sandstone, they average about three inches in diameter with the inner hole 5/8 to 7/8 of an inch wide. They are sometimes referred to as "lava stones." Traditional archaeologists in the U.S. also call these digging stick weights.[6] Make no bones about it: these "digging stick stones" are pure surmise. Why go to the tremendous effort to bore, abrade, and smooth a hard stone into a perfectly symmetrical shape unless the geometric form had some spiritual significance? It would be much easier just to haft a non-worked stone rounded by erosion to the digging stick's shaft.

The Hopi also have a vegetative version of this stone, which is called a *silaqapngöla,* or "...cornhusk wheel, used as part of ceremonial paraphernalia or as a target in a game."[7]

According to one survey of the Chumash tribe's territory in southern California, at least a few archaeologists are cautiously willing to admit to the non-pragmatic explanation of these round stones.

> "Great numbers of perforated stones of steatite and sandstone and looking rather like fossil doughnuts have been found, especially on the islands. They are from 2 to 4 inches in diameter with a hole between ½ inch and one inch. They have been variously described as weights for digging sticks, war club heads, and fishing sinkers. They have been found in fetish bundles with other typical shaman paraphernalia. The neighboring Yokuts used similar stones in rain-making ceremonies and as a game stone."[8]

The game referred to is the hoop-and-pole, apparently similar to the Hopi game played with a cornhusk wheel. Other archaeologists stress the ritual use of the circular stones. "Some donut-shaped artifacts were clearly used in ritual/ceremonial contexts—in death rites, in sacred caches, and in shaman's kits. They have been recovered archaeologically from or near burials and cremations. They are found in both male and female burials."[9]

Old photo of perforated stone slab, loom stones, Four Mile Ruin, Arizona. This may have been a grave stone with a hole for the soul's escape. The hole resembles that in the *Sipapuni.* (See photo top of p. 252.)

The reader may recall the discussion of Hopi cosmology and the illustration of the torus, or doughnut-shape. (See pp. 69-71.) This geometric form allows energy to flow from the *axis mundi* with its roots in the nadir of the previous Hopi Third World and its corn (maize) tassel in the zenith of the stars. The vertical staff of life contains the future as well as the subjective realm of all thoughts, emotions, and desires. This wellspring of energy constantly manifests the objects of the physical world in the present. The energy transference flows toward the past on the horizontal plane of the high desert and ultimately reaches mythical consciousness, where it is again channeled inward toward the heart of matter in a perpetual circuit of numinous awareness.

This torus geometry and its structuring of the temporal domain is radically different from the Judeo-Christian notion of linear time with the past positioned behind, the future in front, and the present somehow interpolated. According to certain Christian eschatologies, we are possibly approaching the End Times, or use the term of the French paleontologist and Jesuit priest Pierre Teilhard de Chardin, the Omega Point. On the other hand, the torus, which permits a perception of time in a far more sophisticated way, may in fact be the key to understanding prophecy. In other words, by using this sacred symbol the ancients could have unlocked the mystery of seeing into the future—essentially, a form of a-somatic time travel.

Prophecy might have even played a part in the orientation of the Orion Correlation in Arizona. (For a complete discussion of this concept, read my book *The Orion Zone*.) It took approximately two-and-a-half centuries to complete the celestial template on the high desert of the American Southwest. (See Google Earth photo on p. 106.) The cliff dwellings in Canyon de Chelly (corresponding to Orion's right foot Saiph) began to be constructed about 1060 AD. The first villages on the three Hopi Mesas (Orion's belt) were built about 40 or 50 years later, and the pueblos at Wupatki near the San Francisco Peaks (Orion's left shoulder Bellatrix) commenced construction about 1120 AD. That is basically the east-west axis.

A little over a century afterward the north-south axis was added. The pueblos at Homol'ovi (Orion's right shoulder

Betelgeuse) near the modern town of Winslow, Arizona, were begun in approximately 1260 AD. Travel due north past the Mesas for a little over 110 miles and you reach Tsegi Canyon, where the spectacular cliff dwellings of Betatakin and Keet Seel are located (Orion's left foot Rigel.) They were constructed between about 1250 and 1285 AD.

In this celestial pattern imposed upon the landscape, Orion's left arm reaches toward Grand Canyon, the Hopi "Place of Emergence" from the previous Third World (Era) to the current Fourth World. It is a summer solstice sunset line with an azimuth of 300°. In other words, if you stood at Wupatki Ruin and looked northwest, you could see the Sun descend into Grand Canyon at nightfall on the first day of summer.

The terrestrial correlation of Pi3 Orionis rests in Grand Canyon. This yellow-white dwarf star with a temperature slightly hotter than our Sun is located in the middle of Orion's shield, bow, or lion's hide that is held aloft by his left arm. Unlike the majority of the stars in the constellation –the belt, for instance, which is about 1500 light-years away– , Pi3 has a distance of only 26 light years. Possibly a binary star, it is listed in the SETI Star Catalogue and is one of Project Phoenix's "Best and Brightest" Candidates for having exo-planets and ET life. Pi3 also ranks among NASA's top 100 target stars for the Terrestrial Planet Finder telescope observatories.[10] Planned launch date: 2012.

Is this, then, the ultimate purpose of the Orion Correlation in Arizona? Did Hopi "star elders" manifest this template in the form of stone villages arranged in a pattern to mirror the Orion constellation? Is their origin identified by Pi3 Orionis, which corresponds on the terrestrial map to the *Sipapuni* in the Grand Canyon? This is the place from which the Hopi ascended out of the underworld to inhabit the Colorado Plateau in the current Fourth World. "The Sípàapuni represents that from which the Hopi, when they became a people, began their journey to find and locate their homeland."[11] Actually called a travertine dome, it is located on the north bank of the Little Colorado River not far from its confluence with the Colorado River. (See photo p. 252.)

[continued on p. 328]

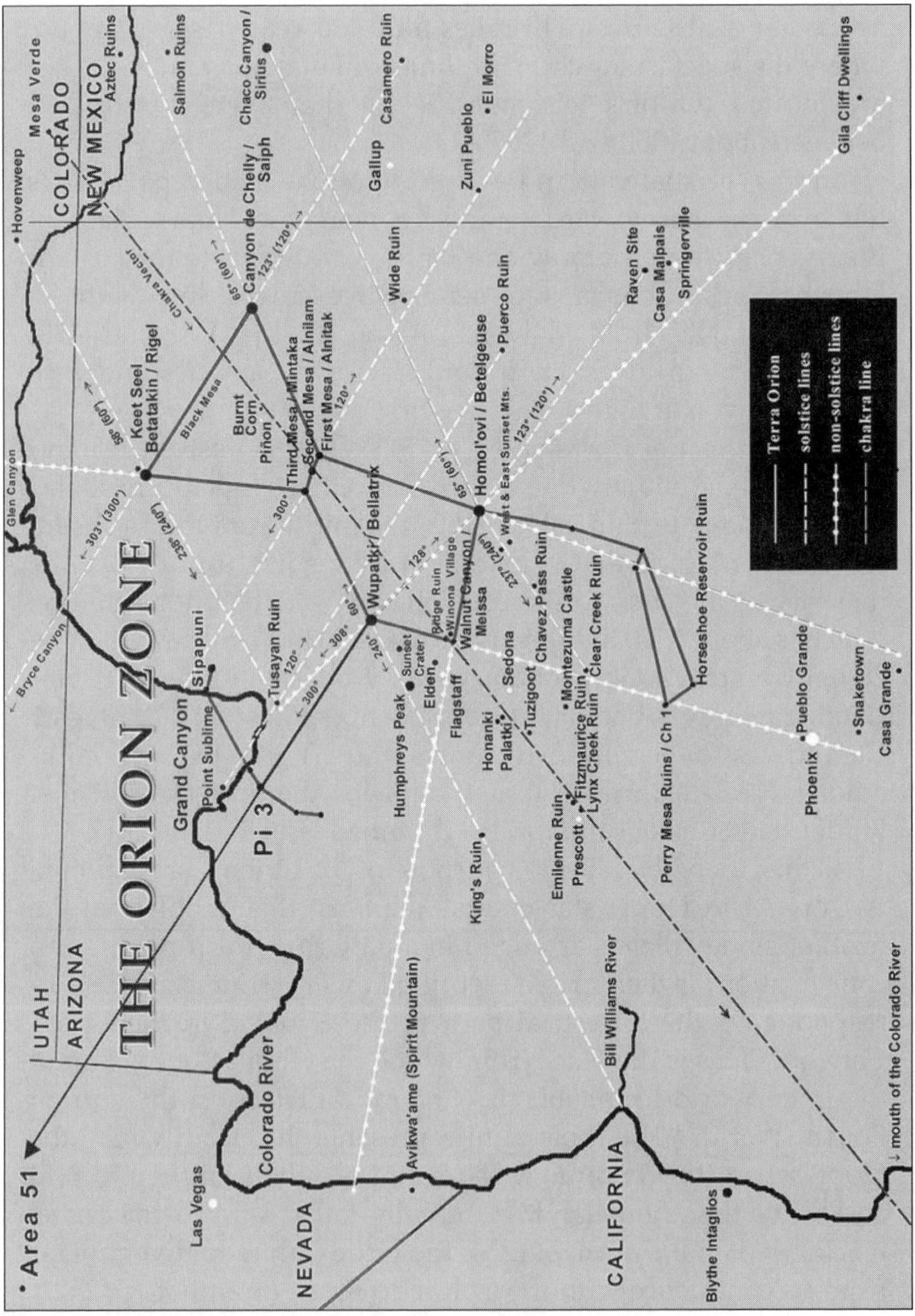
THE ORION ZONE
Area 51
UTAH
ARIZONA
COLORADO
NEW MEXICO
NEVADA
CALIFORNIA
Las Vegas
Colorado River
Grand Canyon
Point Sublime
Sipapuni
Pi 3
Tusayan Ruin
Bryce Canyon
Glen Canyon
Hovenweep
Mesa Verde
Aztec Ruins
Salmon Ruins
Chaco Canyon / Sirius
Canyon de Chelly / Saiph
Keet Seel
Betatakin / Rigel
Black Mesa
Chakra Vector
Burnt Corn
Piñon
Third Mesa / Mintaka
Second Mesa / Alnilam
First Mesa / Alnitak
Wupatki / Bellatrix
Homol'ovi / Betelgeuse
West & East Sunset Mts.
Walnut Canyon / Meissa
Ridge Ruin
Winona Village
Sunset Crater
Elden
Humphreys Peak
Flagstaff
Sedona
Honanki
Palatki
Tuzigoot
Chavez Pass Ruin
Montezuma Castle
Clear Creek Ruin
Fitzmaurice Ruin
Lynx Creek Ruin
Emilenne Ruin
Prescott
King's Ruin
Perry Mesa Ruins / Ch 1
Horseshoe Reservoir Ruin
Phoenix
Pueblo Grande
Snaketown
Casa Grande
Gallup
Casamero Ruin
Wide Ruin
Puerco Ruin
Zuni Pueblo
El Morro
Raven Site
Casa Malpais
Springerville
Gila Cliff Dwellings
Avikwa'ame (Spirit Mountain)
Bill Williams River
Blythe Intaglios
mouth of the Colorado River
Terra Orion
solstice lines
non-solstice lines
chakra line

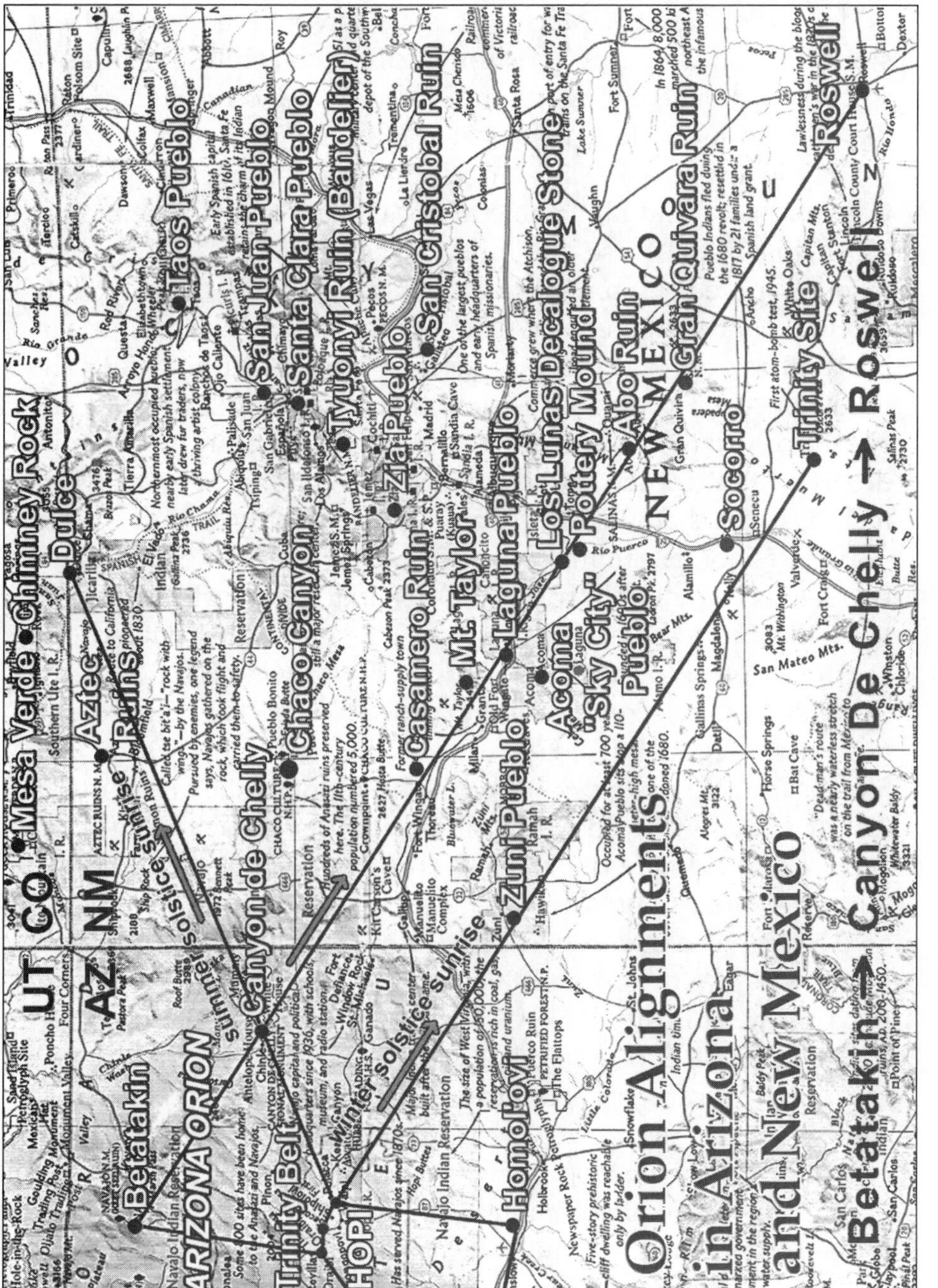
Orion Alignments
in Arizona
and New Mexico
Betatakin → Canyon De Chelly → Roswell
ARIZONA ORION
Trinity Belt
HOPI
Homolovi
Betatakin
Canyon de Chelly
summer solstice sunrise
winter solstice sunrise
UT
CO
AZ
NM
Mesa Verde
Chimney Rock
Aztec Ruins
Dulce
Chaco Canyon
Casamero Ruin
Mt. Taylor
Zuni Pueblo
Laguna Pueblo
Acoma "Sky City" Pueblo
Los Lunas Decalogue Stone
Pottery Mound
Abo Ruin
Gran Quivira Ruin
Socorro
Trinity Site
Roswell
Zia Pueblo
Tyuonyi Ruin (Bandelier)
San Cristobal Ruin
Santa Clara Pueblo
San Juan Pueblo
Taos Pueblo
NEW MEXICO

As a correlative to this geologic feature, the *sipapu* is a small hole on the floor of every kiva that symbolically leads to the underworld. (See Chapter 1.) It is a supreme paradox that the subterranean realm is cosmologically conceptualized as a watery world encompassing the Milky Way and the stars. Thus, the title of this book: "The Kivas of Heaven."

If you extend the line along the arm farther past Grand Canyon, you eventually come to Area 51 in Nevada (see map p. 326). This is, of course, the infamous secret U.S. Air Force base where reputedly alien technology was "back-engineered" to produce saucer-shaped or V-shaped aircraft with incredible aerial abilities beyond currently acknowledged technologies. The intelligence or prophetic vision that originally informed the Hopi had oriented the Orion star configuration on the Arizona desert so that certain specific alignments would be made. This includes sites that would become significant only centuries later.

Please look at the map on p. 327. One line that connects the two feet of Arizona's terrestrial Orion extends southeast to pass very close to Casamero Ruin, which is an outlier pueblo due south of Chaco Canyon, and Mount Taylor, which for the Diné (Navajo) is the Sacred Mountain of the South. This line continues past Laguna Pueblo as well as the Los Lunas Decalogue Stone. The latter is an 80-ton, basalt boulder that measures 26 feet long and is incised with a slightly abbreviated version of the Ten Commandments in paleo-Hebrew and Phoenician scripts with a few additional Greek letters.

The map line then continues past the 14th century ruins of Abo and Gran Quivera in Salinas Pueblo Missions National Monument to terminate at Roswell, New Mexico, famous site of the supposed 1947 UFO crash and retrieval of alien bodies. This vector is significant in part because its azimuth is 120°—that is, the winter solstice sunrise point on the horizon, a crucial period in the Hopi agricultural calendar when the Hopi sun god Tawa enters his Winter House.

A parallel line also running southeast extends from the Hopi Mesas (Trinity Belt) to Trinity Site at White Sands Missile Range in New Mexico—the location of the first atomic bomb detonation, coincidentally found at 33° north latitude. The conquistadors aptly called this desolate volcanic desert the *Jornada del Muerto,* or "Journey of the Dead Man." Were they also looking into the future?

This line also runs close to Socorro, New Mexico, where in 1964 a patrolling police officer named Lonnie Zamora supposedly spotted an egg-shaped metallic craft downed in an arroyo. He originally thought that the two diminutive figures wearing uniforms and standing next to the craft were children, but when he got closer they were no longer visible. Suddenly he heard a loud whoosh and a roar, and he tried to scramble back to his car. The spacecraft then shot off at a low angle, emitting a blue flame, and quickly vanished in the distance.[12]

Another vector connects one of the belt stars, Alnitak, which terrestrially corresponds to First Mesa, with the ruins in Canyon de Chelly, the right foot of Orion. If this line is extended, it passes the major ancient pueblo at Aztec Ruins National Monument and ends at Dulce, New Mexico. As most ufologists and experts on extraterrestrial or alien intelligence know, the Dulce facility is a site fraught with sinister implications. Some believe it is an underground base with multiple levels inside of Archuleta Mesa, which straddles the New Mexico-Colorado border on the Jicarilla Apache Indian Reservation. The grotesque genetic experiments performed here by both humans and entities of non-human origin supposedly rival anything conceived of by the fictional Dr. Moreau. The idea of the Dulce complex where nefarious ETs work in conjunction with secret government agents attracts the extreme fringe element of the conspiracy theorists. Regardless of whether or not this site actually exists, Internet speculations and urban myth nonetheless have turned Dulce into an important contemporary meme.

Aztec Ruins consist of a 500-room, 13th century pueblo on the Animas River located 53 miles directly north of Chaco Canyon. (See p. 224 and p. 226.) Somewhat lesser known than the Roswell crash is the 1948 UFO "soft landing" that occurred on a mesa three miles west of Aztec, New Mexico. Inside the disabled metallic disk measuring 100 feet in diameter and containing portholes were reputedly 16 perfectly formed humanoid bodies measuring 3 to 3½ feet tall. Although an internal fire had apparently charred their bodies, they were reported to have light or gray skin and brownish hair. An autopsy performed at Wright Patterson Air Force Base on one of the crew members showed a greatly convoluted brain that was possibly 200 years old. High strangeness or low hoax?[13]

At any rate, the vector starts at the Hopi village of Walpi, traverses Canyon de Chelly and its offshoot called Canyon del Muerto ("Canyon of the Dead Man"), passes by Aztec, and terminates at Dulce. It is in fact another solstice sunrise line of approximately 60° azimuth, where the Sun rises the farthest north on the first day of summer. It is also where Tawa temporarily rests in his Summer House before starting on the annual journey southward—first toward the equinoctial sunrise point (due east) and then winter solstice sunrise point on the horizon.

The unique orientation of the Arizona Orion Correlation established in the mid-11th through the end of the 13th century AD may have encoded the alignments of these various locations that would become significant in the 20th century. The only means by which this could be accomplished is foreknowledge of events, i.e., prophecy.

Journey of the Dead World

As I write this chapter in July of 2010, the catastrophic oil spill in the Gulf of Mexico keeps wrapping its dark, death-dealing tentacles around the marine wildlife offshore from Louisiana, Mississippi, Alabama, and the Florida Panhandle. Black, viscous waves continue to invade the once-pristine beaches, fouling the environment for generations to come. You can even watch the real-time video feed of the oil gushing from the wellhead. It's become the grim entertainment event of the summer.

On April 20th the Deepwater Horizon oil rig, which was operated by BP (formerly British Petroleum) and owned by Transocean, suddenly exploded, killing eleven crew members and sending up angry plumes of black smoke and fire visible from 35 miles away. Two days later, on the 40th anniversary of Earth Day, the platform sank to the bottom of the ocean.[14]

Apocalyptic scenarios of 2012 fly thick as locusts on the Internet. One recent rumor reported that the *Sangoma* Credo Mutwa addressed a conference in South Africa on January 7, 2010. I did a quick Internet search for exact location of that conference with no luck, indicating perhaps that the original message posted on a forum was a hoax. At any rate, Mutwa's prophecy is not pretty. The reputed attendee stated: "Credo Mutwa apparently just now said half the world's population won't see 2011 at a gathering where I'm attending. Some delegates have walked out because he didn't want to give an acceptable explanation, he just said '…it's no asteroid, comet, plague, ... just OIL…'"[15]

This jibes with an ancient Hopi prophecy that has apparently been known since 1958, when a minister named David Young while driving around the Four Corners region picked up an elder of the Bear Clan named White Feather. The casual conversation about the weather and current local events was punctuated by long periods of silence, which most Native Americans, unlike non-Indians, do not find uncomfortable. Then the Hopi slowly began to reveal a number of dire prophecies that he had received from his ancestors. The old Hopi must have intuitively trusted Young; otherwise, he would not have been so quickly forthcoming about this sacred knowledge. He said his sons had all died, and the Hopi ceremonial cycle was eventually becoming extinct—a casualty of encroaching secular life and the imminent end of the Fourth World. He said that he too would soon journey to the spirit world, and his knowledge would be lost for all time unless he could pass it on to someone.

I will not review all nine of the prophecies that he told Reverend Young, who died in 1976 before he could witness the fulfillment of these signs. (You can google "White Feather Hopi prophecies" and find them easily enough at many websites.) However, the one that pertains to the destruction of the Earth because of darkening oceans is particularly relevant. "This is the Seventh Sign: You will hear of the sea turning black, and many living things dying because of it."[16] The disturbing consequences of a world fueled by an oil-based economy is finally wreaking havoc on our individual survival.

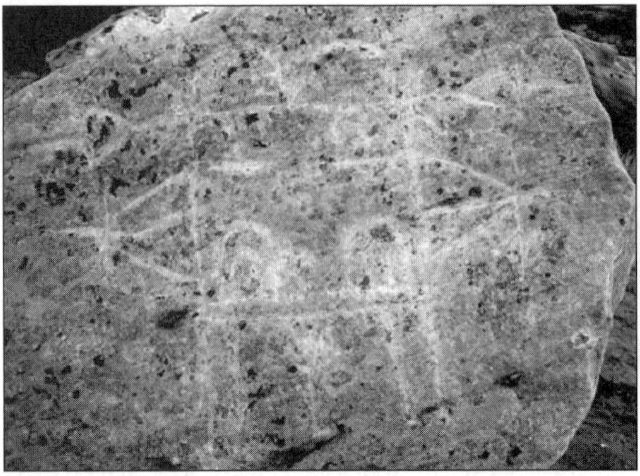

Some say this ancient petroglyph located near Prophecy Rock (see p. 8) represents a spacecraft, but Hopi spiritual elder Grandfather Martin Gashweseoma interprets it as an "instrument" or mechanism by which people can speak to each other all over the world. Is this a prophecy of the Internet carved in stone?

The ninth and final sign describes a "dwelling-place in the heavens" that crashes to the ground, creating a blue star in the sky. (For an examination of the Hopi Blue Star, see the Afterward of my book *Eye of the Phoenix*.) This may be a reference to the Columbia Shuttle disaster on February 1, 2003, or it could indicate the fiery reentry in July, 1979, of Skylab, America's first space station. The debris from the latter landed southeast of Perth, Australia, at about 33° south latitude. Some witnesses said that the craft appeared blue as it descended through the atmosphere.

After the events of the nine omens transpire, the eschatological Purification of the Earth will be squarely upon us. White Feather concluded: "These are the Signs that great destruction is coming. The world shall rock to and fro. The white man will battle against other people in other lands—with those who possessed the first light of wisdom. There will be many columns of smoke and fire such as White Feather has seen the white man make in the deserts not far from here. Only those which come will cause disease and a great dying."

Does the initial part of this revelation refer to the great devastation caused by earthquakes during the first four months of 2010?

January, 12th, Haiti: Magnitude 7.0, Fatalities 222,570
February 27th, Offshore Bio-Bio, Chile: Magnitude 8.8, Fatalities 577
March 8th, Eastern Turkey: Magnitude 6.1, Fatalities 51
April 13th, Southern Quinghai, China: Magnitude 6.9, Fatalities 2,267

There was even a Magnitude 7.2 quake in Baja, California in northern Mexico on Easter Sunday, when, luckily, only 2 people were killed. I felt this quake in northern Arizona over 250 miles away.

Of course, 2004 was not a good year either. We recall with horror that on the day after Christmas, a Magnitude 9.1 earthquake off Sumatra triggered a massive tsunami, which together caused the death of 227,898 people.[17] To experience this earthquake must have seemed like the Apocalypse was truly at hand.

> "And I beheld when he had opened the sixth seal, and, lo, there was a great earthquake; and the sun became black as sackcloth of hair, and the moon became as blood; And the stars of heaven fell unto the earth, even as a fig tree casteth her untimely figs, when she is shaken of a mighty wind. And the heaven departed as a scroll when it is rolled together; and every mountain and island were moved out of their places." (Revelation 6:12-14)

In the second part of White Feather's statement, the land where wisdom first started to shine probably refers to ancient Sumer. The columns of fiery smoke possibly point to the surreal scene of the scores of Kuwaiti oil wells that the late dictator Sadam Hussein set ablaze during the Gulf War in 1991. Or it may refer to the billowing fire clouds rising from the immoral "shock and awe" invasion of Iraq by the U.S. in 2003—just seven weeks after the Shuttle explosion.

Israel's first astronaut named Ilan Ramon was the payload specialist on that fated NASA mission. Son of a Holocaust survivor in Auschwitz, he had also been the youngest F-16A fighter pilot that participated in Operation Babylon. This Israeli air strike on June 7, 1981, destroyed the Osirak nuclear reactor in the heart of Iraq, which was an "Osiris-class" reactor. The French site-name is a portmanteau of "Osiris," Egyptian god of the dead, and "Iraq." The Iraqis called the facility Tammuz 1.

Tammuz was both the Babylonian and the Hebrew month when the summer solstice occurred. The death and resurrection of the eponymous Babylonian god of fertility named Tammuz was commemorated during this time with lamentation and weeping. To ancient Babylonians Tammuz was known as the Month of Orion. "Month of Tammuz: one performs the rites connected with the throwing down the corpse in Babylon." During this period of mourning, the body of Tammuz (in Sumerian, Dumuzid or "the true son") is ritualistically beaten, causing blood to flow as a libation to the underworld. The scholar Alasdair Livingstone has suggested that the blood-red reference might represent the red giant star Betelgeuse.[18] (See Chapter 8.) In pp. 67-69, I noted that Orion symbolically descends to the underworld about eight weeks prior to the summer solstice and is reborn at the heliacal rising of the constellation in mid-July.

Returning to White Feather's martial forecast, this Hopi elder's chilling vision might actually portend a world war looming on the not-too-distant horizon. A recent commentary by Reza Kahlili published in the conservative economic magazine *Forbes* unequivocally declares in its headline: "There Will Be War." Kahlili (a pseudonym for an anonymous ex-CIA spy) notes the current massive buildup of U.S. military muscle, including an armada of 12 U.S. and Israeli aircraft carriers and warships as well as a number of nuclear-armed submarines—all bound for the Persian Gulf. He also describes Iran's strategic response:

> "Meanwhile Iran is busy pursuing its nuclear bomb project and enriching its supply of uranium faster than ever before, with the hope of testing its first nuclear bomb. Accomplishing this will fulfill the prophecy sought by the radical members of the secretive society of Hojjatieh, particularly its leader Ayatollah Mesbah Yazdi, the person responsible for the initial election and fraudulent re-election of Mahmoud Ahmadinejad. The Hojjatieh movement impatiently seeks the end of times and the return of Imam Mahdi, the last messiah."[19]

Also known in Shi'ite doctrine as either the Twelfth (and final) Imam or Muhammad ibn al-Hasan, this messianic descendant of Islam's founder will return from "occultation," where he has been hidden since 872 AD. As both spiritual guardian and political guide for all Muslims, he will arrive on Judgment Day, or Yawm al-Qiyamah, literally, "the Day of Resurrection." Believe it or not, he will be accompanied by Isa (Jesus Christ) in order to purge the world of inequity, injustice, and tyranny.

This viewpoint on the imminence of war does not come merely from the right wing. An aging Fidel Castro was recently just as emphatic, not as a prophet, he said, but simply as a logician. "I have absolutely no doubt that as soon as the American and Israeli warships are deployed –alongside the rest of the American military vessels positioned off the Iranian coasts– and they try to inspect the first merchant ship from that country, there will be a massive launching of missiles in both directions. At that moment exactly the terrible war will begin. It's not possible to estimate how many vessels will be sunk or from what country."[20] And when Comrade Fidel talks about war, he means nuclear war.

During the early to mid-20th century, a number of Hopi prophecies came to light that described the various signs indicating the transition from the Fourth World to the Fifth World. The sources are multiple and fragmentary, given the Hopi reluctance to share privileged, esoteric knowledge with the world at large. Nonetheless, I have tried to assemble some of the major signs in the following list:

1. *People will ride on black ribbons in horseless wagons (cars on asphalt).*
2. *People will speak through spider webs (telegraph, telephone, and now the Web).*
3. *A "gourd of ashes" will fall upon the earth, causing destruction (A-bomb detonation at Trinity Site, Hiroshima and Nagasaki, H-bomb tests in Nevada).*
4. *There will be "roads in the sky" (contrails?) that aerial vehicles travel on.*
5. *Hopi delegates will go four times to the "House of Mica" (the UN building), but their pleas for peace will be ignored.*
6. *Women will wear men's clothing (Women's Liberation Movement).*
7. *People will begin living in the sky (Skylab, MIR, or the International Space Station).*
8. *Floods, famine, earthquakes, and tsunamis will ravage the Earth (climate change).*

9. *An event will happen when America is sleeping, and we will wake up to a thunderous eruption of war (9/11?).*
10. *A blue star will appear in the heavens.*
11. *The Blue Star Kachina will remove his mask during a village dance.*
12. *Hopi ceremonies will cease.*
13. *As a result, the world will be thrown out of balance.*

The Hopi word for this general state of chaos is *Koyaanisqatsi,* or "life out of balance" or "world in turmoil." It also means "life in disintegration" and simply, "crazy life." *Koyaanisqatsi* in essence begs for another way of living.

This plea for a total transformation in our current mode of existence reminds me of a poem by the early 20th century Austrian poet Rainier Maria Rilke.

Archaic Torso of Apollo

We cannot know his legendary head
with eyes like ripening fruit. And yet his torso
is still suffused with brilliance from inside,
like a lamp, in which his gaze, now turned to low,

gleams in all its power. Otherwise
the curved breast could not dazzle you so, nor could
a smile run through the placid hips and thighs
to that dark center where procreation flared.

Otherwise this stone would seem defaced
beneath the translucent cascade of the shoulders
and would not glisten like a wild beast's fur:

would not, from all the borders of itself,
burst like a star: for here there is no place
that does not see you. You must change your life.[21]

Our world has indeed basically lost its head. The stable Apollonian world of culture, civilization, aesthetics, and intellectual pursuits seems to be in total disarray. In spite of instant info on any topic under the sun at our fingertips, both space and time continues to fragment with no counteracting force that acknowledges a unified, cohesive, holistic continuity. Apollo's admonition enshrined at Delphi, *Gnothi Seauton*, "Know thyself," has become a rather quaint atavism in light of our quotidian quandary.

Totally terrifying are the remarks of some Hopi elders, who proclaim that during the final Purification the evil ones refusing to follow the ways of the Creator will be beheaded. Equally appalling is the method that many Muslim fundamentalists dispatch infidels to the afterlife: namely, by slitting their throats. You can even view these sickening decapitations on YouTube. *What* in the world is going on here?

Still, the remaining torso of our civilization possesses sentience. It "sees" with the intrinsic wisdom of some primordial animal whose Dionysian glory finally explodes like a star. We *must* change our life, our lives. Despite the wrecked sculpture of our current Fourth World, we must descend the kiva ladder in order to be purged in the amniotic underworld of the First Time, the Egyptian *Zep Tepi*, the Hopi *Tokpela* ("Endless Sky"). Only then can we reemerge, wet and shining like dew, to be reborn into the resplendent Fifth World.

Chapter 17
The Kivas of 2012

Kiva Maya of Tortuguero

In one Hopi legend the tutelary deity of the earth and death named Masau'u actually walked upon the land, apparently in his physical form, in order to establish the tribe's boundaries. Thus, this may actually be history rather than myth—the latter term used in the modern and pejorative connotation, namely, an untruth. (See a drawing of this god on p. 247.)

> "Masau first traveled south, then circuitously to the eastward until he reached his starting point. He called this area his land. The exact limits are unknown, but it is surmised he started from a point about where Fort Mohave now is situated [near Bullhead City, Arizona], thence south as far as the Isthmus of Panama, skirted eastward along the Gulf of Mexico and northward by the line of the Rio Grande up into Colorado, thence westerly along the thirty-six parallel or thereabouts to the Rio Colorado, meandering along its tributaries and so on southward to his starting point at Fort Mohave. This was Masau's land originally, the land of the Hopitu [Hopi]."[1]

From this description of the journey of Masau'u, we realize that the Hopi territory once extended southward into Mesoamerica and the heartland of the Maya. (Chapter 9 of my book *The Orion Zone* details the parallels between Hopi and Mayan culture.)

According to the Pecos Classification of the ancestral Hopi[2], the Basketmaker III culture (500 AD to 750 AD) and the Pueblo I culture (750 AD to 900 AD) were contemporary with the later part of the Classic Maya culture (250 AD to 900 AD). The Pueblo II culture (900 AD to 1150 AD), the Pueblo III culture (1150 AD to 1350 AD), and the first part of the Pueblo IV culture (1350 AD to 1600 AD) were coeval with the Postclassic Maya period (900 AD to 1500 AD). In short, an inter-flux of goods and ideas via a viable trade network existed for nearly a thousand years between the northern and southern realms.

In a recently published essay called "The Tortuguero Prophecy Unravelled," British 2012-researcher Geoff Stray discusses a series of Mayan glyphs carved into a T-shaped stele discovered at Tortuguero in the Mexican state of Tabasco.[3] (For the global significance of the Tau Cross, see my book *Eye of the Phoenix*. Suffice to say that the Tau was represented by the Mayan glyph *ik*, which means "wind" or "divine breath.")

Surprisingly, this stele known as Monument 6 contains the only known reference to the end of the 13th Baktun—that is, the last cycle in the Mayan Long Count calendar culminating on December 21, 2012 AD. I am certainly no expert on Mayan culture, but it seems that this brief statement made in 669 AD is (pardon the pun) of monumental importance. The glyphs were carved in order to commemorate a building known as a *pibnaah* –basically a steam bath or sweat lodge– erected in 510 AD (coincidentally, at the beginning of the Basketmaker III culture). The Aztecs called this structure a *temazcal*, whereas the Hopi still call it a *söviwa*. The sweats are frequently performed in subterranean kivas.[4]

The left arm of the T-shaped stone is missing, but on the right arm we find the pithy proclamation: "7 days 7 Uinals 0 Tuns and 8 Katuns, previously it happened. On 8 Chuen 9 Mak, it was completed for rebirthing (or nascent becoming), the pibnaah of Ahkal K'uk. It was 2 days, 9 Uinals, 3 Tuns, 8 Katuns and 3 Batuns before the 13th Baktun is completed on 4 Ahau 3 Kankin. Then it will happen - darkness, and Bolon-Yokte will descend to the (???)"

Let's disregard the various terms for the Mayan cycles of time and concentrate on what is actually happening here. Dr. David

Stuart, a renowned epigrapher of Mayan glyphs, provides an alternate translation of the text.

"...(long ago) it happened, the day Eight Chuwen, the ninth of Mak
when the Becoming-Ripe-House was constructed (?).
It was the 'underground house' (shrine) of (the god) Ahkal K'uk'.
It was two and nine-score days, three years, eight-score years and 3 x 400 years
(before) the Thirteenth Pik [Baktun] will end
on Four Ajaw [Ahau], the third of Uniiw [Winal],
when ..?.. will happen,
the ..?.. of B'olon Yookte' at ..?.."[5]

Geoff Stray directly relates this sacred underground house, or *pibnaah,* to the Hopi kiva.

> "Although today's temazcals are above ground, they, and the pibnaahs at Chichen Itza were usually dug five feet into the ground and used a direct fire rather than hot rocks, similar to the method used by Native Americans in California. The design and alignment was [sic] similar to that of a Hopi kiva, or underground ceremonial room. Though today's kivas are often above ground and square, the ancient Anasazi (ancestors of the Hopi) examples are round and mostly below ground. According to Frank Waters's Book of the Hopi, many Hopi regard Aztecs and Maya as 'renegade Hopi clans' that did not finish their migrations, so we may have an insight into the pibnaah."[6]

As one who has participated in intense and very hot Lakota (Sioux) sweat lodges called *inipis,* which were led by bona fide medicine men in the Black Hills of South Dakota, I can truly say that this experience is more about spiritual purification than physical cleansing. It is essentially a rebirthing process on an individual level, whereas the end of the Mayan 13th Baktun is the same sort of spiritual parturition, except that it assumes a mass consciousness-raising goal on a cultural level. The phrase "Becoming-Ripe-House" may be a metaphor for the structure that facilitates this type of spiritual evolution, namely, a kiva.

But who are the Bolon Yokte? (Or B'olon Yookte', also called Bolon Yokte K'u or Bolon-ti-Ku)? This passage says that these beings will descend along with the darkness on 13.0.0.0.0 in the Mayan Long Count—December 21, 2012. Maya scholar J. Eric S. Thompson claims that the name refers to the "the lords of night and the gods of the underworld."[7]

The idea that gods of the netherworld are descending from the heavens is not as problematic as it seems, given that in both Mayan and Hopi cosmologies the underworld –the Mayan *Xibalba* and the Hopi *Maski*– incorporates the celestial realm. For instance, the Quiché Maya phrase "road to Xibalba," or the "Black Road," refers to the dark rift or cleft in the Milky Way.[8] Thus, the term "otherworld" rather than "underworld" might be more appropriate here.

The Mayan word *bolon* means "nine," *y* signifies a plural, *ok* means "foot" and *-te* means "tree." Thus, Bolon-Yokte could mean one or more of the following: "God of the Nine Steps," "Nine Strides," "Nine Support Gods," or simply the "nine gods." The name could refer either to one deity with nine dimensions or nine deities as a collective. The possible pun of *bolon* ("nine") and *balan* ("jaguar," also spelled *balam*) adds another layer of complexity. Thus, Bolon-Yokte also possibly means "Jaguar Foot (or Feet) Tree."[9]

Could the Nine Steps actually be the White Feather's Nine Prophecies referred to in the previous chapter? Nine steps toward the conclusion of the Fourth World? The number nine is actually very significant in Hopi religious symbology. During the course of the year the Hopi perform nine separate ceremonies:

1. Soyalangw—Winter Solstice Ceremony in December (masked)
2. Paamuytotokya—Paamuya Night Dances in January (masked)
3. Powamuy—Katsina Initiation Ceremony in February (masked)
4. Paalölöqangwlalwa—Water Serpent Dance in March (masked)
5. Nímaniw—Niman Home Dance (*katsinam*-go-home) in July (masked)
6. Tsu'—Snake-Antelope Ceremony or Leenangw-Flute Ceremony, alternate years in August (unmasked)

7. Lakòntikive—Women's Basket Dance in September (unmasked)
8. Maraw—Women's Initiation Ceremony in October (unmasked)
9. Wuwtsim—Men's Priesthood Society Initiation Ceremony
(or New Fire Ceremony) in November (unmasked)

This last of the nine ceremonies is said to "belong to Màasaw"(Masau'u).[10] I might add that all the characteristics of Masau'u as god of death, fire, the underworld, the earth plane, hunting, and warfare could equally apply to the Bolon-ti-Ku. In addition, all of the Hopi ceremonies basically have a duration of nine days. In some ways the Hopi and Mayan numerical systems are quite similar. For instance, both systems are vigesimal (based on 20) rather than decimal (based on 10). Richard Maitland Bradfield, a preeminent scholar of the Hopi, explains this correlation as it relates to ceremonies and the calendar structure:

> "The numbers 4, 9, 13, and 20 furnish the key to the Hopi ceremonial day count. That count, it will be remembered, begins *yü'ñya*, 'going in'; this is followed by a first sequence of four days, one for each of the four cardinal directions, and then by a second sequence of four days, making nine days in all. On the ninth day the dance (*ti'kive*) is held, and this initiates the third sequence of four days, during which the leaders of the ceremony (*wi'mi*) fast in the kiva and continue to observe ritual tabus; making a total of thirteen days. The 13-day 'week' [Maya] thus survives among the Hopi in thirteen days of ritual abstinence observed over all major ceremonies, and the 20-day 'month' [Maya] in the twenty days' seclusion to which the new-born child is subject: both periods starting, as among the Maya, with day 0."[11]

Mayan cosmology conceptualizes thirteen layers of heaven and nine layers of the underworld, each with their corresponding reigning deities, or lords. "The Oxlahun ti Ku personify those thirteen heavens just as the Bolon ti Ku personify the nine underworlds, and allegorically they stand in the same relation to one another as light to darkness or good to evil."[12]

[continued on p. 344]

Right: Stylized Mayan Ceiba Tree at the Center of the World. Note 13 levels of heaven and 9 levels of the underworld. The belt of Orion (or sometimes the Cosmic Turtle) rests on the earth plane between the two realms.

Below-left: God L, God M, or Ek Chuuah (deities of the underworld) in the "Orion stance" with a shield and an upraised atlatl, Dresden Codex.

Above-right: kachina doll of the Hopi sky god Sótuknang (a deity of heaven) with warrior symbols on face and lightning-snake in hand.

Left: Mayan drawing from *The Chilam Balam* of Lord of Katun 4 Ahau. Note tripartite feathers on headdress. (See pp. 266-267, p. 275.)

Indeed, Bolon-ti-Ku seems (or if plural, "seem") to have a bad rep. According to Markus Eberl of Tulane University and Christian Prager of the University of Bonn: "The deity Bolon Yokte K'u is shown here to have had a consistent association with underworld, conflict, and war from the beginning of the Classic period into Colonial times."[13] Ergo, we can expect a certain amount of violence when he, or they, descend on the winter solstice of 2012. How this will manifest is the subject of endless speculation in newly published books and on Internet blogs.

It is interesting that the name "Bolon-ti-Ku" has a linguistic parallel with the name of a certain Hopi kachina. There is no "b"sound in Hopi language, so the closest approximation is "p." Palanavantaqa is the "red shirt" kachina, otherwise known as Káhayla (Turtle Kachina, mentioned on p. 297). Palanavantaqa is alternately known as Maakkatsina (Hunter Kachina), which reminds us of the Orion-Hunter-Turtle nexus. The Hopi put dried antelope hooves inside of hollowed-out turtle shells and affix them to their right knees during kachina dances, thereby making a loud, rhythmic clacking sound as they move. The Mayan word *bolon* also echoes the Hopi site-name Palangw, or "a place near Chinle [Arizona, and Canyon de Chelly]; east of Hopi [Mesas]. Witches or sorcerers live or gather there."[14]

Bolon-ti-Ku has been likened to either of two gods that Maya scholars designate as God L and God M. The first one, God L, sometimes wears a jaguar cape and broad-brimmed owl hat—both nocturnal creatures. He also frequently smokes a cigar, which suggests shamanic practice. This aged underworld figure with a prominent nose and a toothless mouth is sometimes depicted brandishing a warrior shield and spear.

God L may have been conflated with the Postclassic God M, also known a Ek Chuuah, or "Black Star." This black merchant god carries a bundle of merchandise on his back and is the patron of the cacao bean, a form of currency in Mesoamerica. Maya scholar Michael J. Grofe points out "…that God L, and the Maize God who defeats him, both preside over different times of the year, with God L ruling over the darker half of the year dedicated to long-distance trade, warfare, and the winter cacao harvest. God L initially defeats the Maize God, but the Maize God's resurrection in the spring hails the defeat of God L and the maize growing season."[15] (See picture of the Maize God on p. 141.) Thus, we can conclude that God L/M, who controls warfare, conflict, wealth, and human sacrifice, also reigns over the winter solstice. We recall that the end of the 13th Baktun falls –hopefully, not in a literal sense!– on the first day of winter in the Northern Hemisphere.

Grofe also suggests a parallel between this god's Nahuatl (Aztec) name Yacatecuhtli and the Mayan underworld god Yokte K'u. He furthermore claims that the Aztec term *pochteca,* the merchant class who traded with the ancestral Hopi in the American Southwest, may have even been derived from the Mayan name.[16]

Maya scholar John Major Jenkins observes that the Mayan god Bolon Yokte, like the Hopi god Masau'u, was present at the beginning of the cycle in 3114 BC (the Creation of the current age) as well as here at the end of this era.

> "Although some scholars have commented that the incomplete text on Tortuguero Monument 6 doesn't tell us much, they have overlooked the obvious: Bolon Yokte's mere presence in the context of a World Age doctrine that sequences forward in intervals of 13 baktuns. This may seem to go without saying, but in fact my work has been criticized for characterizing 2012 as a 'cosmogenesis.' Here the scholars are one step closer to understanding 2012 for what the Maya knew it to be: *a rebirth and the beginning of a new World Age.*"[17]

Note: 1 Baktun = 144,000 days, the exact number also found in the Book of Revelation 7:1-4.

> "And after these things I saw four angels standing on the four corners of the earth, holding the four winds of the earth, that the wind should not blow on the earth, nor on the sea, nor on any tree. And I saw another angel ascending from the east, having the seal of the living God: and he cried with a loud voice to the four angels, to whom it was given to hurt the earth

> and the sea, Saying, Hurt not the earth, neither the sea, nor the trees, till we have sealed the servants of our God in their foreheads. And I heard the number of them which were sealed: and there were sealed *an hundred and forty and four thousand* [italics added] of all the tribes of the children of Israel."

Apparently Bolon Yokte (Bolon-ti-Ku) was present during the cosmogony of each epoch. After the previous Creation of the World (the Third World of the Hopi and the Maya, the Fourth World of Aztecs), a great struggle occurred between Oxlahun-ti-ku, Lord(s) of Heaven, and Bolon-ti-ku, Lord(s) of the Underworld.

The following is a description of these events found in the Mayan book of prophecy called the *Chilam Balam* (*chilam* = "priest" and *balam* = "jaguar"). Written with European script in Yucatec Maya language, the sometimes-cryptic texts date from as early as the Spanish conquest period but allude to much earlier events as well as to those in the future.

> "Then Oxlahun-ti-ku was seized by Bolon-ti-ku. Then it was that fire descended, then the rope descended, then rocks and trees descended. Then came the beating of things with wood and stone. Then Oxlahun-ti-ku was seized, his head was wounded, his face was buffeted, he was spit upon, and he was thrown on his back as well. After that he was despoiled of his insignia [*canhel,* a "serpent" ceremonial staff that perhaps causes lightning] and his smut [either *zabac,* a cloud-making black powder, or the sign of fasting and consecration]. Then shoots of the yaxum tree [either a mangrove or a homonym meaning quetzal plumage] were taken... There would be a sudden rush of water when the theft of the insignia of Oxlahun-ti-ku occurred. Then the sky would fall, it would fall down upon the earth, when the four gods, the four Bacabs, were set up, who brought about the destruction of the world."[18]

Stationed one at each quarter, the Bacabs are bearded old men with upraised arms who hold up the sky. These Atlanteans are also color-coded: Red Bacab = East, Yellow Bacab = South, Black Bacab = West, and White Bacab = North. They correspond to the angels positioned at the four corners of the earth in the

Book of Revelation verses quoted above. One of the Bacabs carries a turtle shell on his back, which, as we saw in Chapter 8, is associated in many cultures with Orion.

Tortuguero, the archaeological site now unfortunately occupied by a cement factory, was where the stele was found that contained the few Mayan glyphs with the only known specific reference to the 12.21.12 date. In fact, the name Tortuguero in Spanish means "turtle" or "Land of the Turtles."

The *Chilam Balam* also describes the state of affairs that existed during the dominion of Bolon-ti-Ku.

> "Then descended greed from the heart of the sky, greed for power, greed for rule ... Compulsion and force were the tidings, when he was seated in authority; compulsion was the tidings, compulsion by misery; it came during his reign, when he arrived to sit upon the mat ... Suddenly on high fire flamed up. The face of the sun was snatched away, taken from earth. This was his garment in his reign. This was the reason for mourning his power, at that time there was too much vigor."[19]

The phrase "heart of the sky" may point to a specific usage in the Mayan pantheon. "Heart-of-the-Sky"refers, in fact, to the god of thunder and lightning named Huracan. (Hurricanes, of course, spawn a lot of electrical storms.)[20] The Hopi sky god Sótuknang is also a deity of thunderbolts. (See photo on p. 343.) Another line from the *Chilam Balam* discusses the Green Rain God named Yax-haal Chac in the context of Bolon-ti-ku. "The drum and rattle of Ah Bolon-yocte shall resound."[21] The Maya frequently used a turtle carapace as a drum; thus, turtles were associated with thunder and rainfall as well as with Orion.

Ahoy, 4 Ahau!

The current Mayan Long Count cycle began August 13, 3114 BC and will end December 21, 2012 AD—the latter date referred to as Katun 4 Ahau 3 Kankin, or the end the 13th Baktun cycle.

The Mayan word *Ahau* means "sun," "lord," "marksman," or "blow-gunner."[22] How, then, is the Egyptian word *ahau* so significant in this context? It variously means "time, period of time, lifetime, a man's age, lifetime upon lifetime." The Egyptian *ahau* also refers to "the gods who measure the lives of men in Ament [i.e., the West, or the land of the dead]" as well as "tomb, sepulchral stele, memorial slab." I'll give you one clue why the Mayan and Egyptian versions of *ahau* are the same: The near-homonym *ahait* means. . . "boat."

The Egyptian word *ahau* also refers to "a crane," perhaps the purple heron, which is the naturalistic version of the *bennu* bird, or the phoenix.[23] This mystical bird rules time, wheel within wheel, and is resurrected in Heliopolis (City of the Sun) at the end of each cycle. This avian spirit is also the *ab* (heart) of Osiris/Orion and the *ba* (soul) of Ra/Sun—the two deities linked by this wordplay.

In *The Egyptian Book of the Dead,* we read: "Re [the sun god] lives, the tortoise is dead, and he who is in the sarcophagus and in the coffin is stretched out."[24] This adversarial relationship is highlighted by the descent of Orion to the *Tuat* (underworld) for a period of 70 days during which he is invisible (see pp. 67-69), or "the tortoise is dead." Orion is essentially blotted out by the Sun until his heliacal rising after the summer solstice. Incidentally, the length of the mummification process is 70 days.

As mentioned in Chapter 9, the Egyptian Turtle-god was named Apesh, whereas "one of the seven stars of Orion" was called Abesh.[25] In addition, Sheta was the "constellation of the Tortoise," while Shethu was "one of the seven stars of Orion."[26] However, these linguistic gymnastics were not mere entertainment. Double entendres instead revealed the multidimensional layers of reality, and their usage was extremely sacrosanct.

John Jay Harper points out that an imposing structure at Abydos named the Osirion resembles a kiva. "…the Osirion [is] an underground ceremonial chamber compared by some archaeologists to a Amerindian Kiva in the U.S. desert Southwest."[27] Constructed of megalithic blocks of rose-colored Aswan granite, much like those of the Valley Temple at Giza, the subterranean Osirion is reputedly the resting place of the phallus of Osiris after the god was dismembered. According to archaeoastronomer Norman Lockyer, it is one of the oldest and holiest places in all of Egypt.[28] Here we can indulge in a little wordplay ourselves: the word *Osirion* contains the anagram "is Orion."

The Maya loved puns just as much as the ancient Egyptians. For instance, the word *ak* means "turtle," while the word *ek* or *eq* means "star." *Bak* is "bone" and *baq* is "meat." *Aq* means "tongue" and *ik* or *iq* means "wind." *Tsak* = "red," *tsaak* = "thunderclap," and *sak* = "white."[29]

Not only were the Maya master wordsmiths with a highly developed system of ideographic glyphs, they were also absolute wizards in regard to the temporal realm. On the other hand, I am mathematically challenged and want to keep this time-stuff to a minimum. So here goes.

The Long Count cycle = 5,125 years, 1/5th of the precessional Great Year, or 25,625 years—some say 25,920 years. (Mark Borcherding adds: "The long count actually uses 360 day TUN cycles or years and thus 5,200 years for each of the 5 ages or Suns on the Aztec Sunstone and 5 x 5,200—26,000 years. Notice the 26,000 fits with the 260 days of the Mayan Tzolkin cycle." Personal email communication.) As mentioned above, a Baktun (or B'ak'tun) = 144,000 days or 394.3 years. A Katun (or K'atun) = 7,200 days or 19.7 years. A Tun = 360 days or 1 year, with five unlucky days left uncounted at the end of each year (like in Egypt). A Winal (or Uinal) = 20 days or 0.055 years. A Kin (or K'in) = 1 day.

Every 13 Katuns (or 256 years) 4 Ahau is repeated. For instance, Katun 4 Ahau occurred in 968 AD, 1224 AD, 1480 AD, 1736 AD, and 1993 AD. Thus, 20-year periods after each of these dates are congruent in tone and substance. In other words, with each time span the specific quotidian details change but the overall mood and general characteristics are similar. The players may be different, but the game is the same.

Hence, 1993-2012 harmonically resonates with 968-988, 1224-1244, 1480-1500, and 1736-1756. For instance, Chichen Itzá in Yucatan was conquered, some say, in about 987 AD (Katun 968-988) by the Toltec king Topiltzin Ce Acatl (a.k.a. Quetzalcoatl) and his army. Earlier this figure had founded the city of Tula (or

Tollan, "Place of the Reeds," a little over 60 miles north-northwest of Mexico City) some time during the 10th century. Others claim that the Toltec influence in architecture and the arts was purely a matter of peaceful trade between the respective cosmopolitan nobilities of the Toltecs and the Maya.[30] During this period the Chichmecs were also establishing their empire at Chaco Canyon in New Mexico. (See Chapter 11.)

In 1224 (Katun 1224-1244) an apotheosized Chichimec chieftain name Xólotl invaded the Valley of Mexico. This god of fire, death, and lightning is frequently depicted with the head of a dog and the body of a man.[31] (Shades of Anubis?)

The last decade of the 15th century (Katun 1480-1500) saw the voyages of Christopher Columbus, which eventually had disastrous and even genocidal consequences for the native populations of America.

In 1736 (Katun 1736-1756) a powerful and cruel ruler named Nader Shah Afshar seized power in Persia (now Iran). Although he idolized Genghis Khan, his military prowess has earned him the title of "Napoleon of Persia."

The current Katun, of course, brought global terror wars in the wake of 9-11, along with the debacles in Afghanistan and Iraq.

Bruce Scofield sums up the basic flavor of Katun 4 Ahau. "There will be scarcities of corn and squash during this katun and this will lead to great mortality. This was the katun during which the settlement of Chichen Itza occurred, when the man-god Kukulkan (Quetzalcoatl) arrived. It is the katun of remembering and recording knowledge."[32]

It is interesting to note that Katun 2 Ahau, which starts on December 23, 2012 (the day after the current cycle ends), has the following attributes: "For half of the katun there will be food, for some misfortunes. This katun brings the end of the 'word of God.' It is a time of uniting for a cause."[33] Will the Catholic Church cease to exist during this time? Some prophets have predicted that the next pope will be the last. Or does this signify that the Christian fundamentalists' "Rapture" will occur during this Katun?

The present Katun –I am writing this in July of 2010– started on April 6, 1993, which Jenkins called a "nexus point," writing a little less than a year before that date.[34] In fact, it happened to be exactly when the Tomsk-7 Explosion occurred in Siberia. *Time* magazine (just a coincidence!) rated this as one of the worst nuclear disasters in history.[35] The town of Tomsk-7 (also known as Seversk) was the site of several nuclear reactors and was the location of a reprocessing and enrichment complex for uranium and plutonium. Nuclear warheads were also stored at the site. On that day a tank being cleaned with nitric acid suddenly exploded, releasing a cloud of radioactive gas over the countryside. This is not a very auspicious beginning to the last Katun period of the Mayan Great Cycle!

The *Chilam Balam* also has a number of prophecies that mention 4 Ahau. "Katun 4 Ahau is the eleventh katun according to the count. The katun is established at Chichen Itzá. The settlement of the Itzá shall take place there. The quetzal shall come, the green bird shall come. Ah Kantenal shall come. Blood-vomit shall come. Kukulcan shall come with them for the second time. It is the word of God. The Itzá shall come."[36] (See drawing on the bottom-left of p. 343.)

Chichen Itzá literally means "mouth of the well of the Itzá." The word Itzá refers to "Sorcerers of Water," or in Spanish, *Brujas del Agua*. The Itzá were most likely a group of Maya from the area of Lake Petén Itzá, Guatemala. The Resplendent Quetzal (*Pharomachrus mocinno*) is the sacred beneficent bird of the Maya that symbolized light, air, and spring growth. "Kantenal" may refer to the *Kante* tree that yields yellow dye, although the meaning is unclear. "Blood-vomit" signifies pestilence, perhaps small pox or yellow fever. Kukulkan is, of course, the Mayan equivalent of the Aztec Quetzalcoatl, the Plumed Serpent. He once came from the East and visited the Maya, teaching them most of the aspects of their culture, then left with a promise to return in the last days of the World Cycle. His Hopi counterpart is Pahana. (See p. 135.)

Other Katun prophecies of 4 Ahau in the *Chilam Balam* are equally disturbing. "4 Ahau was when the pestilence occurred; it was when the vultures entered the houses within the fortress."[37] Also: "4 Ahau was the katun when their souls cried out!" And: "4 Ahau was the name of the katun when occurred the birth of Pauahs, when the rulers descended…."[38]

The Pauahs, or Pauahtuns, are basically the four winds or

four cardinals directions. The late Linda Schele, an epigrapher and artist of the Maya, discovered a Pauahtun on the side of a palanquin found at Uxmal, a major site about 80 miles west of Chichen Itzá. He stands at the center of the façade, his back created by a turtle shell and his round belly forming its underside. He is surrounded by four other Pauahtuns, somewhat like the Bacabs of the four quarters—together making a quincunx.[39]

We are, therefore, not at all surprised to find that in Egypt the tortoise, a personification of evil, was also associated with the "four winds of heaven." This reptile was additionally connected to Thoth, the ibis-headed god of magic, the scribe's reed and palette, calendrics, astrology, astronomy, and judgement of the dead. In *The Book of the Dead,* a deceased soul bemoans his accursed fate: "I have dressed myself like the Tortoise."[40]

The woes of Katun 4 Ahau continue in the *Chilam Balam*.

> "The katun is established at Uuc-yab-nal in Katun 4 Ahau. At the mouth of the well, Uuc-yab-nal, it is established ... It shall dawn in the south. The face of the lord of the katun is covered; his face is dead. There is mourning for water; there is mourning for bread. His mat and his throne shall face the west. Blood-vomit is the charge of the katun. At that time his loin-cloth and his mantle shall be white. Unattainable shall be the bread of the katun. The quetzal shall come; the green bird shall come. The kax tree shall come; the bird shall come. The tapir shall come. The tribute shall be hidden at the mouth of the well."[41]

Uuc-yab-nal is the ancient name of Chichen Itzá. The "well" is the cenote, frequently used for human sacrifice. The "mourning for water and bread" refers to drought and famine. "Blood-vomit" signifies pandemics. The west quite simply symbolizes death. The quetzal is the sacred bird of Quetzalcoatl. The *kax* tree, or possibly *yax-che,* is the green Ceiba tree at the center of the world. (See drawing on the top of p. 343.) It is also known as *yax-cheel-cab,* "first tree of the world." Right now some of us feel that the whole World Tree, the polar *axis mundi,* is shaking, while the precessional epoch shifts from the enervated to the energized, from old modalities to new realities.

During the Creation of the Third World, humans were created

by mixing maize dough with the blood of the pig-like tapir and the serpent.[42] "The Maya associated [the tapir] with other nocturnal animals and the underworld, but also with sexual potency and fertility, probably because the animals require large amounts of water."[43]

Again, chilling prophecies from the *Chilam Balam*: "It shall burn on earth; there shall be a white circle in the sky. Kauil shall be set up; he shall be set up in front in time to come. It shall burn on earth; the very hoof shall burn in that katun, in the time which is to come. Fortunate is he who shall see it when the prophecy is declared, who shall weep over his misfortunes in time to come."[44]

Thompson identifies Kauil as Bolon Dz'acab, or "Nine Generations"—an eternal supreme god of heaven and earth. He is apparently a deity of both vegetation and water and may be associated with the rain god Chac.[45]

As I mentioned on p. 154-155, the term *Baalim* refer to the false gods of the Bible. It is a plural of *Ba'al*, the Phoenician god of rain, storms, and agriculture. On many stelae he is depicted with the "Orion stance." (See codex painting on p. 343.) Is it more than a coincidence, then, that *Baalim* is a homophone of *Balam*, the Mayan word for the fierce nocturnal feline?

As with the prophecies of Nostradamus, the *Chilam Balam* generates many enigmas. "Then it was that the flower sprang up, wide open, to introduce the sin of Bolon-ti-ku. After three years was the time when he said he did not come to create Bolon Dz'acab as the god in hell."[46] The flower mentioned is possibly the Plumeria, which many cultures associate with death, funerals, graveyards, ghosts, vampires, or demons.[47] In this case, it may represent carnal sin. As previously discussed, the Bolon-ti-Ku were the Lords of the Underworld.

I have not yet talked about the identity of the important ruler at Tortuguero named Ahkal K'uk. You will recall that in 669 AD the Maya had carved a series of glyphs on the monument that included the 2012-date—still almost thirteen-and-a-half centuries in their future. The stele commemorated the construction of subterranean *pibnaah* (kiva) belonging to Ahkal K'uk, which had taken place in 510 AD—more than a century-and-a-half in their past. I suppose it is fitting, then, that "The Place of Turtles" should have a divine ruler with a name that literally means "Turtle-Quetzal."[48] Is this some sort of hybrid creature similar to Quetzalcoatl, the feathered snake? Considering Orion's connection to the Cosmic Turtle, we might be facing another great battle with Bolon-ti-ku, the Lord –or Lords– of the Underworld, at the end of the current Katun similar to the one when the previous Long Count cycle terminated.

> "At the end of the Third Creation in Maya mythology, the Hero Twins defeated the Lords of Death and then went to the Ballcourt of Xibalba to resurrect the Maize Gods, who were their fathers. In the imagery of the times, these gods were reborn from the crack in the carapace of the Cosmic Turtle. Like the crocodile tree, the Cosmic Turtle occurred in the sky. It corresponded to the belt of Orion, a constellation that happened to be directly overhead at midnight on this k'atun-ending."[49]

Similar to descent of the Lords of Death at the end of the Third World, the message on the monument claims that on December 21, 2012 AD they will again descend with the darkness to the. . . Unfortunately, the words stop here, and we ourselves are left in darkness in regard to their ultimate meaning.

Sculpture of Tewa "Rain God," Tesuque Pueblo, New Mexico. He is a counterpart to the Mayan rain god Chac. Seated, he holds a ceramic jar. Note enlarged head as well as the big round eyes and mouth. The name "Chac" contains the Mayan word for "turtle," or *ac*. The homonym *ac* also means "dwarf."[50] Will this being descend at the end of the Mayan Long Count calendar? Three days after summer solstice the Tewa of Cochiti Pueblo conduct a sympathetic rain-making ceremony during which pots of water are thrown on the crowd.[51] Sandia Crest near Albuquerque is the Tewa Sacred Mountain of the South. It is named *Oku Pin*, or literally, "Turtle Mountain."[52]

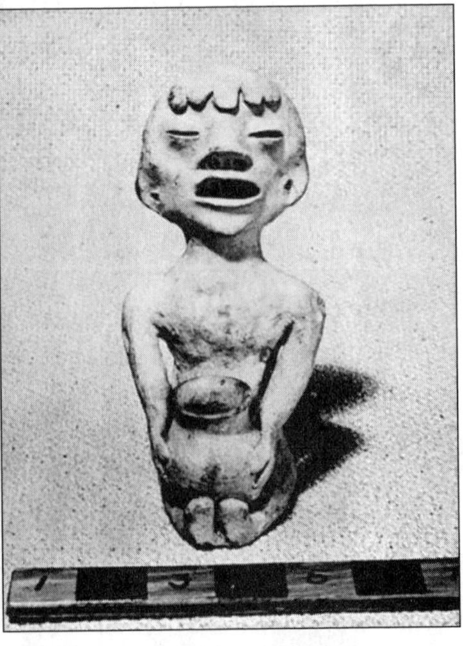

The Orion-Turtle connection is an enduring Mayan tradition. At Chichen Viejo, the oldest section of Chichen Itzá, there is a large, circular altar shaped like a turtle with head, tail, and legs.[56] Nearby is Templo de la Tortuga (Temple of the Turtle), one wing of which is divided into three chambers—symbolic of Orion's belt? At the same site, Templo de los Tres Dinteles (Temple of the Three Lintels) has masks of the rain god Chac positioned on the façade of each of the four corners.[57] At Uxmal, rectangular Casa de las Tortugas (House of the Turtles) has three entrances in each side, while along the roof frieze is a row of sculpted turtles.[58] Also at Uxmal, the large, round-cornered Pyramid of the Magician was built in one night, legends say, by a dwarf sorcerer.[59] He was, by the way, hatched from an egg.

Revolution 9

No one really knows for sure what will happen on December 21st, 2012. (It is, in fact, like the Mystery Egg discussed in Chapter 8.) Some are predicting that the conclusion of the current Mayan Long Count will have catastrophic repercussions and are preparing for the worst. Others say that it will pass, much like Y2K, without either a whimper or a bang. Still others believe that the current social, political, cultural, and environmental chaos is symptomatic of a "2012 era," which extends a decade or two on both sides of the deadline for Operation Endgame.[60]

What is certain, though, is that the Hopi elders of Arizona will be down in their kivas, conducting the winter solstice ceremony—just as they have done for millennia. The Tewa of New Mexico will file out of their kivas and perform the Turtle Dance in the cold village plaza, while Orion hovers above in the clear, frosty sky. With their humble ceremonies they are trying to keep the whole world in balance. For how long? We are not permitted to know.

The Maya say that the turtle weeps for rain during December's dry season. Among the Hopi it is the month of quiet meditation, introspection, fasting, purification, gentle words, and reverence for all life. The belt stars burn fiercely through the longest winter night.

"Three fledglings in a nest high in a tree."[61] The World Tree shudders as we continue to assault our Earth Mother. "...and I saw a star fall from heaven unto the earth..." (Revelation 9:1)

The late Hopi Grandfather Dan Evehema once advised: "On December 21 of each year, you and I will start all over by praying again for everyone and everything in the whole world. We will think again about self-sufficiency, and take whatever steps are necessary to maintain it. To accomplish this, save a few seeds from your crop to plant next Spring."[62] Seeds of redemption? Seeds of joy?

One Lakota (Sioux) Ghost Dance song from December, 1890, proclaims: "The whole world is coming. / A nation is coming. / A nation is coming. / The eagle has returned / with a message to the tribe. / The Father says so. / The Father says so."[63] A new heaven and a new earth?

Will the ninefold Lord of Darkness bring a revolution of enlightened consciousness, or does he descend simply to purge within an alchemical crucible our *massa confusa* symbolized by the Cosmic Turtle?[64] Will the shell of this sky-turtle crack and shift as it did during the previous precessional age? Will the Cosmic Hearthstones be realigned as they were during the Third Creation, when they "marked out a new place in the sky"?[65] Will the primeval Hopi underworld god Masau'u, who is a dead ringer for a modern alien Grey, return at the end of the Fourth World in the guise of the Mayan shade named Bolon Yokte K'u?

I have previously written that the nocturnal god Masau'u is the terrestrial equivalent of Orion, partly because he can journey across the entire earth before dawn arrives.[66] Before the Hopi set out on their migrations at the beginning of the current cycle, he remarked: *Pay pi as nu' mootiy'makyangw pay nu' piw naat nuutungktato*. Translation: "I am the first but I'm also going to be the last."[67]

The Orion temples lie in ruins. Wormwood swells an angry red hue. Flying warrior shields invade our dreams. The ancient stargates are opened. The roots of the Tree of Life water the whole world as the bright morning star begins to rise.

"Surely I come quickly."[68]

Fresco mural at Bonampak, Chiapas. The Dark Lord stands in the center with his staff (*axis mundi*). Behind him are two jaguar priests, two women attendants in white with elongated heads, and one servant. Facing him are six Lords of the Underworld. These nine dominant personages may represent the Bolon-ti-Ku. They are all listening to the kneeling prisoner pleading for his life, while other prisoners await their fate below. On the sky-cartouches above, from left to right, are two copulating peccaries (Gemini), two seated anthropomorphs (Mars and Saturn), and a turtle with with stones on its back (Orion). In his left hand Mars seems to be holding a "prophecy stone" (discussed at the beginning of Chapter 16). Saturn reaches toward Orion with some sort of spear or staff in his right hand. Murals painted in 3 separate rooms c. 800 AD.

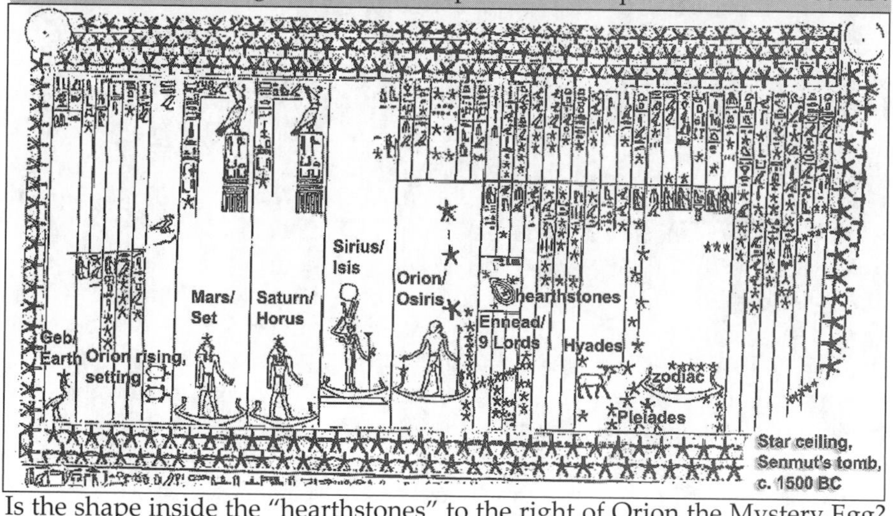

Is the shape inside the "hearthstones" to the right of Orion the Mystery Egg?

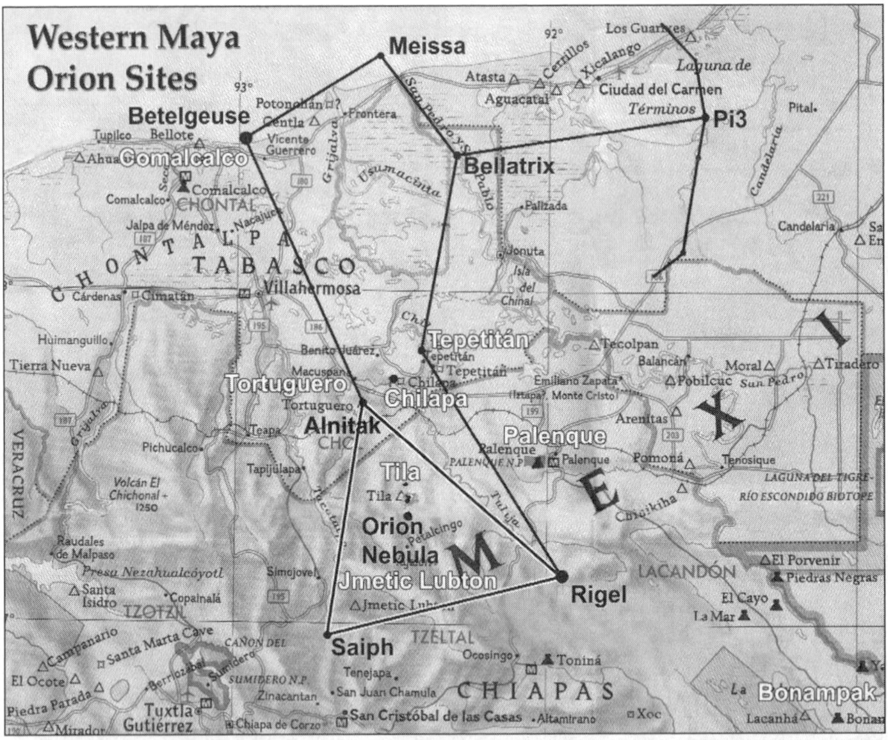

This possible Orion Correlation is located in the Mexican states of Tabasco and Chiapas. Tortuguero corresponds to Alnitak. (The Great Pyramid at Giza and Hopi First Mesa in Arizona also mirror this belt star.) Chilapa corresponds to Alnilam (the middle belt star), and Tepetitán corresponds to Mintaka. Comalcalco corresponds to Betelgeuse, but perhaps only symbolically so. This Mayan city that burgeoned between 700 and 900 AD is unique because its pyramids are constructed of kiln-fired bricks. Moreover, many of the mud bricks had been inscribed with Mayan glyphs, but over 500 of them contain various foreign scripts, such as Phoenician, Egyptian, Libyan, Tifinagh, Chinese, Burmese, and even Ogam.[53] The famous Mayan site of Palenque corresponds to Rigel. However, even if that angle of the constellation is moved north to coincide with the actual site, we still have Tila/Orion Nebula at the center of the three Mayan hearthstones. According to *National Geographic* photographer Stephen Alvarez, the Maya hold a ceremony at Tila dedicated to a black earth god, perhaps Ek Chuuah or God M/L heretofore discussed. "Every June [solstice?] thousands and thousands of people crowd into the Chiapas town of Tila to see the Black Christ which hangs in the Catholic church in town. The town more than triples in size during the pilgrimage. Maya scholars have told me that the Black Christ is an embodiment of a Maya earth lord and that the blending of Catholic and Maya traditions is a prime example of syncretic religion."[54] Jmetic Lubton, which corresponds to Saiph, was a ceremonial city with a carved sculpture of what in Tzotzil means "Our Mother Tired Rock."[55]

Maya Pantheon (*Popol Vuh*)	Hopi Pantheon
Hun Hunahpu — First Father	**Tawa — Sun god**
Huracan — Heart of Heaven	**Sótuknang — Sky god**
Xmucane — Grandmother of Day	**Kokyangwuti — Old Spider Woman**
Xibalba — Lord(s) of Underworld	**Masau'u — Death & Underworld god**
Hunahpu & Xbalanque — Hero Twins	**Pöqanghoya & Palöngawhoya — Warrior Twins**
Xquic — Blood Woman (Blood Moon)	**Huruingwuti — Hard Objects Woman**
Vucub Caquix — Seven Macaw	**Lavaíhoya — Talker Bird**

Two kivas at Mishongnovi village on Second (Middle) Mesa, Arizona
Photo mid-20th century by Milton Snow.
Second Mesa corresponds to Alnilam, middle belt star of Orion.

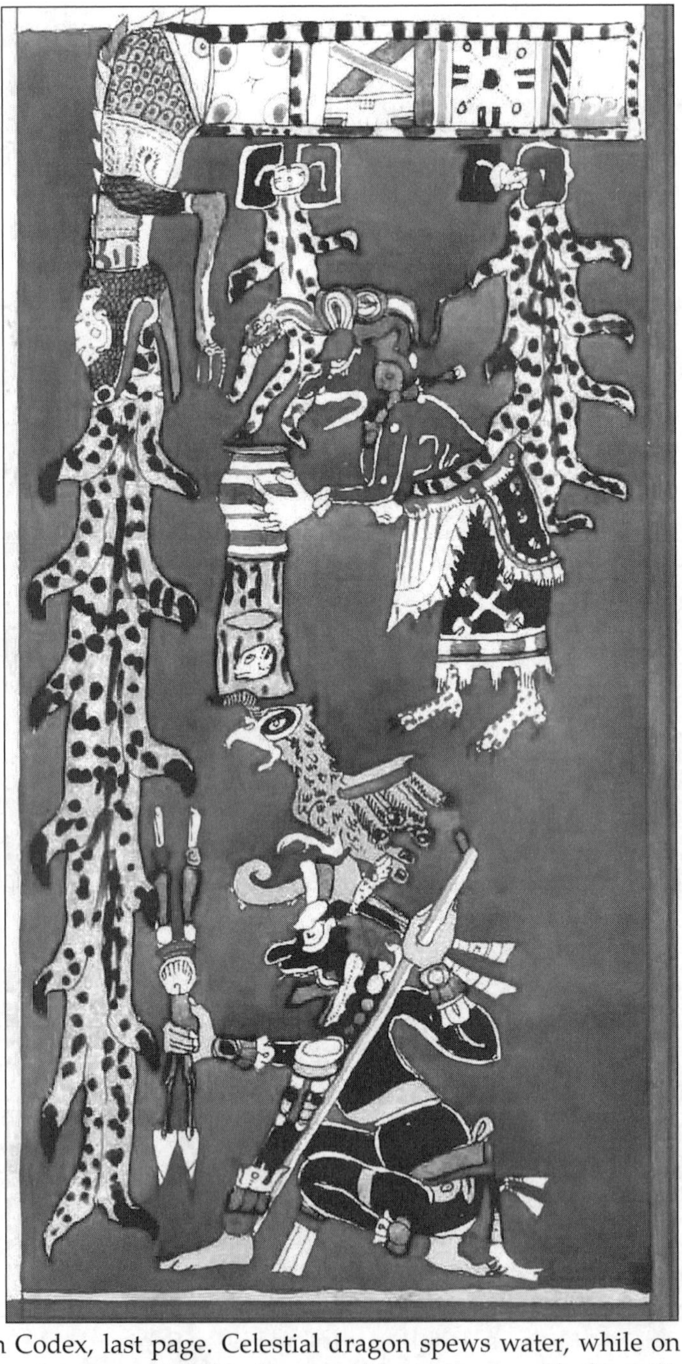

Dresden Codex, last page. Celestial dragon spews water, while on its body torrents stream from glyphs of Sun and Moon. Crone with claws (Xmucane?) pours water from a pot on a dark figure below, probably Bolon Yokte. Unpictured glyphs above panel refer to "black on high" or "black earth."[69]

Endnotes and Bibliography

NB: When typing Web addresses into your browser's toolbar to locate an Internet source, do not use final period of the citation. If needed, divisions of URLs were made between forward slashes in order to prevent spurious hyphenation.

Preface: Bio-Brief and Disclaimer

1. D. H. Lawrence, *Studies In Classic American Literature.*
2. Gary A. David, *The Orion Zone: Ancient Star Cities of the American Southwest* (Kempton, Illinois: Adventures Unlimited Press, 2006) and *Eye of the Phoenix: Mysterious Visions and Secrets of the American Southwest* (Kempton, Illinois: Adventures Unlimited Press, 2008).
3. Benjamin Lee Whorf, "Time, Space, and Language," in Laura Thompson, *Culture In Crisis: a Study of the Hopi Indians* (New York: Harper & Brothers, 1950), p. 156, p. 162.

Chapter 1: What *Is* a Kiva?

1. Dr. E. C. Krupp, *Echoes of the Ancient Skies: the Astronomy of Lost Civilizations* (Cambridge: Harper & Row, 1983), p. 231.
2. Watson Smith, *When Is a Kiva? And Other Questions About Southwestern Archaeology,* edited by Raymond H. Thompson (Tucson: The University of Arizona Press, 1990), p. 59.
3. Watson, Ibid, pp. 56-57.
4. David E. Stuart, *Anasazi America* (Albuquerque: University of New Mexico Press, 2004, 2000), p. 123.
5. Vincent Scully, *Pueblo: Mountain, Village, Dance* (Chicago: The University of Chicago Press, 1989, 1972), p. 15, p. 19.
6. Jon Manchip White, *A World Elsewhere: Life in the American Southwest* (College Station: Texas A&M University Press, 1989, 1975), pp. 55-56.
7. E. Charles Adams, *The Origin and Development of the Pueblo Katsina Cult* (Tucson: The University of Arizona Press, 1991), p. 186.
8. J. McKim Malville, Claudia Putnam, *Prehistoric Astronomy in the Southwest*

(Boulder, Colorado: Johnson Books, 1993, 1989), p. 6.
9. Evan Hadingham, *Early Man and the Cosmos* (Norman: University of Oklahoma Press, 1985, 1984), p. 150.
10. Edward P. Dozier, "Making Inferences From the Present to the Past," *Reconstructing Prehistoric Pueblo Societies*, edited by William A. Longacre (Albuquerque: University of New Mexico Press/School of American Research, 1970), pp. 209-210.
11. Ray A. Williamson, *Living the Sky: The Cosmos of the American Indian* (Norman: University of Oklahoma Press, 1989, 1984), pp. 142-143.
12. Frank Waters and Oswald White Bear Fredericks, *Book of the Hopi* (New York: Penguin Books, 1977, 1963), p. 158, p. 161.
13. "Precession of the equinoxes" is defined as the occurrence of the equinoxes earlier in each successive sidereal year due to a slow wobble in the earth's axial spin that shifts the equinoctial points slightly westward along the ecliptic. The wobble is caused by the pull of the Sun and Moon on the earth's equatorial bulges. Like the spinning of a top, this wobble makes the poles move around a center point (axis of the ecliptic), taking about 25,920 years to return to the same orientation with the stars.
14. Thomas O. Mills, *The Book of Truth: A New Perspective On the Hopi Creation Story* (lulu.com, 2009), p. 74.
15. Richard Hinckley Allen, *Star Names: Their Lore and Meaning* (New York: Dover Publications, Inc., 1963, 1899), pp. 308-309.
16. Richard Maitland Bradfield, *An Interpretation of Hopi Culture* (Derby, England: self-published, 1995), p. 288.
17. Walter Hough, *The Hopi* (Cedar Rapids: Torch Press, 1915) quoted in Hattie Greene Lockett, *The Unwritten Literature of the Hopi*, Social Science Bulletin No. 2, Vol. IV, No. 4 (Tucson: University of Arizona, 1933).
18. Malville and Putnam, *Prehistoric Astronomy in the Southwest*, op. cit., p. 26.
19. Mircea Eliade, *The Sacred and the Profane: the Nature of Religion*, translated by Willard R. Trask, New York: Harcourt, Brace & World, Inc., 1959, 1957), pp. 36-37.
20. Allen, *Star Names*, op. cit., p. 315.
21. Sir William Drummond, *The Oedipus Judaicus* (London: Reeves and Turner, 1866), p. 3., http://books.google.com.
22. Ekkehart Malotki, *Hopi Dictionary: A Hopi-English Dictionary of the Third Mesa Dialect* (Tucson: The University of Arizona Press, 1998), p. 143.
23. J. Walter Fewkes, "The Cave Dwellings of the Old and New Worlds," *Annual Report of the Board of Regents of the Smithsonian Institution, 1910* (Washington: Government Printing Office, 1911), pp. 624-625.
24. Barry Fell, *Saga America* (New York: Times Books, 1980), p. 245.
25. http://www.ping.de/sites/systemcoder/necro/info/sumerian.htm.
26. http://www.jewfaq.org/kabbalah.htm.
27. Fewkes, *Annual Report*, op. cit., p. 626.
28. Sophia Gates, "Star Crossed – Further Thoughts on the Design Sources of Caucasian Rugs," http://www.turkotek.com/salon_00082/salon.html.

29. Malotki, *Hopi Dictionary*, op. cit., p. 123.
30. Barry Fell, *America B.C.: Ancient Settlers in the New World* (New York: Quadrangle/The New York Times Book Co, Inc., 1977, 1976), pp. 190-191.
31. Ralph Blum, *The Book of Runes—A Handbook for the Use of an Ancient Oracle: The Viking Runes* (New York: St. Martin's Press, 1982), p. 86.
32. Gene D. Matlock, "Is the Hopi Deity Kokopelli an Ancient Hindu God?", http://www.viewzone.com/kokopeli.html.
33. John D. Loftin, *Religion and Hopi Life In the Twentieth Century* (Bloomington: Indiana University Press, 1994, 1991), p. 69.

Chapter 2: Stargates In Antiquity

1. Giorgio de Santillana and Hertha von Deschend, *Hamlet's Mill: An Essay Investigating the Origins of Human Knowledge and Its Transmission Through Myth* (Boston: David R. Godine, Publisher, Inc., 1998, 1969), p. 306.
2. Prabhavananda, Swami, and Frederick Manchester, translators, *The Upanishads: The Breath of the Eternal*, (New York: The New American Library, Inc., 1957), p. 36.
3. Adrian Gilbert, *Signs in the Sky* (London: Bantam Books, 2000), p. 209.
4. *The Ancient Egyptian Book of the Dead*, translated by Raymond O. Faulkner (Austin: University of Texas Press), 1990, 1985, 1972), p. 37.
5. Faulkner, Spell 78, Ibid., pp. 77-78.
6. Faulkner, Spell 84, Ibid., pp. 81-82.
7. Faulkner, Ibid., pp. 44-45.
8. Sir. E. A. Wallis Budge, *Egyptian Language: Easy Lessons in Egyptian Hieroglyphics* (New York: Dover Publications, Inc., 1983, 1966, 1910, 1889), p. 66.
9. Zecharia Sitchin, *Stairway to Heaven: Book II of the Earth Chronicles* (New York: Avon Books, 1983, 1980), p. 50.
10. Faulkner, *The Ancient Egyptian Book of the Dead*, op. cit., p. 105, p. 106, p. 110.
11. Faulkner, Ibid., p. 102.
12. Faulkner, Spell 72, Ibid., p. 72.
13. Faulkner, Ibid., p. 102.
14. E. A. Wallis Budge, *The Gods of the Egyptians*, Vol. II (New York: Dover Publications, Inc., 1969, 1904), pp. 94-96.
15. Faulkner, Spell 68, *The Ancient Egyptian Book of the Dead*, op. cit., p. 69.
16. Evelyn Rossiter, *The Book of the Dead: Papyri of Ani, Hunefer, Anhaï* (London: Miller Graphics/Crown Publishers, Inc., 1979, 1978), p. 21.
17. C. G. Jung, *Aion: Researches Into the Phenomenology of the Self*, translated by R.F.C. Hull (Princeton, New Jersey: Princeton University Press/Bollingen Series XX, 1979, 1978, 1968, 1959), p. 122.
18. Jung, Ibid., p. 124.
19. Faulkner, Spell 98, *The Ancient Egyptian Book of the Dead*, op. cit., p. 89.
20. Faulkner, Spell 23, Ibid., pp. 52-53.

21. Faulkner, Spell 69, Ibid., pp. 70-71.
22. Faulkner, Spell 180, Ibid., p. 179.
23. "The Ancient Egypt Site," http://www.ancient-egypt.org/index.html and "An introduction to the history and culture of Pharaonic Egypt," http://nefertiti.iwebland.com/index.html.
24. Re, "form of the sun god at his noon-day strength, often falcon-headed," Faulkner, *The Ancient Egyptian Book of the Dead*, op. cit., p.192.
25. Faulkner, Spell 180, Ibid., p. 180.
26. E.g., Richard Hinckley Allen, *Star Names*, op. cit., p. 308; and Francis Huxley, *The Way of the Sacred: The Rites and Symbols, Beliefs and Tabus, That Men Have Held in Awe and Wonder Through the Ages* (New York: Dell Publishing Co., Inc., Laurel Edition, 1976, reprint 1974), p. 212.
27. Jung, *Aion*, op. cit., p. 65n.
28. Rossiter, *The Book of the Dead*, op. cit., p. 21.
29. Frank Waters, *Masked Gods: Navaho and Pueblo Ceremonialism* (Athens, Ohio: Swallow Press, 1984, 1950), pp. 184-185.
30. Charles H. Lange, *Cochiti: A New Mexico Pueblo, Past and Present* (Albuquerque: University of New Mexico Press, 1990, 1959), pp. 50-51.
31. Alfonso Ortiz, *The Tewa World: Space, Time, Being, and Becoming In a Pueblo Society* (Chicago: The University of Chicago Press, 1969), pp. 13-15.
32. Waters, *Masked Gods*, op. cit., p. 184.
33. Bertha P. Dutton, *American Indians of the Southwest* (Albuquerque: University of New Mexico Press, 1983), p. 26.
34. Edward S. Curtis, Frederick Webb Hodge, editor, *The North American Indian: The Tewa. The Zuñi*, Vol. 17, p. 25, Northwestern University Digital Library Collections, http://curtis.library.northwestern.edu/curtis/ocrtext.cgi?vol=17.
35. "Songs In the Turtle Dance At Santa Clara," *Songs of the Tewa*, translated by Herbert Joseph Spinden, 1933, p. 97, http://www.sacred-texts.com/nam/sw/sot/index.htm.
36. Alfonso Ortiz, "The San Juan Turtle Dance," *Oku Shareh: Turtle Dance Songs of the San Juan Pueblo*, New World Records, 80301-2, liner notes, (New York: New World Records, 1979), http://www.newworldrecords.org/linernotes/80301.pdf.
37. Curtis, *The North American Indian*, Vol. 17, op. cit., p. 40.
38. "Posi-Ouinge: the Greeness Pueblo," BLM, Taos Field Office, New Mexico, http://www.blm.gov.
39. "The Heron and the Turtle," The Electronic Text Corpus of Sumerian Literature, Faculty of Oriental Studies, University of Oxford, 2006, http://www.earth-history.com/Sumer/heron-and-turtle.htm; Jeremy A. Black, *The Literature of Ancient Sumer* (Oxford: Oxford University Press, 2005), pp. 235-236, http://books.google.com.
40. Alexander M. Stephen and Elsie Clew Parsons, editor, *Hopi Journal*, Vol. II (New York: AMS Press, Inc., 1969, reprint 1936), p. 1081.
41. Budge, *The Gods of the Egyptians*, Vol. II, op. cit., p. 376.

42. E. A. Wallis Budge, *From Fetish To God In Ancient Egypt*, (New York: Dover Publications, Inc., 1988, 1934), p. 92.
43. Daniel G. Brinton, *The Walam Olum: Excerpt from The Lenâpé and Their Legends*, 1885, http://www.sacred-texts.com.
44. Frank Russell, *The Pima Indians* (Tucson: The University of Arizona Press, 1980, 1975), p. 306.
45. James George Frazier, *The Golden Bough: A Study in Magic and Religion*, abridged edition (New York: The Macmillan Company, 1940, 1922), pp. 502-504.
46. David Mowaljarlai and Jutta Malnic, *Yorro Yorro: Aboriginal Creation and the Renewal of Nature* (Rochester, Vermont: Inner Traditions, 1993), pp. 80-82, p. 136.
47. "Traditional star lore of Africa," http://www.psychohistorian.org/astronomy/ethnoastronomy/african_star_lore.php.
48. Pete Stewart, *The Spiritual Science of the Stars: A Guide to the Architecture of the Spirit* (Rochester, Vermont: Inner Traditions, 2007), p. 189.
49. J. Eric S. Thompson, *Maya Hieroglyphic Writing: An Introduction* (Norman: University of Oklahoma Press, 1971, 1960), p. 118; Patricia Turner and Charles Russell Coulter, *Dictionary of Ancient Deities*, http://book.google.com.
50. David Freidel, Linda Schele, and Joy Parker, *Maya Cosmos: Three Thousand Years on the Shaman's Path* (New York: William Morrow and Company, Inc., 1993), p. 94.
51. Linda Schele and Peter Matthews, *The Code of Kings: The Language of Seven Sacred Maya Temples and Tombs* (New York: Touchstone Books/Simon & Schuster, 1999, 1998), p. 145.
52. E. Förstemann, "Tortoise and Snall In Maya Literature, Bureau of American Ethnology, Bulletin 28, found in Charles P. Bowditch, *Mexican and Central American Antiquites, Calander Systems, and History*, Pt. 2. (Library reprints, 1904), pp. 423-430.
53. William Sullivan, *The Secret of the Incas: Myth, Astronomy, and the War Against Time* (New York: Three Rivers Press, 1996), p. 70, p. 124, p. 261. —Wari and Tiahuanaco were two pre-Inca, contemporaneous polities with their eponymous capital cities, located north and south respectively. Generally speaking, Wari was oriented toward hegemony and mercantile endeavors, while Tiahuanaco concentrated on religious matters supported by astronomer-priests. Wiraqocha Inca was the traditionalist ruler of an agrarian culture, while his son, Pachakuti Inca, who succeeded him, was the progressive ruler of a warrior culture.
54. http://en.wikipedia.org/wiki/Hypnerotomachia_Poliphili.
55. G.R.S. Mead, *Thrice-Greatest Hermes*, Vol. 1, 1906, pp. 414-415, www.sacred-texts.com.
56. Mead, Ibid., p. 450.

Chapter 3: The Hopi Cosmos

1. Genesis 28: 16-17.
2. Gilbert, *Signs in the Sky*, op. cit., pp. 202-5.
3. Malotki, *Hopi Dictionary*, op. cit., p. 488, p. 39.
4. E. A. Wallis Budge, *An Egyptian Hieroglyphic Dictionary*, Vol. I (New York: Dover Publications, Inc., 1978, 1920), p. 113b, p. 109b.
5. Mircea Eliade, *Rites and Symbols of Initiation: The Mysteries of Birth and Rebirth* (New York: Harper & Row, Publishers, 1975, 1958), p. 14.
6. Mowaljarlai and Malnic, *Yorro Yorro*, op. cit., p. 5.
7. Dennis Tedlock, translator and commentator, *Popol Vuh: The Mayan Book of the Dawn of Life* (New York: Touchtone Books, Simon & Schuster, Inc., 1986, 1985), pp. 63-64.
8. John Major Jenkins, *The 2012 Story: The Myths, Fallacies, and Truth Behind the Most Intriguing Date in History* (New York: Tarcher/Penguin, 2009), p. 137.
9. "Techqua Ikachi: Land and Life, the Traditional View," Issue 44, Newsletters of the Hopi Nation, online publication, www.jnanadana.org/hopi/issue_8.html.
10. Hamilton A. Tyler, *Pueblo Gods and Myths* (Norman, Oklahoma: University of Oklahoma Press, 1984, 1964), pp. 214-216.
11. Katherine Cheshire, "Hopi Teachings," http://www.wolflodge.org/wolflodge/spiritsakes/spirits.htm.
12. Edward S. Curtis, Frederick Webb Hodge, editor, *The North American Indian: Hopi*, Vol. 12 (Norwood, Mass.: The Plimpton Press, 1922), p. 103.
13. J. E. Cirlot, *A Dictionary of Symbols*, tranlated by Jack Sage (New York: Philosophical Library, 1962), p. 332.
14. Tyler, *Pueblo Gods and Myths*, op. cit., p. 33.
15. Benjamin Lee Whorf, John B. Carroll, editor, *Language, Thought, and Reality: Selected Writings of Benjamin Lee Whorf* (Cambridge, Massachusetts: The M.I.T. Press, 1971, 1956), pp. 59-60.

Chapter 4: New Mexico's Orion Kivas

1. Edgar Lee Hewett, *Ancient Life In the American Southwest* (Indianapolis, Indiana: The Bobbs-Merrill Company, 1930), pp. 210-211.
2. Bandelier quoted in Lange, *Cochiti*, op. cit., p. 274.
3. Lange, Ibid., p. 280.
4. Lange, Ibid., p. 416.
5. Ortiz, *The Tewa World*, op. cit., pp. 13-14.
6. Ortiz, Ibid., p. 21.
7. Frank Waters, *The Man Who Killed the Deer* (New York: Pocket Books, 1970), p. 53, p. 188.

Chapter 5: Colorado's Orion Temple

1. Jesse Walter Fewkes, *Excavation and Repair of the Sun Temple, Mesa Verde National Park* (Washington D.C.: Department of the Interior, Government Printing Office, 1914), p. 5, http://openlibrary.org/details/excavationrepair00fewkrich.
2. Robert Bauval and Adrian Gilbert, *The Orion Mystery: Unlocking the Secrets of the Pyramids* (New York: Crown Publishers, Inc., 1994).
3. The "mysterious disappearance of the Anasazi" is merely a canard. Not only are there cultural correlations between the artifacts that archaeologists have found and those of the modern tribe, but geneticists have also determined that the DNA evidence collected from ancient bones corresponds to the DNA of the modern Pueblo tribes. "…the mitochrondrial haplogroup frequency distributions of Anasazi people from Grand Gulch [Utah], dating to 2000 BP [Before Present], are not significantly different from those of modern Pueblo groups, establishing biological as well as cultural continuity." Ripan S. Malhi, Holly M. Mortensen, Jason A. Eshleman, Brian M. Kemp, Joseph G. Lorenz, Frederika A. Kaestle, John R. Johnson, Clara Gorodezky, David Glenn Smith, "Native mtDNA Prehistory in the American Southwest," *American Journal of Physical Anthropology*, 2003, p. 111. https://netfiles.uiuc.edu/malhi/www/MalhiLab/downloads/Malhi%20et%20al%202003.pdf.
—In essence, the two groups are the same, removed in time from each other by at least 800 years.
4. Stephen cited in Ray A. Williamson, *Living the Sky*, op. cit., pp. 79-82.
5. Waters and Fredericks, *Book of the Hopi*, op. cit., p. 160.
6. Waters, and Fredericks, Ibid., p. 96.
7. Waters, and Fredericks, Ibid., p. 90.
8. Rudolf Kaiser, *The Voice of the Great Spirit: Prophecies of the Hopi Indians*, (Boston: Shambala Publications, Inc., 1989, 1991), p. 41. For more on the stone tablets, consult Chapter 17 of David, *Eye of the Phoenix*, op. cit.
9. Thomas E. Mails, *The Pueblo Children of the Earth Mother*, Vol. I (New York: Marlowe & Company, 1983), p. 281.
10. Bradfield, *An Interpretation of Hopi Culture*, op. cit., p. 289.
11. Stephen H. Lekson, *The Chaco Meridian: Centers of Political Power in the Ancient Southwest* (Walnut Creek, California: Altamira Press, 1999).
12. David, *The Orion Zone*, op. cit., p. 190.
13. Malville and Putnam, *Prehistoric Astronomy in the Southwest*, op. cit., p. 92.
14. Anna Sofaer, "The Primary Architecture of the Chacoan Culture: A Cosmological Expression," *Anasazi Architecture and American Design*, edited by Baker H. Morrow and V. B. Price (Albuquerque, New Mexico: University of New Mexico Press, 1997), p. 98.
15. Malville and Putnam, *Prehistoric Astronomy in the Southwest*, op. cit., p. 95.
16. Navajo cosmology designates the following mountains: (1) The Sacred

Mountain of the North is Hesperus Mountain, *Dibé Ntsaa*, Big Mountain Sheep, or Obsidian Mountain (13,232 ft.); (2) the Sacred Mountain of the South is Mount Taylor, *Tsoodzil*, Blue Bead or Turquoise Mountain (11,305 ft.), north of Laguna, New Mexico; (3) the Sacred Mountain of the East is Blanca Peak, *Tsisnaasjini'*, Dawn or White Shell Mountain (14,345 ft.) near Alamosa, Colorado; (4) the Sacred Mountain of the West is Humphreys Peak, *Doko'oosliid*, Abalone Shell Mountain (12,633 ft.) near Flagstaff, Arizona, http://www.lapahie.com/Sacred_Mts.cfm.
17. Author Richard C. Hoagland has noted that the science fiction writer Arthur C. Clarke originally conceived of the famous rectangular Monolith in his book and subsequent movie *2001: A Space Odyssey* "as a large, black tetrahedron," http://www.enterprisemission.com/arthur30.html.
—It is perhaps significant that one of the Navajo names for Hesperus Mountain literally means "Obsidian Mountain."
18. David, *Eye of the Phoenix*, op. cit., pp. 32-37.
19. http://library.nau.edu/speccoll/exhibits/hopitg/Hopilesson4.html.
20. Andy Milroy, "Ultramarathon history over the decades," *Ultra Legends*, adapted by Dan Brannen,
http://www.ultralegends.com/native-american-indians-running-history.

Chapter 6: Hopi Flying Saucers Over Arizona

1. *Fate* magazine article quoted at http://www.burlingtonnews.net/kivas.
2. Michael Lomatuway'ma, Lorena Lomatuway'ma, and Sidney Namingha, Jr., *Hopi Ruin Legends*, collected by Ekkehart Malotki (Lincoln, Nebraska: University of Nebraska, 1993), p. 307.
3. Genesis 6:4.
4. Harold Courlander, *Hopi Voices: Recollections, Traditions, and Narratives of the Hopi Indians* (Albuquerque: University of New Mexico Press, 1982), pp. 200-202.
5. Ekkehart Malotki, *Hopi Stories of Witchcraft, Shamanism, and Magic* (Lincoln, Nebraska: University of Nebraska, 2001), p. xl.
6. Malotki, *Hopi Dictionary*, op. cit., p. 587.
7. H. R. Voth, *Traditions of the Hopi*, Field Columbian Museum Anthropological Publication, Vol. VIII, 1905,
www.sacred-texts.com/nam/hopi/toth/toth042.htm#fn_99.
8. "Dan Katchongva (1865-1972), Hopi,"
http://www.dreamscape.com/morgana/iapetus.htm;
Richard W. Kimball, "The UFO Flap," *The Daily Courier*, Prescott, Arizona, http://members.tripod.com/~drunken_bean/arizona.html.
9. *Prescott Courier*, Sunday, August 9, 1970.
10. *Prescott Courier*, Tuesday, August 11, 1970.
11. "Hopi Elders Messages to the World,"
www.hopiland.net/prophecy/katch-1.htm.

12. *Prescott Courier*, Tuesday, August 18, 1970.
13. http://www.wovoca.com.
14. Rebecca Schubert, "Leupp residents report another UFO sighting in nighttime sky," *Navajo-Hopi Observer*, January 30, 2007, http://www.navajohopiobserver.com/main.asp?SectionID=35&SubSectionID=47&ArticleID=5477; http://www.nuforc.org/webreports/055/S55002.html.

Chapter 7: The Taurus Correlation

1. In addition to the three main pyramids on the Giza Plateau corresponding to the belt stars of Orion, the two pyramids at Dashour to the south, the Red Pyramid and the Bent Pyramid, correspond to Aldebaran and epsilon Tauri respectively. Bauval and Gilbert, *The Orion Mystery*, op. cit., pp. 140-143.
2. http://www.havasupaitribe.com; "Grand Canyon Skywalk," http://www.grandcanyonskywalk.com.
—This tribe has also recently commissioned and co-funded the vertiginous Grand Canyon Skywalk, a translucent, U-shaped walkway perched on the precipice 4,000 feet above the Colorado River.
3. Allen, *Star Names*, op. cit., pp. 381-385; Robert Burnham, Jr., *Burnham's Celestial Handbook: An Observer's Guide to the Universe Beyond the Solar System*, Vol. 3 (New York: Dover Publications, Inc., 1978, reprint, 1966), p. 1807, pp. 1813-1814.
4. William Tyler Olcott, *Star Lore: Myths, Legends, and Facts* (Mineola, New York: Dover Publishing, Inc., 2004, 1911), pp. 339-340.
5. Budge, *An Egyptian Hieroglyphic Dictionary*, Vol. II, op. cit., p. 817b, p. 815b.
6. Revelation 4:7.
7. Cyril Fagan, *Astrological Origins* (St. Paul, Minnesota: Llewellyn Publications, 1971), p. 23.
—Scholarly disputes continue re. the beginning and ending of astrological ages. Graham Hancock, for instance, claims that the Age of Taurus was 4490 BC to 2330 BC. Graham Hancock, *The Mars Mystery: The Secret Connection Between Earth and the Red Planet* (New York: Crown Publishers, Inc., 1998), p. 165.
8. Olcott, *Star Lore*, op. cit., p. 338.
9. Todd Greaves, "The Tau (T) in Escatology and in Religious Architecture around the World, *Pre-Columbiana: A Journal of Long-Distance Contacts*, edited by Stephen C. Jett, Ph.D., Vol. 3, No.4/Vol. 4, Nos. 1 & 2, 2005/2006/2007 (Independence, Missouri: Early Sites Research Society, 2009), p. 211.
David, *Eye of the Phoenix*, op. cit., contains a brief chapter on Hopi-Maya-Egyptian connections to Tau, but it is a substantially lesser contribution to the subject.
10. Andrew Collins, "Göbekli Tepe—Eden, Home of the Watchers,"

http://www.andrewcollins.com/page/articles/
Gobekli_Tepe_interview.htm.
11. Malotki, *Hopi Dictionary*, op. cit., p. 522.
12. Stephen, *Hopi Journal*, op. cit.
13. Waters and Fredericks, *Book of the Hopi*, op. cit., p. 139.
14. David, *The Orion Zone*, op. cit., pp. 90-97.
15. *Prescott Courier*, Friday, August 21, 1970.
16. "Messier 1: Supernova Remnant M1 (NGC 1952) in Taurus, Crab Nebula," http://seds.org/messier/m/m001.html.
17. Sagan quoted in Gerry Zeitlin, "Are Pulsar Signals Evidence of Astro-Engineered Signalling Systems?," *New Frontiers in Science*, Vol. 1 No. 4, Summer 2002, http://www.etheric.com/LaVioletteBooks/Zeitlin-2001.pdf.
18. Zeitlin, Ibid., p. 18.
19. Paul A. LaViolette, "Galactic Cosmic Ray Volleys: A Coming Global Disaster," http://www.etheric.com/GalacticCenter/Galactic.html.
20. Paul A. LaViolette, Ph.D., *Decoding the Message of the Pulsars: Intelligent Communication from the Galaxy* (Rochester, Vermont: Bear & Co., 2006), p. 85.
21. Paul A. LaViolette, "Pulsar Network Transmission of the Fibonacci Series and Golden Mean Ratio," April 17, 2007, http://www.etheric.com/LaVioletteBooks/pulsarupdate3.html.
22. Michio Kaku, "Russia Takes Aim at Asteroids: The dinosaurs never saw what hit them. We can do better," *The Wall Street Journal*, January 5, 2010, http://online.wsj.com/article/
SB10001424052748703580904574638230276797924.html.
23.Erica Ryberg, "Ancient Ruins may give Dalke 'archaeological merit,'" *Read It Here*, December 2006,
http://www.dreamfactoryink.com/Paradise_Subdivided_by_Erica_
Ryberg.pdf; http://paleowest.com/news/enchantedland.htm.
24. Roberta Ruth Hill, "The American Message," *The Ascension Pyramid*, http://theascensionpyramid.webs.com/chapter4.htm.
24. Franklin Barnett, *These Were the Prehistoric Prescott Indians: A History of the Tenure of These Pioneers in Arizona* (Prescott, Arizona: Yavapai Chapter, Arizona Archaeological Society, 2006), p. 20.
25. Barnett, Ibid, p. 34.
26. Franklin Barnett, *Excavation of Main Pueblo At Fitzmaurice Ruin: Prescott Culture in Yavapai County, Arizona* (Flagstaff, Arizona: Museum of Northern Arizona, 1974), p. 12.
27. Barnett, *These Were the Prehistoric Prescott Indians*, op. cit., p. 52.
28. Barnett, *Excavation of Main Pueblo At Fitzmaurice Ruin*, op. cit., p. 95.
29. Franklin Barnett, Ibid, p. 88.
30. Ivar Zapp and George Erikson, *Atlantis In America: Navigators of the Ancient World* (Kempton, Illinois: Adventures Unlimited Press, 1998).

Chapter 8: 2012 Supernova?

1. "Red giant star Betelgeuse is mysteriously shrinking,"e! Science News, June 9, 2009, http://esciencenews.com/articles/2009/06/09/red.giant.star.betelgeuse.mysteriously.shrinking;
Ker Than, "Famous Star Is Shrinking, Puzzling Astronomers," National Geographic News, June 10, 2009, http://news.nationalgeographic.com/news/2009/06/090610-betelgeuse-star-shrinking.html.
2. http://en.wikipedia.org/wiki/SN_1006; http://en.wikipedia.org/wiki/SN_1054.
3. "Red giant star Betelgeuse is mysteriously shrinking," op. cit.
4. Coast to Coast AM radio program, June 10, 2009.
5. Burnham, Jr., *Burnham's Celestial Handbook*, Vol. 2, op. cit., p. 1281.
6. "Mayan Wavespell Analysis," *The Mayan Connection*, http://sexto-sol.net/Mayas/maya2.htm; "The 13-Moon Natural Time Calendar is a universal, modern application of the mathematics of the ancient Mayan Calendar System as deciphered by Dr. José Argüelles, Ph.D. and presented as 'The Dreamspell,'" http://www.13moon.com.
7. Dirk R. Van Tuerenhout, *The Aztecs: New Perspectives* (Santa Barbara, CA: ABC-CLIO, 2005), p. 40, http://books.google.com.
8. http://en.wikipedia.org/wiki/Acamapichtli.
9. http://en.wikipedia.org/wiki/Nezahualcoyotl.
10. "Aztec Poetry, "http://www.carnaval.com/dead/aztec_poetry.htm.
11. See the chapter titled "The Tau (or T-shaped) Cross—Hopi/Maya/Egyptian Connections" in David, *Eye of the Phoenix*, op. cit.
12. Rob Tillett, "The Fixed Stars," http://www.astrologycom.com/fixedstars.html.
13. "The history of the star Betelgeuze," http://www.constellationsofwords.com/stars/Betelgeuse.html.
14. http://en.wikipedia.org/wiki/SN_1987A.
15. Moria Timms, *Beyond Prophecies and Predictions: Everyone's Guide to the Coming Changes* (New York: Ballantine Books, 1994, 1980), p. 302.
16. In Hopi cosmology, a kachina, also spelled *katsina*, is a spirit that can assume the shape of any object or force in the cosmos.
17. Dr. Robert Ghost Wolf quoting anonymous Hopi Elder, "Hopi Prophecy Fulfilled," February, 1997, http://www.wolflodge.org/bluestar/bluestar.htm.
18. Lokmanya Bal Gangadhar Tilak, *Orion: A Search into the Ancientness of Aryan-Vedic Culture* (Delhi, India: Vijay Goel, Millennium Three / 21st Century Edition, 2005, originally published 1893), pp. 69-73.
19. Dan Evehema, "His Final Message to Mankind From Hotevilla, Arizona, USA," http://www.hopiland.net/prophecy/dan-1.htm.
20. Dan Katchongva, "From the Beginning of Life to the Day of

Purification: Teachings, History & Prophecies of the Hopi People" (Los Angeles: California Committee for Traditional Indian Land and Life, 1972), http://www.hopiland.net/prophecy/katch-1.htm.
21. Thomas E. Mails, *The Hopi Survival Kit: The Prophecies, Instructions and Warnings Revealed by the Last Elders* (New York: Stewat, Tabori & Chang, 1997), pp. 209-210.
22. John Major Jenkins, *Maya Cosmogenesis 2012: The True Meaning of the Maya Calendar End-Date* (Santa Fe, New Mexico: Bear & Company Publishing, 1998), pp. 105-114.
23. Susan Milbrath, *Star Gods of the Maya* (Austin: University of Texas Press, 2000), p. 39; "Lacandon Glossary," http://home.planet.nl/~roeli049/gloseng.pdf.
24. J. Eric S. Thompson, *Maya History and Religion* (Norman: University of Oklahoma Press, 1990, 1970) pp. 363-365; also, http://en.wikipedia.org/wiki/Ix_Chel and http://en.wikipedia.org/wiki/Kinich_Ahau.
—For identification of the turtle with Orion in Mayan cosmology, see Freidel, Schele, and Parker, *Maya Cosmos,* op. cit., p. 82.
25. Chris Morton and Ceri Louise Thomas, *The Mystery of the Crystal Skulls: A Real Life Detective Story of the Ancient World* (Santa Fe, New Mexico: Bear & Co, 1998).
26. "Dragonfly crop circle appears in Wiltshire," *The Daily Telegraph,* June 4, 2009, http://www.telegraph.co.uk/news/newstopics/howaboutthat/5443033/Dragonfly-crop-circle-appears-in- Wiltshire.html; http://www.cropcircleconnector.com/2009/yatesbury/yatesbury2009.html.
27. Allen, *Star Names,* op. cit., p. 308.
28. "Phoenix crop circle may predict end of the world," *The Daily Telegraph,* June 15, 2009, http://www.telegraph.co.uk/news/newstopics/howabouthat/5540634/Phoenix-crop-circle-may-predict-end-of-the-world.html; http://www.cropcircleconnector.com/2009/yatesbury2/yatesbury2009b.html.
29. Zechariah 13:8-9: "And it shall come to pass, *that* in all the land, saith the LORD, two parts therein shall be cut off *and* die; but the third shall be left therein. And I will bring the third part through the fire, and will refine them as silver is refined, and will try them as gold is tried: they shall call on my name, and I will hear them: I will say, It *is* my people: and they shall say, The LORD *is* my God." (King James Version)
30. Michael S. Werner, *Concise Encyclopedia of Mexico* (London: Taylor & Francis, 2001), p. 347, http://books.google.com.
31. Bauval and Gilbert, *The Orion Mystery,* op. cit., p. 17.
32. Budge, *An Egyptian Hieroglyphic Dictionary,* Vol. I, op. cit., p. 218a.
33. Cirlot, *Dictionary of Symbols,* op. cit., p 242.
34. http://www.cropcircleconnector.com/2009/baburycastle/barburycastle2009.html.

35. http://en.wikipedia.org/wiki/Maya_calendar.
36. Tedlock, *Popol Vuh*, op. cit., p. 360.
37. http://www.cropcircleconnector.com/2009/milkhill3/milkhill2009c.html.
38. "The Alton Barnes white horse," http://www.wiltshirewhitehorses.org.uk/altonbarnes.html.
39. Justin Kerr, "A Fishy Story," http://www.mayavase.com/fishy.html#graphic1.
40. http://en.wikipedia.org/wiki/Hero_Twins.
41. Tedlock, *Popol Vuh*, op. cit., p. 32.
42. Freidel, Schele, and Parker, *Maya Cosmos*, op. cit., pp. 281-283.
43. http://www.cropcircleconnector.com/2009/westkennett/westkennett2009.htm.
44. http://www.cropcircleconnector.com/2009/roughhill/roughhill2009.html.
45. http://en.wikipedia.org/wiki/Amanita_muscaria; see also Gordon R. Wasson, et al. *The Road to Eleusis: Unveiling the Secret of the Mysteries* (New York: Harcourt, 1978).
46. Jenkins, *Maya Cosmogenesis 2012*, op. cit., pp. 191-193.
47. Joel Snow, "Meso-American Mushroom Stones," 1997, http://physics.lunet.edu/~snow/stone.html.
48. "Nines," 11/9/2006, http://www.halexandria.org/dward091.htm.
49. Annie Khan, "Interpretation of Ancient Navajo Chants," http://www.bci.org/prophecy-fulfilled/navajo.htm; http://altreligion.about.com/od/symbols/ig/Baha-i-Faith-Symbol-Gallery/Nine-Pointed-Star.htm.
—The significance of the number nine is also reflected in the smaller, cruder crop formation that appeared on June 24, 2009 below Milk Hill near Alton Barnes, Wiltshire, http://www.cropcircleconnector.com/2009/milkhill4/milkhill2009d.html. A nine-pointed star crop formation also appeared on August 4, 2007 in Pewsey, England.

Chapter 9: The Wormwood Star

1. http://en.wikipedia.org/wiki/Wormwood_(star).
2. Allen, *Star Names*, op. cit., p. 304.
3. http://en.wikipedia.org/wiki/Baal.
4. Greg Taylor, "The 'God with the Upraised-Arm' in Near Eastern Mythology: An Astronomical Archetype?", 2010, 1999, http://dailygrail.com/features/god-with-the-upraised-arm.
5. "Red giant star Betelgeuse is mysteriously shrinking," op. cit., http://esciencenews.com/articles/2009/06/09/red.giant.star.betelgeuse.mysteriously.shrinking.
6. http://en.wikipedia.org/wiki/Betelgeuse.

7. Alan Oken, *Alan Oken's Complete Astrology*, (Newburyport, Massachusetts: Nicolas Hays, 2006), p. 578, http://books.google.com.
8. Nisar Khan, Lahore, Pakistan, http://www.punjabi.net/talk/messages/3/6795.html.
9. "Sanskrit, Tamil and Pahlavi Dictionaries," http://webapps.uni-koeln.de/tamil.
10. http://en.wikipedia.org/wiki/Nakshatra.
—In Chapter 8, which deals with Betelgeuse, I discussed a crop circle that appeared in Wiltshire, England on June 21, 2009—the summer solstice. One of the primary shapes in this formation was an ovoid or teardrop, which resembled a human head or skull. Another author comments on this symbol: "There is sadness as the symbol of the teardrop suggests. There is a very destructive quality here, but the destruction is necessary to save grace for the future. They [persons affected by Ardra] create destruction and havoc wherever they go, sometimes even destroying themselves. This is the place of the dark night of the soul, for there is a new dawn or new beginning after the seeming tragedy. After the worse storms comes the beautiful sunny day, for the following nakshatra (Purnarvasu) [Gemini] means 'return of the light'." Ashwani Kumar Shukla, "The power of the Nakshatras," 2008, http://ashwani99999.wordpress.com/2008/08/18/the-power-of-the-nakshatras.
11. Saint Isidore, translated by Stephen A. Barney, *The Etymologies of Isidore of Seville* (Cambridge, England: Cambridge University Press, 2006), p. 105, http://books.google.com.
12. http://www.mindfreedom.net/english-mayan_dictionary.htm.
13. Budge, *An Egyptian Hieroglyphic Dictionary*, Vol. I, op. cit., p. 197a , p. 199b.
14. Budge, Vol. I, Ibid., p. 213a.
15. Budge, Vol. I, Ibid., p. 200b.
16. Budge, Vol. I, Ibid., p. 204b.
17. Budge, Vol. I, Ibid., p. 205a.
18. Budge, Vol. I, Ibid., p. 202a.
19. Budge, Vol. I, Ibid., p. 211a.
20. http://www.mindfreedom.net/english-mayan_dictionary.htm.
21. Budge, *An Egyptian Hieroglyphic Dictionary*, Vol. I, op. cit., p. 230b.
22. Budge, Vol. I, Ibid., p. 233b.
23. Budge, Vol. I, Ibid., p. 234a.
24. Budge, Vol. I, Ibid., p. 230b.
25. Sarachandra Dasa, Sarat Chandra Das, Graham Sandberg, A. William Heyde, *A Tibetan-English dictionary with Sanskrit synonyms* (Whitefish, Montana: Kessinger Publishing, 2008), p. 139, http://books.google.com.
26. Jeffrey Hays, "Tibetan Buddhist Sects," *Facts and Details*, http://factsanddetails.com/china.php?itemid=221&catid=6&subcatid=34#04.
27. "16th Karmapa Visits Hopi Nation in Arizona," http://www.youtube.com/watch?v=q8a-OwheAEk.
28. John Hogue, "A Message From the 'Hope' Elders: 'We are the ones we

have been waiting for'," Hogue Prophecy Bulletin 18, April 16, 2001, http://www.hogueprophecy.com/prophecy/hopiprophecy.htm.; Kymberlee Ruff, "The Gates of Shambhala, November 27, 2009, *Hopi/Tibetan Prophecies,* http://www.thegroundcrew.com/hopi_tibetan/2009/112709.html.
29. Malotki, *Hopi Dictionary,* op. cit., p. 369.
30. Alfred F. Whiting, *Ethnobotany of the Hopi* (Flagstaff: Museum of Northern Arizona, 1966, 1939), p. 94.
31. Malotki, *Hopi Dictionary,* op. cit., p. 370.
32. "Sanskrit, Tamil and Pahlavi Dictionaries," http://webapps.uni-koeln.de/tamil.
33. John F. Nunn, *Ancient Egyptian Medicine* (Winnipeg, Canada: Red River Books, 2002, pp. 72-73, http:/books.google.com.
34. Budge, *An Egyptian Hieroglyphic Dictionary,* Vol. II, op. cit., p. 642b.
35. Budge, Vol. II, Ibid., p. 643a.
36. Giorgio de Santillana and Hertha von Deschend, *Hamlet's Mill,* op. cit., p. 166.
37. Budge, *An Egyptian Hieroglyphic Dictionary,* Vol. II, op. cit., p. 638b.
38. Budge, Vol. II, Ibid., p. 638a.
39. Jean Doresse, *The Secret Books of the Egyptian Gnostics: An Introduction to the Gnostic Coptic manuscripts discovered at Chenoboskion* (New York: Inner Traditions/MJF Books, 1986, 1958), p. 162, p. 164, pp. 273-274.
40. Tilak, *Orion,* op. cit., p. 90.
—The period of Orion, which the author Tilak states is 4000–2500 BC (p. 115), may be similar to the Western astrology's Age of Taurus, approximately 4000–2000 BC.
41. "Sanskrit, Tamil and Pahlavi Dictionaries," http://webapps.uni-koeln.de/tamil.
—Gandharvas are male messengers that travel between the gods and humans—similar to the Hopi *katsinam* (kachinas).
42. "Sanskrit Dictionary for Spoken Sanskrit," http://spokensanskrit.de.
43. "Soma, *Indian Divinity,* http://www.webonautics.com/mythology/soma.html.
44. http:/en.wikipedia.org/wiki/Soma.
45. R. C. Zaehner, *Hinduism* (London: Oxford University Press, 1968, 1966), p. 21.
46. Book IX, Hymn XII, verses 3-5, *The Hymns of the Rgveda,* Vol. II, translated by Ralph T. H. Griffith (Varanasi, India: The Chowkhamba Sanskrit Series Office, 1971), pp. 278-279.
47. "Sanskrit, Tamil and Pahlavi Dictionaries," http://webapps.uni-koeln.de/tamil, and *Online Etymology Dictionary,* http://www.etymonline.com/index.php?term=semen.
48. http:/en.wikipedia.org/wiki/Samudra_manthan.
49. "Sanskrit, Tamil and Pahlavi Dictionaries," http://webapps.uni-koeln.de/tamil.
50. Consult pp. 47-50 in regard to the astronomical and cosmological signifi-

cance of the turtle in the Pueblo culture of the American Southwest; see pp. 140-142 and pp. 145-146 for the Mayan take on the same.
51. Budge, *An Egyptian Hieroglyphic Dictionary*, Vol. I, op. cit., p. 118b, p. 119b.
52. Precession of the equinoxes: "…a slow westward shift of the equinoxes along the plane of the ecliptic caused by precession of the Earth's axis of rotation." WordNet Search, 3.0, http://wordnetweb.princeton.edu/perl/webwn?s=precession%20of%20the%20equinoxes.
—Or: "In astronomy, precession refers to a gravity-induced slow but continuous change in an astronomical body's rotational axis or orbital path. In particular, it refers to the gradual shift in the orientation of the Earth's axis of rotation, which, like a wobbling top, traces out a conical shape in a cycle of approximately 26,000 years (called a Great or Platonic year in astrology)." http://en.wikipedia.org/wiki/Precession_(astronomy).
53. Graham Hancock, *Heaven's Mirror: Quest For the Lost Civilization* (New York: Crown Publishers, Inc., 1998), p. 144.
54. Santillana and von Deschend, *Hamlet's Mill*, op. cit., p. 146.
55. Santillana and von Deschend, *Hamlet's Mill*, op. cit., p. 111.
56. "Sanskrit, Tamil and Pahlavi Dictionaries," http://webapps.uni-koeln.de/tamil.
57. Book IX, Hymn II, verse 5, *The Hymns of the Rgveda*, Vol. II, op. cit., p. 270.
58. R. T. Rundle Clark, *Myth and Symbol in Ancient Egypt* (New York: Thames and Hudson, 1991, 1978, 1959), pp. 248-249.
59. Book Ten, Hymn CXXI, *The Hymns of the Rgveda*, Vol. II, op. cit., p. 566.
—Prajapati is also known as "Ka," to which a whole chapter is devoted in David, *Eye of the Phoenix*, op. cit.
—Re. "Mystery Egg": see Chapter 8, the current book.
60. Dr. David Frawley, "The Milky Way and the Cosmic Soma," p. 5, http://www.scribd.com/doc/2849551/The-Milky-Way-and-the-Cosmic-Soma.

Chapter 10: Orion's Copper Connection

1. http://en.wikipedia.org/wiki/Flag_of_Tibet.
2. David, *The Orion Zone*, op. cit., p. 276.
3. Jacqui Menkes, astrologer, http://www.jacquimenkes.com.
4. Ken Croswell, "The Stellar Origin of Copper," April 6, 2007, http://kencroswell.com/Copper.html.
5. http://en.wikipedia.org/wiki/Copper.
6. Kepler also assigned the following: to the tetrahedron, Jupiter and fire; to the dodecahedron, Mars and ether; to the icosahedron, Venus and water; to the octahedron, Mercury and air; and to the sphere, heaven. http://www.newworldencyclopedia.org/entry/Johannes_Kepler.
7. http://www.ptable.com.
8. Huxley, *The Way of the Sacred*, op. cit., p. 212.
9. T. S., (Thomas Swann), "Queen Dido: A Medley," *The Spirit of Sport in*

Nature and Other Poems, (London: Marcus Ward & Co., Ltd., 1883), p. 146, http://books.google.com.
10. http://en.wikipedia.org/wiki/Saturn.
11. *New Larousse Encyclopedia of Mythology* (London: The Hamlyn Publishing Group Limited, 1972, reprint 1959), p. 144; http://en.wikipedia.org/wiki/Hyria_(Boeotia).
12. http://en.wikipedia.org/wiki/Copper.
13. Prash Trivedi, *The 27 Celestial Portals* (Twin Lakes, Wisconsin: Lotus Press, 2005), p. 97, http://books.google.com.
14. "Sanskrit, Tamil and Pahlavi Dictionaries," http://webapps.uni-koeln.de/tamil.
15. Sri Swami Sivananda, "Siva," http://www.dlshq.org/religions/siva.htm.
16. Budge, *An Egyptian Hieroglyphic Dictionary,* Vol. I, op. cit., p. 210a.
17. Homer, *The Odyssey*, Book XI, lines 572-675, translated by Richard Lattimore (New York: Harper & Row, 1967).
18. 1 Samuel 17:4-6.
19. Revelation 1:15-16.
20. *The Koran*, 70:8, translated by N. J. Dawood (London: Penguin Books, 1999, 1956), p. 405.
21. Deuteronomy: 28:23.
22. Albert Pike, *Morals and Dogma of the Ancient and Accepted Scottish Rite of Freemasonry* (Charleston, South Carolina: A. .M. . 5632, 1928, 1906, 1871), pp. 781-782.
23. Megge Hill-Fitz-Randolph, february 22, 2009, "Ancient Alchemy of Fire — Calcinatio," http://metaphysics.suite101.com/article.cfm/calcinatio_first_order_of_alchemy.
24. Online Etymology Dictionary, http://www.etymonline.com/index.php?term=wormwood.
25. "Thujone, Absinthe & Herbs," http://www.paganpath.com/library/articles/93-thujone.html.
26. Than, op. cit., http://news.nationalgeographic.com/news/2009/06/090610-betelgeuse-star-shrinking.html.
27. Waters and Fredericks, *Book of the Hopi*, op. cit., p. 17.
28. In Hopi cosmology, a kachina (also spelled *katsina*) is a spirit that can assume the shape of any object or force in the universe.
29. Evehema, "His Final Message to Mankind," op. cit., http://www.hopiland.net/prophecy/dan-1.htm.
30. Allen, *Star Names*, op. cit., p. 311.
31. Chris Hardaker, "The Hexagon, the Solstice and the Kiva," 2004, http://www.earthmeasure.com/pdf/HexagonSolstice.pdf.
—The science of cymatics involves the visual form of sound waves or vibrations. When the vowel A (as in "ah!"or Alpha) is intoned, quartz sand that is poured on a vibrating "Chladni plate" arranges into a *hexagon* (2D cube), or sometimes a pentagram. When the vowel O (as in "oh!", OM, or Omega) is intoned, a circle is produced. "In his research with the tonoscope, [Hans]

Jenny noticed that when the vowels of the ancient internal languages of Hebrew and Sanskrit were pronounced, the sand took the shape of the written symbols for these vowels, while our modern languages, on the other hand, did not generate the same result. How is this possible? Did the ancient Hebrews and Indians know this? Is there something to the concept of 'sacred language,' which both of these are sometimes called? What qualities do these 'sacred languages,' among which Tibetan, Egyptian and Chinese are often numbered, possess? Do they have the power to influence and transform physical reality, to create things through their inherent power, or, to take a concrete example, through the recitation or singing of sacred texts, to heal a person who has gone 'out of tune'?" http://fusionanomaly.net/cymatics.html.
—Geometers in antiquity squaring the circle or Kepler cubing the sphere? The planet Saturn symbolized as a cube surrounded by its rings? Spirit (circle) encompassing matter (square)? Omega assimilating Alpha? The first kivas, such as those at Chaco Canyon, were circular but encorporated the hexagon into their geometry, as the bottom of p. 182 shows.
32. http://www.mythicalireland.com/highman.
33. Krupp, *Echoes of the Ancient Skies*, op. cit. pp. 315-319.
34. Gerardo Reichel-Dolmatoff, *Amazonian Cosmos: The Sexual and Religious Symbolism of the Tukano Indians* (Chicago: The University of Chicago Press, 1971), p. 100.
35. Reichel-Dolmatoff, Ibid. p. 99.
36. Reichel-Dolmatoff, Ibid. p. 83.
37. Kaj Århem, "Landscape, territory and local belonging in Northwest Amazonia," *Locality and Belonging*, edited by Nadia Lowell (London: Routledge, 1998), p. 85, http://book.google.com.
38. Reichel-Dolmatoff, *Amazonian Cosmos*, op. cit., p. 10.
39. Reichel-Dolmatoff, Ibid., p. 130.
40. John Major Jenkins, "Maya Shamanism and 2012: A Psychedelic Cosmology," http://www.realitysandwich.com/maya_shamanism_and_2012_psychedelic_cosmology.
41. Reichel-Dolmatoff, *Amazonian Cosmos*, op. cit., pp. 104-110.
42 http://en.wikipedia.org/wiki/Copper_mining_in_Arizona.
43. Jefferson Reid and Stephanie Whittlesey, *The Archaeology of Ancient Arizona* (Tucson: The University of Arizona Press, 1997), pp. 111-130.
44. Tom Bahti, *Southwestern Indian Tribes* (Las Vegas: KC Publications, Inc, 1987, 1968), p. 63.
45. Bob "Bubba" Peters, "Powered Paragliding Ancient Geoglyphs," http://www.bubbappg.com/Geoglyphs.htm.
46. Allen, *Star Names*, op. cit., p. 132.
47. Antoon Leon Vollemaere, "Search and Discovery of Aztlan, Tollan, Colhuacan, and Chicomoztoc, 1990–2000," http://users.skynet.be/fa039055/explora2.htm.

48. Olcott, *Star Lore*, op. cit., p. 110.
49. Carl Lumholtz, *New Trails in Mexico: An Account of One Year's Exploration in North-western Sonora, Mexico, and South-western Arizona* (New York: Charles Scribner's Sons, 1912), p. 5, p. 9, p. 142; http://books.google.com.
50. Robert J. Hard, John R. Roney, "Massive Terraced Village Complex in Chihuahua, Mexico, 3000 Years Before Present," http://id-archserve.ucsb.edu/Anth3/Essays/99/mound.html.
51. Jack Andrews, "Nachi Kulik ('Hâ-âk Muerto'): A Cerros de Trincheras megalithic site that may date back thousands of years," http://mysteriousarizona.com/haak.html.
—Some archaeologists see a connection between *cerros de trincheras* and various sites in Mesoamerica and even Oceania. Ben A. Nelson, Ph.D., provides the primary example of La Quemada in Zacatecas as a hilltop ceremonial center and Monte Alban in Oaxaca as "an idealized city on the hill." These were both highly visible places that contained astronomically aligned public architecture, massive walls, ritualized open spaces, residential terraces, staircases, and ceremonial burial grounds which openly glorified the ancestors. Religious rulers used these structures in order to consolidate and amplify their authority. "In any event, placecrafting at hilltop sites is testimony to a spectrum of social power unique to the Americas, but in some ways analogous to the continuum found in Melanesia and Polynesia. There, anthropologists have documented a range of social formations including big-man societies and open, traditional, and stratified chiefdoms. Oceanian strategies of status enhancement emphasized competitive feasting, antagonistic exchange, control of craft specialization, and warfare. Mesoamerican elites and those in the Northwest/Southwest [of Mexico and the U.S. respectively] may also have used all of these strategies." Ben A. Nelson, "Crafting of Places: Mesoamerican Monumentality in Cerros de Trincheras and Other Hilltop Sites, *Trincheras Sites In Time, Space, and Society*, edited by Suzanne K. Fish, Paul R. Fish, and M. Elisa Villalpando (Tucson: The University of Arizona Press, 2007), pp. 238-246.
52. Bethe Hagens, "The Becker-Hagens Grid," 1984, http://www.bibliotecapleyades.net/mapas_ocultotierra/esp_mapa_ocultotierra_12.htm; *Anti-Gravity and the World Grid*, edited by David Hatcher Childress (Stelle, Illinois: Adventures Unlimited Press, 1987); Bethe Hagens, "Basic Instructions for Exploring the UVG Grid with Google Earth," http://www.vortexmaps.com/hagens-grid-google.php.
—With 120 faces, 180 edges, and 62 vertices, the hexakis icosahedron can be conceptualized as a giant earth-crystal.
53. David Hatcher Childress, *Lost Cities & Ancient Mysteries of the Southwest* (Kempton, Illinois: Adventures Unlimited press, 2009), pp. 251-252.
54. "Death on the Border," http://regulus.azstarnet.com/borderdeaths/search.php; "Across the Borderline," lyrics by Ry Cooder.
55. Henriette Mertz, *Gods From the Far East: How the Chinese Discovered*

America, formerly titled *Pale Ink* (New York: Ballantine Book, 1975, 1953), p. 19.
56. quoted in Mertz, Ibid., pp. 44-45.

Chapter 11: Ancient Giants of Earth and Sky

1. Washington Matthews, *Navaho Legends* (Salt Lake: University of Utah Press, 1994, 1897), p. 37, p. 91, pp. 122-123.
2. Harry C. James, *Pages From Hopi History* (Tucson: The University of Arizona Press, 1974), p. 25, p. 27.
3. *Papers on Anthropology of the Western Great Basin* (Berkeley, California: University of California Archaeological Research Facility, Department of Anthropology, No. 7, May 1970).
4. David Hatcher Childress has written extensively about the so-called Lovelock Giants. See his book *Lost Cities of North & Central America* (Stelle, Illinois: Adventures Unlimited Press, 1993, pp. 492-498.
5. Sarah Winnemucca Hopkins, *Life Among the Piutes: Their Wrongs and Claims* (Reno/Las Vegas: University of Nevada Press, 1994), p. 75.
6. Stan Nielsen, "The Cave of the Red Haired Giants," http://www.treasurecenter.com/treasure_diary.htm.
7. Robert F. Heizer, Lewis K. Napton, *Archaeology in the Prehistoric Great Basin Lacustrine Subsistence Regime As Seen From Lovelock Cave, Nevada* (Berkeley, California: University of California Archaeological Research Facility, No. 10, July 1970).
8. "The Lost Race of Lovelock Cave, NV," *Ancient American*, Wayne May, editor, Colfax, Wisconsin, Vol. 13, No. 81.
9. Jared G. Barton, "Secret Chambers in the Rockies," *Ancient American*, Wayne May, editor, Colfax, Wisconsin, Vol. 4, No. 28, http://www.ancientamerican.com/article28p1.htm.
10. Paul Horgan, *Great River: The Rio Grande in North American History* (Middletown, Connecticut: Wesleyan University Press, 1991), p. 35.
11. Harold S. Colton, *Hopi Kachina Dolls with a Key to their Identification* (Albuquerque: University of New Mexico Press, 1990, 1949; Jesse Walter Fewkes, *Hopi Katcinas* (New York: Dover Publications, Inc., 1985, reprint of *Twenty-First Annual Report of the Bureau of American Ethnology*, 1903); Alph H. Secakuku, *Following the Sun and the Moon: Hopi Kachina Tradition* (Flagstaff, Arizona: Northland Publishing, 1998, 1995); Barton Wright, *Hopi Kachinas: The Complete Guide to Collecting Kachina Dolls* (Flagstaff, Arizona: Northland Publishing, 1993, 1977)—all passim.
12. Susan E. James, "Mimetic rituals of child sacrifice in the Hopi Kachina cult," *Journal of the Southwest*, Vol. 44, University of Arizona, Sept. 22, 2002.
13. http:/en.wikipedia.org/wiki/Vagina_dentata.
14. Malotki, *Hopi Stories of Witchcraft, Shamanism, and Magic*, op. cit., pp. 124-135.
15. From Book 14, *The Classic of Mountains and Seas*, quoted in Mertz, *Gods From the Far East*, op. cit., p. 175.

—A rod = 16.5 feet, so the archer may have been over 21 feet tall, according to the account. The mountain referred to is apparently in the vicinity of the Great Luminous Canyon, or Grand Canyon. The ancient Chinese conceptualized the area around the Canis Major as containing the following: *Hou-Chi* (the Bow-and-Arrow, what Western astronomy sees as the hindquarters of the Greater Dog), *T'ien-Kaou* (the Celestial Dog), *T'ien-Lang* (the Celestial Jackal), and *Ye-Ki* (the Wild Cockerel). Thus, found together here are both the archery and canine motifs that are associated with the constellation in cultures around the world. Julius D. W. Staal, *The New Patterns in the Sky: Myths and Legends of the Stars* (Blacksburg, Virginia: The McDonald and Woodwood Publishing Company, 1988), p. 87.

16. Childress, *Lost Cities & Ancient Mysteries of the Southwest,* op. cit., p. 298.

17. D. T. Case, R. J. Hill, C. F. Merbs, M. Fong, "Polydactyly in the Prehistoric American Southwest," *International Journal of Osteoarchaeology,* Vol. 16, Issue 3, 2005, pp. 221-35.

18. Ethne Barnes, "Polydactyly in the Southwest," *Kiva: The Journal of Southwestern Anthropology and History*, Vol. 59, No. 4, 1994, The Arizona Archaeology Society, Tucson, p. 420. See also "Human Skeletal Remains," *The Archaeology of Sand Canyon Pueblo: Intensive Excavations at a Late-Thirteenth-Century Village in Southwestern Colorado*, edited Kristin A. Kuckelman, http://www.crowcanyon.org/researchreports/sandcanyon/text/scpw_humanskeletalremains.asp.

19. Nancy J. Akins, "The Burials of Pueblo Bonito," *Pueblo Bonito: Center of the Chacoan World,* edited by Jill E. Neitzel (Washington: Smithsonian Books, 2003), p. 100.

20. Stephen Plog, *Ancient Peoples of the American Southwest* (London: Thames and Hudson, Ltd., 1997), p. 117.

21. Nancy J. Akins, "Chaco Canyon Mortuary Practices: Archaeological Correlates of Complexity," *Ancient Burial Practices in the American Southwest: Archaeology, Physical Anthropology, and Native American Perspectives,* edited by Douglas R. Mitchell, Judy L. Brunson-Hadley (Albuquerque: University of New Mexico, 2001), p. 184.

22. Steven A. LeBlanc, *Prehistoric Warfare In the American Southwest* (Salt Lake City: The University of Utah Press, 1999), p. 182.

23. Richard D. Fisher, *Grand Canyons Worldwide: the First Encyclopedic View of Earth's Canyonlands* (Tucson, Arizona: Sunracer Publications, 2006), p. 81.

24. Anthropology Laboratories of Northern Arizona Univeristy, http://jan.ucc.nau.edu/d-antlab/Soutwestern%20Arch/Anasazi/pueblo2.htm.

25. Christy G. Turner II and Jacqueline A. Turner, *Man Corn: Cannibalism and Violence in the Prehistoric American Southwest* (Salt Lake City: The University of Utah Press, 1999), p. 3.

26. Turner and Turner, *Man Corn,* Ibid., p. 413.

27. B. Bower, "Ancient Site Holds Cannibalism Clues," *Science News,* September 9, 2000, http://www.articlearchives.com/

science-technology/experimentation-research/366010-1.html; http://www.thefreelibrary.com/ Ancient+Site+Holds+Cannibalism+Clues.(Brief+Article)-a065860845.
28. Turner and Turner, *Man Corn*, op. cit., p. 129.
29. Rina Swentzell, "A Pueblo Woman's Perspective on Chaco Canyon," *In Search of Chaco: New Approaches to an Archaeological Enigma*, edited by David Grant Noble (Santa Fe, New Mexico: School of American Research Press, 2004), p. 50.
30. Swentzell, Ibid., p. 53.
—Hopi spiritual elder Grandfather Martin Gashweseoma talked to Kymberlee Ruff at Prophecy Rock, Third Mesa, Arizona on August 8th, 2008, about the few incidents of cannibalism that occurred when the "two-hearted persons" (Hopi evil sorcerers) caused disease and lack of rain and food together with the arrival of Spanish missionaries in the 17th century. "When they were getting another, Spaniard has been came here, and they were out into this Old Oraibi [village], and put their religious—put aside it. So the Hopi people initiate the Spanish ways and become Christian. So after that there is a lot more rain and have a good harvest every four years. And after four years it's coming down, downward, everything—no, not much rain. So after that four years it's been happen[-ing], then death and starvated [starvation]. And then the people out of food, so there's young ones that's been just playing outside, and some other people they caught them and they killed them, and boiled it up and eat them. So that's what it's been happen… It's just like some movie that's been made like this. Some airplane might be crashed, then they were out of food. And they were… those has been dead, body has been laying there and they cut in their body and they eat them." Ms. Ruff also asked him: "Can you say anything about the Tibetans?" "Well, they are... we are the same. Hopi, Tibetan. And some are Mayans, I will say this. Their knowledge too is like that." "So if we study the Tibetan way that will help?" "Yeah, it will help. It's the same thing… they been pray[-ing] all the time. That's how we been having this. If you don't… must believe in much ways [?], you just keep praying. Let that spirit tell you, and you can notice it from your heart. That's how it will be. That's what happens [on it?] From the beginning, what I could use [?], so I just heard from them, my elders and from my clan, what we have [to] do…" http://www.youtube.com/ watch?v=ZIBvs7wdSdQ&feature=player_embedded#!
(See p. 159 and p. 168 for more on the Hopi-Tibetan connection.)
31. Turner and Turner, *Man Corn*, op. cit., p. 129.
32. Malotki, *Hopi Dictionary*, op. cit., 102.
33. Douglas Preston, "Cannibals of the Canyon," *The New Yorker*, November 30, 1998, p. 88.
34. Robert S. McPherson, *Sacred Land, Sacred View: Navajo Perceptions of the Four Corners Region* (Salt Lake City: Brigham Young University, 1995, 1992), pp. 88-89.

35 Richard M. Begay, "Tsé Bíyah 'Anii'áhí: Chaco Canyon and Its Place in Navajo History," *In Search of Chaco*, op. cit., pp. 55-6.
36. Matthews, *Navaho Legends*, op. cit., pp. 81-87, passim.
37. http://www.firerocknavajocasino.com.
38. Lekson, *The Chaco Meridian*, op. cit., p. 149.
39. McPherson, *Sacred Land, Sacred View*, op. cit., p. 87.
40. Keith Kloor, "Who Were the Anasazi: The Navajo stake a controversial claim to an ancient legacy," *Archaeology*, November/December 2009, p. 18.
41. Aileen O'Bryan, *The Dîné: Origin Myths of the Navaho Indians*, Bureau of American Ethnology Bulletin 163, 1956, p. 62.
http://www.sacred-texts.com/nam/nav/omni/omni04.htm.
42. O'Bryan, Ibid., pp. 62-63.
43. Gene D. Matlock, *The Last Atlantis Book You'll Ever have to Read: The Atlantis-Mexico-India Connection* (Tempe, Arizona: Dandelion Books, 2001), p. 107.
44. Leigh J. Kuwanwisiwma, "Yupköyvi: The Hopi Story of Chaco Canyon," *In Search of Chaco*, op. cit., pp. 46-7.
45. Harold Courlander, *The Fourth World of the Hopis: The Epic Story of the Hopi Indians As Preserved in Their Legends and Traditions* (Albuquerque: University of New Mexico Press, 1991, 1971), p. 37.
46. Read a detailed account in Harry C. James, *Pages From Hopi History*, op. cit., pp. 62-64.
47. Waters, *Masked Gods*, op. cit., pp. 291-292.
48. Malotki, *Hopi Dictionary*, op. cit., p. 487.
49. Rudolph Otto, *The Idea of the Holy: An Inquiry into the non-rational factor in the idea of the divine and its relation to the rational*, tranlated by John W. Harvey (London: Oxford University Press,1971, 1923), pp. 12-30.
50. Florence Cline Lister, Robert Hill Lister, *Earl Morris & Southwestern Archaeology* (Albuquerque: University of New Mexico Press, 1977), p. 32.
51. Brian Fagan, *Chaco Canyon: Archaeologists Explore the Lives Of an Ancient Society* (New York: Oxford University Press, 2005), p. 49.
52. Gordon Brotherston, in collaboration with Ed Dorn, *Image of the New World: The American Continent Portrayed In Native Texts* (London: Thames and Hudson, 1979), p. 188.
53. Bradfield, *An Interpretation of Hopi Culture*, op. cit., p. 289.
54. Bradfield, Ibid., p. 289.
55. Anne Casselman, "Buried Dogs Were Divine 'Escorts' for Ancient Americans," *National Geographic*, April 23,
2008, http://news.nationalgeographic.com/news/2008/04/
080423-dog-burials.html.
56. H. M. Wormington, *Prehistoric Indians of the Southwest* (Denver, Colorado: The Denver Museum of Natural History, 1973, 1947), p. 46.
57. Stuart, *Anasazi America*, op. cit., p. 111.
58. E. Charles Adams, *The Origin and Development of the Pueblo Katsina Cult* (Tucson: The University of Arizona Press, 1991), p. 72.

59. Edward S. Curtis, Frederick Webb Hodge, editor, *The North American Indian: Hopi*, Vol. 12 (Norwood, Mass.: The Plimpton Press, 1922), pp. 90-91.

Chapter 12: Indian Mothman and Sacred Datura

1. Frank C. Hibben, *Kiva Art of the Anasazi at Pottery Mound* (Las Vegas, Nevada: KC Publications, 1975), pp. 10-11.
2. Polly Schaafsma, *Indian Rock Art of the Southwest* (Santa Fe/Albuquerque: School of American Research/University of New Mexico Press, 1980), p. 251.
3. Paul T. Kay, "Ancient Voices…murals and pots speak. DATURA: A Poster Presentation for the 70th Annual Meeting of the Society for American Archaeology,"http://paultkay.info/DATURA_05_08_2006.pdf.
4. CAVEAT—IMPORTANT WARNING FROM A TRUSTED ONLINE SOURCE: "I'd like to point out that there are countless warnings about Datura and reports of horrendous experiences using it throughout this site. More Datura reports fall under the 'Train Wreck' category than any other substance. It is NOT safely used haphazardly. Even with all the warnings and recommendations not to use it, people will continue to do so, often having never read anything about it. Hopefully, the wide variety of information presented here will help some people to take precautions with regard to their safety." http://www.erowid.org/ask/ask.php?ID=227.
5. Andrew Weil, *The Marriage of the Sun and Moon: A Quest for Unity in Consciousness* (Boston: Houghton Mifflin, 1980), p. 166.
6. Clark, *Myth and Symbol In Ancient Egypt*, op. cit., p. 165.
7. Ernst Bibra, and Jonathan Ott, *Plant Intoxicants: A Classic Text on the Use of Mind Altering Plants* (Rochester, Vermont: Inner Traditions/Bear & Company, 1995, originally published 1855), pp. 77-8, http://books.google.com.
8. Lisa W. Huckell and Christine S. Vanpool, "Toloatzin and Shamanic Journeys: Exploring the Ritual Role of Sacred Datura in the Prehistoric Southwest," *Religion In the Prehispanic Southwest*, edited by Christine S. Vanpool, Todd L. Vanpool, and David A Phillips, Jr. (Lanham, Maryland: Altamira Press, 2006), p. 150.
9. Matilda Coxe Stevenson, quoted in Alex Patterson, *A Field Guide to Rock Art Symbols of the Greater Southwest* (Boulder, Colorado: Johnson Books, 1992), p. 80.
10. Carlos Castaneda, *The Teachings of Don Juan: a Yaqui Way of Knowledge* (New York: Pocket Book, 1977, 1974, 1968), p. 128.
11. Castaneda, Ibid., p. 129.
12. Ralph Emerson Twitchell, *The Leading Facts of New Mexican History*, Vol. I (Cedar Rapids, Iowa: The Torch Press, 1917), p. 261, http://books.google.com.
13. Ekkehart Malotki, *Hopi Dictionary*, op. cit., p. 631.
14. Marc Simmons, *Witchcraft in the Southwest: Spanish and Indian Supernaturalism on the Rio Grande* (Lincoln: University of Nebraska Press,

1980, 1974), p. 153.
15. John A. Keel: *The Mothman Prophecies* (New York: Signet/New American Library, 1975), p. 25.
16. Grapevine Canyon is located in the very southern tip of Nevada not far from the casino town of Laughlin. (See location on map, p. 189.) The rugged canyon lies six miles due west of the Colorado River, with the mouth of the canyon roughly facing east. As the largest petroglyph site in southern Nevada, it has had ceremonial significance to the Mojave and other tribes for thousands of years. In Grapevine Canyon the designs carved into the heavily patinated granite cliffs and boulders are predominantly abstract: geometric forms, nets, grids, zigzags, shields, spirals, concentric circles, meandering lines and dots, parallel lines, starbursts, and odd I-shaped or H-shaped forms. I did, however, occasionally find the engravings of a zoomorph (animal form) such as deer or bighorn sheep, and those of snakes. Also stylized anthropomorphs (human forms) appear among the welter of images sometimes densely superimposed as on a palimpsest. Grapevine Canyon may be the ritual location where shamans on a vision quest entered mythic space-time to reenact the cosmic creation. The petroglyphs found here are not mere doodles or idle recreation. On the contrary, these labor-intensive carvings undoubtedly represent the visionary re-creation of mythical or otherworldly dimensions. We may never fully know their true meanings. See more photos at: http://www.theorionzone.com/grapevine_canyon.htm.
—Masau'u figure in collage is adapted from a pen-and-ink drawing by Petra Roeckerath in Ekkehart Malotki and Michael Lomatuway'ma, *Stories of Maasaw, A Hopi God* (Lincoln: University of Nebraska Press, 1987).

Chapter 13: Arizona's Psychic Archaeology

1. Jeffrey Goodman, *Psychic Archaeology: Time Machine to the Past* (New York Berkeley Publishing Corporation, 1977), p. 128.
2. Goodman, Ibid., pp. 120-21.
3. Jeffrey Goodman, Ph.D., *American Genesis: The American Indian and the Origins of Modern Man* (New York: Summit Books, 1981), p. 212.
4. Jeffrey Goodman, Ph.D., *The Genesis Mystery: A Startling New Theory of Outside Intervention in the Development of Modern Man* (New York: Times Books, 1983), p. 218.
5. Goodman, *Psychic Archaeology*, op. cit., p. 118.
6. Stephen C. McCluskey, "Calendar and Symbolism: Functions of Observation in Hopi Astronomy," *Archaeoastronomy (Journal for the History of Astronomy*, xxi), no. 15, 1990), pp. S5-S6.

Chapter 14: Hopi Kachinas and Egyptian Stars

1. Barton Wright, paintings by Cliff Bahnimptewa, *Kachinas: a Hopi Artist's Documentary* (Flagstaff, Arizona: Northland Publishing, 1990, 1973), p. 125.
2. Budge, *An Egyptian Hieroglyphic Dictionary*, Vol. II, op. cit., p. 638b.
3. Jiro Kondo, "Ancient Egyptian Astronomy," http://www.innovations-report.de/html/berichte/physik_astronomie/ancient_egyptian_astronomy_120456.html.
4. Chris Tedder, "An Overview of the Orion Correlation Theory (OCT): Was the angle of observation 52.2 degrees south of east?", Appendix 3 in Robert Bauval, *The Egypt Code* (London: Century, 2006), p. 240.
5. E. A. Wallis Budge, *Osiris and the Egyptian Resurrection*, Vol. I, (New York: Dover Publications, Inc., 1973), p. 121.
6. "The Pyramid Texts," http://www.pyramidtextsonline.com/translation.html.
7. John Anthony West, *The Traveler's Key to Ancient Egypt: A Guide to the Sacred Places of Ancient Egypt* (Adyar, India: Quest Books, 1995), p. 67.
8. "The Pyramid Texts," http://www.pyramidtextsonline.com/translation.html.
9. Faulkner, "Spell 180," *The Ancient Egyptian Book of the Dead*, op. cit., p. 177.
10. Gaston Maspero, *History of Egypt, Chaldea, Syria, Babylonia, and Assyria* , Vol. I, translated by M. L. McClure (London: The Grolier Society, 1903), http://www.gutenberg.org/files/19400/19400-8.txt.
—Maspero relates some interesting information regarding Sopdît (Sirius) and Egyptian cosmology, as well as some downright shocking descriptions of Sahû as hunter, warrior, and even cannibal: "Not content to shine by night only, her bluish rays, suddenly darted forth in full daylight and without any warning, often described upon the sky the mystic lines of the triangle which stood for her name. It was then that she produced those curious phenomena of the zodiacal light which other legends attributed to Horus himself. One, and perhaps the most ancient of the innumerable accounts of this god and goddess, represented Sahû as a wild hunter. A world as vast as ours rested upon the other side of the iron firmament; like ours, it was distributed into seas, and continents divided by rivers and canals, but peopled by races unknown to men. Sahû traversed it during the day, surrounded by genii who presided over the lamps forming his constellation. At his appearing 'the stars prepared themselves for battle, the heavenly archers rushed forward, the bones of the gods upon the horizon trembled at the sight of him,' for it was no common game that he hunted, but the very gods themselves. One attendant secured the prey with a lasso, as bulls are caught in the pastures, while another examined each capture to decide if it were pure and good for food. This being determined, others bound the divine victim, cut its throat, disembowelled it, cut up its carcass, cast the joints into a pot, and superintended their cooking. Sahû did not devour indifferently all that

the fortune of the chase might bring him, but classified his game in accordance with his wants. He ate the great gods at his breakfast in the morning, the lesser gods at his dinner towards noon, and the small ones at his supper; the old were rendered more tender by roasting."
11. Plutarch, *Plutarch's Morals: Theosophical Essays on Isis and Osiris*, translated by Charles William King, 1908, http://www.sacred-texts.com.
12. "The Pyramid Texts," http://www.pyramidtextsonline.com/translation.html.
13. See Bauval and Gilbert, *The Orion Mystery*, op. cit, passim.
14. Budge, *An Egyptian Hieroglyphic Dictionary*, Vol. II, op. cit., p. 638a.
15. A few chapters in David, *Eye of the Phoenix*, op. cit., deal specifically with cultural diffusionism in early times.
16. Malotki and Lomatuway'ma, *Maasaw*, op. cit., p. 69.
17. Ralph Ellis, *Jesus: Last of the Pharaohs* (Dorset, UK: Edfu Books, 1999, 1998), p. 35, http://books.google.com.
18. Budge, *An Egyptian Hieroglyphic Dictionary*, Vol. I, op. cit., p. 485b, p. 548b.
19. Online Etymology Dictionary, http://www.etymonline.com; http://en.wikipedia.org/wiki/Alchemy.
20. Gaston Maspero, *The Dawn of Civilization: Egypt and Chaldæa*, p. 432, http://books.google.com.
21. Waters and Fredericks, *Book of the Hopi*, op. cit., p. 141.
22. Malotki and Lomatuway'ma, *Maasaw*, op. cit., p. 121.
23. Malotki and Lomatuway'ma, Ibid., p. 128.
24. Anne Wright, "Constellations of Words: Explore the etymology and symbolism of the constellations," http://www.constellationsofwords.com/Constellations/Orion.html.
25. Malotki and Lomatuway'ma, *Maasaw*, op. cit., p. 186, p. 188.
26. Gerald Massey, *Ancient Egypt, the Light of the World: a Work of Reclamation and Restitution in Twelve Books*, Vol. I (London: T. Fisher Unwin, 1907), p. 12, http://books.google.com.
27. Malotki, *Hopi Dictionary*, op. cit., p. 195.
28. Mischa Titiev, *Old Oraibi: A Study of the Hopi Indians of Third Mesa* (Albuquerque, New Mexico: University of New Mexico Press, 1992, reprint, 1944), p. 135.
29. Bradfield, *An Interpretation of Hopi Culture*, op. cit., p. 234.
30. "Les Masques,"*Regard Eloigne*, 2006, http://agoras.typepad.fr/regard_eloigne/les-masques.

Chapter 15: Under South African Skies

1. John Parkington, David Morris, and Neil Rusch, *Karoo Rock Engravings: Marking Places in the Landscape* (Cape Town, South Africa: Southern Cross Ventures, August 2008), pp. 17-31.
2. Diffusionist archaeologist Dr Cyril A, Hromník, who was born in

Slovokia, educated at Syacuse University, and lives in Cape Town, South Africa, claims that the word *karu* is actually a Tamil term (Dravidian of southern India) meaning "arid country." Maré Mouton, "'South Africa is denied its rich cultural history'," *Village Life*, No. 15, December 2005-January 2006, p. 21. Hromník further believes that the Khoe (Hottentots), whom he calls the Quena, are descendants of Indian fathers and South African San mothers. "Were Indians the first colonists in SA?", Electronic Mail & Guardian, October 7, 1997,
http://cosmologicaljourneys.com/pdf/Chariot%20for%20cj.pdf.

3. See Rob Milne's excellent book titled *Anecdotes of the Anglo-Boer War* (Johannesburg, South Africa: Covos Day Books, 2000). For photos and explanations of South African rock art, see his website: www.robmilne.com. Also, read his description of an Orion Correlation/engraving site near Lydenburg in Mpumalanga ("rising sun") Province of South Africa, which was published in Appendix 1, David, *Eye of the Phoenix*, op. cit.. Rob's comprehensive book on South African archaeoastronomy titled *Beyond Orion* is forthcoming.

4. McGregor Museum, http://www.museumsnc.co.za/aboutus/depts/archaeology/wildebeestkuil.html.

5. "Traditional star lore of Africa," op. cit.,
http://www.psychohistorian.org/astronomy/ethnoastronomy/african_star_lore.php.

6. The reed is a globally potent motif. For instance, the Hopi refer to the Milky Way by the term *songwuka*, literally "big reed." They have a legend of coming up through a great reed from the previous Third World to the present Fourth World. This perhaps suggests an interstellar journey along the galactic axis.

7. Brenda Sullivan, *Spirit of the Rocks* (Cape Town/Pretoria/Johannesburg, South Africa: Human & Rousseau, 1995), p. 13. For information on the Celtic cross as ancient navigational instrument and architectural tool, see Crichton E M Miller's excellent book *The Golden Thread of Time* (Rugby, Warwickshire, UK: Pendulum Publishing, 2001),
http://www.crichtonmiller.com.

8. David Morris, "Introducing a new interpretation of Driekopseiland," http://www.driekopseiland.itgo.com/about.html; "Cation-Ration Dating of Rock Engravings," *Contested Images: Diversity in Southern African Rock Art Research*, edited by Thomas A Dowson and David Lewis-Williams (Johannesburg: Witwatersrand University Press, 1994), pp. 192-196.

9. Joseph Campbell, *Historical Atlas of World Mythology*, Vol. I, "The Way of the Animal Powers," Part I, "Mythologies of the Primitive Hunters and Gatherers" (New York: Harper & Row, Publishers, Inc., 1988), pp. 88-89.

10. "Capsian culture," http://en.wikipedia.org/wiki/Capsian_culture.

11. Michael Cremo and Richard L. Thompson, *The Hidden History of the Human Race* (Los Angeles: Bhaktivedanta Book Publishing, 1999), pp. 120-122.

12. Brenda Sullivan, *Africa Through the Mists of Time* (Johannesburg, South

Africa, and London: Covos Day Books, 2001), p. 207.
—Corundum (from the Tamil word *kuruntam*, "ruby"), rated 9 on the Mohs scale, may have also been used to incise the rock at Driekopseiland. Large deposits of this gem have been mined in both South Africa and Zimbabwe. Sullivan claims that the Egyptians employed diamond-tipped tools as early as 4000 BC. "Further research revealed that the Egyptians were using diamond- and corundum-tipped copper, or bronze, saws, and jewelled tubular drills, during the time of the Archaic and Old Kingdoms (c. 3200-2723 BCE)." Sullivan, Ibid, p. 57. In discussing the construction of the granite sarcophagus located in the King's Chamber of the Great Pyramid, Graham Hancock quotes the British Egyptologist Flinders Petrie: "Since the granite was extremely hard, he could only assume that these saws must have had bronze blades (the hardest metal then supposedly available) inset with 'cutting points' made of even harder jewels: 'The character of the work would certainly seem to point to diamond as being the cutting jewel; and only the considerations of its rarity in general, and *its absence from Egypt* [italics added], interfere with this conclusion. . .'" Graham Hancock, *Fingerprints of the Gods* (New York: Crown Trade Paperbacks, 1995), p. 331.
—The logical assumption: ancient Egyptians traveled to South Africa in order to obtain their cutting tools. The trade-flow may, however, have gone in both directions. Sullivan notes that the skeleton of a San Bushman dated between 14,000 and 12,000 BC had been found in the Nile Valley. Sullivan, *Spirit of the Rocks*, op. cit., p. 91.
13. David Lewis-Williams and Geoffrey Blundell, *Fragile Heritage: A Rock Art Fieldguide* (Johannesburg, South Africa: Witwatersrand University Press, 1998), pp. 24-25.
—The trance dance is a curing ritual whereby the spirits are contacted. Resembling the Native American Ghost Dance of the late 19th century, it is performed by dancing in a ring, using hyperventilation in order to create a state of transcendent exhaustion. "The !Kung [San] medicine man gradually works himself up into a state of trembling and sweating. When he approaches trance, he feels a rising sensation which he ascribes to the 'boiling' of his medicine (*n/om*); as he enters deep trance, he falls to the ground, sometimes executing a somersault." J. David Lewis-Williams, *A Cosmos In Stone: Interpreting Religion and Society Through Rock Art* (Walnut Creek, California: Altamira Press, 2002), p. 59.
14. Morris, "Introducing a new interpretation of Driekopseiland," op. cit., http://www.driekopseiland.itgo.com/about.html.
15. Lewis-Williams and Blundell, *Fragile Heritage*, op. cit., p. 21.
16. Parkington, Morris, and Rusch, *Karoo Rock Engravings*, op. cit., p. 78.
—The San used to call out to the mythical Water Snake: "Your breast gurgles because it is full of water. The Stars love you—therefore the gemstone gleams on your head." Was this gemstone a diamond? "/Xam astronomical references in G R von Wielligh's *Boesman-Stories*,"
http://www.psychohistorian.org/astronomy/

ethnoastronomy/xam_von_wielligh.php.
17. Lewis-Williams, *A Cosmos In Stone*, op. cit., p. 80.
18. Lewis-Williams and Blundell, *Fragile Heritage*, op. cit., p. 22.
19. Parkington, Morris, and Rusch, *Karoo Rock Engravings*, op. cit., p. 80.
20. Sullivan, *Africa Through the Mists of Time*, op. cit., p. 207.
21. Sullivan, Ibid., p. 11.
22. Laurens van der Post, *The Lost World of the Kalahari* (Middlesex, England: Penguin Books, 1968, 1958), pp. 14-15.
23. Barry Fell, "Ogam Inscriptions from North and South Africa," and Brenda (Sullivan) Wintgen, Ph.D., "Ntethological Analysis of Ogam Script from Driekopseiland Translated and Published by Professor Barry Fell," both articles from *The Epigraphic Society Occasional Publications*, Vol. 6, No. 116, 1979. Brenda Sullivan: "In 1978 I met with Professor Barry Fell, founder of the Epigraphic Society, in Boston, USA. In 1998, I heard of the Mashigo Institute for the Interpretation of Symbols, and became so caught up in this new knowledge that I went on to obtain a Masters degree. By combining my years of self-study and research with the methodology of the advanced courses of Ntethology and Mashigology, I was awarded my Ph.D. for my interpretation of the symbolism of 30 South African rock engravings - a first in this field."
http://www.africanenigmas.co.za/about_us.html.
24. van der Post, *The Lost World of the Kalahari*, op. cit., p. 37.
25. Bruce Trigger, *A History of Archaeological Thought* (Cambridge and New York: Cambridge University Press, 1989), p. 406, cited in David Morris, "Off-beat Conjectures,"
http://www.driekopseiland.itgo.com/catalog.html.
26. Henri A. Junod, *The Life of a South African Tribe*, Vol. II, Mental Life (New Hyde Park, New York: University Books, Inc., 1966), p. 444.
27. Junod, Ibid, pp. 351-352.
28. Henry Callaway, *The Religious System of the Amazulu* (Charleston, South Carolina: Forgotten Books, 2007, 1870), p. 246, http://books.google.com.
29. Henry Callaway, *Nursery Tales, Traditions, and Histories of the Zulus, In Their Own Words, with a Translation Into English, and Notes* (Pietermaritzburg, South Africa: Davis and Sons, 1868), p. 316,
http://books.google.com.
30. http://www.bookrags.com/research/unkulunkulu-eorl-14;
http://www.answers.com/topic/unkulunkulu.
31. Junod, *The Life of a South African Tribe*, Vol. II, op. cit., p. 310.
32. Vusamazulu Credo Mutwa, *Zulu High Sanusi*, edited by Bradford Keeney, Ph.D., (Philadelphia, Pennsylvania: Ringing Rocks Press, 2001), p. 56.
33. Vusamazulu Credo Mutwa, *Zulu Shaman: Dreams, Prophecies, and Mysteries*, edited by Stephen Larsen, original title *Song of the Stars* (Rochester, Vermont: Destiny Books, 2003, 1996), p. 157.
34. Mutwa, Ibid., p. 131.
35. Mutwa, Ibid., p. 133.

36. Mutwa, Ibid., pp. 125-130. For a thorough treatment of the Dogon's relationship to Sirius, see: Robert K. G. Temple, *The Sirius Mystery: New Scientific Evidence of Alien Contact 5,000 Years Ago* (Rochester, Vermont: Destiny Books, 1998).
37. "Vusa'mazulu Credo Mutwa—Biography 04: The Origin of the Gods," http://credomutwa.com/about/biography-04.
38. Mutwa, *Zulu Shaman*, op. cit., p. 133.
39. Wright, *Hopi Kachinas*, op. cit., pp. 110-112; Colton, *Hopi Kachina Dolls*, op. cit., p. 37, p. 54; and Malotki, *Hopi Dictionary*, op. cit., p. 132.
40. Mutwa, *Zulu Shaman*, op. cit., p. 122.
41. "Vusa'mazulu Credo Mutwa—Biography 03: Mysteries of Africa," http://credomutwa.com/about/biography-03.
42. Mutwa, *Zulu Shaman*, op. cit., p. 77.
43. Waters and Fredericks, *Book of the Hopi*, op. cit., pp. 5-7.
44. Hancock, *Fingerprints of the Gods*, op. cit., p. 39.
45. Mutwa, *Zulu High Sanusi*, op. cit., p. 77; and "Vusa'mazulu Credo Mutwa—Biography 06: children of Mars," http://credomutwa.com/about/biography-06.
—The two-toed people, also called the Vadoma, actually have a documented genetic mutation called ectrodactyly, in which the midle three toes are missing. They are also called "ostrich people." "The Two-toed people of Zimbabwe," *Zimbabwe Review: Reflections on Zimbabwe*, April 2, 2007, http://zimreview.wordpress.com/2007/04/02/the-two-toed-people-of-zimbabwe.
46. John E. Mack, M.D., *Passport to the Cosmos: Human Transformation and Alien Encounters* (New York: Crown Publisher, 1999), pp. 196-199.
47. Mack, Ibid., p. 193.
48. Mack, Ibid., p. 192.
49. Mutwa, *Zulu Shaman*, op. cit., p. 144.
"Traditional star lore of Africa," op. cit., http://www.psychohistorian.org/astronomy/ethnoastronomy/african_star_lore.php.
50. Sullivan, *Spirit of the Rocks*, op. cit., p. 25.
51. J. C. Hollmann, "'The Sky Things'" |xam Bushman 'Astrological Mythology' as Recorded in the Bleek and Lloyd Manuscripts," *African Skies/Cieux Africains*, No. 11, July 2007, p. 8.
52. Frederick J. Dockstader, *The Kachina and the White Man: The Influences of White Culture on the Hopi Kachina Religion* (Albuquerque, New Mexico: University of New Mexico Press, 1985, 1954), p. 9.
53. Voth, *Traditions of the Hopi*, op. cit., http://www.sacred-texts.com/nam/hopi/toth/toth023.htm.
54. Zecharia Sitchin, *The 12th Planet* (New York: Avon Books, 1978, 1976), pp. 188-194.
55. Robert H. Eisenman and Michael Wise, *The Dead Sea Scrolls Uncovered: The First Translation and Interpretation of 50 Key Documents Withheld for Over 35 Years* (New York: Penguin Books, 1993), pp. 151-156.

56. E. A. Wallis Budge, *The Gods of the Egyptians*, Vol. I, op. cit., p. 84.
57. "Abedju," http://www.philae.nu/akhet/SoulsPeNekhen.html.
58. Zecharia Sitchin, *The Wars of Gods and Men* (New York: Avon Books, 1985), p. 76.
59. Budge, *An Egyptian Hieroglyphic Dictionary*, Vol. I, op. cit., p. 172b.
60. Sitchin, *The Wars of Gods and Men*, op. cit., p. 38.
61. Budge, *An Egyptian Hieroglyphic Dictionary*, Vol. I, op. cit., p. 401a, p. 403b.
62. Zecharia Sitchin, *When Time Began* (New York: Avon Books, 1993), pp. 82-83.
63. Zecharia Sitchin, *The 12th Planet*, op. cit., p. 171.
64. Zecharia Sitchin, *There Were Giants Upon the Earth: Gods, Demigods, and Human Ancestry: the Evidence of Alien DNA* (Rochester, Vermont: Bear & Co., 2010), p. 84.
65. Christopher Knight and Robert Lomas, *Uriel's Machine: Uncovering the Secrets of Stonehenge, Noah's Flood, and the Dawn of Civilization* (Gloucester, Massachusetts: Fair Winds Press, 2001, 1999), p. 137.
66. Sitchin, *The Wars of Gods and Men*, op. cit., p. 191.
67. Neil Bennun, Wilhelm Heinrich Immanuel Bleek, *The Broken String: the Last Words of an Extinct People* (London, England: Viking/Penguin Books, 2004), p. 33, http://books.google.com.
68. Campbell, *Historical Atlas of World Mythology*, Vol I, Part I, op. cit., p. 91.
69. Bennun and Bleek, *The Broken String*, op. cit., p. 251.
70. J. C. Hollmann, "'The Sky Things'," op. cit., p. 10.
71. Traditional star lore of Africa," op. cit., http://www.psychohistorian.org/astronomy/ethnoastronomy/african_star_lore.php.
72. Rob Milne, "An Introduction to the Orion Mysteries of Boomplaas," http://www.robmilne.com/?q=node/22.
—Rob's DVD of the Boomplaas site in Mpumalanga Province of South Africa is also available at the same website.
73. Traditional star lore of Africa," op. cit., http://www.psychohistorian.org/astronomy/ethnoastronomy/african_star_lore.php.
74. J. C. Hollmann, "'The Sky Things'," op. cit., p. 10.
75. Richard Wade, "Star Lore of South Afrcia," http://www.facebook.com/topic.php?uid=2299284853&topic=2746.
76. "Story: When Bushmen were springbucks and cried," Lucy Lloyd |xam Notebooks, March 1878, The Digital Bleek & Lloyd, http://lloydbleekcollection.cs.uct.ac.za/data/stories/619/index.html; http://lloydbleekcollection.cs.uct.ac.za/data/books/BC_151_A2_1_049/A2_1_49_03905.html.
77. "Story: We do not utter a star man's name," Lucy Lloyd |xam Notebooks, December 1878, The Digital Bleek & Lloyd, http://lloydbleekcollection.cs.uct.ac.za/data/stories/826/index.html.
78. J. F. Thackeray & Jean-Loïc Le Quellec, "A symbolically wounded therianthrope at Melikane Rock Shelter, Lesotho," *Antiquity*, Vol. 81. No. 311

March 2007, http://antiquity.ac.uk/projgall/thackeray1/index.html.
79. "Food of the Gods," The Rock Art Conservation Center: Interpreting, Preserving, and Promoting Tanzanian Rock Art, http://www.racctz.org/FoodofheGods.html.
80. Sullivan, *Africa Through the Mists of Time,* op. cit., p. 208.
81. Sullivan, *Spirit of the Rocks,* op. cit., color Figures 13 and 14 between p. 48 and p. 49.
82. Andrew Lang, *Myth, Ritual and Religion,* Vol. II (London: Longmans, Green, and Co., 1899), p. 36, http://books.google.com.
—Incidentally, this is an extremely bigoted text, with statements describing the Bushmen as "a race on a very low level of development" and "...eternal confusion of savage thought." See Chapter 12 in David, *Eye of the Phoenix,* op. cit., for a discussion of the Nagas.
83. "Have aliens hijacked Voyager 2 spacecraft," *Daily Telegraph,* May 12, 2010, http://www.dailytelegraph.com.au/news/wacky/have-aliens-hijacked-voyager-2-spacecraft/story-e6frev20-1225865566982.

Chapter 16: Ancient Prophecy Now

1. Mutwa, *Zulu Shaman,* op. cit., facing p. 1.
2. Mutwa, *Zulu High Sanusi,* op. cit.
3. Maré Mouton, "'South Africa is denied its rich cultural history'", op. cit., p. 22.
4. Rob Milne, personal email communication, June 6, 2010.
5. Marlize Lombard, Isabele Parsons, and Maria van der Ryst, "'Lentswe La Badimo': Stone of the Ancestors," *The Digging Stick,* Vol. 20, No. 1, April 2003, pp. 5-7.
6. Franklin Barnett, *Dictionary of Prehistoric Indian Artifacts of the American Southwest* (Flagstaff, Arizona: Northland Press, 1973), p. 98.
7. Malotki, *Hopi Dictionary,* op. cit., p. 502.
8. Campbell Grant, *The Rock Paintings of the Chumash: A Study of a California Indian Culture* (Berkeley: University of California Press, 1966), p. 48.
9. Henry Koerper, Mark Q. Sutton, and Polly A. Peterson, "An Unusual Donut-shaped Artifact for CA-LAN-62," *Pacific Coast Archaeological Society Quarterly,* Vol. 43, No. 4, p. 82. http://www.pcas.org/documents/Donut-shapedArtifact434.pdf.
10. http://planetquest.jpl.nasa.gov/TPF/tpf_index.cfm.
11. Malotki, *Hopi Dictionary,* op. cit., p. 504.
12. "The Socorro Incident," UFO Encounters, http://www.ufoencounters.co.uk/TheSocorroIncident.html.
13. Disclose TV, audio, "Professor Robert Carr Discloses Aztec UFO Crash," October 1974, http://www.disclose.tv/action/viewvideo/46631/Professor_Robert_Carr_Discloses_Aztec_UFO_Crash/; Kevin D. Randle and Ronald R. Schmidt, *UFO Crash At Roswell* (New York: Avon Books, 1991), p. 247, pp. 262-263.

14. Also operated by BP, the larger Atlantis oil rig, located 125 miles from New Orleans and 2,000 feet deeper than the mile-deep Deepwater Horizon, was found to have "...incomplete and inaccurate engineering documents, which one official warned could 'lead to catastrophic operator error'...", "BP Was Told of Safety Issues on Another Rig," CBS News, Houston, May 15, 2010. http://www.cbsnews.com/stories/2010/05/15/business/main6487129.shtml; "Another oil disaster waiting to happen?", June 16, 2010, http://www.cnn.com/video/#/video/us/2010/06/16/ac.johns.atlantis.rig.cnn?hpt=C2.
—Given the myth of the Atlantean continent sinking beneath the waves, has any drilling platform ever been so poorly named?
15. Zen Gardner, "Oil Apocalypse Foreseen By Credo Mutwa, Hopi Indians," May 17, 2010, http://beforeitsnews.com/news/45/275/Oil_Apocalypse_Foreseen_By_Credo_Mutwa,_Hopi_Indians.html; Alfred Lambremont Webre, "Web Bot: 1.2 billion dead in BP oil spill, Nov. 2010 nuclear war. Accurate?", June 30, 2010, Seattle Exopolitics Examiner, http://www.examiner.com.
16. http://2012wiki.com/index.php?title=Hopi_Civilization.
17. "Historic World Earthquakes," USGS, http://earthquake.usgs.gov/earthquakes/world/historical.php.
18. Alasdair Livingstone, *Mystical and Mythical Explanatory Works of Assyrian and Babylonian Scholars* (Oxford: Oxford University Press, 2007, 1986), pp. 137-138, p. 148, http://books.google.com.
19. Reza Kahlili, "There Will Be War," *Forbes*, June 21, 2010, http://www.forbes.com/2010/06/21/iran-nuclear-israel-war-opinions-reza-kahlili.html.
20. Fidel Castro Ruz, "Reflections by comrade Fidel: Knowing the Truth Timely," June 27, 2010, http://www.cuba.cu/gobierno/reflexiones/2010/ing/f270610i.html.
21. Rainier Maria Rilke, "Archaic Torso of Apollo," translated by Stephen Mitchell, http://www.poets.org/viewmedia.php/prmMID/15814.

Chapter 17: The Kivas of 2012

1. Alexander M. Stephen, "Hopi Tales," *The Journal of American Folk-Lore*, Vol. 42, No. 163, January-March, 1929, pp. 55-56.
2. http://en.wikipedia.org/wiki/Pecos_Classification.
3. Geoff Stray, "The Tortuguero Prophecy Unravelled," Graham Hancock's Forum, http://www.grahamhancock.com/forum/StrayG1.php.
4. Malotki, *Hopi Dictionary*, op. cit., p. 530.
5. David Stuart, "Translation of rest of Tortuguero 6?", Aztlan, http://www.famsi.org/mailman/htdig/aztlan/2006-August/002533.html.
6. Stray, "The Tortuguero Prophecy Unravelled," op. cit., http://www.grahamhancock.com/forum/StrayG1.php.

7. Thompson, *Maya Hieroglyphic Writing*, op. cit., p. 12.
8. Tedlock, *Popol Vuh*, op. cit., p. 358.
—One wonders if the term "Black Road," which the Lakota medicine man Black Elk used to refer to the east-to-west path of troubles, strive, warfare, and woe, is derived from the Mayan usage. The Black Road of the Sioux is opposed to the north-to-south Red Road, the sacred path of wisdom, fertility, and righteousness.
9. John Major Jenkins, "Comments on the 2012 text of Tortuguero Monument 6 and Bolon Yokte K'u," http://alignment2012.com/bolon-yokte.html.
10. Malotki, *Hopi Dictionary*, op. cit., p. 762.
11. Bradfield, *An Interpretation of Hopi Culture*, op. cit., p. 407.
12. Thompson, *Maya History and Religion*, op. cit., p. 280.
13. Markus Eberl and Christian Prager, "Tortuguero, Monument 6 text," Aztlan, http://www.famsi.org/pipermail/aztlan/2006-April/001978.html.
14. Malotki, *Hopi Dictionary*, op. cit., p. 383.
15. Michael J. Grofe, "The Name of God L: B'olon Yokte' K'uh," *Wayeb Notes*, No. 30, 2009, p. 13, http://www.wayeb.org/notes/wayeb_notes0030.pdf.
16. This trade network was especially vibrant at Chaco Canyon, where recently tested ceramic shards dating from 1000 to 1125 AD showed traces of theobromine, a cacao marker. The nearest cacao trees are 1,200 miles away. The cylindrical, white jars averaging 10 inches in height and painted with black geometric designs were apparently used by the elite to consume liquid chocolate—a custom exactly like that of the Maya. Michael Haederle, "Mystery of Ancient Pueblo Jars Is Solved," *New York Times*, February 3, 2009, http://www.nytimes.com/2009/02/04/us/04cocoa.html?_r=1.
—On the other hand, tests conducted by Sandia National Laboratories on 800-year-old pot shards from various New Mexico pueblos found traces of beer fermentation. Hence, class warfare might be have going on even back then. The chocolate drinkers versus the beer drinkers! Heather Whipps, "Beer Brewed Long Ago By Native Americans," MSNBC, http://www.msnbc.msn.com/id/22421656.
17. John Major Jenkins, "Comments on the 2012 text…", op. cit., http://alignment2012.com/bolon-yokte.html.
18. *The Book of the Chilam Balam of Chumayel*, translated by Ralph L. Roys, Washington, D.C.: Carnegie Institution, 1933), pp. 99-100. http://www.sacred-texts.com/nam/maya/cbc/cbc15.htm.
19. *The Book of the Chilam Balam of Chumayel*, Ibid., p. 103, http://www.sacred-texts.com/nam/maya/cbc/cbc15.htm.
20. Tedlock, *Popol Vuh*, op. cit., p. 341, p. 343.
21. *The Book of the Chilam Balam of Chumayel*, op. cit., p. 133, http://www.sacred-texts.com/nam/maya/cbc/cbc23.htm.
22. John Major Jenkins, "The Importance of April 6th, 1993," May 26, 1992, *Tzolkin: Visionary Perspectives and Calendar Studies*, 1994, 1992, pp. 270-272, http://edj.net/mc2012/fap8.html.

23. Budge, *Egyptian Hieroglyphic Dictionary*, Vol. I, op. cit., p. 133b, p. 134a, p. 134b.
24. *The Egyptian Book of the Dead: The Book of Going Forth by Day*, Chapter 161, translated by Raymond O. Faulkner, Carol Andrews, James Wasserman (San Francisco, California: Chronicle Books, 2008), p. 125.
25. Budge, *Egyptian Hieroglyphic Dictionary*, Vol. I, op. cit., p. 119b, p. 118b.
26. Budge, *Egyptian Hieroglyphic Dictionary*, Vol. II, op. cit., p. 755a, p. 757a.
27. John Jay Harper, "Suns of God, 2012: The Orion Revelation and the Vitruvian Man," http://johnjayharper.com/SunsofGod.pdf.
28. "Abydoss: (Abjou) The Osireion," http://www.ancient-wisdom.co.uk/egyptabydoss.htm
29. Alfred M. Tozzer, *A Maya Grammar* (New York: Dover Publications, Inc.), 1977), passim.
30. Martin Gray, "Chichen Itza Facts," http://www.sacredsites.com/americas/mexico/chichen-itza-facts.html.
31. Paul Westheim, *The Art of Ancient Mexico* (Garden City, New York: Anchor Books/Doubleday & Company, Inc., 1965), p. 104.
32. Bruce Scofield, "The Mayan Katun Prophecies," Alternate Perceptions, Issue 37, 1996, http://www.onereed.com/articles/katun.html.
33. Scofield, Ibid.
34. Jenkins, "The Importance of April 6th, 1993," op. cit., http://edj.net/mc2012/fap8.html.
35. "The Worst Nucelar Diasters," *Time*, http://www.time.com/time/photogallery/0,29307,1887705_1862269,00.html.
36. *The Book of the Chilam Balam of Chumayel*, op. cit., p. 161, http://www.sacred-texts.com/nam/maya/cbc/cbc27.htm.
37. *The Book of the Chilam Balam of Chumayel*, op. cit., p. 138, http://www.sacred-texts.com/nam/maya/cbc/cbc24.htm.
38. *The Book of the Chilam Balam of Chumayel*, op. cit., pp. 139-140, http://www.sacred-texts.com/nam/maya/cbc/cbc25.htm.
39. Schele and Matthews, *The Code of Kings*, op. cit., p. 282.
40. Budge, *Osiris and the Egyptian Resurrection*, Vol. II, op. cit., p. 258.
41. *The Book of the Chilam Balam of Chumayel*, op. cit., p. 133, http://www.sacred-texts.com/nam/maya/cbc/cbc23.htm.
42. Thompson, *Maya History and Religion*, op. cit., p. 335.
43. Hope B. Werness, *The Continuum Encyclopedia of Animal Symbolism in Art* (London: Continuum international Publishing Group, 2004), p. 398.
44. *The Book of the Chilam Balam of Chumayel*, op. cit., p. 165, http://www.sacred-texts.com/nam/maya/cbc/cbc29.htm.
45. Thompson, *Maya History and Religion*, op. cit., pp. 226-227.
46. *The Book of the Chilam Balam of Chumayel*, op. cit., p. 105, http://www.sacred-texts.com/nam/maya/cbc/cbc15.htm.
47. http://en.wikipedia.org/wiki/Plumeria.
48. Sven Gronemeyer, "Tortuguero, Tabasco, Mexico," p. 25, http://www.sven-gronemeyer.de/download/acta-mesoamericana_17.pdf.
49. Schele and Matthews, *The Code of Kings*, op. cit., pp. 144-45.

50. Milbrath, *Star Gods of the Maya*, op. cit., p. 267.
51. Lange, *Cochiti*, op. cit., p. 341 and caption of Plate 21.
52. Ortiz, *The Tewa World*, op. cit., p. 19.
53. Childress, *Lost Cities of North & Central America*, op. cit., p.207; George and Audrey DeLange, "Comalcalco Archaeological Ruins, Tabasco, Mexico," http://www.delange.org/Comalcalco/Comalcalco.htm.
54. Stephen Alvarez, "Tila Pilgrimage: Chiapas, Mexico," April 10, 2008, http://www.picturestoryblog.com/2008/04/tila-pilgrimage.html.
55. Thomas A. Lee, Jr., "Jmetic Lubton: Some Modern and Pre-Hispanic Maya Ceremonial Customs in the Highland of Chiapas, Mexico," Papers of the New World Archaeological Foundation, No. 29, Brigham Young University, Provo, Utah, 1972, p. 1, p. 5.
56. "INAH Uncovers Palace of Elites at Chichen Itza," August 3, 2008, American Egypt, http://www.americanegypt.com/blog/?p=340.
57. Alberto Ruz, Chichen Itza: Official Guide (Mexico, D.F.: Instituto Nacional de Antropologia e Historia, 1963, 1955), p. 45, pp. 47-48.
58. Childress, *Lost Cities of North & Central America*, op. cit., p. 172.
59. John L. Stephens, *Incidents of Travel In Central America, Chiaspas and Yucatan*, Vol. II (New York: Dover Publications, Inc., 1969, 1841), pp. 423-425.
60. "Office of Detention and Removal (DRO) Strategic Plan 2003-2012: Endgame," U.S. Department of Homeland Security, Washington, DC, June 27, 2003, http://www.yuricareport.com/Civil%20Rights/Endgame.pdf.
61. Gemini 23° = Alnilam in the Sabian symbol system. Sabian symbols are a series of 360 brief vignettes --one for each degree of the zodiacal circle-- received in 1925 by San Diego clairvoyant Elsie Wheeler and recorded by astrologist Marc Edmund Jones. Dane Rudhar, *An Astrological Mandala: The Cycle of Transformations and Its 360 Symbolic Phases* (New York: Random House, Inc., 1973), pp. 104-105.
62. Mails, *The Hopi Survival Kit*, op. cit., p. 287.
63. Gary David, *Voices From Inland Island: An Elegy of the Black Hills and the Little Bighorn* (Chino Valley, Arizona: Island Hills Books, 2009), p. 201, http://www.scribd.com/doc/27407175/Voices-From-Inland-Island-An-Elegy-of-the-Black-Hills-and-the-Little-Bighorn.
64. Cirlot, *A Dictionary of Symbols*, op. cit., p. 334.
65. "Cosmic Hearthstones": See sky chart on the bottom of p. 144; "Ak Ek or turtle star relates to ORION and the Mayans say that during the change from the last world cycle to our present world cycle the 3 Hearthstones (ORION) changed position or 'marked out a new place in the sky'." Mark Borcherding, personal email communication, July 16, 2010.
66. David, *The Orion Zone*, op. cit., pp. 47-51.
67. Malotki and Lomatuway'ma, *Maasaw*, op. cit., p. 261.
68. Revelation 22:20.
69. "The Dresden Codex," http://www.crystalinks.com/dresdencodex.html.

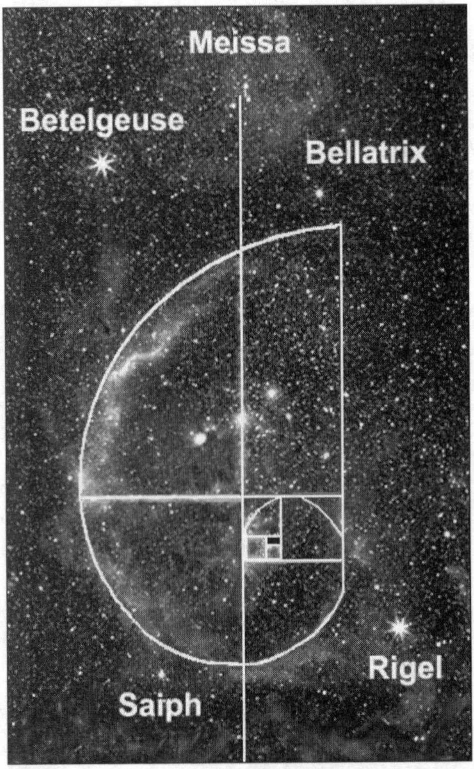

Barnard's Loop is an ionized molecular cloud formed about 2 million years ago in a supernova explosion. It is centered on the Orion Nebula in the shape of a sacred Golden Mean spiral. The vertical axis here starts in Meissa (Orion's head) and runs through Alnilam (middle belt star), and M43/M42 (Orion Nebula). Its diameter is about 300 light years and its distance is about 1,600 light years.

LOST CITIES & ANCIENT MYSTERIES OF AFRICA & ARABIA

by David Hatcher Childress

Childress continues his world-wide quest for lost cities and ancient mysteries. Join him as he discovers forbidden cities in the Empty Quarter of Arabia; "Atlantean" ruins in Egypt and the Kalahari desert; a mysterious, ancient empire in the Sahara; and more. This is the tale of an extraordinary life on the road: across war-torn countries, Childress searches for King Solomon's Mines, living dinosaurs, the Ark of the Covenant and the solutions to some of the fantastic mysteries of the past.

423 PAGES. 6X9 PAPERBACK. ILLUSTRATED. $14.95. CODE: AFA

LOST CITIES OF ATLANTIS, ANCIENT EUROPE & THE MEDITERRANEAN

by David Hatcher Childress

Childress takes the reader in search of sunken cities in the Mediterranean; across the Atlas Mountains in search of Atlantean ruins; to remote islands in search of megalithic ruins; to meet living legends and secret societies. From Ireland to Turkey, Morocco to Eastern Europe, and around the remote islands of the Mediterranean and Atlantic, Childress takes the reader on an astonishing quest for mankind's past. Ancient technology, cataclysms, megalithic construction, lost civilizations and devastating wars of the past are all explored in this book.

524 PAGES. 6X9 PAPERBACK. ILLUSTRATED. $16.95. CODE: MED

LOST CITIES OF CHINA, CENTRAL ASIA & INDIA

by David Hatcher Childress

Like a real life "Indiana Jones," maverick archaeologist David Childress takes the reader on an incredible adventure across some of the world's oldest and most remote countries in search of lost cities and ancient mysteries. Discover ancient cities in the Gobi Desert; hear fantastic tales of lost continents, vanished civilizations and secret societies bent on ruling the world; visit forgotten monasteries in forbidding snow-capped mountains with strange tunnels to mysterious subterranean cities! A unique combination of far-out exploration and practical travel advice, it will astound and delight the experienced traveler or the armchair voyager.

429 PAGES. 6X9 PAPERBACK. ILLUSTRATED. FOOTNOTES & BIBLIOGRAPHY. $14.95. CODE: CHI

LOST CITIES OF ANCIENT LEMURIA & THE PACIFIC

by David Hatcher Childress

Was there once a continent in the Pacific? Called Lemuria or Pacifica by geologists, Mu or Pan by the mystics, there is now ample mythological, geological and archaeological evidence to "prove" that an advanced and ancient civilization once lived in the central Pacific. Maverick archaeologist and explorer David Hatcher Childress combs the Indian Ocean, Australia and the Pacific in search of the surprising truth about mankind's past. Contains photos of the underwater city on Pohnpei; explanations on how the statues were levitated around Easter Island in a clockwise vortex movement; tales of disappearing islands; Egyptians in Australia; and more.

379 PAGES. 6X9 PAPERBACK. ILLUSTRATED. FOOTNOTES & BIBLIOGRAPHY. $14.95. CODE: LEM

EYE OF THE PHOENIX
Mysterious Visions and Secrets of the American Southwest
by Gary David

GaryDavid explores enigmas and anomalies in the vast American Southwest. Contents includes: The Great Pyramids of Arizona; Meteor Crater—Arizona's First Bonanza?; Chaco Canyon—Ancient City of the Dog Star; Phoenix—Masonic Metropolis in the Valley of the Sun; Along the 33rd Parallel—A Global Mystery Circle; The Flying Shields of the Hopi Katsinam; Is the Starchild a Hopi God?; The Ant People of Orion—Ancient Star Beings of the Hopi; Serpent Knights of the Round Temple; The Nagas—Origin of the Hopi Snake Clan?; The Tau (or T-shaped) Cross—Hopi/Maya/Egyptian Connections; The Hopi Stone Tablets of Techqua Ikachi; The Four Arms of Destiny—Swastikas in the Hopi World of the End Times; and more.

348 pages. 6x9 Paperback. Illustrated. Bibliography. $16.95. Code: EOPX

TECHNOLOGY OF THE GODS
The Incredible Sciences of the Ancients
by David Hatcher Childress

Childress looks at the technology that was allegedly used in Atlantis and the theory that the Great Pyramid of Egypt was originally a gigantic power station. He examines tales of ancient flight and the technology that it involved; how the ancients used electricity; megalithic building techniques; the use of crystal lenses and the fire from the gods; evidence of various high tech weapons in the past, including atomic weapons; ancient metallurgy and heavy machinery; the role of modern inventors such as Nikola Tesla in bringing ancient technology back into modern use; impossible artifacts; and more.

356 PAGES. 6x9 PAPERBACK. ILLUSTRATED. BIBLIOGRAPHY. $16.95. CODE: TGOD

VIMANA AIRCRAFT OF ANCIENT INDIA & ATLANTIS
by David Hatcher Childress, introduction by Ivan T. Sanderson

In this incredible volume on ancient India, authentic Indian texts such as the *Ramayana* and the *Mahabharata* are used to prove that ancient aircraft were in use more than four thousand years ago. Included in this book is the entire Fourth Century BC manuscript *Vimaanika Shastra* by the ancient author Maharishi Bharadwaaja. Also included are chapters on Atlantean technology, the incredible Rama Empire of India and the devastating wars that destroyed it.

334 PAGES. 6x9 PAPERBACK. ILLUSTRATED. $15.95. CODE: VAA

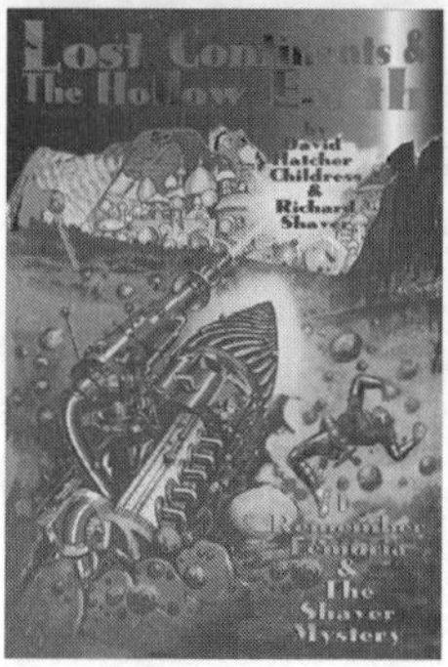

LOST CONTINENTS & THE HOLLOW EARTH
I Remember Lemuria and the Shaver Mystery
by David Hatcher Childress & Richard Shaver

Shaver's rare 1948 book *I Remember Lemuria* is reprinted in its entirety, and the book is packed with illustrations from Ray Palmer's *Amazing Stories* magazine of the 1940s. Palmer and Shaver told of tunnels running through the earth—tunnels inhabited by the Deros and Teros, humanoids from an ancient spacefaring race that had inhabited the earth, eventually going underground, hundreds of thousands of years ago. Childress discusses the famous hollow earth books and delves deep into whatever reality may be behind the stories of tunnels in the earth. Operation High Jump to Antarctica in 1947 and Admiral Byrd's bizarre statements, tunnel systems in South America and Tibet, the underground world of Agartha, the belief of UFOs coming from the South Pole, more.

344 PAGES. 6x9 PAPERBACK. ILLUSTRATED. $16.95. CODE: LCHE

ATLANTIS & THE POWER SYSTEM OF THE GODS

by David Hatcher Childress and Bill Clendenon

Childress' fascinating analysis of Nikola Tesla's broadcast system in light of Edgar Cayce's "Terrible Crystal" and the obelisks of ancient Egypt and Ethiopia. Includes: Atlantis and its crystal power towers that broadcast energy; how these incredible power stations may still exist today; inventor Nikola Tesla's nearly identical system of power transmission; Mercury Proton Gyros and mercury vortex propulsion; more. Richly illustrated, and packed with evidence that Atlantis not only existed—it had a world-wide energy system more sophisticated than ours today.

246 PAGES. 6x9 PAPERBACK. ILLUSTRATED. $15.95. CODE: APSG

THE ANTI-GRAVITY HANDBOOK

edited by David Hatcher Childress

The new expanded compilation of material on Anti-Gravity, Free Energy, Flying Saucer Propulsion, UFOs, Suppressed Technology, NASA Cover-ups and more. Highly illustrated with patents, technical illustrations and photos. This revised and expanded edition has more material, including photos of Area 51, Nevada, the government's secret testing facility. This classic on weird science is back in a new format!

230 PAGES. 7X10 PAPERBACK. ILLUSTRATED. $16.95. CODE: AGH

ANTI–GRAVITY & THE WORLD GRID

Is the earth surrounded by an intricate electromagnetic grid network offering free energy? This compilation of material on ley lines and world power points contains chapters on the geography, mathematics, and light harmonics of the earth grid. Learn the purpose of ley lines and ancient megalithic structures located on the grid. Discover how the grid made the Philadelphia Experiment possible. Explore the Coral Castle and many other mysteries, including acoustic levitation, Tesla Shields and scalar wave weaponry. Browse through the section on anti-gravity patents, and research resources.

274 PAGES. 7X10 PAPERBACK. ILLUSTRATED. $14.95. CODE: AGW

ANTI–GRAVITY & THE UNIFIED FIELD

edited by David Hatcher Childress

Is Einstein's Unified Field Theory the answer to all of our energy problems? Explored in this compilation of material is how gravity, electricity and magnetism manifest from a unified field around us. Why artificial gravity is possible; secrets of UFO propulsion; free energy; Nikola Tesla and anti-gravity airships of the 20s and 30s; flying saucers as superconducting whirls of plasma; anti-mass generators; vortex propulsion; suppressed technology; government cover-ups; gravitational pulse drive; spacecraft & more.

240 PAGES. 7X10 PAPERBACK. ILLUSTRATED. $14.95. CODE: AGU

THE TIME TRAVEL HANDBOOK

A Manual of Practical Teleportation & Time Travel

edited by David Hatcher Childress

The Time Travel Handbook takes the reader beyond the government experiments and deep into the uncharted territory of early time travellers such as Nikola Tesla and Guglielmo Marconi and their alleged time travel experiments, as well as the Wilson Brothers of EMI and their connection to the Philadelphia Experiment—the U.S. Navy's forays into invisibility, time travel, and teleportation. Childress looks into the claims of time travelling individuals, and investigates the unusual claim that the pyramids on Mars were built in the future and sent back in time. A highly visual, large format book, with patents, photos and schematics. Be the first on your block to build your own time travel device!

316 PAGES. 7X10 PAPERBACK. ILLUSTRATED. $16.95. CODE: TTH

MAPS OF THE ANCIENT SEA KINGS
Evidence of Advanced Civilization in the Ice Age
by Charles H. Hapgood

Charles Hapgood has found the evidence in the Piri Reis Map that shows Antarctica, the Hadji Ahmed map, the Oronteus Finaeus and other amazing maps. Hapgood concluded that these maps were made from more ancient maps from the various ancient archives around the world, now lost. Not only were these unknown people more advanced in mapmaking than any people prior to the 18th century, it appears they mapped all the continents. The Americas were mapped thousands of years before Columbus. Antarctica was mapped when its coasts were free of ice!

316 PAGES. 7x10 PAPERBACK. ILLUSTRATED. BIBLIOGRAPHY & INDEX. $19.95. CODE: MASK

PATH OF THE POLE
Cataclysmic Pole Shift Geology
by Charles H. Hapgood

Maps of the Ancient Sea Kings author Hapgood's classic book *Path of the Pole* is back in print! Hapgood researched Antarctica, ancient maps and the geological record to conclude that the Earth's crust has slipped on the inner core many times in the past, changing the position of the pole. *Path of the Pole* discusses the various "pole shifts" in Earth's past, giving evidence for each one, and moves on to possible future pole shifts.

356 PAGES. 6x9 PAPERBACK. ILLUSTRATED. $16.95. CODE: POP

AXIS OF THE WORLD
The Search for the Oldest American Civilization
by Igor Witkowski

Polish author Witkowski's research reveals remnants of a high civilization that was able to exert its influence on almost the entire planet, and did so with full consciousness. Sites around South America show that this was not just one of the places influenced by this culture, but a place where they built their crowning achievements. Easter Island, in the southeastern Pacific, constitutes one of them. The Rongo-Rongo language that developed there points westward to the Indus Valley. Taken together, the facts presented by Witkowski provide a fresh, new proof that an antediluvian, great civilization flourished several millennia ago.

220 pages. 6x9 Paperback. Illustrated. References. $18.95. Code: AXOW

THE FANTASTIC INVENTIONS OF NIKOLA TESLA
by Nikola Tesla with additional material by David Hatcher Childress

This book is a readable compendium of patents, diagrams, photos and explanations of the many incredible inventions of the originator of the modern era of electrification. In Tesla's own words are such topics as wireless transmission of power, death rays, and radio-controlled airships. In addition, rare material on a secret city built at a remote jungle site in South America by one of Tesla's students, Guglielmo Marconi. Marconi's secret group claims to have built flying saucers in the 1940s and to have gone to Mars in the early 1950s! Incredible photos of these Tesla craft are included. •His plan to transmit free electricity into the atmosphere. •How electrical devices would work using only small antennas. •Why unlimited power could be utilized anywhere on earth. •How radio and radar technology can be used as death-ray weapons in Star Wars.

342 PAGES. 6x9 PAPERBACK. ILLUSTRATED. $16.95. CODE: FINT

REICH OF THE BLACK SUN

Nazi Secret Weapons & the Cold War Allied Legend

by Joseph P. Farrell

Why were the Allies worried about an atom bomb attack by the Germans in 1944? Why did the Soviets threaten to use poison gas against the Germans? Why did Hitler in 1945 insist that holding Prague could win the war for the Third Reich? Why did US General George Patton's Third Army race for the Skoda works at Pilsen in Czechoslovakia instead of Berlin? Why did the US Army not test the uranium atom bomb it dropped on Hiroshima? Why did the Luftwaffe fly a non-stop round trip mission to within twenty miles of New York City in 1944? *Reich of the Black Sun* takes the reader on a scientific-historical journey in order to answer these questions. Arguing that Nazi Germany actually won the race for the atom bomb in late 1944,

352 pages. 6x9 paperback. Illustrated. Bibliography. $16.95. Code: ROBS

THE GIZA DEATH STAR

The Paleophysics of the Great Pyramid & the Military Complex at Giza

by Joseph P. Farrell

Was the Giza complex part of a military installation over 10,000 years ago? Chapters include: An Archaeology of Mass Destruction, Thoth and Theories; The Machine Hypothesis; Pythagoras, Plato, Planck, and the Pyramid; The Weapon Hypothesis; Encoded Harmonics of the Planck Units in the Great Pyramid; High Fregquency Direct Current "Impulse" Technology; The Grand Gallery and its Crystals: Gravito-acoustic Resonators; The Other Two Large Pyramids; the "Causeways," and the "Temples"; A Phase Conjugate Howitzer; Evidence of the Use of Weapons of Mass Destruction in Ancient Times; more.

290 pages. 6x9 Paperback. Illustrated. $16.95. code: GDS

THE GIZA DEATH STAR DEPLOYED

The Physics & Engineering of the Great Pyramid

by Joseph P. Farrell

Farrell expands on his thesis that the Great Pyramid was a maser, designed as a weapon and eventually deployed—with disastrous results to the solar system. Includes: Exploding Planets: A Brief History of the Exoteric and Esoteric Investigations of the Great Pyramid; No Machines, Please!; The Stargate Conspiracy; The Scalar Weapons; Message or Machine?; A Tesla Analysis of the Putative Physics and Engineering of the Giza Death Star; Cohering the Zero Point, Vacuum Energy, Flux: Feedback Loops and Tetrahedral Physics; and more.

290 Pages. 6x9 Paperback. Illustrated. $16.95. Code: GDSD

THE GIZA DEATH STAR DESTROYED

The Ancient War For Future Science

by Joseph P. Farrell

Farrell moves on to events of the final days of the Giza Death Star and its awesome power. These final events, eventually leading up to the destruction of this giant machine, are dissected one by one, leading us to the eventual abandonment of the Giza Military Complex—an event that hurled civilization back into the Stone Age. Chapters include: The Mars-Earth Connection; The Lost "Root Races" and the Moral Reasons for the Flood; The Destruction of Krypton: The Electrodynamic Solar System, Exploding Planets and Ancient Wars; Turning the Stream of the Flood: the Origin of Secret Societies and Esoteric Traditions; The Quest to Recover Ancient Mega-Technology; Non-Equilibrium Paleophysics; Monatomic Paleophysics; Frequencies, Vortices and Mass Particles; "Acoustic" Intensity of Fields; The Pyramid of Crystals; tons more.

292 pages. 6x9 paperback. Illustrated. $16.95. Code: GDES

THE ORION ZONE
Ancient Star Cities of the American Southwest
by Gary A. David

This book on ancient star lore explores the mysterious location of Pueblos in the American Southwest, circa 1100 AD, that appear to be a mirror image of the major stars of the Orion constellation. Packed with maps, diagrams, astronomical charts, and photos of ruins and rock art, *The Orion Zone* explores this terrestrial-celestial relationship and its astounding global significance. Chapters include: Leaving Many Footprints—The Emergence and Migrations of the Anazazi; The Sky Over the Hopi Villages; Orion Rising in the Dark Crystal; The Cosmo-Magical Cities of the Anazazi; Windows Onto the Cosmos; To Calibrate the March of Time; They Came from Across the Ocean—The Patki (Water) Clan and the Snake Clan of the Hopi; Ancient and Mysterious Monuments; Beyond That Fiery Day; more.

346 pages. 6x9 Paperback. Illustrated. $19.95. Code: OZON

THE CRYSTAL SKULLS
Astonishing Portals to Man's Past
by David Hatcher Childress and Stephen S. Mehler

Childress introduces the technology and lore of crystals, and then plunges into the turbulent times of the Mexican Revolution form the backdrop for the rollicking adventures of Ambrose Bierce, the renowned journalist who went missing in the jungles in 1913, and F.A. Mitchell-Hedges, the notorious adventurer who emerged from the jungles with the most famous of the crystal skulls. Mehler shares his extensive knowledge of and experience with crystal skulls. Having been involved in the field since the 1980s, he has personally examined many of the most influential skulls, and has worked with the leaders in crystal skull research, including the inimitable Nick Nocerino, who developed a meticulous methodology for the purpose of examining the skulls.

294 pages. 6x9 Paperback. Illustrated. $18.95. Code: CRSK

LOST CITIES & ANCIENT MYSTERIES OF THE SOUTHWEST
By David Hatcher Childress

Join David as he searches for the lost mines and stumbles upon a hollow mountain with a billion dollars of gold bars hidden deep inside it! In Arizona he investigates tales of Egyptian catacombs in the Grand Canyon, cruises along the Devil's Highway, and tackles the century-old mystery of the Lost Dutchman mine. In Nevada and California Childress checks out the rumors of mummified giants and weird tunnels in Death Valley, plus the mysterious remains of ancient dwellers alongside lakes that dried up tens of thousands of years ago.

486 Pages. 6x9 Paperback. Illustrated. $19.95. Code: LCSW

SUNKEN REALMS
A Survey of Underwater Ruins Around the World
By Karen Mutton

Australian researcher Mutton starts with the underwater cities in the Mediterranean, and then moves into Europe and the Atlantic. She continues with chapters on the Caribbean and then moves through the extensive sites in the Pacific and Indian Oceans. Places covered in this book include: Tartessos; Cadiz; Morocco; Alexandria; Cyprus; Malta; Thule & Hyperborea; Celtic Realms Lyonesse, Ys, and Hy Brasil; Canary and Azore Islands; Bahamas; Cuba; Bermuda; Mexico; Peru; Micronesia; California; Japan; Indian Ocean; Sri Lanka Land Bridge; India; Sumer; Lake Titicaca; more.

320 Pages. 6x9 Paperback. Illustrated. $20.00. Code: SRLM

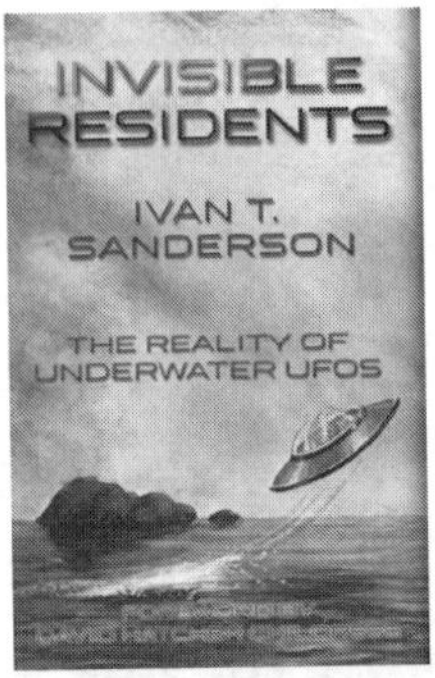

INVISIBLE RESIDENTS
The Reality of Underwater UFOS
by Ivan T. Sanderson

In this book, Sanderson, a renowned zoologist with a keen interest in the paranormal, puts forward the curious theory that "OINTS"—Other Intelligences—live under the Earth's oceans. This underwater, parallel, civilization may be twice as old as Homo sapiens, he proposes, and may have "developed what we call space flight." Sanderson postulates that the OINTS are behind many UFO sightings as well as the mysterious disappearances of aircraft and ships in the Bermuda Triangle. What better place to have an impenetrable base than deep within the oceans of the planet? Sanderson offers here an exhaustive study of USOs (Unidentified Submarine Objects) observed in nearly every part of the world.

298 PAGES. 6x9 PAPERBACK. ILLUSTRATED. BIBLIOGRAPHY. INDEX. $16.95. CODE: INVS

THE ENERGY GRID
Harmonic 695, The Pulse of the Universe
by Captain Bruce Cathie

This is the breakthrough book that explores the incredible potential of the Energy Grid and the Earth's Unified Field all around us. Cathie's first book, *Harmonic 33*, was published in 1968 when he was a commercial pilot in New Zealand. Since then, Captain Bruce Cathie has been the premier investigator into the amazing potential of the infinite energy that surrounds our planet every microsecond. Cathie investigates the Harmonics of Light and how the Energy Grid is created. In this amazing book are chapters on UFO Propulsion, Nikola Tesla, Unified Equations, the Mysterious Aerials, Pythagoras & the Grid, Nuclear Detonation and the Grid, Maps of the Ancients, an Australian Stonehenge examined, more.

255 PAGES. 6x9 TRADEPAPER. ILLUSTRATED. $15.95. CODE: TEG

THE BRIDGE TO INFINITY
Harmonic 371244
by Captain Bruce Cathie

Cathie has popularized the concept that the earth is crisscrossed by an electromagnetic grid system that can be used for anti-gravity, free energy, levitation and more. The book includes a new analysis of the harmonic nature of reality, acoustic levitation, pyramid power, harmonic receiver towers and UFO propulsion. It concludes that today's scientists have at their command a fantastic store of knowledge with which to advance the welfare of the human race.

204 PAGES. 6x9 TRADEPAPER. ILLUSTRATED. $14.95. CODE: BTF

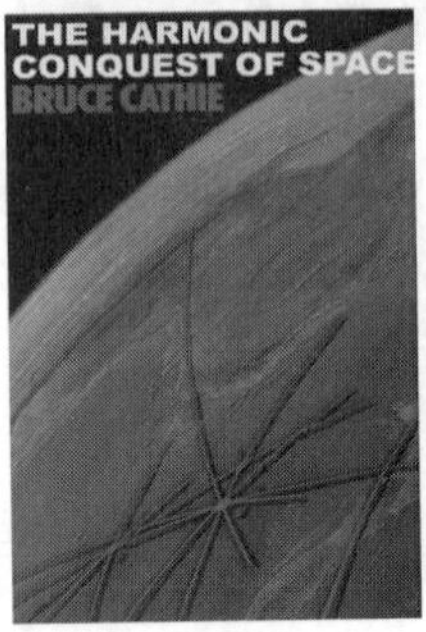

THE HARMONIC CONQUEST OF SPACE
by Captain Bruce Cathie

Chapters include: Mathematics of the World Grid; the Harmonics of Hiroshima and Nagasaki; Harmonic Transmission and Receiving; the Link Between Human Brain Waves; the Cavity Resonance between the Earth; the Ionosphere and Gravity; Edgar Cayce—the Harmonics of the Subconscious; Stonehenge; the Harmonics of the Moon; the Pyramids of Mars; Nikola Tesla's Electric Car; the Robert Adams Pulsed Electric Motor Generator; Harmonic Clues to the Unified Field; and more. Also included are tables showing the harmonic relations between the earth's magnetic field, the speed of light, and anti-gravity/gravity acceleration at different points on the earth's surface. New chapters in this edition on the giant stone spheres of Costa Rica, Atomic Tests and Volcanic Activity, and a chapter on Ayers Rock analysed with Stone Mountain, Georgia.

248 PAGES. 6x9. PAPERBACK. ILLUSTRATED. BIBLIOGRAPHY. $16.95. CODE: HCS

PIRATES & THE LOST TEMPLAR FLEET
The Secret Naval War Between the Templars & the Vatican
by David Hatcher Childress

Childress takes us into the fascinating world of maverick sea captains who were Knights Templar (and later Scottish Rite Free Masons) who battled the ships that sailed for the Pope. The lost Templar fleet was originally based at La Rochelle in southern France, but fled to the deep fiords of Scotland upon the dissolution of the Order by King Phillip. This banned fleet of ships was later commanded by the St. Clair family of Rosslyn Chapel (birthplace of Free Masonry). St. Clair and his Templars made a voyage to Canada in the year 1298 AD, nearly 100 years before Columbus! Later, this fleet of ships and new ones to come, flew the Skull and Crossbones, the symbol of the Knights Templar.

320 Pages. 6x9 Paperback. Illustrated. $16.95. Code: PLTF

THE MYSTERY OF THE OLMECS
by David Hatcher Childress

The Olmecs were not acknowledged to have existed as a civilization until an international archeological meeting in Mexico City in 1942. Now, the Olmecs are slowly being recognized as the Mother Culture of Mesoamerica, having invented writing, the ball game and the "Mayan" Calendar. But who were the Olmecs? Where did they come from? What happened to them? How sophisticated was their culture? Why are many Olmec statues and figurines seemingly of foreign peoples such as Africans, Europeans and Chinese? Is there a link with Atlantis? In this heavily illustrated book, join Childress in search of the lost cities of the Olmecs! Chapters include: The Mystery of Quizuo; The Mystery of Transoceanic Trade; The Mystery of Cranial Deformation; more.

296 Pages. 6x9 Paperback. Illustrated. Bibliography. Color Section. $20.00. Code: MOLM

THE LAND OF OSIRIS
An Introduction to Khemitology
by Stephen S. Mehler

Was there an advanced prehistoric civilization in ancient Egypt who built the great pyramids and carved the Great Sphinx? Did the pyramids serve as energy devices and not as tombs for kings? Mehler has uncovered an indigenous oral tradition that still exists in Egypt, and has been fortunate to have studied with a living master of this tradition, Abd'El Hakim Awyan. Mehler has also been given permission to present these teachings to the Western world, teachings that unfold a whole new understanding of ancient Egypt . Chapters include: Egyptology and Its Paradigms; Asgat Nefer—The Harmony of Water; Khemit and the Myth of Atlantis; The Extraterrestrial Question; more.

272 Pages. 6x9 Paperback. Illustrated. Color Section. Bibliography. $18.00 Code: LOOS

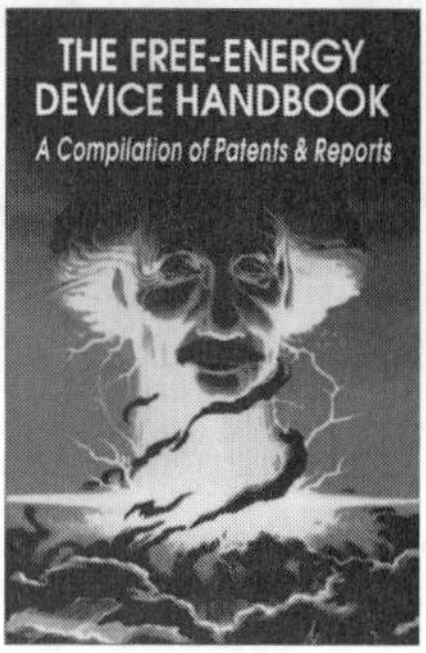

THE FREE-ENERGY DEVICE HANDBOOK
A Compilation of Patents and Reports
by David Hatcher Childress

A large-format compilation of various patents, papers, descriptions and diagrams concerning free-energy devices and systems. *The Free-Energy Device Handbook* is a visual tool for experimenters and researchers into magnetic motors and other "over-unity" devices. With chapters on the Adams Motor, the Hans Coler Generator, cold fusion, superconductors, "N" machines, space-energy generators, Nikola Tesla, T. Townsend Brown, and the latest in free-energy devices. Packed with photos, technical diagrams, patents and fascinating information, this book belongs on every science shelf.

292 Pages. 8x10 Paperback. Illustrated. $16.95. Code: FEH

ORDER FORM

10% Discount When You Order 3 or More Items!

One Adventure Place
P.O. Box 74
Kempton, Illinois 60946
United States of America
Tel.: 815-253-6390 • Fax: 815-253-6300
Email: auphq@frontiernet.net
http://www.adventuresunlimitedpress.com

ORDERING INSTRUCTIONS

- ✓ Remit by USD$ Check, Money Order or Credit Card
- ✓ Visa, Master Card, Discover & AmEx Accepted
- ✓ Paypal Payments Can Be Made To: info@wexclub.com
- ✓ Prices May Change Without Notice
- ✓ 10% Discount for 3 or more Items

SHIPPING CHARGES

United States

- ✓ Postal Book Rate { $4.00 First Item; 50¢ Each Additional Item
- ✓ POSTAL BOOK RATE Cannot Be Tracked!
- ✓ Priority Mail { $5.00 First Item; $2.00 Each Additional Item
- ✓ UPS { $6.00 First Item; $1.50 Each Additional Item

NOTE: UPS Delivery Available to Mainland USA Only

Canada

- ✓ Postal Air Mail { $10.00 First Item; $2.50 Each Additional Item
- ✓ Personal Checks or Bank Drafts MUST BE US$ and Drawn on a US Bank
- ✓ Canadian Postal Money Orders OK
- ✓ Payment MUST BE US$

All Other Countries

- ✓ Sorry, No Surface Delivery!
- ✓ Postal Air Mail { $16.00 First Item; $6.00 Each Additional Item
- ✓ Checks and Money Orders MUST BE US$ and Drawn on a US Bank or branch.
- ✓ Paypal Payments Can Be Made in US$ To: info@wexclub.com

SPECIAL NOTES

- ✓ RETAILERS: Standard Discounts Available
- ✓ BACKORDERS: We Backorder all Out-of-Stock Items Unless Otherwise Requested
- ✓ PRO FORMA INVOICES: Available on Request

ORDER ONLINE AT: www.adventuresunlimitedpress.com

Please check: ☑

☐ This is my first order ☐ I have ordered before

Name

Address

City

State/Province | Postal Code

Country

Phone day | Evening

Fax | Email

Item Code	Item Description	Qty	Total

Please check: ☑

Subtotal ▸

Less Discount-10% for 3 or more items ▸

☐ Postal-Surface — Balance ▸

☐ Postal-Air Mail (Priority in USA) — Illinois Residents 6.25% Sales Tax ▸

Previous Credit ▸

☐ UPS (Mainland USA only) — Shipping ▸

Total (check/MO in USD$ only) ▸

☐ Visa/MasterCard/Discover/American Express

Card Number

Expiration Date

10% Discount When You Order 3 or More Items!